Yamaha XJ600S & XJ600N

Service and Repair Manual

by Alan Ahlstrand
and John H Haynes Member of the Guild of Motoring Writers

(2145-208-6AI5)

Models covered
Yamaha XJ600S Diversion. 598cc. UK 1992 to 2003
Yamaha XJ600S Seca II. 598cc. US 1992 to 1999
Yamaha XJ600N. 598cc. UK 1995 to 2003

ABCDE
FGH

© Haynes Publishing 2009

A book in the **Haynes Service and Repair Manual Series**

ISBN **978 1 78521 048 8**

Library of Congress Control Number 2004106944

British Library Cataloguing in Publication Data
A catalogue record for this book is available from the British Library.

Printed in Malaysia

Haynes Publishing
Sparkford, Yeovil, Somerset BA22 7JJ, England

Haynes North America, Inc
859 Lawrence Drive, Newbury Park, California 91320, USA

Printed using NORBRITE BOOK 48.8gsm (CODE: 40N6533) from NORPAC; procurement system certified under Sustainable Forestry Initiative standard. Paper produced is certified to the SFI Certified Fiber Sourcing Standard (CERT - 0094271)

Contents

LIVING WITH YOUR YAMAHA XJ

Introduction

Daily (pre-ride) checks

MAINTENANCE

Routine maintenance and servicing

Contents

REPAIRS AND OVERHAUL

Engine, transmission and associated systems

Chassis components

Electrical system

Wiring diagrams

REFERENCE

Index

Yamaha
Musical instruments to Motorcycles

The Yamaha Motor Company

The Yamaha name can be traced back to 1889, when Torakusu Yamaha founded the Yamaha Organ Manufacturing Company. Such was the success of the company, that in 1897 it became Nippon Gakki Limited and manufactured a wide range of reed organs and pianos.

During World War II, Nippon Gakki's manufacturing base was utilised by the Japanese authorities to produce propellers and fuel tanks for their aviation industry. The end of the war brought about a huge public demand for low cost transport and many firms decided to utilise their obsolete aircraft tooling for the production of motorcycles. Nippon Gakki's first motorcycle went on sale in February 1955 and was named the 125 YA-1 Red Dragonfly. This machine was a copy of the German DKW RT125 motorcycle, featuring a single cylinder two-stroke engine with a four-speed gearbox. Due to the

The FS1-E - first bike of many sixteen year olds in the UK

outstanding success of this model the motorcycle operation was separated from Nippon Gakki in July 1955 and the Yamaha Motor Company was formed.

The YA-1 also received acclaim by winning two of Japan's biggest road races, the Mt. Fuji Climbing race and the Asama Volcano race. The high level of public demand for the YA-1 led to the development of a whole series of two-stroke singles and twins.

Having made a large impact on their home market, Yamahas were exported to the USA in 1958 and to the UK in 1962. In the UK the signing of an Anglo-Japanese trade agreement during 1962 enabled the sale of Japanese lightweight motorcycles and scooters in Britain. At that time, competition between the many motorcycle producers in Japan had reduced numbers significantly and by the end of the sixties, only the big-four which are familiar with today remained.

Yamaha Europe was founded in 1968 and based in Holland. Although originally set up to market marine products, the Dutch base is now the official European Headquarters and distribution centre. Yamaha motorcycles are built at factories in Holland, Denmark, Norway, Italy, France, Spain and Portugal. Yamahas are imported into the UK by Yamaha Motor UK Ltd, formerly Mitsui Machinery Sales (UK) Ltd. Mitsui and Co. were originally a trading house, handling the shipping, distribution and marketing of Japanese products into western countries. Ultimately Mitsui Machinery Sales was formed to handle Yamaha motorcycles and outboard motors.

Based on the technology derived from its motorcycle operation, Yamaha have produced many other products, such as automobile and lightweight aircraft engines, marine engines and boats, generators, pumps, ATVs, snowmobiles, golf cars, industrial robots, lawnmowers, swimming pools and archery equipment.

Two-strokes first

Part of Yamaha's success was a whole string of innovations in the two-stroke world. Autolube engine lubrication, pressed steel monocoque frame, electric starting, torque induction, multi-ported engines, reed valves and power valves kept their two-strokes at the forefront of technology.

In the 1960s and 70s the two-stroke engined YAS3 125, YDS1 to YDS7 250 and YR5 350 formed the core of Yamaha's range. By the mid-70s they had been superseded by the RD (Race-Developed) 125, 250, and 350 range of two-stroke twins, featuring improved 7 port engines with reed valve induction. Braking was improved by the use of an hydraulic brake on the front wheel of DX models, instead of the drum arrangement used previously, and cast alloy wheels were available as an option on later RD models. The RD350 was replaced by the RD400 in 1976.

Running parallel with the RD twins was a range of single-cylinder two-strokes. Used in a variety of chassis types, the engine was used in the popular 50 cc FS1-E moped, the V50 to 90 step-thrus, RS100 and 125, YB100 and the DT trail range.

The air-cooled single and twin cylinder RD models were eventually replaced by the LC series in 1980, featuring liquid-cooled engines, radical new styling, spiral pattern cast wheels and cantilever rear suspension (Yamaha's Monoshock). Of all the LC models, the RD350LC, or RD350R as it was later known, has made the most impact in the market. Later models had YPVS (Yamaha Power Valve System) engines, another first for Yamaha - this was essentially a valve located in the exhaust ports which was electronically operated to alter port timing to achieve maximum power output. The RD500LC was the largest two-stroke made by Yamaha and differed from the other LCs by the use of its vee-four cylinder engine.

With the exception of the RD350R, now manufactured in Brazil, the LC range has been discontinued. Two-stroke engined models have given way to environmental pressure, and thus with a few exceptions, such as the TZR125 and TZR250, are used only in scooters and small capacity bikes.

The Four-strokes

Yamaha concentrated solely on two-stroke models until 1970 when the XS1 was produced, their first four-stroke motorcycle. It was perhaps Yamaha's success with two-strokes that postponed an earlier move into the four-stroke motorcycle market, although their work with Toyota during the

The distinctive paintwork and trim of the RD models

1960s had given them a sound base in four-stroke technology.

The XS1 had a 650 cc twin-cylinder SOHC engine and was later to become known as the XS650, appearing also in the popular SE custom form. Yamaha introduced a three cylinder 750 cc engine in 1976, fitted in a sport-tourer frame and called the XS750, TX750 in the USA. The XS750 established itself well in the sport tourer class and remained in production with very few changes until uprated to 850 cc in 1980.

Other four-strokes followed in 1976, with the introduction of the XS250/360/400 series twins. The XS range was strengthened in 1978 by the four-cylinder XS1100.

The 1980s saw a new family of four-strokes, the XJ550, 650, 750 and 900 Fours. Improvements over the XS range amounted to a slimmer DOHC engine unit due to the relocation of the alternator behind the cylinders, electronic ignition and uprated braking and suspension systems. Models were available mainly in standard trim, although custom-styled Maxims were produced especially for the US market. The XJ650T was the first model from Yamaha to have a turbo-charged engine. Although these early XJ models have now been discontinued, their roots live on in the XJ600S and XJ900S Diversion (Seca II) models.

The FZR prefix encompasses the pure sports Yamaha models. With the exception of the 16-valve FZR400 and FZR600 models, the FZ/FZR750 and FZR1000 used 20-valve engines, two exhaust valves and three inlet valves per cylinder. This concept was called Genesis and gave improved gas flow to the combustion chambers. Other features of the new engine were the use of down-draught carburetors and the engine's inclined angle in the frame, plus the change to liquid-cooling. Lightweight Deltabox design aluminium frames and uprated suspension improved the bikes's handling. The Genesis engine lives on in the YZF750 and 1000 models.

The vee-twin engine has been the mainstay of the XV Virago range. Since 1981 XVs have

The XS650 led the way for Yamaha's four-stroke range

Yamaha's XS750 was produced from 1976 to 1982 and then uprated to 850 cc

been produced in 535, 700, 750, 920, 1000 and 1100 engine sizes, all using the same basic air-cooled sohc vee-twin engine. Other uses of vee engines have been in the XZ550 of the early 1980s, the XVZ12 Venture and the mighty VMX-12 V-Max.

Anti-lock braking, engine management, catalytic converters and hub center steering are all features found on present-day models, ensuring that Yamaha remain at the forefront of technology.

The XJ600S and XJ600N

Yamaha's XJ range goes back to the XJ650 of 1980, introduced to replace the ageing XS series of four-strokes. The XJs have appeared in 550, 600, 750 and 900 cc form, with an XJ400 for the Japanese home market.

The Diversion is not a retro version of the old XJ or XS Yamahas, but an uncomplicated and affordable middleweight bike. Launched in 1992, the Diversion soon established itself as a firm favourite with riders wanting a good all-round motorcycle which was relatively cheap to insure and run. Its success was so great that it wasn't long before this approach was seen on other manufacturers' models,

A new family of four-strokes was released in 1980 with the introduction of the XJ range

like Suzuki's popular 600 Bandit. Yamaha carried the Diversion formula onto a 900 cc bike when the ageing XJ900F was replaced in 1994.

The Diversion, or Seca II, as it is named in the USA, uses a two valve DOHC air-cooled engine like the previous XJ models, but the engine is tilted 35° forwards in the frame to lower the centre of gravity. Angling the engine in this way allows the use of straight inlet tracts and downdraft Mikuni carburettors as seen on the Genesis-engined FZR bikes. One of the engine's most distinctive features is the crossover exhaust header pipes; the pipes from cylinders 2 and 3 connect to the right-hand silencer, whereas the pipe from cylinder no. 4 crosses over to join the no. 1 cylinder pipe in the left-hand silencer.

Without the added complexity of liquid cooling and a 16- or 20-valve head, the Diversion is a DIY mechanics dream; easy to service and with all components very accessible. Transmission is by a six speed gearbox with chain drive to the rear wheel. The three-spoke cast aluminium wheels, 17 inch front and 18 inch rear, carry tubeless tyres.

Suspension is by straightforward 38 mm telescopic forks at the front and a Monoshock linkage with preload adjustment at the rear linked to an oval section steel swingarm. Braking is all hydraulic, using a single twin piston sliding caliper at the front and an opposed caliper at the rear. The engine is rubber-mounted in a steel tube double cradle frame, painted the same colour as the fuel

The XJ600S Diversion model

tank and bodywork on many models. The US Seca II model has the benefit of a colour-matched belly pan or chin fairing.

In 1995 Yamaha responded to the need for a 'naked' style bike by producing the XJ600N – one of the most notable models being the yellow bodywork and yellow framed version. The only difference between this model and the Diversion was that it lacked a fairing and according was fitted with a chrome round headlamp and chrome instrument pods. However, the Diversion still remains the most popular of the two models, with most riders preferring its looks and the wind protection offered by its fairing.

Apart from colour and graphics there were very few changes until 1996 (UK) or 1997 (US) when the XJ600S received a new style fairing and windshield. Both models were fitted with new rear bodywork, identified by the small black fillet between the tank and side cover. Less obvious changes included a handlebar-mounted choke lever, rather than the operating knob on the carburettors, and European models received an oil cooler, electric fuel pump, throttle position switch and revised carburettor heater system. Later European models were fitted with twin front disc brakes and hazard warning lights.

Acknowledgements

Our thanks are due to Mitsui Machinery Sales (UK) Ltd for permission to reproduce certain illustrations used in this manual and for supplying some of the cover photographs. We would also like to thank NGK Spark Plugs (UK) Ltd for supplying the colour spark plug condition photos and the Avon Rubber Company for supplying information on tyre fitting.

Special thanks to Doreen DeMello for supplying the XJ600S used in these photographs; to Dave Jewell for organising and performing the teardown; and to both Dave and Denny Jewell for the technical expertise that comes from their years of experience as motorcycle mechanics and racers. Thanks are also due to Taylors Motorcycles of Misterton, Crewkerne, who supplied the later model XJ600S.

About this manual

The aim of this manual is to help you get the best value from your motorcycle. It can do so in several ways. It can help you decide what work must be done, even if you choose to have it done by a dealer; it provides information and procedures for routine maintenance and servicing; and it offers diagnostic and repair procedures to follow when trouble occurs.

We hope you use the manual to tackle the work yourself. For many simpler jobs, doing it yourself may be quicker than arranging an appointment to get the vehicle into a dealer and making the trips to leave it and pick it up. More importantly, a lot of money can be saved by avoiding the expense the dealer must pass on to you to cover its labour and overhead costs. An added benefit is the sense of satisfaction and accomplishment that you feel after doing the job yourself.

References to the left or right side of the motorcycle assume you are sitting on the seat, facing forward.

We take great pride in the accuracy of information given in this manual, but motorcycle manufacturers make alterations and design changes during the production run of a particular motorcycle of which they do not inform us. No liability can be accepted by the authors or publishers for loss, damage or injury caused by any errors in, or omissions from, the information given.

Professional mechanics are trained in safe working procedures. However enthusiastic you may be about getting on with the job at hand, take the time to ensure that your safety is not put at risk. A moment's lack of attention can result in an accident, as can failure to observe simple precautions.

There will always be new ways of having accidents, and the following is not a comprehensive list of all dangers; it is intended rather to make you aware of the risks and to encourage a safe approach to all work you carry out on your bike.

Asbestos

● Certain friction, insulating, sealing and other products - such as brake pads, clutch linings, gaskets, etc. - contain asbestos. Extreme care must be taken to avoid inhalation of dust from such products since it is hazardous to health. If in doubt, assume that they do contain asbestos.

Fire

● Remember at all times that petrol is highly flammable. Never smoke or have any kind of naked flame around, when working on the vehicle. But the risk does not end there - a spark caused by an electrical short-circuit, by two metal surfaces contacting each other, by careless use of tools, or even by static electricity built up in your body under certain conditions, can ignite petrol vapour, which in a confined space is highly explosive. Never use petrol as a cleaning solvent. Use an approved safety solvent.

● Always disconnect the battery earth terminal before working on any part of the fuel or electrical system, and never risk spilling fuel on to a hot engine or exhaust.

● It is recommended that a fire extinguisher of a type suitable for fuel and electrical fires is kept handy in the garage or workplace at all times. Never try to extinguish a fuel or electrical fire with water.

Fumes

● Certain fumes are highly toxic and can quickly cause unconsciousness and even death if inhaled to any extent. Petrol vapour comes into this category, as do the vapours from certain solvents such as trichloro-ethylene. Any draining or pouring of such volatile fluids should be done in a well ventilated area.

● When using cleaning fluids and solvents, read the instructions carefully. Never use materials from unmarked containers - they may give off poisonous vapours.

● Never run the engine of a motor vehicle in an enclosed space such as a garage. Exhaust fumes contain carbon monoxide which is extremely poisonous; if you need to run the engine, always do so in the open air or at least have the rear of the vehicle outside the workplace.

The battery

● Never cause a spark, or allow a naked light near the vehicle's battery. It will normally be giving off a certain amount of hydrogen gas, which is highly explosive.

● Always disconnect the battery ground (earth) terminal before working on the fuel or electrical systems (except where noted).

● If possible, loosen the filler plugs or cover when charging the battery from an external source. Do not charge at an excessive rate or the battery may burst.

● Take care when topping up, cleaning or carrying the battery. The acid electrolyte, even when diluted, is very corrosive and should not be allowed to contact the eyes or skin. Always wear rubber gloves and goggles or a face shield. If you ever need to prepare electrolyte yourself, always add the acid slowly to the water; never add the water to the acid.

Electricity

● When using an electric power tool, inspection light etc., always ensure that the appliance is correctly connected to its plug and that, where necessary, it is properly grounded (earthed). Do not use such appliances in damp conditions and, again, beware of creating a spark or applying excessive heat in the vicinity of fuel or fuel vapour. Also ensure that the appliances meet national safety standards.

● A severe electric shock can result from touching certain parts of the electrical system, such as the spark plug wires (HT leads), when the engine is running or being cranked, particularly if components are damp or the insulation is defective. Where an electronic ignition system is used, the secondary (HT) voltage is much higher and could prove fatal.

Remember...

✗ **Don't** start the engine without first ascertaining that the transmission is in neutral.

✗ **Don't** suddenly remove the pressure cap from a hot cooling system - cover it with a cloth and release the pressure gradually first, or you may get scalded by escaping coolant.

✗ **Don't** attempt to drain oil until you are sure it has cooled sufficiently to avoid scalding you.

✗ **Don't** grasp any part of the engine or exhaust system without first ascertaining that it is cool enough not to burn you.

✗ **Don't** allow brake fluid or antifreeze to contact the machine's paintwork or plastic components.

✗ **Don't** siphon toxic liquids such as fuel, hydraulic fluid or antifreeze by mouth, or allow them to remain on your skin.

✗ **Don't** inhale dust - it may be injurious to health (see Asbestos heading).

✗ **Don't** allow any spilled oil or grease to remain on the floor - wipe it up right away, before someone slips on it.

✗ **Don't** use ill-fitting spanners or other tools which may slip and cause injury.

✗ **Don't** lift a heavy component which may be beyond your capability - get assistance.

✗ **Don't** rush to finish a job or take unverified short cuts.

✗ **Don't** allow children or animals in or around an unattended vehicle.

✗ **Don't** inflate a tyre above the recommended pressure. Apart from overstressing the carcass, in extreme cases the tyre may blow off forcibly.

✔ **Do** ensure that the machine is supported securely at all times. This is especially important when the machine is blocked up to aid wheel or fork removal.

✔ **Do** take care when attempting to loosen a stubborn nut or bolt. It is generally better to pull on a spanner, rather than push, so that if you slip, you fall away from the machine rather than onto it.

✔ **Do** wear eye protection when using power tools such as drill, sander, bench grinder etc.

✔ **Do** use a barrier cream on your hands prior to undertaking dirty jobs - it will protect your skin from infection as well as making the dirt easier to remove afterwards; but make sure your hands aren't left slippery. Note that long-term contact with used engine oil can be a health hazard.

✔ **Do** keep loose clothing (cuffs, ties etc. and long hair) well out of the way of moving mechanical parts.

✔ **Do** remove rings, wristwatch etc., before working on the vehicle - especially the electrical system.

✔ **Do** keep your work area tidy - it is only too easy to fall over articles left lying around.

✔ **Do** exercise caution when compressing springs for removal or installation. Ensure that the tension is applied and released in a controlled manner, using suitable tools which preclude the possibility of the spring escaping violently.

✔ **Do** ensure that any lifting tackle used has a safe working load rating adequate for the job.

✔ **Do** get someone to check periodically that all is well, when working alone on the vehicle.

✔ **Do** carry out work in a logical sequence and check that everything is correctly assembled and tightened afterwards.

✔ **Do** remember that your vehicle's safety affects that of yourself and others. If in doubt on any point, get professional advice.

● If in spite of following these precautions, you are unfortunate enough to injure yourself, seek medical attention as soon as possible.

Frame and engine numbers

The frame serial number is stamped into the steering head and printed on a label affixed to the right front portion of the frame. The engine number is stamped into the right upper side of the crankcase. Both of these numbers should be recorded and kept in a safe place so they can be furnished to law enforcement officials in the event of a theft.

The frame serial number, engine serial number and carburettor identification number should also be kept in a handy place (such as with your driver's licence) so they are always available when purchasing or ordering parts for your machine.

Buying spare parts

Once you have found all the identification numbers, record them for reference when buying parts. Since the manufacturers change specifications, parts and vendors (companies that manufacture various components on the machine), providing the ID numbers is the only way to be reasonably sure that you are buying the correct parts.

Whenever possible, take the worn part to the dealer so direct comparison with the new component can be made. Along the trail from the manufacturer to the parts shelf, there are numerous places that the part can end up with the wrong number or be listed incorrectly.

The two places to purchase new parts for your motorcycle – the accessory shop and the franchised dealer – differ in the type of parts they carry. While dealers can obtain virtually every part for your motorcycle, the accessory shop is usually limited to normal high wear items such as shock absorbers, filters, various engine gaskets, cables, chains, brake pads, etc. Rarely will an accessory outlet have major suspension components, cylinders, transmission gears, or cases.

Used parts can be obtained for roughly half the price of new ones, but you can't always be sure of what you're getting. Once again, take your worn part to the breaker (wrecking yard) for direct comparison.

Whether buying new, used or rebuilt parts, the best course is to deal directly with someone who specialises in parts for your particular make.

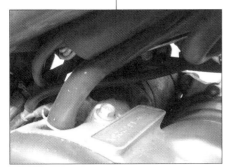

The engine number is stamped into the right side of the crankcase

The frame number is printed on a decal on the frame . . .

. . . and stamped in the right side of the steering head

Note: *The daily (pre-ride) checks outlined in the owner's manual covers those items which should be inspected on a daily basis.*

1 Engine/transmission oil level check

Before you start:

✔ Start the engine and allow it to reach normal operating temperature.

Caution: Do not run the engine in an enclosed space such as a garage or workshop.

✔ Stop the engine and allow the machine to sit undisturbed in a level position for about five minutes. Place the bike on the centrestand (if equipped) or prop it securely in an upright position.

Bike care:

● If you have to add oil frequently, you should check whether you have any oil leaks. If there is no sign of oil leakage from the joints and gaskets, the engine could be burning oil (see *Fault Finding*).

The correct oil

● Modern, high-revving engines place great demands on their oil. It is very important that the correct oil for your bike is used.

● Always top up with a good quality oil of the specified type and viscosity and do not overfill the engine.

Oil type	API grade SE, SF or SG
Oil viscosity - below 15°C (60°F)	SAE 10W30
Oil viscosity - above 5°C (40°F)	SAE 20W40

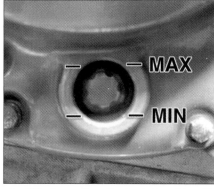

1 With the engine off, check the oil level in the window located at the lower part of the right crankcase cover. The oil level should be between the Maximum and Minimum level marks next to the window.

2 If the level is below the Minimum mark, remove the oil filler cap from the right side of the crankcase.

3 Add enough oil of the recommended grade and type to bring the level up to the Maximum mark. Do not overfill the crankcase.

2 Brake fluid level checks

 Warning: Brake hydraulic fluid can harm your eyes and damage painted surfaces, so use extreme caution when handling and pouring it and cover surrounding surfaces with rag. Do not use fluid that has been standing open for some time, as it absorbs moisture from the air which can cause a dangerous loss of braking effectiveness.

Before you start:
✔ With the motorcycle on the centrestand or held upright, turn the handlebars until the top of the front master cylinder is as level as possible.
✔ Make sure that you have the correct DOT 4 hydraulic fluid (or as directed on reservoir cap). Do not mix different brands of brake fluid in the reservoir, as they may not be compatible.
✔ Before removing the front brake reservoir cover, place a rag over the front of the fuel tank to protect it from brake fluid spills (which will damage the paint) and remove all dust and dirt from the area around the cover.
✔ Remove the right side cover to access the rear brake fluid reservoir (see Chapter 7).

Bike care:
● The fluid in the front and rear brake master cylinder reservoirs will drop slightly as the brake pads wear down.
● If any fluid reservoir requires repeated topping-up this is an indication of a leak somewhere in the system, which should be investigated immediately.
● Check for signs of fluid leakage from the hydraulic hoses and components – if found, rectify immediately.
● Check the operation of both brakes before taking the machine on the road; if there is evidence of air in the system (spongy feel to lever or pedal), it must be bled (see Chapter 6).

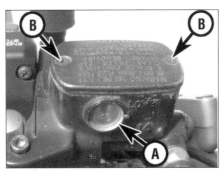

1 The front brake fluid level is checked via the inspection window in the master cylinder reservoir. Make sure that the fluid level is above the LOWER mark on the reservoir (A). If the level is too low remove the screws (B) . . .

2 . . . and lift off the cover and rubber diaphragm to allow topping up.

3 Top up with the recommended brake fluid.

4 Ensure that the diaphragm is folded correctly . . .

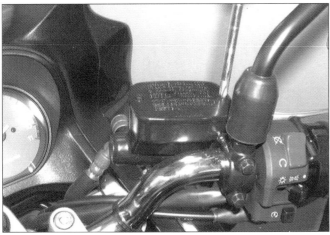

5 . . . then fit the cover and tighten its screws securely.

6 The rear brake fluid level can be checked by looking through the plastic reservoir. The fluid must be above the LOWER mark on the reservoir. Unscrew the cap to permit topping up.

3 Suspension, steering and final drive check

Suspension and steering:
● Check that the front and rear suspension operates smoothly without binding.
● Check that the rear suspension is adjusted as required.
● Check that the steering moves smoothly from lock-to-lock.

Final drive:
● Check that the drive chain slack isn't excessive, and adjust if necessary (see Chapter 1).
● If the chain looks dry, lubricate it (see Chapter 1).

4 Legal and safety checks

Lighting and signalling:
● Take a minute to check that the headlight, taillight, brake light, instrument lights and turn signals all work correctly.
● Check that the horn sounds when the switch is operated.
● A working speedometer, graduated in mph, is a statutory requirement in the UK.

Safety:
● Check that the throttle grip rotates smoothly and snaps shut, when released, in all steering positions.
● Check that the engine shuts off when the kill switch is operated.
● Check that the clutch lever operates smoothly and with the correct amount of freeplay.
● Check that the sidestand return spring holds the stand securely up when retracted. The same applies to the centrestand.

Fuel:
● This may seem obvious, but check that you have enough fuel to complete your journey. If you notice signs of fluid leakage rectify the cause immediately.
● Ensure you use the correct grade unleaded fuel – see Chapter 3 Specifications. Don't overfill the fuel tank – only fill up to the bottom edge of the filler tube.

5 Tyre checks

The correct pressures:
● The tyres must be checked when **cold**, not immediately after riding. Note that low tyre pressures may cause the tyre to slip on the rim or come off. High tyre pressures will cause abnormal tread wear and unsafe handling.
● Use an accurate pressure gauge.

1 Check the tyre pressures when the tyres are **cold** and keep them properly inflated.

● Proper air pressure will increase tyre life and provide maximum stability and ride comfort.

Tyre care:
● Check the tyres carefully for cuts, tears, cracks, bulges, embedded nails or other sharp objects and excessive wear. Operation of the motorcycle with excessively worn tyres is extremely hazardous, as traction and handling are directly affected.
● Check the condition of the tyre valve and ensure the dust cap is in place.
● Pick out any stones or nails which may have become embedded in the tyre tread. If left, they will eventually penetrate through the casing and cause a puncture.

● If tyre damage is apparent, or unexplained loss of pressure is experienced, seek the advice of a tyre fitting specialist without delay.

Tyre tread depth:
● At the time of writing UK law requires that tread depth must be at least 1 mm over 3/4 of the tread breadth all the way around the tyre, with no bald patches. Many riders, however, consider 2 mm tread depth minimum to be a safer limit.
● Many tyres now incorporate wear indicators in the tread. Identify the triangular pointer on the tyre sidewall to locate the indicator bar and replace the tyre if the tread has worn down to the bar.

Loading/speed	Front	Rear
Up to 90 kg (198 lbs)	29 psi (2.0 Bars)	33 psi (2.25 Bars)
Above 90 kg (198 lbs) or high speed riding	29 psi (2.0 Bars)	36 psi (2.50 Bars)

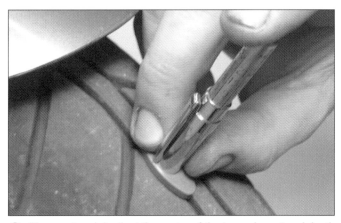

2 Measure tread depth at the centre of the tyre using a tread depth gauge.

3 Tyre tread wear indicator bar and its location marking (usually either an arrow, a triangle or the letters TWI) on the sidewall.

Notes

Chapter 1
Routine maintenance and servicing

Contents

Degrees of difficulty

Easy, suitable for novice with little experience	**Fairly easy,** suitable for beginner with some experience	**Fairly difficult,** suitable for competent DIY mechanic	**Difficult,** suitable for experienced DIY mechanic	**Very difficult,** suitable for expert DIY or professional 

Specifications

Engine

Spark plugs	
Type	
US models	NGK CR7E or CR8E, ND U22ESR-N or U24ESR-N
UK models	NGK CR7E, CR8E or CR9E, ND U22ESR-N, U24ESR-N or U27ESR-N
Gap	0.7 to 0.8 mm (0.028 to 0.031 inch)
Valve clearances (COLD engine)	
Intake	0.11 to 0.15 mm (0.004 to 0.006 inch)
Exhaust	0.21 to 0.25 mm (0.008 to 0.010 inch) (Note 1)
Engine idle speed	
US models	1200 to 1400 rpm
UK models (1992-95)	1150 to 1250 rpm
UK models (1996-on)	1200 to 1300 rpm
Cylinder compression pressure (at sea level)	10.6 Bars (156 psi)
Carburettor synchronisation	
Engine vacuum at idle speed	
US models	220 to 230 mm Hg (8.06 to 9.66 inches Hg)
UK models (1992-95)	260 to 270 mm Hg (10.24 to 10.64 inches Hg)
UK models (1996-on)	230 mm Hg (9.66 inches Hg)
Maximum vacuum difference between cylinders	10 mm Hg (0.4 inch Hg)
Cylinder numbering (from left side to right side of bike)	1-2-3-4

Cycle parts

Disc brake pad thickness

Front

    Standard – 1992-97 UK models, all US models . . . . 6.2 mm (1/4 inch)

    Standard – 1998-on UK models . . . . 5.5 mm (7/32 inch)

    Minimum . . . . 0.8 mm (1/32 inch)

Rear

    Standard . . . . 5.5 mm (7/32 inch)

    Minimum . . . . 0.8 mm (1/32 inch)

Brake pedal position (below top of footpeg) . . . . 40 mm (1-19/32 inch)

Freeplay adjustments

Throttle grip . . . . 3 to 7 mm (1/8 to 9/32 inch)

Clutch lever

    1992-95 UK models, 1992-96 US models (at lever stock) . . . . 2 to 3 mm (5/64 to 19/64 inch)

    1996-on UK models, 1997-on US models (at lever end) . . . . 10 to 15 mm (0.4 to 0.6 inch)

Front brake lever . . . . see text

Drive chain slack . . . . 30 to 40 mm (1-13/64 to 1-19/32 inch)

Tyre pressures and tread depth . . . . see *Daily (pre-ride) checks*

Torque settings

Oil drain plug . . . . 43 Nm (31 ft-lbs)

Oil filter . . . . 17 Nm (144 in-lbs)

Spark plugs . . . . 12.5 Nm (108 in-lbs)

Exhaust pipe flange nuts . . . . 15 Nm (132 in-lbs) (Note 2)

Steering head bearing ring nut

Initial torque . . . . 52 Nm (37 ft-lbs) (Note 3)

Final torque . . . . 18 Nm (156 in-lbs) (Note 3)

Valve cover bolts . . . . 10 Nm (86 in-lbs)

Fork caps . . . . 23 Nm (17 ft-lbs)

Recommended lubricants and fluids

Engine/transmission

Type . . . . API grade SE, SF or SG

Viscosity

Up to 15°C (60°F) . . . . SAE 10W-30

Above 5°C (40°F) . . . . SAE 20W-40

Capacity – all US models, 1992-95 UK models

With filter change . . . . 2.5 litres (2.6 US qts, 4.4 Imperial pts)

Oil change only . . . . 2.2 litres (2.3 US qts, 3.8 Imperial pts)

Capacity – 1996-on UK models

With filter change . . . . 2.6 litres (2.7 US qts, 4.6 Imperial pts)

Oil change only . . . . 2.3 litres (2.4 US qts, 4.0 Imperial pts)

Brakes

Fluid type . . . . DOT 4 (DOT 3 may be used if DOT 4 is unavailable)

Front forks

Type . . . . SAE 10W fork oil

Capacity

1992-95 UK models, 1992-96 US models . . . . 379 cc (12.8 US fl oz, 13.3 Imperial fl oz)

1996-98 UK models, 1997-on US models . . . . 375 cc (12.7 US fl oz, 13.2 Imperial fl oz)

1999-on UK models . . . . 463 cc (16.3 Imperial fl oz)

Oil level (Note 4)

1992-95 UK models, 1992-96 US models . . . . 111 mm (4.37 inches)

1996-98 UK models, 1997-on US models . . . . 116 mm (4.57 inches)

1999-on UK models . . . . 120 mm (4.72 inches)

Cycle parts

Drive chain . . . . SAE 30 to 50W engine oil

Wheel and steering head bearings . . . . Medium weight, lithium-based multi-purpose grease

Swingarm pivot bearings . . . . Medium weight, lithium-based waterproof wheel bearing grease

Cables and lever pivots . . . . Chain and cable lubricant or 10W30 motor oil

Sidestand/centrestand pivots . . . . Medium-weight, lithium-based multi-purpose grease

Brake pedal/shift lever pivots . . . . Chain and cable lubricant or 10W30 motor oil

Throttle grip . . . . Multi-purpose grease or dry film lubricant

Notes

1. To minimise valve noise it may be possible to reduce the exhaust valve clearance to 0.18 mm (0.007 inch).

2. Lubricate the threads with anti-seize compound.

3. Using Yamaha ring nut wrench YU-33975 and a torque wrench placed at a right angle to the ring nut wrench.

4. Fork oil level is measured from the top of the fork tube, with the fork fully compressed and the spacer, spring seat and spring removed.

Note: *The pre-ride inspection outlined in the owner's manual covers checks and maintenance that should be carried out on a daily basis. it's condensed and included here to remind you of its importance. Always perform the pre-ride inspection at every maintenance interval (in addition to the procedures listed). The intervals listed below are the shortest intervals recommended by the manufacturer for each particular operation during the model years covered in this manual. Your owner's manual may have different intervals for your model.*

Daily (pre-ride) checks

☐ See *Daily (pre-ride) checks* at the beginning of this manual.

After the initial 600 miles (1000 km)

Note: *This check is usually performed by a Yamaha dealer after the first 600 miles (1000 km) from new. Thereafter, maintenance is carried out according to the following intervals of the schedule.*

Every 500 miles (800 km)

☐ Check/adjust and lubricate the drive chain (Section 1)

Every 4000 miles (6000 km) or 6 months

Note: *Carry out all the items above plus the following:*
☐ Change the engine/transmission oil (Section 2)
☐ Clean the air filter element and replace it if necessary (Section 3)
☐ Clean and gap the spark plugs (Section 4)
☐ Check/adjust the idle speed and throttle cable freeplay (Section 5)
☐ Check/adjust the carburettor synchronisation (Section 6)
☐ Check the brake discs and pads (Section 7)
☐ Lubricate brake pad edges and caliper cavities* (Section 7)
☐ Check/adjust the brake pedal and lever position and check the brake light (Section 8)
☐ Check the clutch cable freeplay (Section 9)
☐ Lubricate the clutch and brake lever pivots (Section 10)
☐ Lubricate the shift/brake lever pivots and the sidestand/centrestand pivots (Section 10)
☐ Lubricate the cables (Section 10)
☐ Check the front forks for proper operation and fluid leaks (Section 11)
☐ Inspect the rear shock absorber (Section 11)
☐ Check the wheels and tyres (Section 12)
☐ Check the exhaust system for leaks (Section 13)
☐ Check the tightness of the fasteners (Section 14)

Every 4000 miles (6000 km) or 6 months (continued)

☐ Check the cleanliness of the fuel system and the condition of the fuel lines and vacuum hoses (Section 15)
☐ Inspect the crankcase breather system (Section 16)
☐ Check the operation of the sidestand switch (Section 17)
Required in the UK and recommended wherever salt is used on the roads

Every 8000 miles (12,000 km) or 12 months

Note: *Carry out all the items under the previous mileage headings plus the following:*
☐ Change the engine/transmission oil and oil filter (Section 18)
☐ Check and adjust the steering head bearings (Section 19)

Every 12,000 miles (18,000 km) or 18 months

Note: *Carry out all the items under the 4000 mile (6000 km) heading plus the following:*
☐ Inspect the evaporative emission control system (California models) (Section 20)

Every 16,000 miles (24,000 km) or two years

Note: *Carry out all the items under the 8000 mile (12,000 km) heading plus the following:*
☐ Change the brake fluid (Section 21)
☐ Overhaul the brake master cylinders and calipers (Section 22)
☐ Clean and repack the steering head bearings (Section 23)
☐ Lubricate the swingarm bearings and rear suspension pivot points (Section 24)
☐ Adjust the valve clearances (Section 25)

Non-scheduled maintenance

☐ Check the battery (Section 26)
☐ Check the cylinder compression (Section 27)
☐ Replace the fork oil (Section 28)

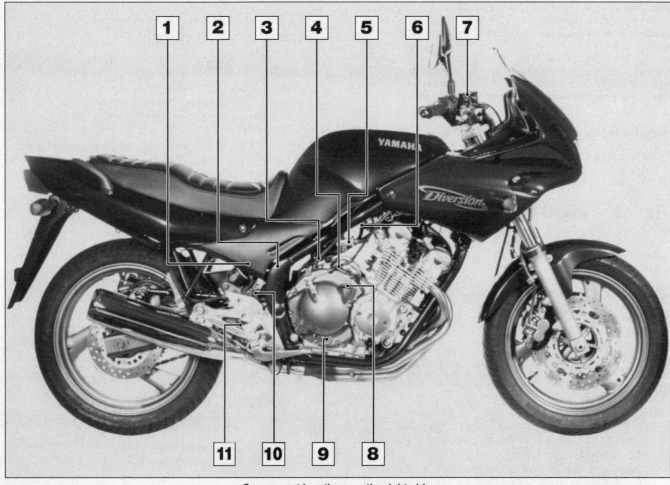

Component locations on the right side

1 Rear brake fluid reservoir
2 Emission control canister (California models)
3 Crankcase breather hose
4 Clutch cable lower adjuster
5 Fuel filter
6 Idle speed adjuster
7 Front brake fluid reservoir
8 Engine/transmission oil filler cap
9 Engine/transmission oil level window
10 Rear brake light switch
11 Rear brake pedal height adjuster

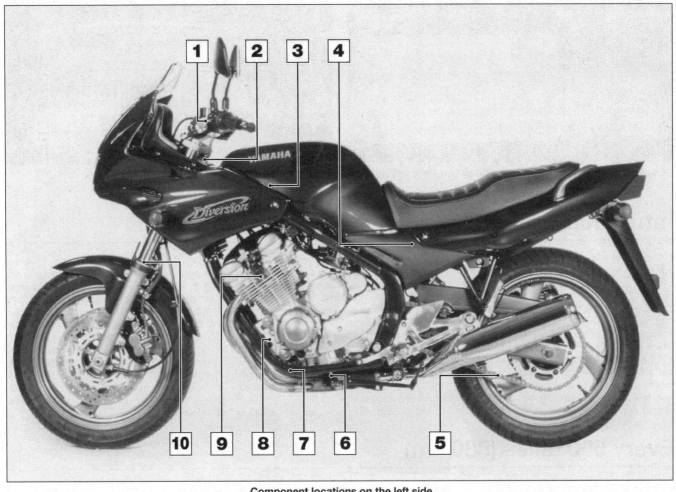

Component locations on the left side

1 Clutch cable upper adjuster
2 Steering head bearings
3 Air filter
4 Battery

5 Drive chain
6 Sidestand switch
7 Engine/transmission oil drain plug

8 Engine/transmission oil filter
9 Spark plugs
10 Fork seals

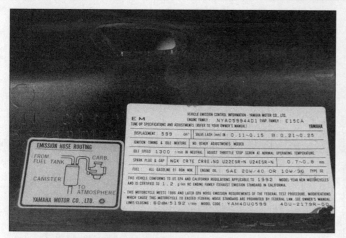

Maintenance labels on the bike provide oil types and settings . . .   . . . and maximum load limit details

Introduction

1 This Chapter is designed to help the home mechanic maintain his/her motorcycle for safety, economy, long life and peak performance.

2 Deciding where to start or plug into the routine maintenance schedule depends on several factors. If you have a motorcycle on which the warranty has recently expired, and if it has been maintained according to the warranty standards, you may want to pick-up routine maintenance as it coincides with the next mileage or calendar interval. If you have owned the machine for some time but have never performed any maintenance on it, then you may want to start at the nearest interval and include some additional procedures to ensure that nothing important is overlooked. If you have just had a major engine overhaul, then you may want to start the maintenance routine from the beginning. If you have a used machine and have no knowledge of its history or maintenance record, you may desire to combine all the checks into one large service initially and then settle into the maintenance schedule prescribed.

3 Before beginning any maintenance or repair, the machine should be cleaned thoroughly, especially around the oil filter, spark plugs, valve cover, side covers, carburettors, etc. Cleaning will help ensure that dirt does not contaminate the engine and will allow you to detect wear and damage that could otherwise easily go unnoticed.

4 Certain maintenance information is sometimes printed on decals attached to the motorcycle. If the information on the decals differs from that included here, use the information on the decal **(see illustrations)**.

Every 500 miles (800 km)

1 Drive chain and sprockets – check, adjustment and lubrication

Check

1 A neglected drive chain won't last long and can quickly damage the sprockets. Routine chain adjustment and lubrication isn't difficult and will ensure maximum chain and sprocket life.

2 To check the chain, place the bike on its centrestand (if equipped) or prop it securely in an upright position. Shift the transmission into Neutral. Make sure the ignition switch is Off.

3 Push up on the bottom run of the chain and measure the slack midway between the two sprockets **(see illustration)**, then compare your measurements to the value listed in this Chapter's Specifications. As wear occurs, the chain will actually stretch, which means adjustment usually involves removing some slack from the chain. In some cases where lubrication has been neglected, corrosion and galling may cause the links to bind and kink, which effectively shortens the chain's length. If the chain is tight between the sprockets, rusty or kinked, it's time to replace it with a new one. **Note:** *Repeat the chain slack measurement along the length of the chain – ideally, every inch or so. If you find a tight area, mark it with felt pen or paint and repeat the measurement after the bike has been ridden. If the chain is still tight in the same area, it may be damaged or worn. Because a tight or kinked chain can damage the transmission output shaft bearing, it's a good idea to replace it.*

4 Remove the chain guard **(see illustration)**.

1.3 Push up on the lower run of the chain and measure how far it deflects – if it's not within the specified limits, adjust the slack in the chain

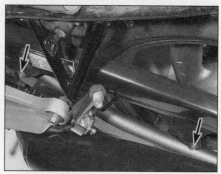

1.4a The chain guard is secured by screws at the front and rear (arrowed)

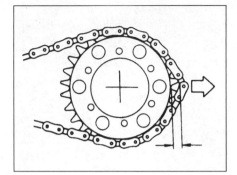

1.4b If the chain can be pulled more than half the length of a tooth away from the sprocket, it's worn and should be replaced

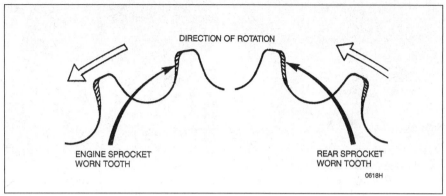

1.5 Check the sprockets in the areas indicated to see if they're worn excessively

Check the entire length of the chain for damaged rollers, loose links and pins. Pull the chain rearward, away from the centre of the rear sprocket **(see illustration)**. If the chain pulls away by more than half the length of a sprocket tooth, it's worn and should be replaced. Rotate the wheel and repeat this check at several places on the chain, since it may wear unevenly. **Note:** *Never install a new chain on old sprockets, and never use the old chain if you install new sprockets – replace the chain and sprockets as a set.*

5 Remove the engine sprocket cover (see Chapter 5). Check the teeth on the engine sprocket and the rear sprocket for wear **(see illustration)**.

Adjustment

6 Rotate the rear wheel until the chain is positioned with the least amount of slack present.

7 Remove the cotter pin from the axle nut and loosen the nut **(see illustration)**.

8 Loosen and back-off the locknuts on the adjuster bolts.

9 Turn the axle adjusting bolts on both sides of the swingarm until the proper chain tension is obtained (get the adjuster on the chain side close, then set the adjuster on the opposite side). Be sure to turn the adjusting bolts evenly to keep the rear wheel in alignment. If the adjusting bolts reach the end of their travel, the chain is excessively worn and should be replaced with a new one (see Chapter 6).

10 When the chain has the correct amount of slack, make sure the marks on the adjusters correspond to the same relative marks on each side of the swingarm **(see illustration 1.7)**. Tighten the axle nut to the torque listed in the Chapter 6 Specifications, then install a new cotter pin and bend it properly **(see illustration)**. If necessary, turn the nut an additional amount to line up the cotter pin hole with the castellations in the nut – don't loosen the nut to do this.

11 Tighten the chain adjuster locknuts securely.

Lubrication

Note: *If the chain is extremely dirty, it should be removed and cleaned before it's lubricated (see Chapter 5).*

12 The best time to lubricate the chain is after the motorcycle has been ridden. When the chain is warm, the lubricant will penetrate the joints between the side plates, pins, bushings and rollers to provide lubrication of the internal load bearing areas. **Note:** *Yamaha specifies SAE 30 to SAE 50 engine oil only; you can use aerosol chain lube, but make sure it is suitable for O-ring chains.*

13 Apply the oil to the area where the side plates overlap – not the middle of the rollers. After applying the lubricant, let it soak in a few minutes before wiping off any excess.

> **HAYNES HINT**
> *Apply the oil to the top of the lower chain run, so centrifugal force will work the oil into the chain when the bike is moving.*

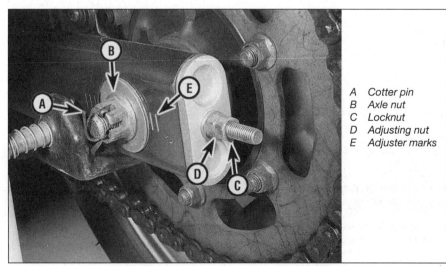

A Cotter pin
B Axle nut
C Locknut
D Adjusting nut
E Adjuster marks

1.7 Remove the cotter pin and loosen the axle nut

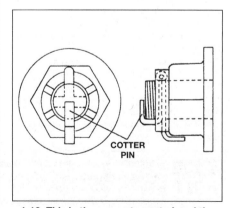

1.10 This is the correct way to bend the axle nut cotter pin – always use a new cotter pin whenever the old one is removed

2.5 Remove the oil drain plug

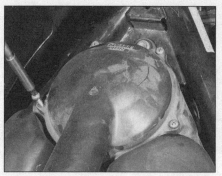

3.2 Remove the cover screws and lift off the cover . . .

3.3 . . . noting the position of the cover O-ring (A), then remove the filter element (B) from the air box

Every 4000 miles (6000 km) or 6 months

2 Engine/transmission oil – change

1 Consistent routine oil changes are the single most important maintenance procedure you can perform on a motorcycle. The oil not only lubricates the internal parts of the engine, transmission and clutch, but it also acts as a coolant, a cleaner, a sealant, and a protectant. Because of these demands, the oil takes a terrific amount of abuse and should be replaced often with new oil of the recommended grade and type. Saving a little money on the difference in cost between a good oil and a cheap oil won't pay off if the engine is damaged.

2 Before changing the oil, warm up the engine so the oil will drain easily.

⚠ **Warning: Be careful when draining the oil, as the exhaust pipes, the engine, and the oil itself can cause severe burns.**

3 Put the motorcycle on the centrestand (if equipped) or prop it securely upright. Place a clean drain pan beneath the crankcase drain plug. Remove the oil filler cap to vent the crankcase and to serve as a reminder that there is no oil in the engine.

4 If the bike has a lower fairing, remove it (see Chapter 7).

5 Next, remove the drain plug from the engine **(see illustration)** and allow the oil to drain into the pan. Discard the sealing washer on the drain plug; it should be replaced whenever the plug is removed.

6 Before refilling the engine, check the old oil carefully.

7 If the inspection of the oil turns up nothing unusual, refill the crankcase to the proper level with the recommended oil and install the filler cap (see *Daily (pre-ride) checks*). Start the engine and let it run for two or three minutes. Shut it off, wait a few minutes, then check the oil level. If necessary, add more oil to bring the level up to the Maximum mark. Check around the drain plug and filter housing for leaks.

8 The old oil drained from the engine cannot be reused in its present state and should be disposed of. Check with your local refuse disposal company, disposal facility or environmental agency to see whether they will accept the used oil for recycling. Don't pour used oil into drains or onto the ground. After the oil has cooled, it can be drained into a suitable container (capped plastic jugs, topped bottles, milk cartons, etc.) for transport to one of these disposal sites.

Note: It is antisocial and illegal to dump oil down the drain. In the UK, call this number free to find the location of your local oil recycling bank. In the USA, note that any oil supplier must accept used oil for recycling.

3 Air filter element – servicing

1 Remove the fuel tank (see Chapter 3).

2 Remove the cover screws and lift off the housing cover **(see illustration)**. Inspect the cover O-ring and replace it if it's damaged or deteriorated.

3 Remove the element **(see illustration)**. Wipe out the housing with a clean rag.

4 Tap the element on a hard surface to shake out dirt. If compressed air is available, use it to clean the element by blowing from the outside in. If the element is extremely dirty or torn, replace it with a new one.

5 Reinstall the filter by reversing the removal procedure. Make sure the element is seated properly in the filter housing before installing the cover.

4 Spark plugs – replacement

1 This motorcycle is equipped with spark plugs that have a 16 mm wrench hex. Make sure your spark plug socket is the correct size before attempting to remove the plugs.

2 Rotate the spark plug caps back-and-forth to loosen them, then pull them off the plugs and check them for brittleness and cracking. If available, use compressed air to blow any accumulated debris from around the spark plugs. Remove the plugs **(see illustration)**.

3 Inspect the electrodes for wear. Both the centre and side electrodes should have square edges and the side electrode should be of uniform thickness. Look for excessive deposits and evidence of a cracked or chipped insulator around the centre electrode.

4.2 Use an extension and a deep socket to remove the spark plugs

If the oil is drained into a clean pan, small pieces of metal or other material can be easily detected. If the oil is very metallic coloured, then the engine is experiencing wear from break-in (new engine) or from insufficient lubrication. If there are flakes or chips of metal in the oil, then something is drastically wrong internally and the engine will have to be disassembled for inspection and repair. If there are pieces of fibre-like material in the oil, the clutch is wearing excessively and should be checked.

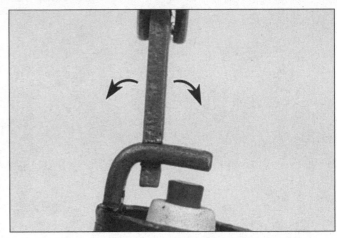

4.6a Spark plug manufacturers recommend using a wire type gauge when checking the gap

4.6b To change the gap, bend the side electrode only, as indicated by the arrows

Compare your spark plugs to the colour spark plug chart on the inside of the back cover. Check the threads, the washer and the ceramic insulator body for cracks and other damage.

4 If the electrodes are not excessively worn, and if the deposits can be easily removed with a wire brush, the plugs can be re-gapped and reused (if no cracks or chips are visible in the insulator). If in doubt concerning the condition of the plugs, replace them with new ones, as the expense is minimal.

5 Cleaning spark plugs by sandblasting is permitted, provided you clean the plugs with a high flash-point solvent afterwards.

6 Before installing new plugs, make sure they are the correct type and heat range. Check the gap between the electrodes, as they are not preset. For best results, use a wire-type gauge rather than a flat gauge to check the gap **(see illustration)**. If the gap must be adjusted, bend the side electrode only and be very careful not to chip or crack the insulator nose **(see illustration)**. Make sure the washer is in place before installing each plug.

7 Since the cylinder head is made of aluminium, which is soft and easily damaged, thread the plugs into the heads by hand.

> **HAYNES HiNT** *Since the plugs are recessed, slip a short length of hose over the end of the plug to use as a tool to thread it into place. The hose will grip the plug well enough to turn it, but will start to slip if the plug begins to cross-thread in the hole – this will prevent damaged threads and the resultant repair costs.*

8 Once the plugs are finger tight, the job can be finished with a socket. If a torque wrench is available, tighten the spark plugs to the torque listed in this Chapter's Specifications. If you do not have a torque wrench, tighten the plugs finger tight (until the washers bottom on the cylinder head) then use a wrench to tighten them an additional 1/4 turn. Regardless of the method used, do not over-tighten them.

9 Reconnect the spark plug caps and reinstall all components removed for access.

---

5 Idle speed and throttle cable freeplay – check and adjustment

Idle speed

1 The idle speed should be checked and adjusted before and after the carburettors are synchronised and when it is obviously too high or too low. Before adjusting the idle speed, make sure the valve clearances and spark plug gaps are correct. Also, turn the handlebars back-and-forth and see if the idle speed changes as this is done. If it does, the throttle cable may not be adjusted correctly, or it may be worn out. This is a dangerous condition that can cause loss of control of the bike. Be sure to correct this problem before proceeding.

2 The engine should be at normal operating temperature, which is usually reached after 10 to 15 minutes of stop and go riding. Place the motorcycle on the centrestand (if equipped) or prop it securely upright and make sure the transmission is in Neutral. If necessary for access to the pilot air screw or idle speed screw (US models), remove the upper fairing.

3 If you're working on a UK model (or a US model with the pilot air screw covers removed) refer to Chapter 3 and adjust the pilot air screw to the setting listed in the Chapter 3 Specifications.

4 With the engine idling, turn the throttle stop screw **(see illustration 6.9)** until the idle speed listed in this Chapter's Specifications is obtained.

5 Snap the throttle open and shut a few times, then recheck the idle speed. If necessary, repeat the adjustment procedure.

6 If a smooth, steady idle can't be achieved, the fuel/air mixture may be incorrect. Refer to Chapter 3 for additional carburettor information.

7 After making the adjustment adjust throttle cable freeplay.

Throttle check

8 Make sure the throttle grip rotates easily from fully closed to fully open with the front wheel turned at various angles. The grip should return automatically from fully open to fully closed when released. If the throttle sticks, check the throttle cables for cracks or kinks in the housings. Also, make sure the inner cables are clean and well-lubricated.

9 Check for a small amount of freeplay at the grip and compare the freeplay to the value listed in this Chapter's Specifications **(see illustration)**. If adjustment is necessary, adjust the idle speed first (see above).

Throttle cable adjustment

10 Freeplay adjustments are made at the handlebar end of the accelerator cable using the mid-line adjuster, then at the carburettor end if necessary. The decelerator cable isn't adjustable.

11 Make sure the throttle grip is in the fully closed position.

12 Make sure the throttle linkage lever contacts the idle adjusting screw when the throttle grip is in the closed throttle position.

5.9 Throttle cable freeplay is measured at the grip flange

5.13 To adjust throttle freeplay, pull back the rubber boot from the mid-line adjuster, loosen the locknut, turn the adjuster (arrowed), then tighten the locknut

5.14 Loosen the locknut (arrowed) to adjust the carburettor end of the cable

13 At the throttle grip, loosen the locknut **(see illustration)**. Turn the adjuster to achieve the correct freeplay, then tighten the locknut.

 Warning: Turn the handlebars all the way through their travel with the engine idling. Idle speed should not change. If it does, the cables may be routed incorrectly. Correct this dangerous condition before riding the bike.

14 If correct freeplay can't be achieved at the handlebar adjuster, loosen the locknut at the carburettor end of the cable **(see illustration)**. Reposition the cable as necessary, then tighten the locknuts.

6 Carburettor synchronisation – check and adjustment

 Warning: Gasoline (petrol) is extremely flammable, so take extra precautions when you work on any part of the fuel system. Don't smoke or allow open flames or bare light bulbs near the work area, and don't work in a garage where a natural gas-type appliance (such as a water heater or clothes dryer) is present. Since gasoline is carcinogenic, wear latex gloves when there's a possibility of being exposed to fuel, and, if you spill any fuel on your skin, rinse it off immediately with soap and water. When you perform any kind of work on the fuel system, wear safety glasses and have a fire extinguisher suitable for a Class B type fire (flammable liquids) on hand.

1 Carburettor synchronisation is simply the process of adjusting the carburettors so they pass the same amount of fuel/air mixture to each cylinder. This is done by measuring the vacuum produced in each cylinder. Carburettors that are out of synchronisation will result in decreased fuel mileage, increased engine temperature, less than ideal throttle response and higher vibration levels.

2 To properly synchronise the carburettors,

you will need some sort of vacuum gauge set-up, preferably with a gauge for each cylinder, or a manometer, which is a calibrated tube arrangement to indicate engine vacuum. Because of the nature of the synchronisation procedure and the need for special instruments, most owners leave the task to a dealer service department or a reputable motorcycle repair shop.

3 Remove the seat and side covers (see Chapter 7).

4 Remove the fuel tank to provide access to the carburettors (see Chapter 3). Position the fuel tank on a bench alongside the motorcycle (at the same height as normal) and run longer fuel and vacuum lines from the tank to their unions.

5 Start the engine and let it run until it reaches normal operating temperature, then shut it off.

6 Detach the screws from the vacuum ports on the intake manifolds and install vacuum fittings **(see illustrations)**, then hook up the vacuum gauge set or the manometer according to the manufacturer's instructions.

6.6a Remove the vacuum fitting screws (arrowed) . . .

6.6b . . . and install vacuum fittings so a test gauge set-up can be installed (two of four carburettors shown)

6.9 The throttle stop screw and synchronising screws are accessible from the rear of the carburettor assembly

A   Throttle stop screw
B   Synchronising screw for no. 1 and 2 carburettors
C   Synchronising screw for no. 3 and 4 carburettors
D   Centre synchronising screw

7.2 Front caliper - check to see if the pad grooves (arrowed) are nearly worn away; if they are, the pads are worn

Make sure there are no leaks in the set-up, as false readings will result.

7 Start the engine and make sure the idle speed is correct. If it isn't, adjust it (see Section 5).

8 The vacuum readings for all of the cylinders should be the same, or at least within the tolerance listed in this Chapter's Specifications. If the vacuum readings vary, adjust as necessary.

9 To perform the adjustment, synchronise the carburettors for no. 1 and no. 2 cylinders by turning the synchronising screw, as needed, until the vacuum is identical or nearly identical for both cylinders **(see illustration)**. Snap the throttle open and shut 2 or 3 times, then recheck the adjustment and readjust as necessary.

10 Next synchronise the carburettors for no. 3 and no. 4 cylinders to each other by turning the synchronising screw for those two carburettors **(see illustration 6.9)**.

11 Finally, turn the centre synchronising screw to synchronise the two pairs of carburettors to each other.

12 When the adjustment is complete, recheck the vacuum readings and idle speed, then stop the engine. Remove the vacuum gauge or manometer and attach the hoses or caps to the fittings on the carburettors.

7   Brakes pads – check

Note: *In addition to the visual wear checks described in this Section, minimum brake pad*

thicknesses are listed in this Chapter's Specifications.

1 The front and rear brake pads should be checked at the recommended intervals and replaced with new ones when worn beyond the limit described in this Section.

2 To check the front brake pads, reach up and operate the brake lever while you look at the wear indicator grooves in the pad friction material **(see illustration)**.

3 If the grooves are nearly worn away, the pads are worn excessively and must be replaced with new ones (see Chapter 6).

4 The rear brake pad wear indicators may be grooves in the friction material or raised corners of the metal backing **(see illustrations)**. Have an assistant press the brake pedal firmly while you look at the pads through the back of the caliper. If the pads are

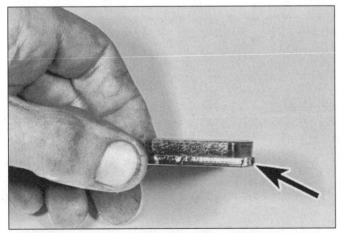

7.4a Rear caliper - if the pad backing metal is equipped with raised corners (arrowed) and the corners are close to the disc, the pads are worn

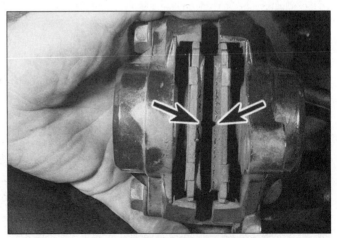

7.4b Rear caliper - if the pads have wear grooves (arrowed), check to see if they are nearly worn away

8.2 To adjust the front brake lever position, align one of the adjuster notches with the dot on the lever pivot (arrowed)

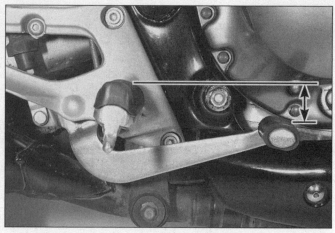
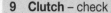

8.3a Measure brake pedal height from the top of the footpeg

equipped with raised corners and they're close to the disc, replace the pads (see Chapter 6). If the pads don't have raised corners, the caliper must be removed so the wear grooves can be inspected (see Chapter 6).

5 On UK models, remove the brake pads and lubricate the edges of the pad backing plates and the pad cavities in the calipers with special lubricants (see *Brake pads – replacement* in Chapter 6).

8 Brake system – checks and adjustment

Front brake lever

1 The front brake lever can be adjusted to vary its distance from the handlebar according to rider preference.

2 Push the lever forward. At the same time, turn the adjuster and align one of the notches on the adjuster with the mark on the top of the lever **(see illustration)**. There are two notches, directly opposite each other on the adjuster.

Rear brake pedal

3 Check pedal height (measured down from the top of the footpeg to the tip of the pedal) and compare it to the value listed in this Chapter's Specifications **(see illustration)**. Adjust it if necessary by loosening the locknuts on the adjusting bolt, turning the adjusting bolt as needed and tightening the locknuts **(see illustration)**.

4 If necessary, adjust the brake light switch (see Section 8).

General checks

5 A routine general check of the brakes will ensure that any problems are discovered and remedied before the rider's safety is jeopardised.

6 Check the brake lever and pedal for loose connections, excessive play, bends, and other damage. Replace any damaged parts with new ones (see Chapter 6).

7 Make sure all brake fasteners are tight.

Check the brake pads for wear (see Section 7) and make sure the fluid level in the reservoirs is correct (see *Daily (pre-ride) checks*). Look for leaks at the hose connections and check for cracks in the hoses. If the lever or pedal is spongy, bleed the brakes as described in Chapter 6.

8 Make sure the brake light operates when the brake lever or pedal is depressed, just before the rear brake takes effect.

9 If adjustment is necessary, hold the switch and turn the adjusting nut on the switch body **(see illustration)** until the brake light is activated when required. If the switch doesn't operate the brake lights, check it as described in Chapter 8.

10 The front brake light switch is not adjustable. If it fails to operate properly, replace it with a new one (see Chapter 8).

9 Clutch – check

1 Clutch cable freeplay is measured at the

8.3b To adjust the brake pedal height, loosen the locknut (arrowed) and turn the adjusting bolt

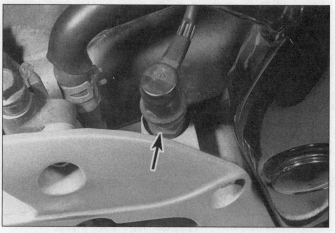

8.9 Hold the switch body and turn the plastic nut (arrowed) to adjust switch position

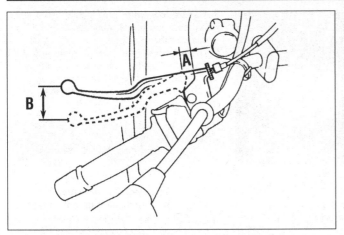

9.1 Clutch cable freeplay measurement point

A   *1992-95 UK models, 1992-96 US models*
B   *1996-on UK models, 1997-on US models*

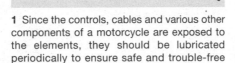

9.2 Pull back the rubber boot to access the upper adjuster; loosen the lock wheel (A) and turn the adjuster (B), then tighten the lock wheel

handlebar lever **(see illustration)**. On 1992-95 UK models and 1992-96 US models, pull the clutch lever gently towards the handlebar until all freeplay is taken up and tension is felt in the cable, then measure the distance from the lever blade to the lever stock. If this is not within the specification, the clutch cable must be adjusted. On 1996-on UK models and 1997-on US models, hold a ruler against the ball end of the clutch lever, then pull the lever gently towards the handlebar until all freeplay is taken up and tension is felt in the cable, and measure the movement of the lever's ball end from its original position.

2 Starting at the lever end of the cable, loosen the locknut and turn the adjuster in or out as required **(see illustration)**.

3 Don't back the adjuster out too far, if you can't adjust freeplay to specifications with the handlebar adjuster, loosen the two nuts on the cable lower adjuster and reposition the adjuster in its bracket. Re-lock the two nuts to secure the housing into its final position **(see illustration)**.

4 Start the bike, release the clutch and ride off, noting the position of the clutch lever when the clutch begins to engage. If it's too close to the handlebar with freeplay correctly adjusted, check the cable and clutch components for wear and damage (see Chapter 2).

10 Lubrication – general

1 Since the controls, cables and various other components of a motorcycle are exposed to the elements, they should be lubricated periodically to ensure safe and trouble-free operation.

2 The footpegs, clutch and brake levers, brake pedal, shift lever and side and centrestand (if equipped) pivots should be lubricated frequently. In order for the lubricant to be applied where it will do the most good, the component should be disassembled. However, if chain and cable lubricant is being used, it can be applied to the pivot joint gaps and will usually work its way into the areas where friction occurs. If motor oil or light grease is being used, apply it sparingly as it may attract dirt (which could cause the controls to bind or wear at an accelerated rate). **Note:** *One of the best lubricants for the control lever pivots is a dry-film lubricant (available from many sources by different names).*

3 To lubricate the throttle cables, clutch cable and choke cable (if equipped), disconnect the cable at the lower end, then lubricate the cable with a pressure lube adapter **(see illustration)**. See Chapter 3 for the throttle and choke cable removal procedure and Chapter 2 for the clutch cable removal procedure. **Note:** *Yamaha recommends that the throttle grip be removed and lubricated whenever the throttle cables are lubricated. Refer to the handlebars section of Chapter 5.*

4 The speedometer cable should be removed from its housing and lubricated with motor oil or cable lubricant.

9.3 Clutch cable lower adjuster; loosen the nuts (arrowed) to reposition the cable in its bracket

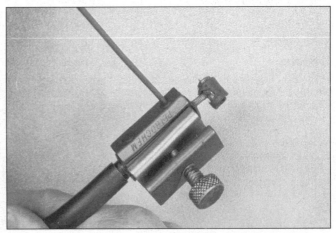

10.3 Lubricating a cable with a pressure lube adapter (make sure the tool seats around the inner cable)

11 Suspension – check

1 The suspension components must be maintained in top operating condition to ensure rider safety. Loose, worn or damaged suspension parts decrease the vehicle's stability and control.

Front suspension

2 While standing alongside the motorcycle, hold the front brake on and push on the handlebars to compress the forks several times. See if they move up-and-down smoothly without binding. If binding is felt, the forks should be disassembled and inspected as described in Chapter 5.
3 Carefully inspect the area around the fork seals for any signs of fork oil leakage **(see illustration)**. If leakage is evident, the seals must be replaced as described in Chapter 5.
4 Check the tightness of all front suspension nuts and bolts to be sure none have worked loose.

Rear suspension

5 Inspect the rear shock for fluid leakage and tightness of the mounting fasteners. If leakage is found, the shock should be replaced.
6 Set the bike on its centrestand (if equipped) or support it securely upright with the rear wheel off the ground. Grab the swingarm on each side, just ahead of the axle. Rock the swingarm from side to side – there should be no discernible movement at the rear. If there's a little movement or a slight clicking can be heard, make sure the pivot shaft nuts are tight. If the pivot nuts are tight but movement is still noticeable, the swingarm will have to be removed and the bearings replaced as described in Chapter 5.
7 Inspect the tightness of the rear suspension nuts and bolts.

12 Wheels and tyres – general check

Wheels

1 The cast wheels used on these machines are virtually maintenance free, but they should be kept clean and checked periodically for cracks and other damage. Never attempt to repair damaged cast wheels; they must be replaced with new ones.
2 Check the valve stem locknuts to make sure they are tight. Also, make sure the valve stem cap is in place and tight. If it is missing, install a new one made of metal or hard plastic.

Tyres

3 Check tyre condition and tread depth thoroughly – see *Daily (pre-ride) checks*.

11.3 Check above and below the fork seals (arrowed) for signs of oil leakage

13 Exhaust system – check

1 Periodically check all of the exhaust system joints for leaks and loose fasteners. The lower fairing (if equipped) will have to be removed to do this properly (see Chapter 7). If tightening the clamp bolts fails to stop any leaks, replace the gaskets with new ones (a procedure which requires disassembly of the system).
2 The exhaust pipe flange nuts at the cylinder heads are especially prone to loosening, which could cause damage to the head. Check them frequently and keep them tight (see Chapter 3).

14 Fasteners – check

1 Since vibration of the machine tends to loosen fasteners, all nuts, bolts, screws, etc. should be periodically checked for proper tightness.
2 Pay particular attention to the following:
Spark plugs
Engine oil drain plug
Oil filter
Gearshift lever
Footpegs, sidestand and centrestand (if equipped)
Engine mount bolts
Shock absorber mount bolts
Front axle and clamp bolt
Rear axle nut
Swingarm pivot shaft nut

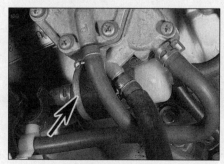

15.6a Fuel filter location (arrowed) – 1992-95 UK and all US models

3 If a torque wrench is available, use it along with the torque specifications at the beginning of this, or other, Chapters.
4 Should you find certain fasteners that do come loose periodically, apply a non-hardening liquid thread locking agent to the threads and reassemble to the proper torque.

15 Fuel system – check and filter replacement

⚠️ *Warning: Gasoline (petrol) is extremely flammable, so take extra precautions when you work on any part of the fuel system. Don't smoke or allow open flames or bare light bulbs near the work area, and don't work in a garage where a natural gas-type appliance (such as a water heater or clothes dryer) is present. Since gasoline is carcinogenic, wear latex gloves when there's a possibility of being exposed to fuel, and, if you spill any fuel on your skin, rinse it off immediately with soap and water. When you perform any kind of work on the fuel system, wear safety glasses and have a fire extinguisher suitable for a Class B type fire (flammable liquids) on hand.*

1 Check the fuel tank, the tank breather hose, the fuel tap, the lines and the carburettors for leaks and evidence of damage.
2 If carburettor gaskets are leaking, the carburettors should be disassembled and rebuilt by referring to Chapter 3.
3 If the fuel tap is leaking, tightening the screws may help. If leakage persists, the tap should be disassembled and repaired or replaced with a new one (see Chapter 3).
4 If the fuel lines are cracked or otherwise deteriorated, replace them with new ones.
5 Check the vacuum hose connected to the fuel tap. If it is cracked or otherwise damaged, replace it with a new one.
6 The fuel filter should be replaced periodically. To do so, loosen the hose clamps and slide them down the hoses, away from the filter. Pry the hoses off each end of the filter and connect a new filter in its place **(see illustrations)**.

15.6b Fuel filter location (arrowed) – 1996-on UK models

7 Check that there is no sign of leakage from the fuel pump. Check that the fuel pump line connections are secure and on early models with a vacuum type fuel pump check the condition of the vacuum hose.

16 Crankcase breather system – inspection

1 Remove the fuel tank (see Chapter 3) and disconnect the large-bore crankcase breather hose from the rear of the air cleaner housing **(see illustration 12.2c in Chapter 3)**. Disconnect the other end of the hose from the top of the crankcase on the right side **(see illustration 5.8 in Chapter 2)**.

2 Blow through the hose to clear any emulsified oil or sludge present and check that the hose is not pinched at any point nor perished. If necessary renew the hose. Reconnect the hose and secure it with the spring clips.

3 Trace the drain hose from the base of the air cleaner housing on the left side **(see illustration 12.2a in Chapter 3)** and make sure the hose is clear. Some models have an in-line filter in the hose – ensure that this is not blocked.

17 Sidestand switch – operation check

1 The sidestand switch is a safety component, designed to prevent the motorcycle being ridden with the sidestand in the down (extended) position. Conduct the following test to determine if the side stand and clutch switches are working correctly.

2 Make sure that the engine kill switch is in the RUN position and turn the ignition (main) switch ON. Shift the transmission into a gear. Ensure that the sidestand is UP, then pull in the clutch lever and press the starter button – the engine should start. If it doesn't, the clutch switch should be checked as described in Chapter 8. With the engine idling and the clutch lever still held in, extend the sidestand – the engine should stop. If it doesn't the sidestand switch should be checked as described in Chapter 8.

Every 8000 miles (12,000 km) or 12 months

18 Engine/transmission oil and filter – change

1 Consistent routine oil and filter changes are the single most important maintenance procedure you can perform on a motorcycle. The oil not only lubricates the internal parts of the engine, transmission and clutch, but it also acts as a coolant, a cleaner, a sealant, and a protectant. Because of these demands, the oil takes a terrific amount of abuse and should be replaced often with new oil of the recommended grade and type. Saving a little money on the difference in cost between a good oil and a cheap oil won't pay off if the engine is damaged.

2 Before changing the oil and filter, warm up the engine so the oil will drain easily.

 ⚠ ***Warning: Be careful when draining the oil, as the exhaust pipes, the engine, and the oil itself can cause severe burns.***

3 Put the motorcycle on the centrestand (if equipped) or prop it securely upright. Place a clean drain pan beneath the crankcase drain plug and filter housing. Remove the oil filler cap to vent the crankcase and to serve as a reminder that there is no oil in the engine.

4 If the bike has a lower fairing, remove it (see Chapter 7).

5 Next, remove the drain plug from the engine **(see illustration 2.5)** and allow the oil to drain into the pan. Discard the sealing washer on the drain plug; it should be replaced whenever the plug is removed.

6 Make sure the oil drain pan is under the oil filter, then unscrew the filter element with a ratchet and filter wrench **(see illustrations)**. If additional maintenance is planned for this time period, check or service another component while the oil is allowed to drain completely.

7 Apply a film of oil to the gasket on the new filter **(see illustration)**. Thread the filter onto the adapter and tighten it to the torque listed in this Chapter's Specifications.

8 Slip a new sealing washer over the oil drain plug, then install and tighten it to the torque listed in this Chapter's Specifications. Avoid overtightening, as damage to the engine case will result.

9 Before refilling the engine, check the old oil carefully (see Section 2).

10 If the inspection of the oil turns up nothing unusual, refill the crankcase to the proper level with the recommended oil and install the filler cap. Start the engine and let it run for two or three minutes. Shut it off, wait a few minutes, then check the oil level. If necessary, add more oil to bring the level up to the Maximum mark. Check around the drain plug and filter housing for leaks.

11 The old oil drained from the engine cannot be reused in its present state and should be disposed of (see Section 2).

19 Steering head bearings – check and adjustment

1 This vehicle is equipped with caged-ball type steering head bearings which can become dented, rough or loose during normal use of the machine. In extreme cases, worn or loose steering head bearings can cause steering wobble that is potentially dangerous.

18.6a This tool is used to remove the oil filter . . .

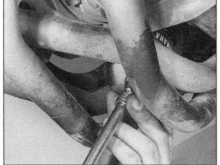

18.6b . . . you'll need an extension, and possibly a universal joint adapter, to reach between the exhaust pipes

18.7 Apply a film of clean engine oil to the filter gasket (arrowed)

19.4 Grasp the front wheel and try to pull it back and forth; if it moves, the steering head bearings are loose and in need of adjustment

19.5 Loosen the lower triple clamp bolts on each fork

19.7 The ring nut can be tightened with a spanner wrench (C-spanner)

Check

2 To check the bearings, place the motorcycle on the centrestand and block the machine so the front wheel is in the air.

3 Point the wheel straight ahead and slowly move the handlebars from side-to-side. Dents or roughness in the bearing races will be felt and the bars will not move smoothly.

4 Next, grasp the wheel and try to move it forward and backward **(see illustration)**. Any looseness in the steering head bearings will be felt as front-to-rear movement of the fork legs. If play is felt in the bearings, adjust the steering head as follows:

Adjustment

5 Loosen the lower triple clamp bolts **(see illustration)**. This allows the necessary vertical movement of the steering stem in relation to the fork tubes.

6 Remove the handlebars, steering stem nut (and washer – later models), upper triple clamp, ring nut lockwasher, upper ring nut

and rubber washer **(see illustration 7.4a in Chapter 5, components 12, 11, 3, 4 and 5)**. Adjust freeplay as described in Step 7 or 8 below.

7 Carefully tighten the lower ring nut to eliminate any freeplay, but not so much that there is any loading on the bearings **(see illustration)**. After adjustment make sure that the steering is still able to swing smoothly from lock-to-lock and all freeplay has been removed.

8 If the Yamaha service tool (pt no. YU-33975 or 90890-01403) is available this can be attached to the lower ring nut and a torque wrench applied to its square hole; the torque wrench handle must be at 90° to the service tool and the initial torque figure applied. The lower ring nut is then slackened one full turn and retightened to the final torque setting using the service tool. After adjustment make sure that the steering is still able to swing smoothly from lock-to-lock and all freeplay has been removed.

9 Turn the steering from lock to lock and

check for binding. If there is any, remove the bearings for inspection (see Chapter 5).

10 Install the rubber washer and upper ring nut, tightening the nut by hand so that its slots align with those of the lower ring nut. If they don't align, hold the lower ring nut with a C-spanner and tighten the upper nut against it until the slots align – be careful not to disturb the bearing freeplay setting. Fit the lockwasher tangs into the nuts slots **(see illustration 7.5a in Chapter 5)**, then fit the upper triple clamp, steering head nut (with washer – later models) and handlebars (see Chapter 5).

11 Recheck the steering head bearings for play again (see Step 4). The handlebars should move from a full turn to the full opposite turn with just a tap on the end of the handlebar. If necessary, repeat the adjustment procedure. Reinstall all parts previously removed. Tighten the steering stem nut, triple clamp bolts and handlebar bolts to the torques listed in the Chapter 5 Specifications.

Every 12,000 miles (18,000 km) or 18 months

20 Evaporative emission control system (California models only) – check

1 This system, installed on California models to conform to stringent emission control standards, routes fuel vapours from the fuel system into the engine to be burned, instead of letting them evaporate into the atmosphere. When the engine isn't running, vapours are stored in a carbon canister.

2 To begin the inspection of the system, remove the seat (see Chapter 7) and fuel tank (see Chapter 3). Inspect the hoses from the fuel tank and carburettors to the canister for cracking, kinks or other signs of deterioration **(see illustration)**.

3 Label and disconnect the hoses, then remove the canisters from the machine.

4 Inspect the canister for cracks or other signs of damage. Tip the canister so the nozzle points down. If fuel runs out

of the canister, it is probably damaged internally, so it would be a good idea to replace it.

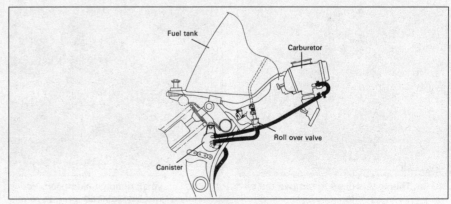

20.2 Evaporative emission control system details

24.1 Lubricate the swingarm through the grease fittings (arrowed)

25.5 Remove the bolts and detach the signal generator cover from the left side of the engine . . .

25.6 . . . and turn the crankshaft with a wrench on the turning bolt to align the T mark on the timing rotor with the protrusion on the pick-up coil

Every 16,000 miles (24,000 km) or two years

21 Brake fluid – change

1 Refer to the brake bleeding section in Chapter 6, noting that all old fluid must be pumped from the fluid reservoir and hydraulic line before filling with new fluid.

 Old brake fluid is invariably much darker in colour than new fluid, making it easy to see when all old fluid has been expelled from the system.

22 Brake master cylinders and calipers – overhaul

1 Refer to Chapter 6 and dismantle the front and rear brake calipers and master cylinders. Inspect the components for wear and contamination and then rebuild each

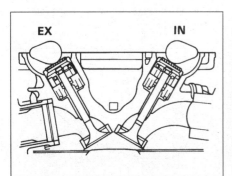

25.7 Make sure the cam lobes for no. 1 cylinder point away from each other as shown (the no. 4 cylinder cam lobes will point toward each other)

assembly using new seals. Renew the dust and fluids seals which seal the piston in the caliper and the piston/seal assembly in the master cylinder.

23 Steering head bearings – lubrication

1 Periodic cleaning and repacking of the steering head bearings is recommended by the manufacturer. Refer to Chapter 5 for steering head bearing lubrication and replacement procedures.

24 Swingarm bearings and rear suspension pivot points – lubrication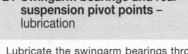

1 Lubricate the swingarm bearings through the grease fittings, using a grease gun **(see illustration)**. Note that some models may not be fitted with grease fittings, in which case the swingarm must be removed for greasing of the bearings (see Chapter 5).

25.8 Slip a feeler gauge between the cam lobe and valve adjusting shim – it should pull out with a slight drag

25 Valve clearances – check and adjustment

Checking

1 The engine must be completely cool for this maintenance procedure, so let the machine sit overnight before beginning.
2 Disconnect the cable from the negative terminal of the battery.
3 Remove the seat (see Chapter 7) and the fuel tank (see Chapter 3).
4 Remove the valve cover (see Chapter 2).
5 Remove the signal generator cover to provide access to the crankshaft rotation bolt **(see illustration)**.
6 Position the no. 1 piston (at the left side of the engine) at Top Dead Centre (TDC) on the compression stroke. Rotate the engine with a wrench placed on the timing rotor bolt or by pushing the bike with the transmission in high gear until the no. 1 and no. 4 cylinder TDC mark on the timing rotor aligns with the line on the pick-up coil **(see illustration)**.
7 Now, check the position of the no. 1 cylinder cam lobes – they should be pointing away from each other **(see illustration)**. Piston no. 1 is now at TDC compression. If the cam lobes are pointing toward each other, no. 1 cylinder is at TDC exhaust, in which case turn the crankshaft one full turn.
8 Start with the no. 1 intake valve clearance (the intake valve is on the carburettor side of the engine). Insert a feeler gauge of the thickness listed in this Chapter's Specifications between the cam lobe and valve adjusting shim **(see illustration)**. Pull the feeler gauge out slowly – you should feel a slight drag. If there's no drag, the clearance is too loose. If there's a heavy drag, the clearance is too tight.
9 If the clearance is incorrect, write down the actual measured clearance. You'll need this

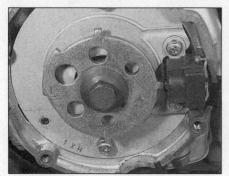

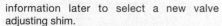

25.11 When the signal generator rotor tab opposite the T mark is aligned with the pick-up coil protrusion, no. 2 and 3 cylinders are at TDC; the valves for the cylinder which is on its compression stroke can be adjusted

25.17 The valve lifter notch (arrowed) should be toward the centre of the engine

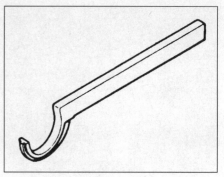

25.18 The Yamaha valve adjusting tool

information later to select a new valve adjusting shim.

10 Now measure the no. 1 exhaust valve clearance, following the same procedure you used for the intake valve. Be sure to use a feeler gauge of the specified thickness and write down the actual clearances of any valves that aren't within the Specifications.

11 Rotate the crankshaft exactly one-half turn to place piston no. 2 at TDC compression. The no. 2 and 3 cylinder TDC mark on the timing rotor should now be aligned with the line on the pick-up coil (see illustration). Also, the cam lobes for no. 2 cylinder should now point away from each other (see illustration 25.7).

12 Measure the clearances of both valves on cylinder no. 2 and write down any that aren't within the Specifications.

13 Rotate the crankshaft another half turn to place cylinder no. 4 at TDC (no. 1 and 4 cylinder TDC mark lined up with the pick-up coil; no. 4 cam lobes pointing away from each other). Measure its valve clearances.

14 Rotate the engine another half turn to place cylinder no. 3 at TDC and measure its valve clearances.

15 If any of the clearances need to be adjusted, go to Step 18 or Step 20.

16 If all the clearances were within the Specifications, go to Step 28.

17 Check the positions of the valve lifter notches. They should be turned so the intake and exhaust notches are facing each other (see illustration).

Adjustment with the Yamaha valve adjusting tool

18 If you're using the Yamaha valve adjusting tool (US part no. YM-04125, UK part no. 90890-04125), install the tool on the valve lifter and press it down so there's a gap between the shim and cam lobe (see illustration). Note: *Be sure the tool bears against the lifter only, not the adjusting shim.*

19 Take the shim out with a magnet (see illustration). If necessary, slip a small screwdriver into the lifter notch, under the shim, and pry the shim up out of the lifter.

Adjustment with a universal valve adjusting tool

20 If you don't have access to the special Yamaha tool, you can use a universal valve adjusting tool (see illustration).

21 Push the wedge of the valve adjusting tool between the cam lobe and adjusting shim so it pushes the lifter down slightly. Slip the holder between the camshaft and lifter, then pull out the wedge.

22 Slip the wedge tool between the adjusting shim and the lifter. This will dislodge the adjusting shim.

23 Take the shim out with a magnet (see illustration 25.19).

Shim selection

24 Determine the thickness of the shim you removed. It should be marked on the bottom of the shim (see illustration), but the ideal way is to measure it with a micrometer. Shims are available in increments of 0.05 mm (0.002 inch); ie a number 200 shim is 2.00 mm (0.079 inch) thick and a number 320 shim is 3.20 mm (0.130 inch) thick. Note: *If the number on the shim does not end in 0 or 5, round it off to the nearest zero or 5. For example, if the number on the shim is 258, round it off to 260. If it's 254, round it off to 255.*

25 If the clearance (measured and written down earlier) was too large, you need a thicker shim. If the clearance was too small, you need a thinner shim. Calculate the thickness of the replacement shim by referring to the accompanying charts (see illustrations).

26 Install the new shim and recheck the clearance. If it's within the Specifications, the valve is properly adjusted. Note: *Always install the shim with the number down against the valve lifter.*

27 Adjust any remaining valves that were not within the Specifications. Perform the adjustments in the same order as the cylinder firing order (1-2-4-3).

28 Install the valve cover.

29 Reconnect the negative cable to the battery.

30 Install all components removed for access.

25.19 Lift the shim out with a magnet

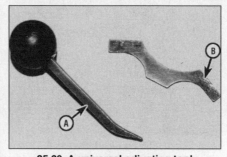

25.20 A universal adjusting tool (A – wedge, B – holder) can be used to change the shims

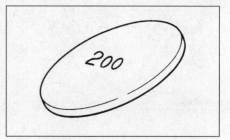

25.24 There's a thickness mark on the underside of each valve shim (be sure to place the marked side of the shim down during installation)

INSTALLED PAD NUMBER

MEASURED CLEARANCE	200	205	210	215	220	225	230	235	240	245	250	255	260	265	270	275	280	285	290	295	300	305	310	315	320
0.00~0.05			200	205	210	215	220	225	230	235	240	245	250	255	260	265	270	275	280	285	290	295	300	305	310
0.06~0.10		200	205	210	215	220	225	230	235	240	245	250	255	260	265	270	275	280	285	290	295	300	305	310	315
0.11~0.15	STANDARD CLEARANCE																								
0.16~0.20	205	210	215	220	225	230	235	240	245	250	255	260	265	270	275	280	285	290	295	300	305	310	315	320	
0.21~0.25	210	215	220	225	230	235	240	245	250	255	260	265	270	275	280	285	290	295	300	305	310	315	320		
0.26~0.30	215	220	225	230	235	240	245	250	255	260	265	270	275	280	285	290	295	300	305	310	315	320			
0.31~0.35	220	225	230	235	240	245	250	255	260	265	270	275	280	285	290	295	300	305	310	315	320				
0.36~0.40	225	230	235	240	245	250	255	260	265	270	275	280	285	290	295	300	305	310	315	320					
0.41~0.45	230	235	240	245	250	255	260	265	270	275	280	285	290	295	300	305	310	315	320						
0.46~0.50	235	240	245	250	255	260	265	270	275	280	285	290	295	300	305	310	315	320							
0.51~0.55	240	245	250	255	260	265	270	275	280	285	290	295	300	305	310	315	320								
0.56~0.60	245	250	255	260	265	270	275	280	285	290	295	300	305	310	315	320									
0.61~0.65	250	255	260	265	270	275	280	285	290	295	300	305	310	315	320										
0.66~0.70	255	260	265	270	275	280	285	290	295	300	305	310	315	320											
0.71~0.75	260	265	270	275	280	285	290	295	300	305	310	315	320												
0.76~0.80	265	270	275	280	285	290	295	300	305	310	315	320													
0.81~0.85	270	275	280	285	290	295	300	305	310	315	320														
0.86~0.90	275	280	285	290	295	300	305	310	315	320															
0.91~0.95	280	285	290	295	300	305	310	315	320																
0.96~1.00	285	290	295	300	305	310	315	320																	
1.01~1.05	290	295	300	305	310	315	320																		
1.06~1.10	295	300	305	310	315	320																			
1.11~1.15	300	305	310	315	320																				
1.16~1.20	305	310	315	320																					
1.21~1.25	310	315	320																						
1.26~1.30	315	320																							
1.31~1.35	320																								

25.25a Intake valve shim selection chart

Valve clearance (cold): 0.11 to 0.15 mm (0.004 to 0.006 inch)
Example: Installed pad is 250
Measured clearance is 0.23 mm (0.009 inch)
Replace 250 pad with 260 pad
Pad numbers (example)
  250 is 2.50 mm (0.098 inch) thick
  255 is 2.55 mm (0.100 inch) thick

INSTALLED PAD NUMBER

MEASURED CLEARANCE	200	205	210	215	220	225	230	235	240	245	250	255	260	265	270	275	280	285	290	295	300	305	310	315	320
0.00~0.05				200	205	210	215	220	225	230	235	240	245	250	255	260	265	270	275	280	285	290	295	300	305
0.06~0.10			200	205	210	215	220	225	230	235	240	245	250	255	260	265	270	275	280	285	290	295	300	305	310
0.10~0.15		200	205	210	215	220	225	230	235	240	245	250	255	260	265	270	275	280	285	290	295	300	305	310	315
0.16~0.20	200	205	210	215	220	225	230	235	240	245	250	255	260	265	270	275	280	285	290	295	300	305	310	315	320
0.21~0.25	STANDARD CLEARANCE																								
0.26~0.30	210	215	220	225	230	235	240	245	250	255	260	265	270	275	280	285	290	295	300	305	310	315	320		
0.31~0.35	215	220	225	230	235	240	245	250	255	260	265	270	275	280	285	290	295	300	305	310	315	320			
0.36~0.40	220	225	230	235	240	245	250	255	260	265	270	275	280	285	290	295	300	305	310	315	320				
0.41~0.45	225	230	235	240	245	250	255	260	265	270	275	280	285	290	295	300	305	310	315	320					
0.46~0.50	230	235	240	245	250	255	260	265	270	275	280	285	290	295	300	305	310	315	320						
0.51~0.55	235	240	245	250	255	260	265	270	275	280	285	290	295	300	305	310	315	320							
0.56~0.60	240	245	250	255	260	265	270	275	280	285	290	295	300	305	310	315	320								
0.61~0.65	245	250	255	260	265	270	275	280	285	290	295	300	305	310	315	320									
0.66~0.70	250	255	260	265	270	275	280	285	290	295	300	305	310	315	320										
0.71~0.75	255	260	265	270	275	280	285	290	295	300	305	310	315	320											
0.76~0.80	260	265	270	275	280	285	290	295	300	305	310	315	320												
0.81~0.85	265	270	275	280	285	290	295	300	305	310	315	320													
0.86~0.90	270	275	280	285	290	295	300	305	310	315	320														
0.91~0.95	275	280	285	290	295	300	305	310	315	320															
0.96~1.00	280	285	290	295	300	305	310	315	320																
1.01~1.05	285	290	295	300	305	310	315	320																	
1.06~1.10	290	295	300	305	310	315	320																		
1.11~1.15	295	300	305	310	315	320																			
1.16~1.20	300	305	310	315	320																				
1.21~1.25	305	310	315	320																					
1.26~1.30	310	315	320																						
1.31~1.35	315	320																							
1.36~1.40	320																								

25.25b Exhaust valve shim selection chart

Valve clearance (cold): 0.21 to 0.25 mm (0.008 to 0.010 inch)
Example: Installed pad is 250
Measured clearance is 0.32 mm (0.013 inch)
Replace 250 pad with 265 pad
Pad numbers (example)
  250 is 2.50 mm (0.098 inch) thick
  255 is 2.55 mm (0.100 inch) thick

26.2 Battery positive terminal (left arrow) and negative terminal (right arrow)

27.2 Check cylinder compression with a compression gauge and screw-in type adapter

28.5 Unscrew the fork cap bolt

26 Battery – check

Note: *The battery fitted as original equipment is of the maintenance-free type and therefore does not require electrolyte level or specific gravity checks like a conventional battery. It is, however, advised that you periodically check that the battery leads are secure and free of corrosion.*

1 Remove the seat (see Chapter 7).
2 Brush off any corrosion from the battery terminals and tighten them if their connecting bolts are loose. Smear petroleum jelly over the metal terminals (with the leads connected) to prevent future corrosion and fit the plastic cover over the positive terminal **(see illustration)**.
3 If the motorcycle will be stored for an extended time, fully charge the battery and leave the negative cable disconnected after the battery is reinstalled.

27 Cylinder compression – check

1 A compression test will provide useful information about an engine's condition, and if performed regularly, can give warning of trouble before any other symptoms become apparent.
2 Refer to the procedure under the *Fault Finding Equipment* heading in the Reference section of this manual **(see illustration)**. The cylinder compression figure is given in the Specifications at the beginning of this Chapter.

28 Fork oil – replacement

Note: *On 1992-94 models the forks are equipped with drain screws in the bottom outer face of each fork slider. On later models the drain screws are omitted, and the forks must be removed from the triple clamps to drain the oil.*

1 Move the machine onto the centrestand (if equipped) or prop it securely upright.
2 On 1992-94 models place a drain pan under each fork. Remove the fork drain screw from the bottom of each fork **(see illustration 6.2 in Chapter 5)**. Be prepared for the oil to shoot out forcefully and position the drain pan accordingly.
3 Carefully pump the front-end up and down to remove the remaining oil from the fork. Return the drain screws to their respective holes, using new sealing washers if necessary. Tighten them securely.
4 For 1995-on models, slacken off the fork cap bolts at the top of the fork legs a few turns, then remove the forks from the triple clamps as described in Chapter 5.
5 On all models, remove the cap bolt at the top of the fork tube **(see illustration)**. The spring will be under a moderate amount of pressure, so be careful!
6 Remove the spacer, spring seat and fork spring from the fork tube **(see illustration 6.2 in Chapter 5)**.
7 On 1995-on models, invert the fork and pour the oil out; pump the leg to expel as much oil as possible.
8 On all models pour in the specified amount of approved fork oil. Slowly pump the forks up and down several times to distribute the oil.
9 Fully compress the forks and use a ruler or length of welding rod to measure the distance from the top of the fork tube to the oil. Compare this with the fork oil level specified at the beginning of this Chapter and add or remove oil until the level is correct; it is important that the level is the same in each fork tube.
10 Install the spring, spring seat, spacer and cap bolt. Tighten the cap to the torque listed in this Chapter's Specifications, noting that on 1995-on models this is easier once the forks have been installed in the triple clamps.
11 On 1995-on models install the forks in the triple clamps (see Chapter 5).

Chapter 2
Engine, clutch and transmission

Contents

Degrees of difficulty

Easy, suitable for novice with little experience	**Fairly easy,** suitable for beginner with some experience	**Fairly difficult,** suitable for competent DIY mechanic 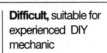	**Difficult,** suitable for experienced DIY mechanic	**Very difficult,** suitable for expert DIY or professional

Specifications

General
Bore .... 58.5 mm (2.30 inches)
Stroke .... 55.7 mm (2.19 inches)
Displacement .... 598.8 cc
Compression ratio .... 10 to 1

Camshaft
Lobe height (intake)
  Standard .... 35.75 to 35.85 mm (1.404 to 1.411 inches)
  Minimum .... 35.7 mm (1.4 inches)
Lobe height (exhaust)
  Standard .... 35.45 to 35.55 mm (1.396 to 1.400 inches)
  Minimum .... 35.4 mm (1.4 inches)
Base circle (intake and exhaust)
  Standard .... 27.95 to 28.05 mm (1.100 to 1.104 inches)
  Minimum .... 27.9 mm (1.1 inches)
Bearing oil clearance .... 0.020 to 0.054 mm (0.0008 to 0.0021 inch)
Journal diameter .... 24.967 to 24.980 mm (0.9830 to 0.9835 inch)
Bearing bore .... 25.000 to 25.021 mm (0.9843 to 0.9859 inch)
Camshaft runout limit .... 0.05 mm (0.002 inch)

Cylinder head, valves and valve springs
Cylinder head warpage limit .... 0.03 mm (0.0012 inch)
Valve stem bend limit .... 0.03 mm (0.0012 inch)
Valve head diameter
  Intake .... 29.9 to 30.1 mm (1.177 to 1.185 inches)
  Exhaust .... 25.9 to 26.1 mm (1.020 to 1.028 inches)
Valve stem diameter
  Standard
    Intake .... 4.975 to 4.990 mm (0.1959 to 0.1965 inches)
    Exhaust .... 4.960 to 4.975 mm (0.1953 to 0.1959 inches)
  Minimum
    Intake .... 4.945 mm (0.195 inch)
    Exhaust .... 4.920 mm (0.194 inch)
Valve stem clearance
  Standard
    Intake .... 0.010 to 0.037 mm (0.0004 to 0.0015 inch)
    Exhaust .... 0.025 to 0.052 mm (0.0010 to 0.0020 inch)
  Maximum .... 0.10 mm (0.004 inch)
Valve margin thickness (intake and exhaust) .... 1.0 mm (0.039 inch)
Valve guide inside diameter (intake and exhaust)
  Standard .... 5.000 to 5.012 mm (0.1969 to 0.1973 inch)
  Maximum
    Intake .... 5.045 mm (0.199 inch)
    Exhaust .... 5.020 mm (0.198 inch)
Valve seat width (intake and exhaust) .... 0.9 to 1.1 mm (0.035 to 0.043 inch)
Valve face width (intake and exhaust) .... 2.26 mm (0.089 inch)
Valve seat angles 45, 60, 75-degrees
Valve spring free length (intake and exhaust)
  Outer spring .... 38.52 mm (1.52 inches)
  Inner spring .... 38.33 mm (1.51 inches)
Valve spring installed height (intake and exhaust)
  Outer spring .... 33.4 mm (1.31 inches)
  Inner spring .... 32.5 mm (1.28 inches)
Valve spring bend limit .... 1.7 mm (0.067 inch)
Valve clearances .... see Chapter 1

Crankshaft, connecting rods and bearings
Main bearing oil clearance .... 0.014 to 0.053 mm (0.0006 to 0.0021 inch)
Connecting rod side clearance
  Standard .... 0.160 to 0.262 mm (0.0063 to 0.0103 inch)
  Maximum .... 0.5 mm (0.020 inch)
Connecting rod bearing oil clearance
  Standard .... 0.026 to 0.060 mm (0.0010 to 0.0024 inch)
  Maximum .... 0.08 mm (0.003 inch)
Crankshaft runout limit .... 0.03 mm (0.0012 inch)

Cylinder block
Bore diameter .... 58.505 to 58.545 mm (2.3033 to 2.3049 inches)
Taper limit .... 0.05 mm (0.002 inches)
Out of round limit .... 0.01 mm (0.0004 inch)
Bore measuring points .... Top, centre and bottom

Pistons
Piston diameter
  Standard .... 58.47 to 58.51 mm (2.302 to 2.304 inches)
Diameter measuring point .... 4.0 mm (5/32 inch) from bottom of skirt
Piston-to-cylinder clearance
  Standard .... 0.025 to 0.045 mm (0.0010 to 0.0018 inch)
  Maximum .... 0.15 mm (0.006 inch)
Ring side clearance
  Top ring
    Standard .... 0.035 to 0.070 mm (0.0014 to 0.0028 inch)
    Maximum .... 0.15 mm (0.006 inch)
  Second ring
    Standard .... 0.02 to 0.06 mm (0.0008 to 0.0024 inch)
    Maximum .... 0.15 mm (0.006 inch)
  Oil ring .... Not specified
Ring thickness
  Top ring .... 1.0 mm (0.0394 inch)
  Second ring .... 1.2 mm (0.047 inch)
  Oil ring (spacer and rails) .... 2.8 mm (0.11 inch)
Ring end gap
  Top ring
    Standard (1998-on UK models) .... 0.1 to 0.2 mm (0.004 to 0.008 inch)
    Standard (all other models) .... 0.15 to 0.30 mm (0.006 to 0.012 inch)
    Maximum .... 0.7 mm (0.028 inch)
  Second ring
    Standard .... 0.15 to 0.35 mm (0.006 to 0.014 inch)
    Maximum .... 0.7 mm (0.028 inch)
  Oil ring .... 0.20 to 0.70 mm (0.008 to 0.028 inch)

Lubrication system
Oil pump
  Inner to outer rotor clearance
    Standard .... 0.09 to 0.15 mm (0.0035 to 0.0059 inch)
    Maximum .... 0.2 mm (0.008 inch)
  Outer rotor to housing clearance
    Standard .... 0.03 to 0.08 mm (0.0012 to 0.0031 inch)
    Maximum .... 0.15 mm (0.006 inch)
Bypass valve setting pressure .... 0.78 to 1.17 Bars (11.4 to 17.1 psi)
Relief valve opening pressure .... 4.4 to 5.38 Bars (64 to 78.2 psi)
Oil pressure (hot) .... 0.78 Bars (11.4 psi) at 1200 rpm

Clutch
Friction plate thickness
  Standard .... 2.9 to 3.1 mm (0.114 to 0.122 inch)
  Minimum .... 2.7 mm (0.106 inch)
Steel plate thickness .... 1.5 to 1.7 mm (0.060 to 0.067 inch)
Steel plate warpage limit .... 0.15 mm (0.006 inch)
Spring free length
  Standard .... 42.8 mm (1.69 inches)
  Minimum .... 41.8 mm (1.65 inches)

Transmission
Driveshaft and mainshaft runout limit .... 0.08 mm (0.0031 inch)
Shift fork guide bar bend limit .... 0.08 mm (0.0031 inch)
Primary reduction ratio .... 23/24 x 65/28 (2.225)
Gear ratios (no. of teeth)
  1st gear 2.733 (41/15T)
  2nd gear 1.778 (32/18T)
  3rd gear 1.333 (28/21T)
  4th gear 1.074 (29/27T)
  5th gear 0.913 (21/23T)
  6th gear 0.821 (22/28T)

Torque settings

Cam chain tensioner cap bolt	20 Nm (168 in-lbs)
Cam chain tensioner mounting bolts	10 Nm (86 in-lbs)
Camshaft bearing cap bolts	10 Nm (86 in-lbs) (1)
Camshaft sprocket bolts	24 Nm (17 ft-lbs)
Clutch boss nut	70 Nm (50 ft-lbs)
Clutch cover bolts	10 Nm (86 in-lbs)
Clutch pressure plate bolts	8 Nm (70 in-lbs)
Connecting rod cap nuts	25 Nm (18 ft-lbs) (2)
Crankcase bolts	24 Nm (17 ft-lbs) (3)
Crankcase plugs (M10)	12 Nm (105 in-lbs)
Cylinder block to crankcase nut	20 Nm (168 in-lbs)
Cylinder block to cylinder head nuts	10 Nm (86 in-lbs)
Cylinder head cap nuts	22 Nm (16 ft-lbs) (3)
Engine mount bolts	
Front	60 Nm (43 ft-lbs)
Rear	88 Nm (64 ft-lbs)
Oil filter adapter bolt	50 Nm (36 ft-lbs)
Oil pan mounting bolts	10 Nm (86 in-lbs)
Oil pick-up bolts	10 Nm (86 in-lbs)
Oil pump assembly screw	7 Nm(61 in-lbs)
Oil pump mounting screws	7 Nm (61 in-lbs)
Oil pump screws	7 Nm (61 in-lbs)
Primary drive gear nut	50 Nm (36 ft-lbs)
Shift cam retaining plate screws	7 Nm (61 in-lbs) (4)
Shift cam stopper screw	22 Nm (16 ft-lbs) (4)
Shift lever pinch bolt	10 Nm (86 in-lbs) (4)
Shift pedal linkage locknuts	10 Nm (86 in-lbs)
Starter chain guide bolts	8 Nm (70 in-lbs) (4)
Starter chain tensioner bolts	10 Nm (86 in-lbs) (4)
Starter clutch Allen bolts	25 Nm (18 ft-lbs)
Valve cover bolts	10 Nm (86 in-lbs)
Oil cooler adapter central bolt	50 Nm (36 ft-lbs)
Oil cooler banjo bolts (at radiator)	32 Nm (24 ft-lbs)
Oil cooler radiator mounting bolt nut	10 Nm (86 in-lbs)
Oil cooler pipes-to-adapter bolts	10 Nm (86 in-lbs)
Oil cooler clamp plate bolt	10 Nm (86 in-lbs)

1 *Apply engine oil to the threads and tighten evenly in three stages.*
2 *Apply molybdenum disulphide grease to the threads and tighten in a continuous motion.*
3 *Apply engine oil to the threads and tighten in the specified sequence (see text).*
4 *Apply non-permanent thread locking agent to the threads.*

1 General information

The engine/transmission is an air-cooled, in-line four cylinder unit. The valves (one intake and one exhaust per cylinder) are operated by double overhead camshafts which are chain driven off the crankshaft. The engine/transmission assembly is constructed from aluminium alloy. The crankcase is divided horizontally.

The crankcase incorporates a wet sump, pressure-fed lubrication system which uses a gear-driven, single-rotor oil pump, an oil filter, relief valves and an oil level switch. Also contained in the crankcase is the starter motor clutch.

Power from the crankshaft is routed to the transmission via the clutch, which is of the coil spring, wet multi-plate type and is gear-driven off the crankshaft. The transmission is a six-speed, constant-mesh unit.

2 Operations possible with the engine in the frame

The components and assemblies listed below can be removed without having to remove the engine from the frame. If, however, a number of areas require attention at the same time, removal of the engine is recommended.

Gear selector mechanism external
  components
Starter motor
Alternator
Clutch assembly
Oil pump
Valve cover, camshafts and lifters
Cam chain tensioner
Cylinder head
Cylinder block and pistons

3 Operations requiring engine removal

It is necessary to remove the engine/transmission assembly from the frame and separate the crankcase halves to gain access to the following components:

Oil pan and relief valves
Crankshaft, connecting rods and bearings
Transmission shafts
Shift cam and forks
Camshaft chain and starter chain
Starter clutch and idle gears

4 Major engine repair – general note

1 It is not always easy to determine when or if an engine should be completely overhauled, as a number of factors must be considered.

2 High mileage is not necessarily an indication that an overhaul is needed, while low mileage, on the other hand, does not preclude the need for an overhaul. Frequency of servicing is probably the single most important consideration. An engine that has regular and frequent oil and filter changes, as well as other required maintenance, will most likely give many miles of reliable service. Conversely, a neglected engine, or one which has not been broken in properly, may require an overhaul very early in its life.

3 Exhaust smoke and excessive oil consumption are both indications that piston rings and/or valve guides are in need of attention. Make sure oil leaks are not responsible before deciding that the rings and guides are bad. Refer to Chapter 1 and perform a cylinder compression check to determine for certain the nature and extent of the work required.

4 If the engine is making obvious knocking or rumbling noises, the connecting rod and/or main bearings are probably at fault.

5 Loss of power, rough running, excessive valve train noise and high fuel consumption rates may also point to the need for an overhaul, especially if they are all present at the same time. If a complete tune-up does not remedy the situation, major mechanical work is the only solution.

6 An engine overhaul generally involves restoring the internal parts to the specifications of a new engine. During an overhaul the piston rings are replaced and the cylinder walls are bored and/or honed. If a rebore is done, then new pistons are also required. The main and connecting rod bearings are generally replaced with new ones and, if necessary, the crankshaft is also replaced. Generally the valves are serviced as well, since they are usually in less than perfect condition at this point. While the engine is being overhauled, other components such as the carburettors and the starter motor can be rebuilt also. The end result should be a like-new engine that will give as many trouble-free miles as the original.

7 Before beginning the engine overhaul, read through all of the related procedures to familiarise yourself with the scope and requirements of the job. Overhauling an engine is not all that difficult, but it is time consuming. Plan on the motorcycle being tied up for a minimum of two weeks. Check on the availability of parts and make sure that any necessary special tools, equipment and supplies are obtained in advance.

8 Most work can be done with typical shop hand tools, although a number of precision measuring tools are required for inspecting parts to determine if they must be replaced. Often a dealer service department or motorcycle repair shop will handle the inspection of parts and offer advice concerning reconditioning and replacement. As a general rule, time is the primary cost of an overhaul so it doesn't pay to install worn or substandard parts.

9 Any machine shop type operations (valve job, resurfacing, cylinder boring, etc.) should be performed by a speciality shop familiar with motorcycle applications.

10 As a final note, to ensure maximum life and minimum trouble from a rebuilt engine, everything must be assembled with care in a spotlessly clean environment.

5 Engine – removal and installation

Note: Engine removal and installation should be done with the aid of an assistant to avoid damage or injury that could occur if the engine is dropped. A hydraulic floor jack should be used to support and lower the engine if possible (they can be rented at low cost).

Removal

1 Set the bike on its centrestand (if equipped) or support it securely upright.

2 Remove the upper fairing (and lower fairing, if equipped) (see Chapter 7).

3 Remove the fuel tank (see Chapter 3).

4 Drain the engine oil and remove the oil filter (see Chapter 1). On 1996-on UK models, disconnect the oil pipes from the cooler unit and remove the oil cooler radiator from the frame (see Section 32).

5 Disconnect both battery cables from the battery.

⚠️ Warning: Always disconnect the negative cable first and reconnect it last to prevent a battery explosion. Remove the battery and battery case (see Chapter 8).

6 Remove the exhaust system (see Chapter 3).

7 Remove the air cleaner housing, fuel pump, carburettors and intake manifolds (see Chapter 3) and plug the intake openings with rags.

8 Remove the crankcase ventilation hose and unbolt the battery ground (earth) cable (see illustration).

9 Refer to Chapters 4 and 8 and disconnect the following electrical connectors:

a) Alternator
b) Pick-up coil
c) Neutral switch
d) Oil level switch
e) Starter motor
f) Sidestand switch

10 Remove the starter motor (see Chapter 8).

11 Remove the oil cooler and lines, if applicable (see Section 32).

12 If you're working on a California model, unbolt the evaporative emission canister and secure it with a piece of wire so it's out of the way.

13 Remove the clutch cable (see Section 19).

14 Remove the shift pedal (see Section 20).

15 Remove the engine sprocket cover and engine sprocket (see Chapter 5). It isn't necessary to remove the drive chain completely, but if the engine sprocket is difficult to remove, loosen the rear axle nut and chain adjusters, then push the rear wheel forward to create slack in the chain (see Chapter 1 for details).

16 Place a floor jack and a wood block beneath the oil pan and raise the jack just enough to support the oil pan (see illustration). Pad the frame with rags so it won't be scratched when the engine is removed (see illustration).

5.8 Remove the crankcase ventilation hose and disconnect the ground (earth) cable (arrowed)

5.16a Support the engine with a jack and a block of wood . . .

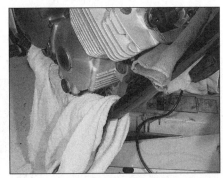

5.16b . . . and pad the frame with a thick layer of rags so it won't be scratched as the engine is removed

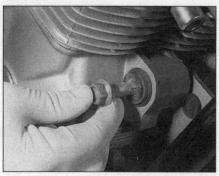

5.17a With the engine supported by a jack, remove the engine mounting bolts at the upper front . . .

5.17b . . . lower front . . .

5.17c . . . and rear (arrowed)

17 Remove the engine front and rear mounting bolts **(see illustrations)**.
18 Make sure no wires or hoses are still attached to the engine assembly.

Warning: The engine is heavy and may cause injury if it falls. Be sure it's securely supported. Have an assistant help you steady the engine as you remove it.

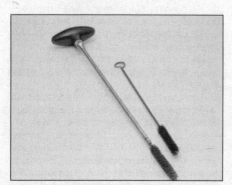

6.2a A selection of brushes is required for cleaning holes and passages in the engine components

19 Raise the engine so that the oil pan is level with the frame, then slide the engine out through the right side of the frame and set it on the floor.

Installation

20 Installation is the reverse of removal. Note the following points:
  a) *Don't tighten any of the engine mounting bolts until they all have been installed.*
  b) *Use new gaskets at all exhaust pipe connections.*
  c) *Tighten the engine mount bolts to the torques listed in this Chapter's Specifications.*
  d) *Adjust the drive chain, clutch and throttle cables following the procedures in Chapter 1.*
  e) *Refill the engine with oil.*

6 Engine disassembly and reassembly – general information

1 Before disassembling the engine, clean the exterior with a degreaser and rinse it with water. A clean engine will make the job easier

and prevent the possibility of getting dirt into the internal areas of the engine.
2 In addition to the precision measuring tools mentioned earlier, you will need a torque wrench, a valve spring compressor, valve spring compressor adapter, oil gallery brushes, a piston ring removal and installation tool, a piston ring compressor and a clutch holder tool (which is described in Section 18). Some new, clean engine oil of the correct grade and type, some engine assembly lube (or moly-based grease), a tube of Yamaha bond or equivalent, and a tube of RTV (silicone) sealant will also be required. Although it may not be considered a tool, some Plastigauge (type HPG-1) should also be obtained to use for checking bearing oil clearances **(see illustrations)**.
3 An engine support stand make from short lengths of 2 x 4's bolted together will facilitate the disassembly and reassembly procedures **(see illustration)**. The perimeter of the mount should be just big enough to accommodate the engine oil pan. If you have an automotive-type engine stand, an adapter plate can be made from a piece of plate, some angle iron and a few nuts and bolts.

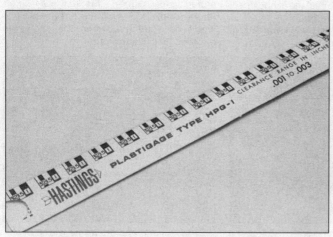

6.2b Type HPG-1 Plastigauge is needed to check the crankshaft, connecting rod and camshaft oil clearances

6.3 An engine stand can be made from short lengths of 2 x 4 wood and lag bolts or nails

7.5 Remove the valve cover bolts

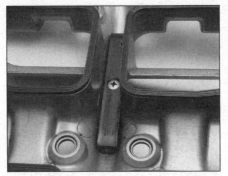

7.7 Replace the upper cam chain guide inside the valve cover if it's worn or damaged

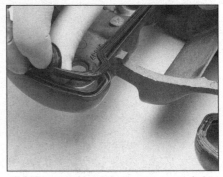

7.9 Be sure the gasket seats securely in the groove

4 When disassembling the engine, keep 'mated' parts together (including gears, cylinders, pistons, valves, etc. that have been in contact with each other during engine operation). These 'mated' parts must be reused or replaced as an assembly.

5 Engine/transmission disassembly should be done in the following general order with reference to the appropriate Sections.

Remove the camshafts
Remove the cylinder head
Remove the cylinder block
Remove the pistons
Remove the clutch
Remove the oil pan
Remove the external shift mechanism
Remove the alternator and starter (see Chapter 8)
Separate the crankcase halves
Remove the crankshaft and connecting rods
Remove the transmission shafts/gears
Remove the shift cam/forks
Remove the starter clutch and idle gears

6 Reassembly is accomplished by reversing the general disassembly sequence.

7 Valve cover – removal and installation

Note: *The valve cover can be removed with the engine in the frame. If the engine has been removed, ignore the steps which don't apply.*

Removal

1 Set the bike on its centrestand (if equipped) or support it securely upright.
2 Remove the seat (see Chapter 7).
3 Remove the fuel tank, air cleaner housing and carburettors (see Chapter 3).
4 Disconnect the spark plug wires from the plugs (see Chapter 1).
5 Remove the valve cover bolts **(see illustration)**. Loosen the bolts in a criss-cross pattern, 1/4 turn at a time, until all of the bolts are loose, then remove the bolts and their rubber seals. If access is difficult with the oil

cooler radiator in place on 1996-on UK models, remove it as described in Section 32.
6 Lift the cover off the cylinder head. If it's stuck, don't attempt to pry it off – tap around the sides with a plastic hammer to dislodge it. **Note:** *Pay attention to the locating dowels as you remove the cover – if they fall into the engine, major disassembly may be required to get them out.*

Installation

7 Peel the rubber gasket from the cover. If it's cracked, hardened, has soft spots or shows signs of general deterioration, replace it with a new one. Inspect the upper cam chain guide inside the valve cover and replace it if it's worn or damaged **(see illustration)**.
8 Clean the mating surfaces of the cylinder head and the valve cover with lacquer thinner, acetone or brake system cleaner.
9 Install the gasket to the cover. Make sure it fits completely into the cover groove **(see illustration)**.
10 Position the cover on the cylinder head, making sure the gasket doesn't slip out of place.
11 Check the rubber seals on the valve cover bolts, replacing them if necessary. Install the bolts with their seals and washers, tightening them evenly to the torque listed in this Chapter's Specifications.
12 The remainder of installation is the reverse of removal.

8.1 Loosen the tensioner cap bolt (A) and remove the tensioner mounting bolts (B)

8 Camshaft chain tensioner – removal and installation

Removal

1 Loosen the tensioner cap bolt while the tensioner is still installed **(see illustration)**.
2 Remove the tensioner mounting bolts and take it off the engine.
3 Remove the cap, sealing washer and spring from the tensioner. Check the tensioner parts for wear and damage and replace them as necessary.

Installation

4 Check the sealing washer on the adjusting bolt for cracks or hardening. It's a good idea to replace this washer whenever the tensioner cap is removed.
5 Lift the tensioner latch, compress the tensioner piston into the body and release the latch to hold the piston in **(see illustration)**.
6 Install the tensioner on the cylinder block, using a new gasket. The latch and the ratchet teeth on the tensioner must face down.
Caution: The tensioner will fit into the engine upside down, but the tensioner body will crack if the bolts are tightened in this position.

8.5 Lift the latch (arrowed), compress the tensioner piston and release the latch – the piston must be retracted like this to prevent damage when the tensioner is installed (also, the latch must face down when installing the tensioner)

9.6 The camshaft bearing end caps are numbered (left arrow), the inner caps have an arrow pointing to the clutch end of the engine (right arrow) and all caps are marked I or E for intake or exhaust . . .

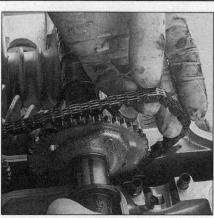

9.8a Lift the chain off the sprockets and remove the camshafts

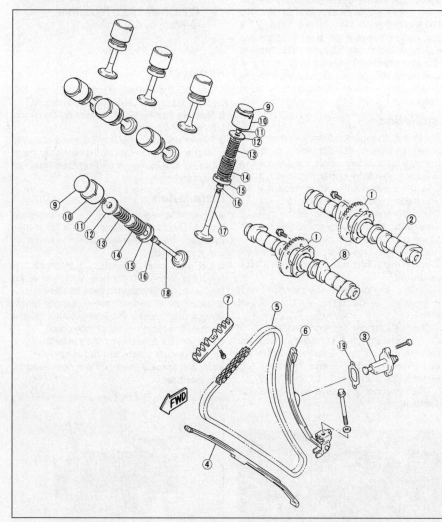

9.8b Camshafts, valves and cam chain tensioner – exploded view

1 Cam sprocket	8 Exhaust camshaft	14 Outer valve spring
2 Intake camshaft	9 Valve adjusting shim	15 Valve spring seat
3 Cam chain tensioner	10 Valve lifter	16 Valve stem oil seal
4 Exhaust side chain guide	11 Valve keepers/collets	17 Intake valve
5 Cam chain	12 Valve spring retainer	18 Exhaust valve
6 Intake side chain guide	13 Inner valve spring	19 Gasket
7 Upper chain guide		

7 Tighten the mounting bolts to the torque listed in this Chapter's Specifications.
8 Install the tensioner spring, sealing washer and cap. Tighten the cap bolt to the torque listed in this Chapter's Specifications.

9 Camshafts and lifters – removal, inspection and installation

Note: *This procedure can be performed with the engine in the frame.*

Camshafts

Removal

1 Set the bike on its centrestand (if equipped) or support it securely upright.
2 Remove the valve cover (see Section 7). On 1996-on UK models removal of the oil cooler radiator is advised for easier access to the camshafts (see Section 32).
3 Turn the engine to position no. 1 cylinder at TDC (top dead centre) on the compression stroke (see Chapter 1, *Valve clearances – check and adjustment*). To ease reassembly, make alignment marks on the sprockets, chain and camshafts with a felt pen. The no. 1 cam lobes will face each other when no. 1 cylinder is at TDC **(see illustration 25.7 in Chapter 1)**.
4 Remove the camshaft chain tensioner (see Section 8).
5 If you're planning to remove the sprockets from the camshafts, hold the camshafts from turning with an open-end wrench on the camshaft hex and loosen the sprocket bolts. The sprockets need not be removed unless the sprockets or camshafts are being replaced.
6 Loosen the camshaft bearing cap bolts for the intake and exhaust camshafts, a little at a time, working from the outside toward the centre, until all of the bolts are loose **(see illustration)**.
Caution: If the bearing cap bolts aren't loosened evenly, the camshaft may bind. Note that each bearing cap is labelled with the letter I for intake or E for exhaust and the no. 1 and no. 4 bearing caps are numbered.
7 Remove the bolts and lift off the bearing caps. The dowel pins may come off with the caps or stay in the engine – don't lose them.
8 Slip the camshafts out of the chain, then remove them **(see illustrations)**.
9 While the camshafts are out, don't allow the chain to go slack – the chain may fall and bind between the crankshaft and case, which could damage these components. Tie the chain up with a piece of wire to prevent it from dropping down into the crankcase. Also, cover the top of the cylinder head with a rag to prevent foreign objects from falling into the engine.

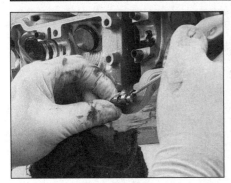

9.10 Lift out the exhaust-side cam chain guide

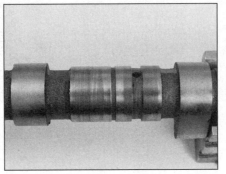

9.12a Check the journal surfaces of the camshaft for scratches or wear

9.12b Check the lobes of the camshaft for wear – here's a good example of damage which will require replacement (or repair) of the camshaft

10 Lift out the exhaust side chain guide (see illustration).

Inspection

Note: *Before replacing camshafts or the cylinder head and bearing caps because of damage, check with local machine shops specialising in motorcycle engine work. In the case of the camshafts, it may be possible for cam lobes to be welded, reground and hardened, at a cost far lower than that of a new camshaft. If the bearing surfaces in the cylinder head are damaged, it may be possible for them to be bored out to accept bearing inserts. Due to the cost of a new cylinder head it is recommended that all options be explored before condemning it as trash!*

11 Inspect the cam bearing surfaces of the head and the bearing caps. Look for score marks, deep scratches and evidence of spalling (a pitted appearance).

12 Check the camshaft bearing surfaces and lobes for heat discoloration (blue appearance), score marks, chipped areas, flat spots and spalling **(see illustrations)**. Measure the height of each lobe with a micrometer **(see illustration)** and compare the results to the minimum lobe height listed in this Chapter's Specifications. If damage is noted or wear is excessive, the camshaft must be replaced.

13 Next, check the camshaft bearing oil clearances. Clean the camshafts, the bearing surfaces in the cylinder head and the bearing

caps with a clean, lint-free cloth, then lay the cams in place in the cylinder head.

14 Cut eight strips of Plastigauge (type HPG-1) and lay one piece on each bearing journal, parallel with the camshaft centreline.

15 Make sure the bearing cap dowels are installed. Install the bearing caps in their proper positions. The arrows on the caps must face toward the right side of the engine. The numbers on the cap must correspond with the cylinder number (1 through 4, counting from the left side of the engine). The caps labelled I must go on the intake side of the engine and the caps labelled E must go on the exhaust side. Tighten the bolts in three steps to the torque listed in this Chapter's Specifications.

Caution: Tighten the bearing caps evenly to specifications. While tightening, DO NOT let the camshafts rotate! Use an open end wrench on the hex to hold them steady.

16 Now unscrew the bolts evenly, a little at a time, and carefully lift off the bearing caps.

17 To determine the oil clearance, compare the crushed Plastigauge (at its widest point) on each journal to the scale printed on the Plastigauge container **(see illustration)**. Compare the results to this Chapter's Specifications. If the oil clearance is greater than specified, measure the diameter of the cam bearing journal with a micrometer **(see illustration)**. If the journal diameter is less

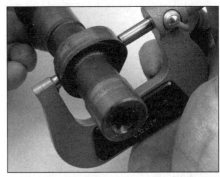

9.12c Measure the height of the camshaft lobes with a micrometer

than the specified limit, replace the camshaft with a new one and recheck the clearance. If the clearance is still too great, replace the cylinder head and bearing caps with new parts (see the Note that precedes Step 11).

18 Except in cases of oil starvation, the camshaft chain wears very little. If the chain has stretched excessively, which makes it difficult to maintain proper tension, replace it with a new one (see Section 27).

19 Check the sprockets for wear, cracks and other damage, replacing them if necessary. If the sprockets are worn, the chain is also worn, and also the sprocket on the crankshaft (which can only be remedied by replacing the crankshaft). If wear this severe is apparent,

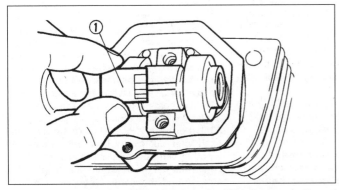

9.17a Compare the width of the crushed Plastigauge to the scale (1) on the Plastigauge container to obtain the clearance

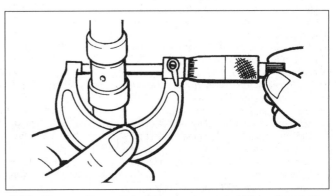

9.17b Measure the camshaft bearing journals with a micrometer

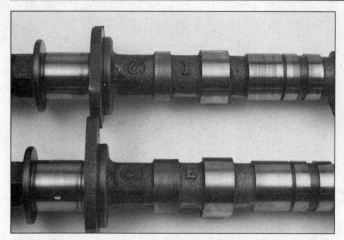

9.24a The camshafts are marked I for intake and E for exhaust

9.24b With the camshaft at TDC, the punch mark (left arrow) will be visible through the hole in the bearing cap (right arrow) (camshaft and bearing cap removed for clarity)

the entire engine should be disassembled for inspection.

20 Check the upper chain guide (see Section 27) and exhaust side chain guide for wear or damage. If they're worn or damaged, the chain may be worn out or improperly adjusted. Replacement of the chain requires removal of the crankshaft (see Section 25).

Installation

21 Make sure the crankshaft is still at no. 1 TDC (refer to Chapter 1, *Valve clearances – check and adjustment*).

22 Install the camshaft sprockets if they were removed and tighten the bolts to the torque listed in this Chapter's Specifications.

23 Make sure the bearing surfaces in the cylinder head and the bearing caps are clean, then apply a light coat of engine assembly lube or moly-based grease to each of them.

24 Apply a coat of moly-based grease to the camshaft lobes. Make sure the camshaft bearing journals are clean, then lay the camshafts in the cylinder head. The camshaft with the I mark goes on the intake side (the same side as the carburettors) and the camshaft with the EX mark goes on the exhaust side **(see illustration)**. Make sure the small punch mark on each camshaft (next to the no. 2 bearing cap) is straight up **(see illustration)**.

25 Carefully set all of the bearing caps in place with the small arrowhead cast in the top of each cap pointing toward the right (clutch) end of the engine. Make sure the caps are in their proper positions.

   a) *All caps are marked with the letter I (intake) or E (exhaust). Intake caps go on the intake side of the engine (closest to the carburettors). Exhaust caps go on the exhaust side of the engine (closest to the exhaust ports).*

   b) *The no. 1 caps (at the left end of the engine) are marked with the number 1 next to the letter I or E.*

   c) *The no. 2 and no. 3 caps are don't have number marks, but can be distinguished from each other by their shapes.*

   d) *The no. 4 caps (at the right end of the engine) are marked with the number 4 next to the letter I or E.*

26 Tighten the caps evenly, in three stages, to the torque listed in this Chapter's Specifications.

27 Recheck the camshaft alignment mark (small punch mark) on the exhaust camshaft. It should be aligned with the hole in the top of the no. 2 bearing cap **(see illustration 9.24b)**. Once you've done this, engage the sprocket with the cam chain. The sprocket should rest against its mounting flange on the camshaft, but don't install the sprocket bolts yet.

28 Turn the exhaust sprocket clockwise (viewed from the left end of the engine) to eliminate all slack in the cam chain. While the punch mark on the intake camshaft is aligned with the hole in the no. 2 bearing cap, install the sprocket bolt in the exposed hole and tighten it slightly with a wrench. **Note:** *If the sprocket bolt holes don't line up, reposition the sprocket in the cam chain.*

29 Rotate the intake sprocket clockwise (viewed from the left side of the engine) to take up all the slack in the chain. Make sure the camshaft punch marks are still aligned with the holes in the no. 2 bearing caps, then install the sprocket bolt in the exposed hole and tighten it slightly with a wrench. If the bolt holes aren't lined up properly, disengage sprocket from the chain and make the needed adjustment.

30 Recheck to make sure all timing marks – those on the signal generator, camshafts and no. 2 bearing caps – are aligned correctly.

Caution: If the marks are not aligned exactly as described, the valve timing will be incorrect and the valves may contact the pistons, causing extensive damage to the engine. Be sure to recheck the timing mark on the signal generator to make sure it hasn't shifted.

31 Pour clean engine oil over the cam chain and along the camshafts. Use enough that it flows down onto the sprockets and the valve area.

32 Install the exhaust side cam chain guide and cam chain tensioner.

33 Turn the engine slowly counterclockwise with a wrench on the crankshaft turning bolt. If you feel a sudden increase in resistance, stop turning. The valves may be hitting the pistons due to incorrect assembly. Find the problem and fix it before turning the engine any further, or serious damage may occur. Once again, check the alignment of the camshaft punch marks with the holes in the no. 2 bearing caps and the crankshaft timing marks.

34 Continue turning until the remaining camshaft sprocket bolt holes are exposed. Install the remaining two sprocket bolts and tighten all four bolts to the torque listed in this Chapter's Specifications.

35 The remainder of installation is the reverse of removal.

Valve lifters

Removal

36 Remove the camshafts following the procedure given above. Be sure to keep tension on the camshaft chain.

37 Make a holder with a separate section for each lifter and its valve adjusting shim (an egg carton or box will work). Label the sections according to cylinder number (1, 2, 3 or 4) and whether the lifter belongs with an intake or exhaust valve. The lifters form a wear pattern with their bores and must be returned to their original locations if reused.

38 Label each lifter and shim set and pull each lifter out of the bore with a magnet together with its valve adjusting shim **(see illustration)**. If the lifters are stuck, spray the area around them with carburettor cleaner and let it soak in. Place the lifters in order in their holder or box.

9.38 Mark the lifters and shims with a felt tip pen to identify their locations, then remove the lifters from their bores

10.8 Remove the nuts and washers attaching the front of the head to the cylinder block (also remove the two nuts on the other side of the head)

Inspection

39 Check the lifters and their bores for wear, scuff marks, scratches or other damage. Yamaha doesn't provide specifications or wear tolerances for the lifters or their bores, but if the bores are seriously out-of-round or tapered, replace the lifters and cylinder head as a set.

Installation

40 Coat the lifters and their bores with clean engine oil. Place a small dab of moly-based grease or assembly lube onto the adjusting shims prior to camshaft reinstallation.
41 The remainder of installation is the reverse of the removal steps.

10 Cylinder head – removal and installation

Caution: The engine must be completely cool before beginning this procedure or the cylinder head may become warped.

Note: *This procedure can be performed with the engine in the frame. If the engine has been removed, ignore the steps which don't apply.*

Removal

1 Remove the valve cover (see Section 7). On 1996-on UK models remove the oil cooler radiator (see Section 32).
2 Remove the exhaust system (see Chapter 3).
3 Turn the engine to position no. 1 cylinder at TDC compression (see Chapter 1, *Valve clearances – check and adjustment).*
4 Remove the camshaft chain tensioner (see Section 8).
5 Remove the camshafts (see Section 9).
6 The lifters can be left in their bores or removed (see Section 9). If you're planning work that includes turning the head upside down, such as valve service or measuring the gasket surface warpage, remove the lifters.
7 Remove the exhaust-side cam chain guide (see Section 9).
8 Remove the nuts and washers from the front of the cylinder head **(see illustration)**.

9 Remove the nuts and washers from the rear of the cylinder head.
10 Loosen the cylinder head nuts, 1/2 turn at a time, working in the reverse of the tightening sequence **(see illustration)**.
11 Once all of the nuts are loose, remove the nuts and washers. The two washers on the right (clutch) end of the engine are copper. The others are steel.
12 Pull the cylinder head off the cylinder block studs. If the head is stuck, tap up with a rubber mallet to jar it loose, or use two wooden dowels inserted into the intake or exhaust ports to rock the head back and forth slightly (its movement will be limited by the studs). Don't attempt to pry the head off by inserting a screwdriver between the head and the cylinder block – you'll damage the sealing surfaces.
13 Lift the head gasket off the cylinder block. Stuff a clean rag into the cam chain tunnel to prevent the entry of debris.
14 Remove the dowel pins and O-rings **(see illustration)**.
15 Check the cylinder head gasket and the

10.10 Cylinder head nut TIGHTENING sequence

10.14 Remove the dowel pins and O-rings from the corners of the cylinder block (arrowed)

mating surfaces on the cylinder head and block for leakage, which could indicate warpage. Refer to Section 12 and check the flatness of the cylinder head.

16 Clean all traces of old gasket material from the cylinder head and block. Be careful not to let any of the gasket material fall into the crankcase, the cylinder bores or the oil passages.

Installation

17 Install the dowels on the cylinder head studs. Use new O-rings on the two studs at the clutch end of the block **(see illustration 10.14)**.

18 Lay the new head gasket in place on the cylinder block. The gasket only goes one way; if all of the holes don't line up with the holes in the cylinder block, the gasket is upside down. Never re-use the old gasket.

19 Carefully lower the cylinder head over the studs. It's helpful to have an assistant support the camshaft chain with a piece of wire so it doesn't fall and become kinked or detached from the crankshaft. When the head is resting against the cylinder block, wire the cam chain to another component to keep tension on it.

20 Lubricate the threads with engine oil, then install the head washers and nuts. Install new copper washers onto the outer studs on the right side of the engine. Using the proper sequence **(see illustration 10.10)**, tighten the nuts to approximately half of the torque listed in this Chapter's Specifications.

21 Using the same sequence, tighten the nuts to the torque listed in this Chapter's Specifications.

22 Lubricate the threads with engine oil, then install the small cylinder block-to-cylinder head nuts, tightening them to the torque listed in this Chapter's Specifications.

23 Install the exhaust side and upper cam chain guides.

24 Install the camshafts, tensioner and the valve cover (see Sections 9, 8 and 7).

25 Change the engine oil (see Chapter 1).

26 The remainder of installation is the reverse of the removal steps.

11 Valves/valve seats/valve guides – servicing

1 Because of the complex nature of this job and the special tools and equipment required, servicing of the valves, the valve seats and the valve guides (commonly known as a valve job) is best left to a professional.

2 The home mechanic can, however, remove and disassemble the head, do the initial cleaning and inspection, then reassemble and deliver the head to a dealer service department or properly equipped motorcycle repair shop for the actual valve servicing. Refer to Section 12 for those procedures.

3 The dealer service department will remove the valves and springs, recondition or replace the valves and valve seats, replace the valve guides, check and replace the valve springs, spring retainers and keepers/collets (as necessary), replace the valve seals with new ones and reassemble the valve components.

4 After the valve job has been performed, the head will be in like-new condition. When the head is returned, be sure to clean it again very thoroughly before installation on the engine to remove any metal particles or abrasive grit that may still be present from the valve service operations. Use compressed air, if available, to blow out all the holes and passages.

12 Cylinder head and valves – disassembly, inspection and reassembly

1 As mentioned in the previous Section, valve servicing and valve guide replacement should be left to a dealer service department or motorcycle repair shop. However, disassembly, cleaning and inspection of the valves and related components can be done

(if the necessary special tools are available) by the home mechanic. This way no expense is incurred if the inspection reveals that service work is not required at this time.

2 To properly disassemble the valve components without the risk of damaging them, a valve spring compressor is absolutely necessary. If your valve spring compressor is not designed to fit inside the lifter bores, you'll need a special adapter to compress the valve springs and retainers in order not to damage the bores **(see illustrations)**.

Disassembly

3 Remove the lifters and their shims if you haven't already done so (see Section 9). Store the components so they can be returned to their original locations without getting mixed up.

4 Before the valves are removed, scrape away any traces of gasket material from the head gasket sealing surface. Work slowly and do not nick or gouge the soft aluminium of the head. Gasket removing solvents, which work very well, are available at most motorcycle shops and auto parts stores.

5 Carefully scrape all carbon deposits out of the combustion chamber area. A hand-held wire brush or a piece of fine emery cloth can be used once most of the carbon has been scraped away. Do not use a wire brush mounted in a drill motor, or one with extremely stiff bristles, as the head material is soft and may be eroded away or scratched by the wire brush. Be careful not to disturb the head surface finish, any scratches or gouges will require that the head be resurfaced.

6 Before proceeding, arrange to label and store the valves along with their related components so they can be kept separate and reinstalled in the same valve guides they are removed from (labelled plastic bags work well for this).

7 Compress the valve spring on the first valve with a spring compressor, then remove the keepers/collets and the retainer from the valve assembly **(see illustration 12.2b and the**

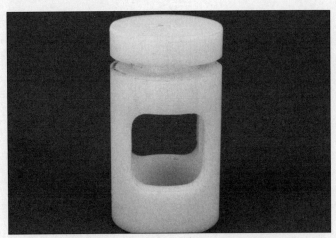

12.2a This is one type of adapter used with a standard valve spring compressor to remove the valves

12.2b Attach the compressor like this

accompanying illustration). Don't compress the springs any more than is absolutely necessary. Carefully release the valve spring compressor and remove the springs and the valve from the head. If the valve binds in the guide (won't pull through), push it back into the head and deburr the area around the keeper groove with a very fine file or whetstone (see illustration).

8 Repeat the procedure for the remaining valves. Remember to keep the parts for each valve together so they can be reinstalled in the same location.

9 Once the valves have been removed and labelled, pull off the valve stem seals with pliers and discard them (the old seals should never be reused), then remove the steel valve spring seats.

10 Next, clean the cylinder head with solvent and dry it thoroughly. Compressed air will speed the drying process and ensure that all holes and recessed areas are clean.

11 Clean all of the valve springs, keepers, retainers and spring seats with solvent and dry them thoroughly. Do the parts from one valve at a time so that no mixing of parts between valves occurs.

12 Scrape off any deposits that may have formed on the valve, then use a motorised wire brush to remove deposits from the valve heads. Again, make sure the valves don't get mixed up.

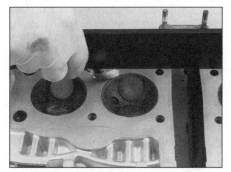

12.14a Lay a precision straight-edge across the cylinder head and try to slide a feeler gauge of the specified thickness (equal to the maximum allowable warpage) under it

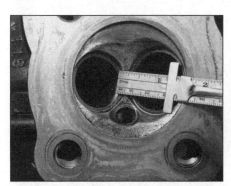

12.15 Measure the valve seat width with a ruler (or for greater precision use a vernier caliper)

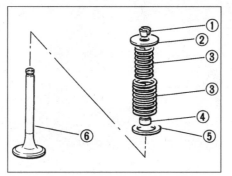

12.7a Valve components – exploded view

1 Valve keepers
   (collets)
2 Spring retainer
3 Valve springs
4 Stem oil seal
5 Spring seat
6 Valve

Inspection

13 Inspect the head very carefully for cracks and other damage. If cracks are found, a new head will be required. Check the cam bearing surfaces for wear and evidence of seizure. Check the camshafts and lifters for wear as well (see Section 9).

14 Using a precision straight-edge and a feeler gauge, check the head gasket mating surface for warpage. Lay the straight-edge lengthways, across the head and diagonally (corner-to-corner), intersecting the head stud holes, and try to slip a feeler gauge under it, on either side of each combustion chamber (see illustrations). The gauge should be the

12.14b Measure along these lines

12.16a Insert a small hole gauge into the valve guide and expand it so there's a slight drag when it's pulled out

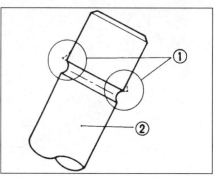

12.7b Check the area around the keeper groove for burrs and remove any that you find

1 Burrs (remove with a file)
2 Valve stem

same thickness as the cylinder head warpage limit listed in this Chapter's Specifications. If the feeler gauge can be inserted between the head and the straight-edge, the head is warped and must either be machined or, if warpage is excessive, replaced with a new one.

15 Examine the valve seats in each of the combustion chambers. If they are pitted, cracked or burned, the head will require valve service that's beyond the scope of the home mechanic. Measure the valve seat width (see illustration) and compare it to this Chapter's Specifications. If it is not within the specified range, or if it varies around its circumference, valve service work is required.

16 Clean the valve guides to remove any carbon build-up, then measure the inside diameters of the guides (at both ends and the centre of the guide) with a small hole gauge and a 0-to-1-inch micrometer (see illustrations). Record the measurements for future reference. These measurements, along with the valve stem diameter measurements, will enable you to compute the valve stem-to-guide clearance. This clearance, when compared to the Specifications, will be one factor that will determine the extent of the valve service work required. The guides are measured at the ends and at the centre to determine if they are worn in a bell-mouth

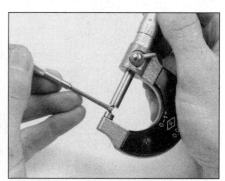

12.16b Measure the small hole gauge with a micrometer

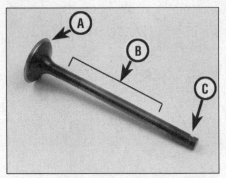

12.17 Check the valve face (A), stem (B) and keeper/collet groove (C) for signs of wear and damage

12.18a Measure the valve stem diameter with a micrometer

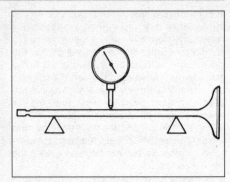

12.18b Check the valve stem for bends with a V-block (or blocks, as shown here) and a dial gauge

pattern (more wear at the ends). If they are, guide replacement is an absolute must.

17 Carefully inspect each valve face for cracks, pits and burned spots. Check the valve stem and the keeper groove area for cracks **(see illustration)**. Rotate the valve and check for any obvious indication that it is bent. Check the end of the stem for pitting and excessive wear and make sure the bevel is the specified width. The presence of any of the above conditions indicates the need for valve servicing.

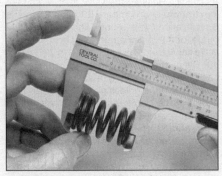

12.19a Measure the free length of the valve springs

18 Measure the valve stem diameter **(see illustration)**. By subtracting the stem diameter from the valve guide diameter, the valve stem-to-guide clearance is obtained. If the stem-to-guide clearance is greater than listed in this Chapter's Specifications, the guides and valves will have to be replaced with new ones. Also check the valve stem for bending. Set the valve in a V-block with a dial gauge touching the middle of the stem **(see illustration)**. Rotate the valve and note the reading on the gauge. If the stem runout exceeds the value listed in this Chapter's Specifications, replace the valve.

19 Check the end of each valve spring for wear and pitting. Measure the free length **(see illustration)** and compare it to this Chapter's Specifications. Any springs that are shorter than specified have sagged and should not be reused. Stand the spring on a flat surface and check it for squareness **(see illustration)**.

20 Check the spring retainers and keepers/collets for obvious wear and cracks. Any questionable parts should not be reused, as extensive damage will occur in the event of failure during engine operation.

21 If the inspection indicates that no service

work is required, the valve components can be reinstalled in the head.

Reassembly

22 Before installing the valves in the head, they should be lapped to ensure a positive seal between the valves and seats. This procedure requires coarse and fine valve lapping compound (available at auto parts stores) and a valve lapping tool. If a lapping tool is not available, a piece of rubber or plastic hose can be slipped over the valve stem (after the valve has been installed in the guide) and used to turn the valve.

23 Apply a small amount of coarse lapping compound to the valve face **(see illustration)**, then slip the valve into the guide. **Note:** *Make sure the valve is installed in the correct guide and be careful not to get any lapping compound on the valve stem.*

24 Attach the lapping tool (or hose) to the valve and rotate the tool between the palms of your hands. Use a back-and-forth motion rather than a circular motion. Lift the valve off the seat and turn it at regular intervals to distribute the lapping compound properly. Continue the lapping procedure until the valve face and seat contact area is of uniform width

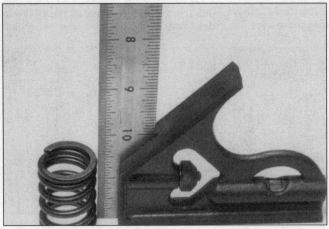

12.19b Check the valve springs for squareness

12.23 Apply the lapping compound very sparingly, in small dabs, to the valve face only

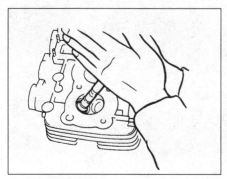

12.24a After lapping, the valve face should exhibit a uniform, unbroken pattern . . .

12.24b . . . and the seat should be the specified width (arrowed) with a smooth, unbroken appearance

12.28a Install the springs with their closely spaced coils down (against the cylinder head)

and unbroken around the entire circumference of the valve face and seat **(see illustrations)**.

25 Carefully remove the valve from the guide and wipe off all traces of lapping compound. Use solvent to clean the valve and wipe the seat area thoroughly with a solvent-soaked cloth.

26 Repeat the procedure with fine valve lapping compound, then repeat the entire procedure for the remaining valves.

27 Lay the spring seats in place in the cylinder head, then install new valve stem seals on each of the guides. Use an appropriate size deep socket to push the seals into place until they are properly seated. don't twist or cock them, or they will not seal properly against the valve stems. Also, don't remove them again or they will be damaged.

28 Coat the valve stems and valve face with assembly lube or moly-based grease, then install one of them into its guide. Next, install the springs and retainers, compress the springs and install the keepers. **Note:** *Install the springs with the tightly wound coils at the bottom (next to the spring seat)* **(see illustration)**; *Yamaha advise installing the inner spring so that its coils run in a counterclockwise direction and the outer spring with its coils running in a clockwise direction (both as viewed from above).* When compressing the springs with the valve spring compressor, depress them only as far as is absolutely necessary to

slip the keepers/collets into place. Apply a small amount of grease to the keepers (collets) **(see illustration)** to help hold them in place as the pressure is released from the springs. Make certain that the keepers/collets are securely locked in their retaining grooves.

29 Support the cylinder head on blocks so the valves can't contact the workbench top, then very gently tap each of the valve stems with a soft-faced hammer. This will help seat the keepers/collets in their grooves.

> **HAYNES HiNT** *Check for proper valve sealing by pouring a small amount of solvent into each of the valve ports. If the solvent leaks past the valve(s) into the combustion chamber area, disassemble the valve(s) and repeat the lapping procedure, then reinstall the valve(s) and repeat the check.*

13 Cylinder block – removal, inspection and installation

Removal

1 Following the procedure given in Section 10, remove the cylinder head. Make sure the crankshaft is positioned at Top Dead Centre (TDC) for cylinder no. 1.

2 Remove the nut from the stud that secures the block to the crankcase **(see illustration)**.

3 Lift the cylinder block straight up to remove it. If it's stuck, tap around its perimeter with a soft-faced hammer. Don't attempt to pry between the block and the crankcase, as you will ruin the sealing surfaces. As you lift, note the location of the dowel pins. Be careful not to let these drop into the engine.

4 Stuff clean shop towels around the pistons and remove the gasket and all traces of old gasket material from the surfaces of the cylinder block and the cylinder head.

Inspection

5 Don't attempt to separate the liners from the cylinder block.

6 Check the cylinder walls carefully for scratches and score marks.

7 Using the appropriate precision measuring tools, check each cylinder's diameter. Measure near the top, centre and bottom of the cylinder bore, parallel to the crankshaft axis **(see illustration)**. Next, measure each cylinder's diameter at the same three locations across the crankshaft axis. Compare the results to this Chapter's

12.28b A small dab of grease will help hold the keepers (collets) in place on the valve spring while the valve is released

13.2 Remove the nut from the single stud at the front of the cylinder block

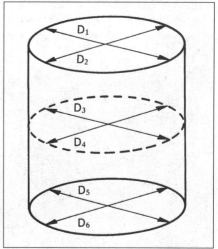

13.7 Measure the cylinder bore with a telescoping gauge at these six points (then measure the gauge with a micrometer)

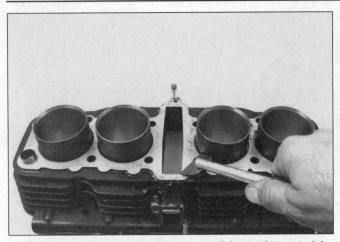

13.12 Use a scraper to remove any remaining gasket material from the bottom of the cylinder block

13.13a Install a new O-ring around the base of each cylinder and press it completely into its groove. . .

Specifications. If the cylinder walls are tapered, out-of-round, worn beyond the specified limits, or badly scuffed or scored, have them rebored and honed by a dealer service department or a motorcycle repair shop. If a rebore is done, oversize pistons and rings will be required as well.

8 As an alternative, if the precision measuring tools are not available, a dealer service department or motorcycle repair shop will make the measurements and offer advice concerning servicing of the cylinders.

9 If they are in reasonably good condition and not worn to the outside of the limits, and if the piston-to-cylinder clearances can be maintained properly (see Section 14), then the cylinders do not have to be rebored; honing is all that is necessary.

10 To perform the honing operation you will need the proper size flexible hone with fine stones, or a bottle-brush type hone, plenty of light oil or honing oil, some shop towels and an electric drill motor. Hold the cylinder block sideways (bore 90° to the vice jaws) in a vice (cushioned with soft jaws or wood blocks) when performing the honing operation. Mount the hone in the drill motor, compress the stones and slip the hone into the cylinder. Lubricate the cylinder thoroughly, turn on the drill and move the hone up and down in the cylinder at a pace which will produce a fine crosshatch pattern on the cylinder wall with the crosshatch lines intersecting at approximately a 60° angle. Be sure to use plenty of lubricant and do not take off any more material than is absolutely necessary to produce the desired effect. Do not withdraw the hone from the cylinder while it is running. Instead, shut off the drill and continue moving the hone up and down in the cylinder until it comes to a complete stop, then compress the stones and withdraw the hone. Wipe the oil out of the cylinder and repeat the procedure on the other cylinders. Remember, do not remove too much material from the cylinder wall. If you do not have the tools, or do not desire to perform the honing operation, a dealer service department or motorcycle repair shop will generally do it for a reasonable fee.

11 Next, the cylinders must be thoroughly washed with warm soapy water to remove all traces of the abrasive grit produced during the honing operation. Be sure to run a brush through the bolt holes and flush them with running water. After rinsing, dry the cylinders thoroughly and apply a coat of light, rust-preventative oil to all machined surfaces.

Installation

12 Ensure that the bottom gasket surface is clean (see illustration) before you lubricate the cylinder bores with clean engine oil. Apply a thin film of engine oil to the piston skirts.

13 Install the dowel pins, then place a new cylinder base gasket on the cylinder block. Install new O-rings on the base of each cylinder. Install new O-rings around the two cylinder block dowels at the right end of the engine (see illustrations).

14 Slowly rotate the crankshaft until two of the pistons are up and two down. Be extremely careful not to jam the timing chain in the case.

15 Attach four piston ring compressors to the pistons and compress the piston rings. Large hose clamps can be used instead – just make sure they don't scratch the pistons, and don't tighten them too much.

13.13b . . . then, install the new gasket between the block and cylinder assembly, making sure the UP mark is up . . .

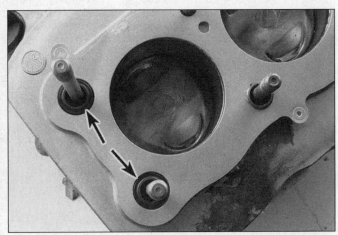

13.13c . . . and new O-rings at the clutch end of the engine

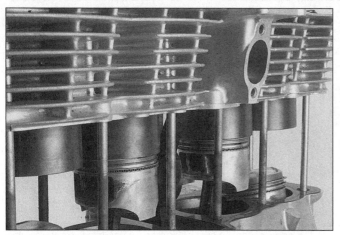

13.16 If you're very careful, you can install the cylinder block over the pistons without using ring compressors, but it's advised to use them

14.3a Mark the cylinder numbers on the piston crowns – also note the arrow, which must point to the front

16 Install the cylinder block over the pistons and carefully lower it down until the piston crowns fit into the cylinder liners **(see illustration)**. While doing this, pull the camshaft chain up, using a hooked tool or a piece of coat hanger or previously attached piece of wire. Also keep an eye on the cam chain guide to make sure it doesn't wedge against the block. Push down on the cylinder block, making sure the pistons don't get cocked sideways, until the bottoms of the cylinder liners slide down past the piston rings. A wood or plastic hammer handle can be used to gently tap the block down, but don't use too much force or the pistons will be damaged.

17 Once the cylinders have passed over the rings of the two pistons, rotate the crankshaft so the remaining pistons are up and install the cylinder block over them.

18 Remove the piston ring compressors or hose clamps (if used), being careful not to scratch the pistons. Remove the rods from under the pistons.

19 The remainder of installation is the reverse of removal.

14 Pistons – removal, inspection and installation

1 The pistons are attached to the connecting rods with piston pins that are a slip fit in the pistons and rods.

2 Before removing the pistons from the rods, stuff a clean shop towel into each crankcase hole, around the connecting rods. This will prevent the circlips from falling into the crankcase if they are inadvertently dropped.

Removal

3 Using a sharp scribe, scratch the number of each piston into its crown (or use a felt pen if the piston is clean enough). Each piston should also have an arrow pointing toward the front of the engine **(see illustration)**. If not, scribe an arrow into the piston crown before removal. Support the first piston, grasp the circlip with needle-nose pliers and remove it from the groove **(see illustration)**.

4 Push the piston pin out from the opposite

14.3b Remove the circlip from one side of the piston – wear eye protection and be careful not to let it fly out

end to free the piston from the rod **(see illustration)**. You may have to deburr the area around the groove to enable the pin to slide out (use a triangular file for this procedure). If the pin won't come out, remove the remaining circlip. Fabricate a piston pin removal tool from threaded stock, nuts, washers and a piece of pipe **(see illustration)**. Repeat the procedure for the other pistons.

14.4a Push the piston pin out until you can grasp it, then pull it out the rest of the way

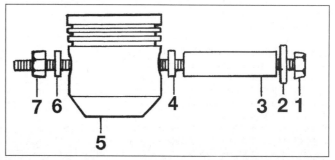

14.4b The piston pin should come out with hand pressure, but if not this removal tool can be fabricated from readily available parts

1 Bolt	6 Washer (B)	B Small enough to
2 Washer	7 Nut (B)	fit through pin
3 Tubing or pipe (A)	A Large enough for	bore in piston
4 Padding (A)	piston pin to fit	
5 Piston	through	

14.6 Remove the piston rings with a ring removal and installation tool

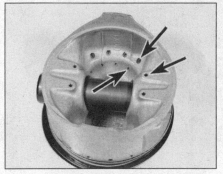

14.11 Check the piston pin bore and the piston skirt for wear, and make sure the internal holes are clear (arrowed)

14.13 Measure the piston ring-to-groove clearance with a feeler gauge

Inspection

5 Before the inspection process can be carried out, the pistons must be cleaned and the old piston rings removed.

6 Using a piston ring removal and installation tool, carefully remove the rings from the pistons **(see illustration)**. Do not nick or gouge the pistons in the process.

7 Scrape all traces of carbon from the tops of the pistons. A hand-held wire brush can be used once most of the deposits have been scraped away. Do not, under any circumstances, use a wire brush mounted in a drill motor to remove deposits from the pistons; the piston material is soft and will be eroded away by the wire brush.

8 Use a piston ring groove cleaning tool to remove any carbon deposits from the ring grooves. If a tool is not available, a piece broken off the old ring will do the job. Be very careful to remove only the carbon deposits. Do not remove any metal and do not nick or gouge the top and bottom of the ring lands (the metal ridges between the ring grooves).

9 Once the deposits have been removed, clean the pistons with solvent and dry them thoroughly. Make sure the oil return holes below the oil ring grooves are clear.

10 If the pistons are not damaged or worn excessively and if the cylinders are not rebored, new pistons will not be necessary. Normal piston wear appears as even, vertical wear on the thrust surfaces of the piston and slight looseness of the top ring in its groove. New piston rings, on the other hand, should always be used when an engine is rebuilt.

11 Carefully inspect each piston for cracks around the skirt, at the pin bosses and at the ring lands **(see illustration)**.

12 Look for scoring and scuffing on the thrust faces of the skirt, holes in the piston crown and burned areas at the edge of the crown. If the skirt is scored or scuffed, the engine may have been suffering from overheating and/or abnormal combustion, which caused excessively high operating temperatures. The oil pump and oil cooler (if equipped) should be checked thoroughly. A hole in the piston crown, an extreme to be sure, is an indication that abnormal combustion (pre-ignition) was

occurring. Burned areas at the edge of the piston crown are usually evidence of spark knock (detonation). If any of the above problems exist, the causes must be corrected or the damage will occur again.

13 Measure the piston ring-to-groove clearance by laying a new piston ring in the ring groove and slipping a feeler gauge in beside it **(see illustration)**. Check the clearance at three or four locations around the groove. Be sure to use the correct ring for each groove; they are different. If the clearance is greater than specified, new pistons will have to be used when the engine is reassembled.

14 Check the piston-to-bore clearance by measuring the bore (see Section 13) and the piston diameter. Make sure that the pistons and cylinders are correctly matched. Measure the piston across the skirt on the thrust faces at a 90° angle to the piston pin, at the distance from the bottom of the skirt listed in this Chapter's Specifications **(see illustration)**. Subtract the piston diameter from the bore diameter to obtain the clearance. If it is greater than specified, the cylinders will have to be rebored and new oversized pistons and rings installed.

15 If the appropriate precision measuring tools are not available, the piston-to-cylinder clearances can be obtained, though not quite as accurately, using feeler gauge stock. Feeler gauge stock comes in 12-inch lengths and

various thicknesses and is generally available at auto parts stores. To check the clearance, select a feeler gauge of the same thickness as the piston clearance listed in this Chapter's Specifications and slip it into the cylinder along with the appropriate piston. The cylinder should be upside down and the piston must be positioned exactly as it normally would be. Place the feeler gauge between the piston and cylinder on one of the thrust faces (90° to the piston pin bore). The piston should slip through the cylinder (with the feeler gauge in place) with moderate pressure. If it falls through, or slides through easily, the clearance is excessive and a new piston will be required. If the piston binds at the lower end of the cylinder and is loose toward the top, the cylinder is tapered, and if tight spots are encountered as the feeler gauge is placed at different points around the cylinder, the cylinder is out-of-round.

16 Repeat the procedure for the remaining pistons and cylinders. Be sure to have the cylinders and pistons checked by a dealer service department or a motorcycle repair shop to confirm your findings before purchasing new parts.

17 Apply clean engine oil to the pin, insert it into the piston and check for freeplay by rocking the pin back-and-forth **(see illustration)**. If the pin is loose, new pistons and pins must be installed.

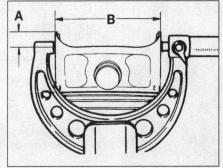

14.14 Measure the piston diameter with a micrometer

A Specified distance from bottom of piston
B Piston diameter

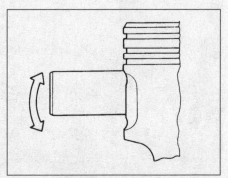

14.17 Slip the pin into the piston and try to rock it back-and-forth; if it's loose, replace the piston and pin

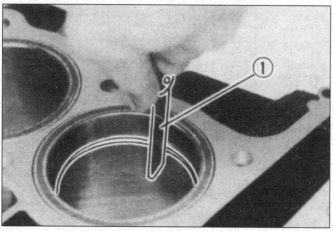

15.3 Square the ring in the bore by turning the piston upside down and tapping on the ring, then check the piston ring end gap with a feeler gauge (1)

15.5 If the end gap is too small, clamp a file in a vice and file the ring ends (from the outside in only) to enlarge the gap slightly

18 Refer to Section 15 and install the rings on the pistons.

Installation

19 Install the pistons in their original locations with the arrows pointing to the front of the engine. Lubricate the pins and the rod bores with clean engine oil. Install new circlips in the grooves in the inner sides of the pistons (don't reuse the old circlips). Push the pins into position from the opposite side and install new circlips. Compress the circlips only enough for them to fit in the piston. Make sure the clips are properly seated in the grooves and that the open of the circlip is away from the removal notch.

15 Piston rings – installation

1 Before installing the new piston rings, the ring end gaps must be checked.
2 Lay out the pistons and the new ring sets so the rings will be matched with the same piston and cylinder during the end gap measurement procedure and engine assembly.

3 Insert the top (No. 1) ring into the bottom of the first cylinder and square it up with the cylinder walls by pushing it in with the top of the piston. Since the bottom of the cylinder experiences the least amount of wear, the ring should be about one inch above the bottom edge of the cylinder. To measure the end gap, slip a feeler gauge between the ends of the ring **(see illustration)** and compare the measurement to this Chapter's Specifications.
4 If the gap is larger or smaller than specified, double check to make sure that you have the correct rings before proceeding.
5 If the gap is too small, it must be enlarged or the ring ends may come in contact with each other during engine operation, which can cause serious damage. The end gap can be increased by filing the ring ends very carefully with a fine file **(see illustration)**. When performing this operation, file only from the outside in.
6 Excess end gap is not critical unless it is greater than 0.040 in (1 mm). Again, double check to make sure you have the correct rings for your engine. Too little end gap can cause the rings to seize to the cylinder walls.
7 Repeat the procedure for each ring that will be installed in the first cylinder and for each ring in the remaining cylinders. Remember to

keep the rings, pistons and cylinders matched up.
8 Once the ring end gaps have been checked/corrected, the rings can be installed on the pistons.
9 The oil control ring (lowest on the piston) is installed first. It is composed of three separate components. Slip the expander into the groove, then install the upper side rail **(see illustrations)**. Don't use a piston ring installation tool on the oil ring side rails as they may be damaged. Instead, place one end of the side rail into the groove between the spacer expander and the ring land. Hold it firmly in place and slide a finger around the piston while pushing the rail into the groove. Next, install the lower side rail in the same manner.
10 After the three oil ring components have been installed, check to make sure that both the upper and lower side rails can be turned smoothly in the ring groove.
11 Install the second (middle) ring next. It can be readily distinguished from the top ring by its cross-section shape **(see illustration)**. Do not mix the top and middle rings.
12 To avoid breaking the ring, use a piston ring installation tool and make sure that the identification mark is facing up **(see**

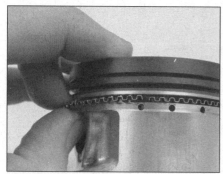

15.9a Installing the oil ring expander – make sure the ends don't overlap

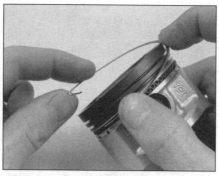

15.9b Installing an oil ring side rail – don't use a ring installation tool to do this

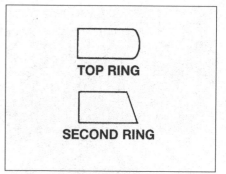

15.11 Don't confuse the top ring with the second ring

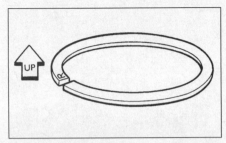

15.12 Make sure the marks on the rings face up when the rings are installed on the pistons

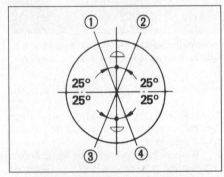

15.15 Arrange the ring gaps like this

1 Top compression ring
2 Oil ring lower rail
3 Oil ring upper rail
4 Second compression ring

illustration). Fit the ring into the middle groove on the piston. Do not expand the ring any more than is necessary to slide it into place.

13 Finally, install the top ring in the same manner. Make sure the identifying mark is facing up.

14 Repeat the procedure for the remaining pistons and rings. Be very careful not to confuse the top and second rings.

15 Once the rings have been properly installed, stagger the end gaps, including those of the oil ring side rails (see illustration).

16 Apply a liberal coating of engine oil on the pistons prior to installation.

16 Oil pan and relief valves – removal, relief valve inspection and installation

Removal

1 Remove the engine (see Section 5).

2 Remove the oil pan bolts and detach the pan from the crankcase (see illustration 17.2b and the accompanying illustration).

3 Remove all traces of old gasket material from the mating surfaces of the oil pan and crankcase.

4 Remove the strainer from the oil pick-up and inspect for debris (see illustration).

5 Unbolt the pick-up from the crankcase (see illustration).

6 Remove all traces of old gasket material from the pick-up and crankcase.

7 Remove the pressure relief valves from the crankcase (see illustrations). The oil pressure valve should pull out with light hand pressure. If it's stuck, rock it back and forth slightly while you pull on it. The starter chain tensioner relief valve should be unscrewed with a wrench or socket.

Relief valve inspection

8 Push the plunger into the relief valve and check for free movement (see illustration). If the valve sticks, perform the following steps to disassemble and inspect it.

9 Straighten the cotter pin and pull it out (see illustration).

10 Remove the spring retainer, spring and plunger.

11 Check all parts for wear and damage. Clean the parts thoroughly, reassemble the valve and recheck its movement. If the valve still sticks, replace it.

Caution: If you reuse the relief valve, install a new cotter pin before reinstalling the relief valve in the engine.

12 Repeat the same steps for the starter chain tensioner relief valve.

Installation

13 Install the starter chain tensioner relief valve with a new sealing washer.

16.2 Remove the oil pan bolts around the edge of the pan

16.4 Remove the oil strainer from the pick-up; the arrow on the strainer points toward the rear of the engine

16.5 Remove the pick-up bolts and detach the pick-up from the engine

16.7a Pull the main oil relief valve out of the crankcase . . .

16.7b . . . and unscrew the starter chain relief valve

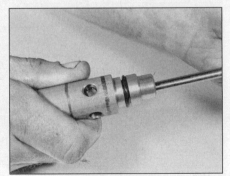

16.8 Push in on the relief valve plunger to make sure it moves freely

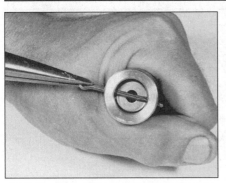

16.9 Straighten the ends of the cotter pin and pull it out

17.2a Remove the snap-ring and the oil pump drive gear

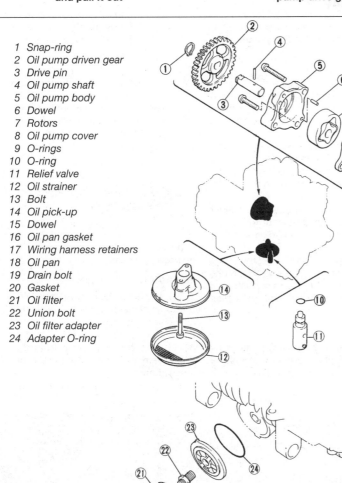

1 Snap-ring
2 Oil pump driven gear
3 Drive pin
4 Oil pump shaft
5 Oil pump body
6 Dowel
7 Rotors
8 Oil pump cover
9 O-rings
10 O-ring
11 Relief valve
12 Oil strainer
13 Bolt
14 Oil pick-up
15 Dowel
16 Oil pan gasket
17 Wiring harness retainers
18 Oil pan
19 Drain bolt
20 Gasket
21 Oil filter
22 Union bolt
23 Oil filter adapter
24 Adapter O-ring

17.2b Oil pump and pan (exploded view)

14 Install the oil pan dowels. Install the oil pressure relief valves in the crankcase, using new O-rings.
15 Install the oil pick-up and tighten the bolts to the torque listed in this Chapter's Specifications. Install the strainer on the pick-up with its open end toward the rear of the engine.
16 Position a new gasket on the oil pan. A thin film of sealant can be used to hold the gasket in place. Install the oil pan and bolts, tightening the bolts to the torque listed in this Chapter's Specifications, using a criss-cross pattern. Reinstall the wiring harness clips on the appropriate bolts.
17 The remainder of installation is the reverse of removal. Install a new oil filter and fill the crankcase with oil (see Chapter 1), then run the engine and check for leaks.

17 Oil pump – removal, inspection and installation

Note: *The oil pump can be removed with the engine in the frame.*

Removal

1 Remove the clutch (see Section 18).
2 Remove the snap-ring and take off the oil pump driven gear **(see illustrations)**.
3 Remove the oil pump mounting screws and lift the pump away from the engine **(see illustration)**. Remove the O-rings **(see illustration)**.

17.3a Remove the three mounting screws (arrowed) and take the pump off

17.3b Remove the O-rings (arrowed)

17.8 Insert a feeler gauge between the outer rotor and pump body to measure the clearance

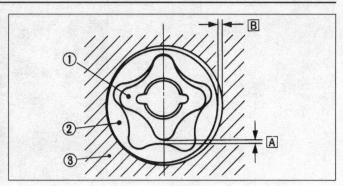

17.9 Measure the clearance between the outer rotor tip and the inner rotor with a feeler gauge

1	Inner rotor	A	Inner rotor to outer rotor clearance
2	Outer rotor	B	Outer rotor to pump body clearance
3	Pump body		

Inspection

4 Wash the oil pump in solvent, then dry it off.
5 Remove the pump cover screw (use an impact driver if it's tight).
6 Lift off the cover.
7 Check the pump body and rotors for

17.10 Insert the pin in the shaft and make sure it's centred

scoring and wear. If any damage or uneven or excessive wear is evident, replace the pump (individual parts aren't available). If you're rebuilding the engine, it's a good idea to install a new oil pump.
8 Measure the clearance between the outer rotor and pump body with a feeler gauge and compare it to the value listed in this Chapter's Specifications **(see illustration)**. If it's excessive, replace the pump.
9 Measure the clearance between the inner and outer rotors **(see illustration)**. Again, replace the pump if the clearance is excessive.
10 If the pump is good, reverse the disassembly steps to reassemble it. Make sure the pin is centred in the rotor shaft so it will align with the slot in the inner rotor **(see illustration)**.

Installation

11 Before installing the pump, prime it by pouring oil into it while turning the shaft by hand – this will ensure that it begins to pump oil quickly.

12 Installation is the reverse of removal, with the following additions:
  a) Make sure the O-rings are in place.
  b) Tighten the pump mounting screws to the torque listed in this Chapter's Specifications.

18 Clutch – removal, inspection and installation

Note: The clutch can be removed with the engine in the frame.

Removal

1 Set the bike on its centrestand (if equipped) or prop it securely upright. Remove the lower fairing (if equipped).
2 Drain the engine oil (see Chapter 1).
3 Detach the clutch cable from the lever, then remove the clutch cover **(see illustrations)**.
4 Loosen the clutch pressure plate bolts

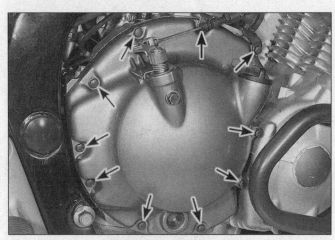

18.3a Loosen the clutch cover bolts (arrowed) evenly in a criss-cross pattern . . .

18.3b . . . and pry gently at the pry point (arrowed) to separate the cover from the engine

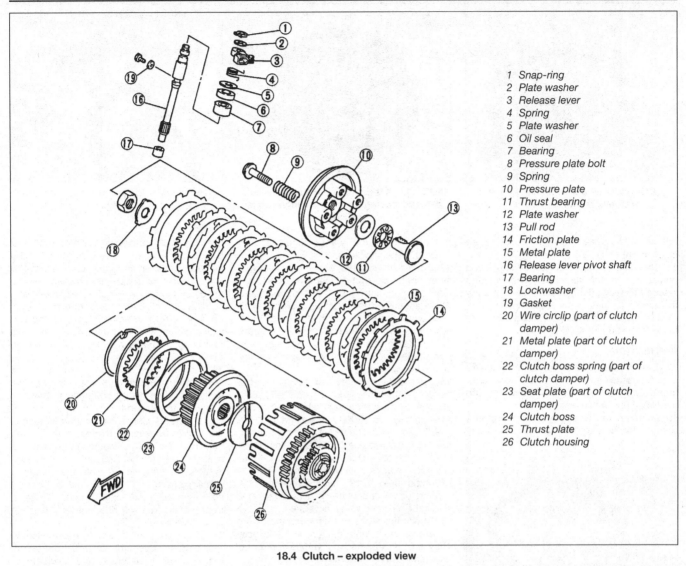

1 Snap-ring
2 Plate washer
3 Release lever
4 Spring
5 Plate washer
6 Oil seal
7 Bearing
8 Pressure plate bolt
9 Spring
10 Pressure plate
11 Thrust bearing
12 Plate washer
13 Pull rod
14 Friction plate
15 Metal plate
16 Release lever pivot shaft
17 Bearing
18 Lockwasher
19 Gasket
20 Wire circlip (part of clutch damper)
21 Metal plate (part of clutch damper)
22 Clutch boss spring (part of clutch damper)
23 Seat plate (part of clutch damper)
24 Clutch boss
25 Thrust plate
26 Clutch housing

18.4 Clutch – exploded view

evenly in a criss-cross pattern, then remove the bolts and washers **(see illustration)**.
5 Remove the clutch springs.
6 Remove the pressure plate.
7 Remove the pull rod, thrust bearing and plate washer from the pressure plate **(see illustration)**.

8 Remove the friction plates and steel plates as a set.
9 Bend back the lockwasher tab on the clutch boss nut **(see illustration)**. Remove the nut, using a special holding tool or equivalent (Yamaha tool no. YM-91402 in the US; 90890-04086 in the UK) to prevent the clutch

housing from turning. An alternative to this tool can be fabricated from some steel strap, bent at the ends and bolted together in the middle **(see Tool Tip)**. Remove the lockwasher and discard it. Use a new one during installation.
10 Remove the clutch boss, clutch

18.7 Remove the pull rod, release bearing and washer from the pressure plate

18.9a Bend the tab on the clutch boss lockwasher (arrowed) away from the nut, then remove the nut

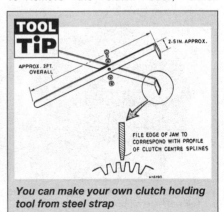

You can make your own clutch holding tool from steel strap

18.10 Slide the clutch housing off and remove the thrust washer

18.12 Check the clutch boss for wear and damage, paying special attention to the splines

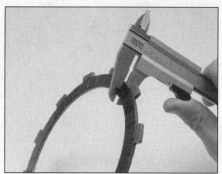

18.14 Measure the thickness of the friction plates

housing and rear thrust washer **(see illustration)**.

11 The clutch damper can be left in position unless the clutch has been experiencing severe chattering (juddering). If it's necessary to remove it, remove the wire retainer ring, metal plate, clutch boss spring and seat plate **(see illustration 18.4)**.

Inspection

12 Examine the splines on both the inside and the outside of the clutch boss **(see illustration)**. If any wear is evident, replace the clutch hub with a new one.

13 Measure the free length of the clutch springs. Replace the springs as a set if any

18.15 Check the metal plates for warpage

are not within the values listed in this Chapter's Specifications.

14 If the lining material of the friction plates smells burnt or if it's glazed, new parts are required. If the steel clutch plates are scored or discoloured, they must be replaced with new ones. Measure the thickness of each friction plate **(see illustration)** and compare the results to this Chapter's Specifications. Replace the friction plates as a set if any are near the wear limit.

15 Lay the metal plates, one at a time, on a perfectly flat surface (such as a piece of plate glass) and check for warpage by trying to slip a gauge between the flat surface and the plate **(see illustration)**. The feeler gauge should be the same thickness as the warpage limit listed in this Chapter's Specifications. Do this at several places around the plate's circumference. If the feeler gauge can be slipped under the plate, it is warped and should be replaced with a new one.

16 Check the tabs on the friction plates for excessive wear and mushroomed edges. They can be cleaned up with a file if the deformation is not severe.

17 Check the edges of the slots in the clutch housing for indentations made by the friction plate tabs. If the indentations are deep they can prevent clutch release, so the housing should be replaced with a new one. If the indentations can be removed easily with a file, the life of the housing can be prolonged to an

extent. Check the driven gear on the back of the clutch housing, as well as the oil pump rive gear, for wear or damaged teeth. If the oil pump drive gear is worn or damaged, remove the snap-ring and take it off **(see illustration)**.

18 Check the clutch pressure plate, clutch boss, wire retainer, clutch boss spring and seat plate for wear and damage (if they were removed). Replace any worn or damaged parts.

19 Check the release bearing **(see illustration)** and clutch housing thrust plate for wear, damage or roughness. Replace them if their condition is uncertain or obviously bad. Check the bearing surface in the clutch housing and replace the clutch housing if it's worn or damaged. Inspect the slots in the clutch housing and the drive dogs in the oil pump gear and replace any worn or damaged parts.

20 Clean all traces of old gasket material from the clutch cover and its mating surface on the crankcase.

21 Check the clutch release mechanism in the clutch cover for smooth operation. Disassemble it to clean and lubricate or replace components as necessary **(see illustration)**.

Installation

22 Install the oil pump drive gear on the clutch housing, using a new snap-ring.

23 Coat the inside of the clutch housing with

18.17 Remove the snap-ring (arrowed) and take off the oil pump drive gear if its damaged

18.19 Check the release bearing for worn or damaged rollers

18.21 If necessary, remove the snap-ring and retaining bolt (arrowed) to remove the release mechanism from the clutch cover

engine oil and install it on the transmission shaft. Coat the thrust washer with engine oil, then install the thrust washer and clutch boss. Install a *new* clutch boss lockwasher and the nut. Hold the clutch boss with one of the methods used in Step 9, then tighten the nut to the torque listed in this Chapter's Specifications. Bend the lockwasher against the nut to secure it.

24 Install the clutch damper components (seat, clutch boss spring, clutch plate and wire retainer) if they were removed. Be sure both ends of the wire retainer fit into the hole in the clutch hub **(see illustration)**.

25 Coat one of the friction plates with engine oil and install it on the clutch housing. Engage the tabs on the friction plate with the slots in the clutch housing.

26 Install a metal plate on top of the friction plate.

27 Coat the remaining friction plates with engine oil, then install alternating friction plates and metal plates until they're all installed (don't forget to stagger the metal plate tabs).

28 Coat the release bearing with oil and install the plate washer, bearing and pull rod in the pressure plate **(see illustration 18.7)**. Make sure the gear teeth on the pull rod will face the rear of the engine when the pressure plate is installed.

29 Install the pressure plate, aligning the marks on pressure plate and clutch boss **(see illustration)**.

30 Install the clutch springs, washers and pressure plate bolts, then tighten the bolts evenly in a criss-cross pattern to the torque listed in this Chapter's Specifications.

31 Make sure the clutch cover dowels are in position and install a new gasket. Make sure the gear teeth on the pull rod face the rear of the engine **(see illustration)**, then install the clutch cover and push the release lever in to position the cover for tightening.

32 Tighten the clutch cover bolts evenly to

18.24 If you removed the clutch damper, be sure the wire retainer fits securely in its groove and both ends are fitted all the way through the hole (arrowed)

the torque listed in this Chapter's Specifications.

33 Fill the crankcase with the recommended type and amount of engine oil (see Chapter 1 and *Daily (pre-ride) checks*).

34 The remainder of installation is the reverse of the removal steps.

19 Clutch cable – removal and installation

1 Loosen the clutch cable nuts on the right side of the engine **(see illustration 9.3 in Chapter 1)**. Disconnect the lower end of the cable from the release lever and the bracket on the engine.

2 Pull back the rubber cover from the clutch adjuster at the handlebar **(see illustration 9.2 in Chapter 1)**. Loosen the lockwheel and the adjusting nut to create slack in the cable.

3 Pull the adjuster out of its slot in the clutch lever bracket, then rotate the cable to align it with the slot in the clutch lever and lower the cable end out of the clutch lever.

4 Installation is the reverse of the removal

18.29 Align the dots on the pressure plate and clutch boss (arrowed)

steps. Adjust the clutch lever freeplay (see Chapter 1).

20 Shift pedal and linkage – removal and installation

1 These models use a shift pedal and linkage rod connected to the shift shaft.

2 Set the bike on its centrestand (if equipped) or prop it securely upright.

3 Where necessary for access, remove the left footpeg bracket.

4 Look for an alignment mark on the end of the shift shaft next to the gap in the lever **(see illustration)**. If it isn't visible, make your own.

5 Remove the pinch bolt and detach the shift lever from the shift shaft. Remove the shift pedal Allen bolt and take the pedal off.

6 Installation is the reverse of the removal steps. Tighten the bolt to the torque listed in this Chapter's Specifications.

7 To adjust the shift pedal height, loosen the locknuts, turn the knurled adjuster on the shaft and tighten the locknuts **(see illustration 20.4)**. **Note:** *The rear locknut has left-hand threads (loosens clockwise).*

18.31 Before installing the clutch cover, make sure the pull rod gear teeth face the rear of the engine (arrowed)

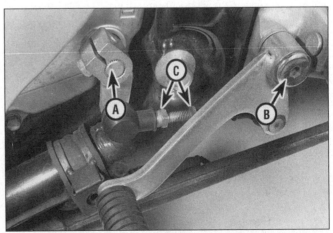

20.4 There should be a punch mark on the end of the shift shaft aligned with the lever gap (A); the shift pedal is secured by an Allen bolt (B); adjust the linkage with the adjusting nuts (C)

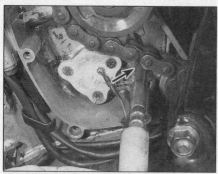

21.3 Remove the plastic spacer and check the condition of the seal (arrowed)

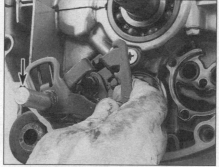

21.5a Pull the change lever away from the shift cam and slide the shift shaft (arrowed) out of the crankcase . . .

21.5b . . . and remove the washer

21 External shift mechanism – removal, inspection and installation

Removal

1 Remove the shift pedal and linkage (see Section 20).
2 Remove the engine sprocket cover (see Chapter 5).
3 Remove the plastic spacer from the shift shaft **(see illustration)**.
4 Remove the clutch (see Section 18).
5 Pull the change lever away from the shift cam and slide the shift shaft and washer out of the crankcase **(see illustrations)**.

Inspection

6 Inspect the shift shaft return springs. If they are worn or damaged, replace them.
7 Check the change shaft for bends and damage to the splines. If the shaft Is bent, you can attempt to straighten it, but if the splines are damaged it will have to be replaced. Inspect the pawl and springs on the change shaft and replace the shaft if they're worn or damaged.
8 Check the condition of the stopper lever and spring. Replace the stopper lever if it's

worn where it contacts the shift cam. Replace the spring if it's distorted.
9 Inspect the straight detent pins on the end of the shift cam. If they're worn or damaged, you'll have to disassemble the crankcase to replace the shift cam.
10 Check the condition of the seal on the right side of the engine case. If it has been leaking, pry it out **(see illustration 21.3)**. It's a good idea to replace it regardless of its condition, since gaining access to it requires a fair amount of work. Install a new seal with its closed side facing out. It should be possible to install the seal with thumb pressure, but if necessary, drive it in with a socket or piece of tubing the same diameter as the seal.

Installation

11 Remove the circlip and flat washer from the end of the shift shaft. Make sure the large washer is still on the shaft, positioned against the change lever.
12 Apply high-temperature grease to the lip of the seal. Wrap the splines of the shift shaft with electrical tape, so the splines won't damage the seal as the shaft is installed.
13 Slide the shaft into the crankcase. Engage the pawls with the pins on the shift cam and position the return spring over its guide bar **(see illustration)**.

14 The remainder of installation is the reverse of the removal steps.
15 Refill the engine oil (see Chapter 1 and *Daily (pre-ride) checks*).

22 Crankcase – disassembly and reassembly

1 To examine and repair or replace the crankshaft, starter chain and camshaft chain, connecting rods, bearings, transmission components, starter idler gears or starter motor clutch, the crankcase must be separated into two parts.

Disassembly

2 If the crankcase is being separated to remove the crankshaft, remove the cylinder head, cylinder block and pistons (see Sections 10, 13 and 14). If you're only separating the crankcase halves to disassemble the transmission shafts or remove the internal shift linkage, there's no need to remove the top-end components. In all cases, remove the clutch (see Section 18).
3 Remove the oil pan and remove the oil pressure relief valves from the crankcase (see Section 16). Unbolt the oil filter adapter for access to one of the case bolts **(see illustration)**;

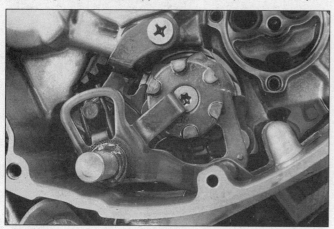

21.13 The shift mechanism should look like this when it's assembled

22.3 Remove the oil filter adapter bolt (arrowed) – you'll find one of the crankcase bolts behind the adapter

22.5 Bend back the lockwasher (A) and remove the primary drive gear nut. Remove the bearing retainer by unscrewing the two Allen bolts (B), then pull off the gear and spacer

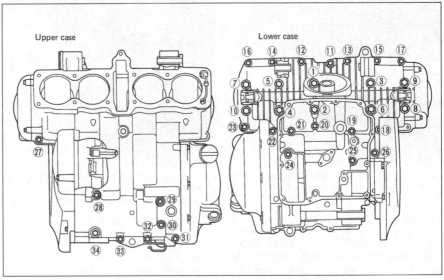

22.6 Crankcase bolt TIGHTENING sequence

on later UK models which have an oil cooler, remove the cooler assembly as described in Section 32.

4 Remove the timing plate and rotor (see Chapter 4) and alternator rotor (see Chapter 8).

5 Check the primary drive gear for wear or damage **(see illustrations)**. If necessary, bend back the tabs of the lockwasher and remove the nut, then slide the gear off.

6 Remove the upper crankcase bolts, then the lower crankcase bolts, working in a sequence *opposite* that of the tightening sequence **(see illustration)**.

7 Carefully separate the crankcase halves. Pry slowly at the single pry point **(see illustration)**. If the halves won't come apart easily, make sure all fasteners have been removed. Don't use force or the cases will break. Don't pry against the crankcase mating surfaces or they will leak after reassembly.

8 Refer to Sections 23 through 29 for

information on the internal components of the crankcase.

Reassembly

9 Remove all traces of sealant from the crankcase mating surfaces. Be careful not to let any fall into the case as this is done. Check to make sure the O-rings and dowel pins are in place in their holes in the mating surface of the lower crankcase half **(see illustration)**.

10 A common method of assembling motorcycle crankcases is to position the engine upside down and install the crankshaft and transmission shafts in it, then install the lower crankcase half on top of the upper crankcase half. Yamaha recommends that on these models, the shift forks and transmission shafts be installed in the upper case half and the crankshaft and connecting rods in the lower case half, then the upper case half be lowered onto the lower case half. This means that the transmission shafts will have to be

held in position until the upper case half is installed.

11 Pour some engine oil over the transmission gears, the crankshaft main bearings and the shift drum. Don't get any oil on the crankcase mating surfaces.

12 Apply a thin, even bead of Yamaha bond sealant or equivalent to the crankcase mating surfaces.

Caution: Don't apply an excessive amount of sealant. Don't let it contact the oil gallery O-ring. Don't apply it within 2 to 3 mm (5/64 to 1/8 inch) of the bearing inserts, as it will ooze out when the case halves are assembled and may obstruct oil passages and prevent the bearings from seating.

13 Check the position of the shift cam, shift forks and transmission shafts – make sure they're in the neutral position. In this condition it will be possible to rotate each pair of gears independently of the other gears on the shafts.

22.7 Pry slowly at the pry point

22.9 The dowel inside the case has an O-ring (arrowed)

22.14a If the end seal has a lip, make sure it's seated securely in its groove . . .

22.14b . . . non-lipped replacement seals like this one can be removed and installed without separating the crankcase halves

22.14c Coat the outer circumference of the end plug with a thin layer or sealant (arrowed)

14 Carefully assemble the crankcase halves over the dowels and the blind plug and seal at the ends of the crankshaft **(see illustrations)**. While doing this, make sure the shift forks fit into their gear grooves. Make sure the crankshaft blind plug and seal are positioned correctly in the case grooves. Check the input and output shaft bearings to ensure that the bearing retainers are installed correctly. *Caution: The crankcase halves should fit together completely without being forced. If they're slightly apart, DO NOT force them together by tightening the crankcase bolts. The most likely reason they're apart is that the transmission bearing pins aren't aligned with their holes. If the pins are forced against the crankcase halves, the cases will crack and have to be replaced.*
15 Install the crankcase bolts (and washers, if equipped) in the correct holes **(see illustration 22.6)**. Bolt 32 secures a wiring harness retainer. Tighten the bolts in two or three steps, in the correct sequence, to the torque listed in this Chapter's Specifications.
16 Install the oil pan (see Section 16).
17 Turn the transmission shafts to make sure they turn freely. Also make sure the crankshaft turns freely.
18 The remainder of installation is the reverse of removal, with the following additions:
a) *Once the external shift linkage is installed, shift the transmission through all the gear positions and back to Neutral.*

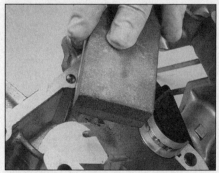

23.3 Small burrs can be removed from the gasket surfaces with a fine file or sharpening stone (be sure to remove any grit or metal particles when you're done)

b) *Use a new lockwasher on the primary gear (if removed) and tighten its nut to the torque listed in this Chapter's Specifications.*
c) *Be sure to refill the engine with oil (see Chapter 1 and Daily (pre-ride) checks).*

23 Crankcase components – inspection and servicing

1 After the crankcases have been separated and the crankshaft, shift cam and forks and transmission components removed, the crankcases should be cleaned thoroughly with new solvent and dried with compressed air.
2 Remove any oil passage plugs that haven't already been removed. All oil passages should be blown out with compressed air.
3 All traces of old gasket sealant should be removed from the mating surfaces. Minor damage to the surfaces can be cleaned up with a fine file or sharpening stone **(see illustration)**.
Caution: Be very careful not to nick or gouge the crankcase mating surfaces or leaks will result. Check both crankcase halves very carefully for cracks and other damage.
4 Check the starter chain and cam chain guides for wear (see Section 27). If they appear to be worn excessively, replace them.
5 If any damage is found that cannot be repaired, replace the crankcase halves as a set.

24 Main and connecting rod bearings – general note

1 Even though main and connecting rod bearings are generally replaced with new ones during the engine overhaul, the old bearings should be retained for close examination as they may reveal valuable information about the condition of the engine.
2 Bearing failure occurs mainly because of lack of lubrication, the presence of dirt or

other foreign particles, overloading the engine and/or corrosion. Regardless of the cause of bearing failure, it must be corrected before the engine is reassembled to prevent it from happening again.
3 When examining the bearings, remove the main bearings from the case halves and the rod bearings from the connecting rods and caps and lay them out on a clean surface in the same general position as their location on the crankshaft journals. This will enable you to match any noted bearing problems with the corresponding crankshaft journal.
4 Dirt and other foreign particles get into the engine in a variety of ways. It may be left in the engine during assembly or it may pass through filters or breathers. It may get into the oil and from there into the bearings. Metal chips from machining operations and normal engine wear are often present. Abrasives are sometimes left in engine components after reconditioning operations such as cylinder honing, especially when parts are not thoroughly cleaned using the proper cleaning methods. Whatever the source, these foreign objects often end up imbedded in the soft bearing material and are easily recognised. Large particles will imbed in the bearing and will score or gouge the bearing and journal. The best prevention for this cause of bearing failure is to clean all parts thoroughly and keep everything spotlessly clean during engine reassembly. Frequent and regular oil and filter changes are also recommended.
5 Lack of lubrication or lubrication breakdown has a number of interrelated causes. Excessive heat (which thins the oil), overloading (which squeezes the oil from the bearing face) and oil leakage or throw off (from excessive bearing clearances, worn oil pump or high engine speeds) all contribute to lubrication breakdown. Blocked oil passages will also starve a bearing and destroy it. When lack of lubrication is the cause of bearing failure, the bearing material is wiped or extruded from the steel backing of the bearing. Temperatures may increase to the point where the steel backing and the journal turn blue from overheating.
6 Riding habits can have a definite effect on bearing life. Full throttle low speed operation,

or lugging (labouring) the engine, puts very high loads on bearings, which tend to squeeze out the oil film. These loads cause the bearings to flex, which produces fine cracks in the bearing face (fatigue failure). Eventually the bearing material will loosen in pieces and tear away from the steel backing. Short trip driving leads to corrosion of bearings, as the engine doesn't have a chance to reach temperatures sufficient to drive off the condensed water and corrosive gases that are produced. These products collect in the engine oil, forming acid and sludge. As the oil is carried to the engine bearings, the acid attacks and corrodes the bearing material.

7 Incorrect bearing installation during engine assembly will lead to bearing failure as well. Tight fitting bearings which leave insufficient bearing oil clearances result in oil starvation. Dirt or foreign particles trapped behind a bearing insert result in high spots on the bearing which lead to failure.

8 To avoid bearing problems caused during initial start-up, clean all parts thoroughly before reassembly, double check all bearing clearance measurements and lubricate the new bearings with engine assembly lube or moly-based grease during installation.

25 Crankshaft and main bearings – removal, inspection and installation

Crankshaft removal

1 Before removing the crankshaft check the endplay, using a dial gauge mounted in line with the crankshaft. Yamaha doesn't provide endplay specifications, but if the endplay is excessive (more than about 0.15 mm or 0.006 inch), consider replacing the case halves.
2 Remove the starter clutch (see Section 31).
3 Lift the crankshaft out, together with the connecting rods, cam chain and starter chain and set them on a clean surface **(see illustration)**.
4 The main bearing inserts can be removed from their saddles by pushing their centres to the side, then lifting them out **(see illustration)**. Keep the bearing inserts in order. The main bearing oil clearance should be checked, however, before removing the inserts.

Inspection

5 If you haven't already done so, mark and remove the connecting rods from the crankshaft (see Section 26).
6 Clean the crankshaft with solvent, using a rifle-cleaning brush to scrub out the oil passages. If available, blow the crank dry with compressed air. Check the main and connecting rod journals for uneven wear, scoring and pits. Rub a copper coin across the journal several times – if a journal picks up copper from the coin, it's too rough. Replace the crankshaft.

7 Check the camshaft chain sprocket and starter chain sprocket on the crankshaft for chipped teeth and other wear. If any undesirable conditions are found, replace the crankshaft. Check the chains as described in Section 27. Check the rest of the crankshaft for cracks and other damage. It should be Magnafluxed to reveal hidden cracks – a dealer service department or motorcycle machine shop should handle this procedure.
8 Set the crankshaft on V-blocks and check the runout with a dial gauge touching each of the main journals, comparing your findings with this Chapter's Specifications. If the runout exceeds the limit, replace the crank.

Main bearing selection

9 To check the main bearing oil clearance, clean off the bearing inserts (and reinstall them, if they've been removed from the case) and lower the crankshaft into the upper half of the case. Cut four pieces of Plastigauge (type

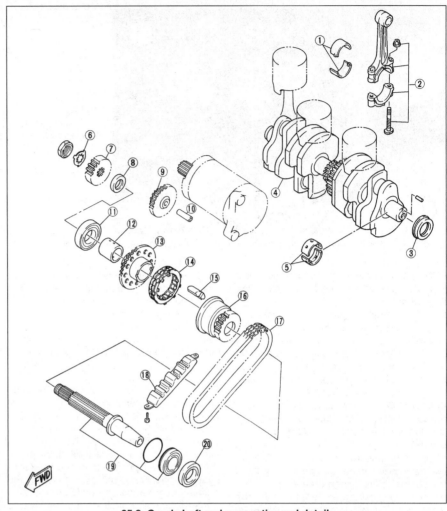

25.3 Crankshaft and connecting rod details

1 Connecting rod bearings	8 Spacer	15 Damper segment
2 Connecting rod	9 Idle gear	16 Driven gear
3 Oil seal	10 Idle gear shaft	17 Starter chain
4 Crankshaft	11 Bearing	18 Starter chain upper guide
5 Main bearings	12 Spacer	19 Starter clutch shaft
6 Lockwasher	13 Starter clutch gear	20 Oil seal
7 Primary drive gear	14 Starter clutch	

25.4 Push the centres of the bearing inserts to the side to tilt them out of their saddles

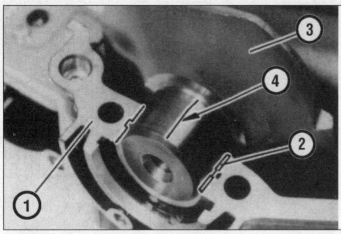

1 Crankcase
2 Bearing
3 Crankshaft
4 Plastigauge

25.9 Lay the Plastigauge strips on the journals, parallel to the crankshaft centreline

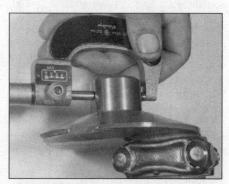

25.11 Measuring the width of the crushed Plastigauge (be sure to use the correct scale – standard and metric are included)

25.14 Measure the diameter of each crankshaft journal at several points to detect taper and out-of-round conditions

HPG-1) and lay them on the crankshaft main journals, parallel with the journal axis **(see illustration)**.

10 Very carefully, guide the lower case half down onto the upper case half. Install the crankshaft retaining bolts (case bolts 1 through 10) and tighten them, using the recommended sequence, to the torque listed in this Chapter's Specifications (see Section 22 and illustration 22.6).
Caution: DO NOT tighten the bolts unless the case halves fit together completely. Don't rotate the crankshaft during this procedure!

11 Now, remove the bolts and carefully lift the lower case half off. Compare the width of the crushed Plastigauge on each journal or bearing to the scale printed on the Plastigauge envelope to obtain the main bearing oil clearance **(see illustration)**. Write down your findings, then remove all traces of Plastigauge from the journals or bearings, using your fingernail or the edge of a credit card.

12 If the oil clearance falls into the specified range, no bearing replacement is required (provided they are in good shape). If the clearance is more than the standard range, but within the service limit, replace the bearing inserts with new ones of the same thickness and check the oil clearance once again. Replace all of the inserts, as a set, at the same time.
13 The clearance should be within the range listed in this Chapter's Specifications.
14 If the clearance is greater than the service limit listed in this Chapter's Specifications, measure the diameter of the crankshaft journals with a micrometer **(see illustration)**. Yamaha doesn't provide journal diameter or wear specifications, but by measuring the diameter at a number of points around each journal's circumference, you'll be able to determine whether or not the journal is out-of-round. Take the measurement at each end of the journal, near the crank throws, to determine if the journal is tapered. Out-of-round and taper should not exceed 0.04 millimetres (0.001 inch).
15 If any crank journal is out-of-round or tapered or the bearing clearance is beyond the limit listed in this Chapter's Specifications with new bearings, replace the crankshaft and bearings as a complete set.

16 Use the number marks on the crankshaft and on the case to determine the bearing sizes required. The first five numbers on the crankshaft web are the main journal numbers, starting with the left journal **(see illustrations)**. These correspond with the numbers at the rear of the upper crankcase half **(see illustration)**. **Note:** *Where only one size code number is found on the upper crankcase half this indicates that all five bearings are the same code.* To determine the bearing number for each bearing, subtract the crankshaft number from the case number. For example, the crankshaft number for journal no. 1 is 2 and the case number for journal no. 1 is 4. Subtracting 2 from 4 produces 2, which

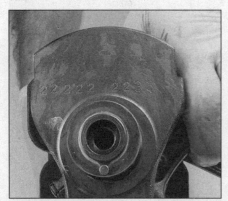

25.16a These numbers on the crankshaft indicate journal thickness; reading from left to right, the first five numbers correspond with main bearing journals no. 1 through 5 – the next four numbers correspond with connecting rod journals no. 1 through 4

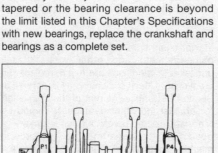

25.16b The main and rod journals are numbered from the left to the right side of the engine (J = main bearing journal; P = pin – crankpin or connecting rod journal)

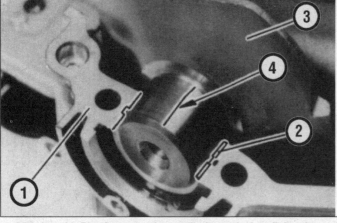

25.16c The numbers on the crankcase correspond with the crankshaft main journals no. 1 through 5

Bearing color code	
No. 1	Blue
No. 2	Black
No. 3	Brown
No. 4	Green
* No. 5	Yellow

* No. 5 applies only to the crankshaft main bearing selection.

25.16d Calculate the bearing number by subtracting the crankshaft number from the crankcase number, then use the bearing number to select a colour code

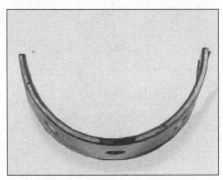

25.16e The colour codes painted on the sides of the bearings identify bearing thickness

is the bearing number for journal no. 1. According to the accompanying chart, bearing no. 2 is colour-coded black **(see illustration)**. The colour codes are painted on the edges of the bearings **(see illustration)**.

Installation

17 Clean the bearing saddles in the case halves, then install the bearing inserts in their saddles in the case **(see illustrations)**. When installing the bearings, use your hands only – don't tap them into place with a hammer! Do not get fingerprints on the front or rear of the bearings.
18 Lubricate the bearing inserts with engine assembly lube or moly-based grease.
19 You can install the connecting rods on the crankshaft at this point if the top end was removed from the engine (see Section 26).
20 Loop the camshaft chain and the starter chain over the crankshaft and lay them onto their sprockets.
21 If the connecting rods are in the engine, place short pieces of hose over the studs to protect the crankshaft as you remove them.
22 Carefully lower the crankshaft into place. If the connecting rods are in the engine, guide them onto the crankshaft journals and refit their caps (see Section 26).
23 Assemble the case halves (see Section 22) and check to make sure the crankshaft and the transmission shafts turn freely.

25.17a Make sure the oil holes are clear (arrowed) . . .

26 Connecting rods and bearings – removal, inspection and installation

Removal

1 Before removing the connecting rods from the crankshaft, measure the side clearance of each rod with a feeler gauge **(see illustration)**. If the clearance on any rod is greater than that listed in this Chapter's Specifications, that rod may have to be replaced with a new one. Check the crankshaft journal for excessive, if excessive wear is evident, replace the crankshaft and/or the connecting rods as a set.

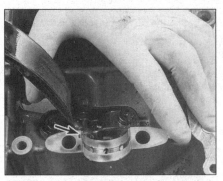

25.17b . . . then install the bearings in their saddles – engage the locating tab securely in its slot (arrowed)

2 Use a centre punch or number stamp to mark the position of each rod and cap, relative to its position on the crankshaft **(see illustration)**. The printed numbers on the rods don't indicate cylinder number; they're used for bearing selection. Yamaha specifies that the letter 'A' cast in the side of each connecting rod face the right side of the engine. If you find another mark, such as the letter 'C' **(see illustration)**, carefully note which end of the crankshaft it faces before removing the connecting rod cap.
3 Unscrew the bearing cap nuts, separate the cap from the rod, then detach the rod from the crankshaft. If the cap is stuck, tap on the

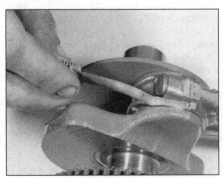

26.1 Measure the clearance between the crankshaft and the connecting rod with a feeler gauge

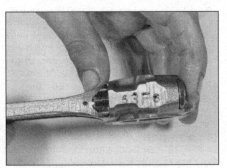

26.2a Make a cylinder number mark on the connecting rod; the letter stamped across the rod cap is a guide for reassembly; the number is used in bearing selection

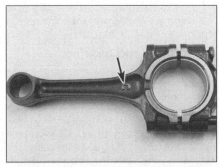

26.2b If there's an A mark on the side of the connecting rod, it faces the right side of the engine; if there's any other mark, carefully note which way it faces before removing the connecting rod

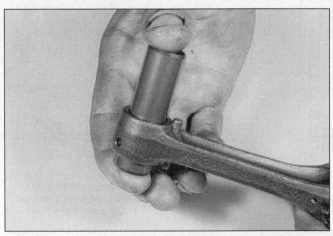

26.5 Slip the piston pin into the rod and rock it back-and-forth to check for looseness

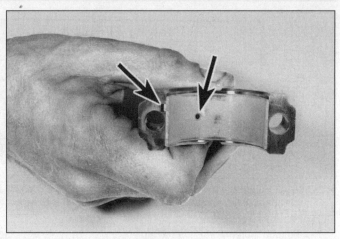

26.20 Be sure the tab fits in the notch and the oil hole in the upper bearing aligns with the hole in the connecting rod (arrowed)

ends of the rod bolts with a soft-faced hammer to free them.

4 Separate the bearing inserts from the rods and caps, keeping them in order so they can be reinstalled in their original locations. Wash the parts in solvent and dry them with compressed air, if available.

Inspection

5 Check the connecting rods for cracks (this may require taking the rods to a machine shop) and other obvious damage. Lubricate the piston pin for each rod, install it in the proper rod and check for play (see illustration). If it wobbles, replace the connecting rod and/or the pin.

6 Refer to Section 24 and examine the connecting rod bearing inserts. If they are scored, badly scuffed or appear to have been seized, new bearings must be installed. Always replace the bearings in the connecting rods as a set. If they're badly damaged, check the corresponding crankshaft journal. Evidence of extreme heat, such as discoloration, indicates that lubrication failure has occurred. Be sure to thoroughly check the oil passages, oil pump and pressure relief valves as well as all oil holes and passages for debris before reassembling the engine.

7 Have the rods checked for twist and bend at a dealer service department or motorcycle repair shop.

Connecting rod bearing selection

8 If the bearings and journals appear to be in good condition, check the oil clearances as follows:

9 Start with the rod for the no. 1 cylinder. Wipe the bearing inserts and the connecting rod and cap clean, using a lint-free cloth.

10 Install the bearing inserts in the connecting rod and cap. Make sure the tab on the bearing engages with the notch in the rod or cap.

11 Wipe off the connecting rod journal with a lint-free cloth. Lay a strip of Plastigauge (type

HPG-1) across the top of the journal, parallel with the journal axis (see illustration 25.9).

12 Position the connecting rod on the bottom of the journal, then install the rod cap and nuts. Tighten the nuts to the torque listed in this Chapter's Specifications, but don't allow the connecting rod to rotate at all.

13 Unscrew the nuts and remove the connecting rod and cap from the journal, being very careful not to disturb the Plastigauge. Compare the width of the crushed Plastigauge to the scale printed in the Plastigauge envelope (see illustration 25.11) to determine the bearing oil clearance.

14 If the clearance is within the range listed in this Chapter's Specifications and the bearings are in perfect condition, they can be reused. If the clearance is beyond the standard range, replace the bearing inserts with new inserts that have the same colour code, then check the oil clearance once again. Always replace all of the inserts at the same time.

15 The clearance should be within the range listed in this Chapter's Specifications.

16 If the clearance is greater than the maximum clearance listed in this Chapter's Specifications, measure the diameter of the connecting rod journal with a micrometer. As with the main bearing journals, Yamaha doesn't provide diameter or wear limit specifications, but by measuring the diameter at a number of points around the journal's circumference, you'll be able to determine whether or not the journal is out-of-round. Take the measurement at each end of the journal to determine if the journal is tapered.

17 If any journal is tapered or out-of-round or bearing clearance is beyond the maximum listed in this Chapter's Specifications, replace the crankshaft.

18 Each connecting rod has a 3 or 4 stamped on it in ink (see illustration 26.2a). Subtract this number from the connecting rod journal number on the crankshaft to get a bearing number (see illustrations 25.16a and 25.16b). For example, the number on the connecting rod shown in illustration 26.2a is 3.

The corresponding number for that connecting rod's journal, stamped into the crankshaft, is 2. Subtracting 2 from 3 produces 1, which is the bearing number for that journal. According to the chart in illustration 25.16d, bearing no. 1 is colour-coded blue. The colour codes are painted on the edges of the bearings (see illustration 25.16e).

19 Repeat the bearing selection procedure for the remaining connecting rods.

Installation

20 Wipe off the bearing inserts, connecting rods and caps. Install the inserts into the rods and caps, using your hands only, making sure the tabs on the inserts engage with the notches in the rods and caps and the oil holes in rod and bearing line up (see illustration). When all the inserts are installed, lubricate them with engine assembly lube or moly-based grease. don't get any lubricant on the back side of the bearings in the rod or cap.

21 Assemble each connecting rod to its proper journal, referring to the previously applied cylinder numbers. Make sure the letter on the rod is facing the proper direction (see Step 2). Also, the letter present at the rod/cap seam on one side of the connecting rod should fit together perfectly when the rod and cap are assembled (see illustration 26.2a). If it doesn't, the wrong cap is on the rod. Fix this problem before assembling the engine any further.

22 When you're sure the rods are positioned correctly, lubricate the threads of the rod bolts with moly-based grease and tighten the nuts to the torque listed in this Chapter's Specifications. Note: Tighten the nuts in a continuous motion. If you must stop before the nuts are fully tightened, loosen them completely, then retighten them to the specified torque.

23 Turn the rods on the crankshaft. If any of them feel tight, tap on the bottom of the connecting rod caps with a soft-faced hammer – this should relieve stress and free

27.7 This bolt secures the cam chain rear (intake side) guide; don't remove it unless you plan to separate the case halves

27.8a The starter chain upper guide is secured by two bolts (arrowed); use non-permanent thread locking agent on the bolts during installation

27.8b The starter chain lower guide is secured to its bracket by a clip and pivot pin; the bracket is secured to the case by two Allen bolts

them up. If it doesn't, recheck the bearing clearance.

24 As a final step, recheck the connecting rod side clearances (see Step 1). If the clearances aren't correct, find out why before proceeding with engine assembly.

27 Starter chain, camshaft chain and guides – removal, inspection and installation

Removal

Starter chain and camshaft chain

1 Remove the engine (see Section 5).
2 Separate the crankcase halves (see Section 22).
3 Remove the starter clutch shaft (see Section 31).
4 Remove the crankshaft (see Section 25).
5 Remove the chains from the crankshaft.

Chain guides

6 The exhaust side (front) cam chain guide can be lifted from the cylinder head **(see illustration 9.8b)**.
7 The cam chain rear guide is held in position by a bolt that's accessible from outside the crankcase **(see illustration)**. **Note:** *Don't remove this bolt unless you plan to disassemble the crankcase; there's no way to*

install it unless the crankcase halves are separated.
8 The starter chain guides in the upper and lower case halves are secured by two bolts each **(see illustrations)**.

Starter chain tensioner

9 Remove the Allen bolts and lift off the starter chain upper guide **(see illustration 27.8b)**. Remove the piston and spring from the tensioner **(see illustration)**. Remove the tensioner Allen bolts and detach the tensioner from the crankcase.

Inspection

Starter chain and camshaft chain

10 Check the chains for binding and obvious damage. Lay the starter drive chain onto a flat surface. The inner edges of the chain should not touch **(see illustration)**. If they do, or if the chain appears worn, replace it. The camshaft drive chain should be checked for cracks and stiff links and to see if the rollers are in good working order.

Starter chain tensioner

11 Check the tensioner piston for wear and the spring for weakness or breakage, replacing them as necessary. Blow air through the metal oil tube to make sure it's clear.

Chain guides

12 Check the guides for deep grooves,

cracking and other obvious damage, replacing them if necessary.

Installation

13 Installation of these components is the reverse of the removal procedure, with the following additions:
a) *When installing the starter chain guide, apply a non-hardening thread locking compound to the threads of the bolts. Tighten the bolts to the torque listed in this Chapter's Specifications.*
b) *Apply engine oil to the faces of the guides and to the chains.*
c) *Use a new sealing washer on the exhaust side cam chain guide bolt. Tighten the bolt securely, but take care not to strip out the threads in the case.*

28 Transmission shafts – removal and installation

Removal

1 Remove the engine and clutch, then separate the case halves (see Sections 5, 18 and 22).
2 Lift out the mainshaft, then the driveshaft **(see illustration)**. If they are stuck, use a soft-faced hammer and gently tap on the bearings

27.9 The starter chain tensioner piston is secured to the crankcase by two Allen bolts

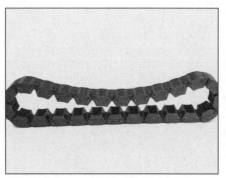

27.10 Replace the starter chain if it's worn or damaged – when it's in this position the inner edges shouldn't touch

28.2 Lift out the mainshaft (upper arrow) and the driveshaft (lower arrow)

28.4 Be sure the bearing retainer half-rings (A) are pushed down into their slots; there's one at the end of each shaft – engage the shift forks (B) with the sliding gear grooves as the transmission shafts are installed

on the ends of the shafts to free them. Be careful not to lose the bearing end caps and bearing retainer half-rings.

3 Refer to Section 29 for information pertaining to transmission shaft service and Section 30 for information pertaining to the shift cam and forks.

Installation

4 Carefully lower each shaft into place, making sure the shift forks engage the grooves in the gears **(see illustration 28.2)**. The bearing end caps should be held in place with a little moly lube. The bearing retainer half-rings should fit into the locating grooves in the crankcase and the ball bearing outer races **(see illustration)**.
Caution: If the rings are out of position and you try to force the crankcase halves together by tightening the bolts, the crankcase halves will crack and will have to be replaced.
5 The remainder of installation is the reverse of removal.
6 Make sure the gears are in the neutral

position. When this occurs, each pair of gears can be rotated independently of the others.

29 Transmission shafts – disassembly, inspection and reassembly

 When disassembling the transmission shafts, place the parts on a long rod or thread a wire through them to keep them in order and facing the proper direction.

1 Remove the shafts from the case (see Section 28).
2 A hydraulic press is required at several points to disassemble and reassemble the shafts. If you don't have one, it may be more

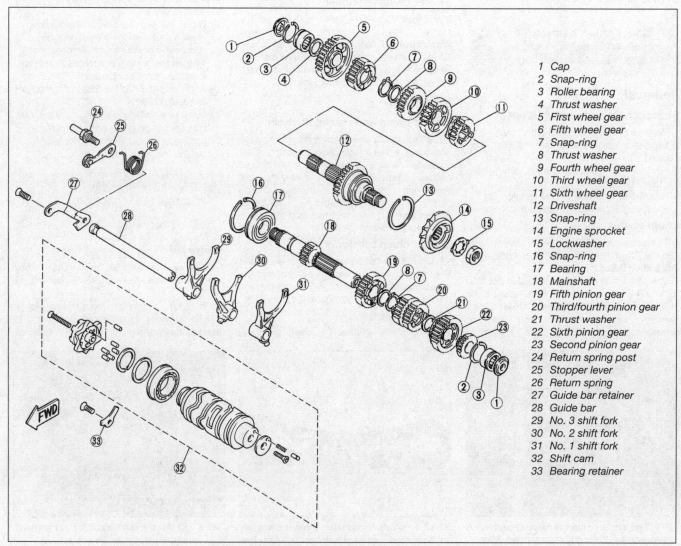

1 Cap
2 Snap-ring
3 Roller bearing
4 Thrust washer
5 First wheel gear
6 Fifth wheel gear
7 Snap-ring
8 Thrust washer
9 Fourth wheel gear
10 Third wheel gear
11 Sixth wheel gear
12 Driveshaft
13 Snap-ring
14 Engine sprocket
15 Lockwasher
16 Snap-ring
17 Bearing
18 Mainshaft
19 Fifth pinion gear
20 Third/fourth pinion gear
21 Thrust washer
22 Sixth pinion gear
23 Second pinion gear
24 Return spring post
25 Stopper lever
26 Return spring
27 Guide bar retainer
28 Guide bar
29 No. 3 shift fork
30 No. 2 shift fork
31 No. 1 shift fork
32 Shift cam
33 Bearing retainer

29.3a Transmission gears and shafts – exploded view

29.3b Remove the bearing and snap-ring from the end of the shaft

29.4 Press the shaft out of the sixth and second gears

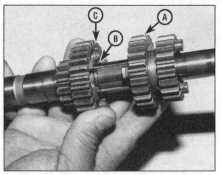

29.5 Remove the third-fourth pinion gear (A), snap-ring and thrust washer (B) and the fifth pinion gear (C)

convenient to have a dealer do the disassembly and reassembly.

Mainshaft

Disassembly

3 Slide the bearing off the mainshaft and remove the snap-ring **(see illustrations)**.
4 Press the second and sixth pinion gears loose from the shaft together, then remove them from the shaft **(see illustration)**.
5 Slide the third and fourth gear off the shaft **(see illustration)**. Remove the snap-ring and thrust washer, then slide the fifth pinion gear off the shaft.

Inspection

6 Wash all of the components in clean solvent and dry them off.   Rotate the ball bearing on the shaft, feeling for tightness, rough spots and excessive looseness and listening for noises. If the bearing is defective, press it off the shaft **(see illustration)**.
7 Inspect the roller bearings for pitting and scoring and replace it if its condition seems at all doubtful.
8 Check the gear teeth for cracking and other obvious damage. Check the gear bushings and the surface in the inner diameter of each gear for scoring or heat discoloration **(see illustration)**. If the gear or bushing is damaged, replace it. First pinion gear is integral with the mainshaft; the mainshaft must be replaced if the gear is defective.

29.6 If the bearing needs to be replaced, press it off the shaft

9 Inspect the dogs and the dog holes in the gears for excessive wear. Replace the paired gears as a set if necessary.
10 Place the shaft in V-blocks and check runout with a dial gauge. Replace the shaft if runout exceeds the value listed in this Chapter's Specifications.

Reassembly

11 Reassembly of the mainshaft is the reverse of disassembly, with the following additions:
a) Always use new snap-rings. The sharp side of the snap-ring faces away from the thrust washer; the rounded side faces towards the thrust washer.
b) With fifth pinion gear, the thrust washer and snap-ring and third-fourth pinion gear

29.8 Replace the gears if their internal bushings (arrowed) are worn or damaged

on the mainshaft, press sixth and second gears onto the mainshaft together **(see illustration)**. Check the side clearance between the gears to be sure they aren't pressed against each other.
c) If the ball bearing was pressed off, press it on with the snap-ring groove away from the gears **(see illustration)**.
d) Check the positions of the gears on the assembled shaft to make sure they are correct **(see illustration 28.2)**.

Driveshaft

Disassembly

12 To disassemble the driveshaft, refer to illustration 29.3a and the accompanying illustrations.

29.11a With fifth gear, its thrust washer and snap-ring and third-fourth gear on the shaft, press on sixth and second gears

29.11b Position the bearing so its snap-ring groove is away from the gears, then press it onto the shaft

29.12a Remove the cup, bearing and thrust washer from the end of the shaft . . .

29.12b . . . slide off first wheel gear . . .

29.12c . . . fifth wheel gear . . .

29.12d . . . remove the snap-ring and thrust washer . . .

29.12e . . . slide off fourth wheel gear . . .

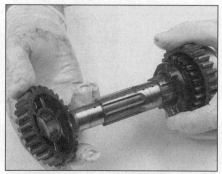

29.12f . . . third wheel gear . . .

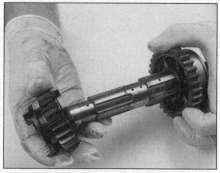

29.12g . . . and sixth wheel gear

Inspection

13 Refer to Steps 6 through 10 above to inspect the driveshaft components. If the ball bearing and seal collar need to be replaced, remove them with a press; otherwise, they can be left on the shaft.

Reassembly

14 Assembly is the reverse of the disassembly procedure. Use new snap-rings and lubricate the components with engine oil before assembling them. Check the assembled shaft to make sure the gears are in the correct positions **(see illustration 28.2)**.

30 Shift cam and forks – removal, inspection and installation

Removal

1 Remove the engine, separate the crankcase halves and remove the transmission shafts (see Sections 5, 22 and 28).
2 Support the shift forks and pull the guide bar out.
3 Lift out the shift forks and place them in their installed positions on the guide bar so they can be reinstalled correctly **(see illustration)**.
4 Remove the shift cam retainers from the left side of the case **(see illustration)**. Remove the neutral switch from the right side of the case (see Chapter 8).
5 Pull the shift cam out of the case.

Inspection

6 Check the edges of the grooves in the shift cam for signs of excessive wear. Check the pins on each end of the shift cam for wear and damage. If undesirable conditions are found,

30.3 Reassemble the forks onto the guide bar so they don't get mixed up; the number on each fork faces the right side of the engine when the forks are installed

30.4 Bend back the lockwasher tabs and unscrew the return spring post (A); you'll probably need an impact driver to remove the screws (B)

31.3a Remove the Torx screws (arrowed) and bearing retainer

31.3b Remove the oil nozzle (arrowed)

31.4 Remove the bearing housing, together with the oil seal

replace the shift cam and pins as an assembly.

7 Check the shift forks for distortion and wear, especially at the fork tips. If they are discoloured or severely worn they are probably bent. If damage or wear is evident, check the shift fork groove in the corresponding gear as well. Inspect the guide pins and the shaft bore for excessive wear and distortion and replace any defective parts with new ones.

8 Check the shift fork guide bar for evidence of wear, galling and other damage. Make sure the shift forks move smoothly on the bar. If the bar is worn or bent, replace it with a new one.

Installation

9 Installation is the reverse of removal, noting the following points:

a) Lubricate all parts with engine oil before installing them.
b) The shift forks are numbered 1 through 3, starting from the right side of the engine. The numbers cast in the forks face the right side of the engine.
c) Engage the follower pin on each shift fork with the shift cam as you pass the guide bar through the fork.
d) Apply a non-permanent locking agent to the threads of the shift cam retainer screws and tighten them to the torque listed in this Chapter's Specifications.

31 Starter clutch assembly –
removal, inspection and installation

Removal

1 Remove the engine, separate the crank-case halves and remove the transmission shafts (see Sections 5, 22 and 28).
2 Refer to Section 22 and remove the primary drive gear, then remove the bearing retainer from behind the gear **(see illustration 22.5)**.
3 On the other side of the engine, remove the bearing retainer bolts with a T30 Torx bit, then remove the retainer and oil spray nozzle **(see illustrations)**.
4 Remove the bearing housing from the case. Hold the starter clutch with one hand and pull out the starter clutch shaft **(see illustration)**.
5 Lift the starter idler gear from the case.
6 Lift the starter clutch from the chain and lift it out **(see illustration)**.
7 Remove the Allen bolts that hold the starter chain tensioner pad to the case and remove the tensioner pad **(see illustration 27.8b)**.
8 Remove the Allen bolts that hold the starter chain tensioner piston **(see illustration 27.9)** and unscrew the oil pressure relief valve used to secure the oil supply line (see Section 16).
9 Note how the starter idler gear is installed, then pull out its shaft with a magnet and remove the gear **(see illustrations)**.

31.6 Lift the starter clutch out of the crankcase

Inspection

10 Separate the starter clutch components **(see illustration 25.3)**. Check all parts for wear and damage and replace as necessary.
11 Inspect the rollers and replace any that show wear or damage **(see illustration)**. Place the wheel gear in the starter clutch and try to turn it in both directions. It should only turn in one direction. If it turns both ways or neither way, remove the starter clutch snap-ring, then install a new starter clutch and snap-ring. Note the direction the rollers face and be sure to install the new starter clutch the same way. After installation, try to turn the wheel gear again; if it turns the wrong way, the starter clutch is installed backwards.
12 Rotate the bearing on the starter clutch shaft and check for roughness, looseness or

31.9a The idler gear should look like this when it's installed . . .

31.9b . . . pull its shaft out of the case with a magnet and lift out the gear

31.11 Lift the gear and spacer out of the starter clutch and inspect the rollers (arrowed)

31.16 Check the starter clutch damper (arrowed) for damage

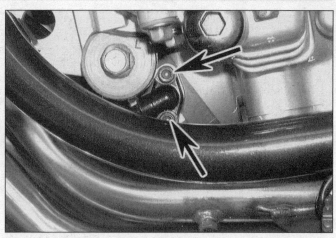

32.3 The oil pipes are secured to the cooler by two bolts on each side (arrowed)

noise. If the bearing is bad, have it pressed off the shaft and a new one pressed on by a Yamaha dealer or machine shop.

13 The oil seal in the bearing housing should be replaced if it's worn. Since the seal is inexpensive and a good deal of work is required to get to it, it's a good idea to replace the seal as a matter of course. Tap the seal out of the housing with a hammer and a

32.4a Oil pipe clamp bolt (arrowed)

bearing driver or socket, then install a new one with the same tools.

14 Pull the piston and spring assembly from the starter drive chain tensioner housing.

15 Use a pair of pliers to remove the oil pipe from the bottom of the tensioner housing. Be sure to replace the O-ring whenever the oil pipe is removed.

16 Check the damper for wear or damage and replace it if problems are found **(see illustration)**.

Installation

17 Installation is the reverse of the removal steps. Use non-permanent thread locking agent on the threads of the starter chain guide bolts, starter chain tensioner bolts and the bearing housing screws.

32 Oil cooler –
removal and installation
(1996-on UK models)

1 The engine/transmission oil is cooled by

routing it from the oil filter adapter on the front of the crankcase to a cooler radiator mounted on the frame. The oil is cooled by air flow through the radiator and returned to the other side of the filter adapter.

Removal

2 Drain the engine/transmission oil as described in Chapter 1. Remove the upper fairing as described in Chapter 7.

3 Remove the two bolts from each side of the oil filter adapter to free the oil pipes, noting the O-ring on each side **(see illustration)**. It was necessary to remove one of the engine mounting bolt nuts on the right side to provide clearance for the oil pipe bolts to be withdrawn.

4 Remove the single bolt and spacer to free the pipe clamp **(see illustration)**. Remove the two mounting bolts which retain the oil cooler radiator to the frame, then free the peg from its lug in the frame and carefully withdraw the oil cooler complete with pipes **(see illustrations)**.

5 If required, the oil cooler pipes can be

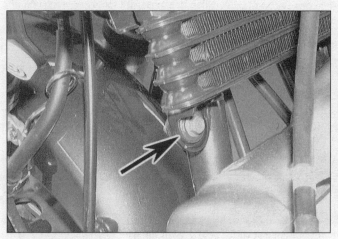

32.4b The oil cooler is retained to the frame by a bolt on each side (arrowed) . . .

32.4c . . . and by a peg on the top edge

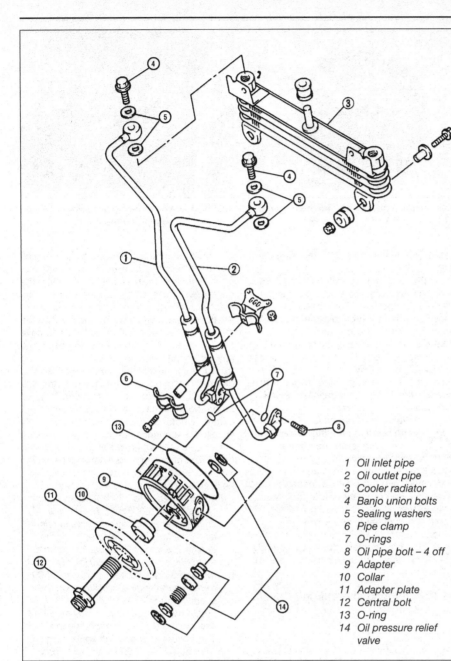

1 Oil inlet pipe
2 Oil outlet pipe
3 Cooler radiator
4 Banjo union bolts
5 Sealing washers
6 Pipe clamp
7 O-rings
8 Oil pipe bolt – 4 off
9 Adapter
10 Collar
11 Adapter plate
12 Central bolt
13 O-ring
14 Oil pressure relief
   valve

32.5 Oil cooler

32.6a Unscrew the oil filter

32.6b Remove the central bolt . . .

disconnected from the radiator by removing their banjo union bolts **(see illustration)**.
6 To remove the oil cooler adapter from the engine first unscrew the oil filter (see Chapter 1) **(see illustration)**. Remove the central bolt and the cooler assembly **(see illustrations)**.
7 To dismantle the cooler, lift off the adapter plate and collar **(see illustrations)**. Remove the O-ring from the back of the adapter; a new one should be obtained for installation.
8 The cooler contains a pressure relief valve **(see illustration)**. To dismantle the valve, remove the circlip from each side of the cooler and taken careful note of the fitted position of all components **(see illustration 32.5)**.

32.6c . . . to free the oil cooler assembly

32.7a Lift off the adapter plate . . .

32.7b . . . and remove the collar

32.8 Pressure relief valve location (arrowed)

32.9a Install a new O-ring (arrowed) on the back of the oil cooler

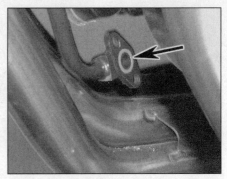

32.9b Use a new O-ring (arrowed) at each oil pipe connection

Installation

9 Installation is a reverse of the removal procedure, noting the following points:

a) *Ensure that the pressure relief valve components are assembled correctly.*

b) *Use a new O-ring on the back of the cooler (see illustration) and on the back of the adapter plate.*

c) *Assemble the cooler, collar and adapter plate, meshing the tab on the adapter plate against the triangular lug on the front of the cooler. Install the cooler assembly on the engine so that the tab on its finned section is approximately in the 12 o'clock position and engages the crankcase fins.*

d) *Tighten all bolts to the specified torque.*

e) *Use new O-rings between the oil pipes and adapter (see illustration).*

f) *Use new sealing washers on each side of the oil pipe unions at the radiator connections.*

g) *Refill the engine with oil as described in Chapter 1 and 'Daily (pre-ride) checks'.*

33 Initial start-up after overhaul

1 Make sure the engine oil level is correct. Pull the caps off the spark plugs and connect four auxiliary spark plugs into the caps; rest the metal plug bodies on the cylinder head – it is important that they make good ground (earth) contact. Place the engine kill switch in the RUN position, shift the transmission into neutral and make sure that the sidestand is UP.

2 Turn the ignition (key) switch ON and crank the engine over with the starter several times to build up oil pressure. Turn the ignition OFF, remove the auxiliary spark plugs and push the caps back on the installed spark plugs.

3 Make sure there is fuel in the tank, then turn the fuel tap to the ON position and operate the choke.

4 Start the engine and allow it to run at a moderately fast idle until it reaches operating temperature.

 Warning: If the oil level indicator light comes on while the engine is running, stop the engine immediately.

5 Check carefully for oil leaks and make sure the transmission and controls, especially the brakes, function properly before road testing the machine. Refer to Section 34 for the recommended break-in procedure.

6 Upon completion of the road test, and after the engine has cooled down completely, recheck the valve clearances (see Chapter 1).

34 Recommended break-in procedure

1 Any rebuilt engine needs time to break-in, even if parts have been installed in their original locations. For this reason, treat the machine gently for the first few miles to make sure oil has circulated throughout the engine and any new parts installed have started to seat.

2 Even greater care is necessary if the engine has been rebored or a new crankshaft has been installed. In the case of a rebore, the engine will have to be broken in as if the machine were new. This means greater use of the transmission and a restraining hand on the throttle until at least 500 miles (800 km) have been covered. There's no point in keeping to any set speed limit – the main idea is to keep from lugging (labouring) the engine and to gradually increase performance until the 500 mile (800 km) mark is reached. These recommendations can be lessened to an extent when only a new crankshaft is installed. Experience is the best guide, since it's easy to tell when an engine is running freely. The following recommendations, which Yamaha provides for new motorcycles, can be used as a guide:

a) *0 to 90 miles (0 to 150 km): Keep engine speed below 5,000 rpm. Turn off the engine after each hour of operation and let it cool for 5 to 10 minutes. Vary the engine speed and don't use full throttle.*

b) *90 to 300 miles (150 to 500 km): Don't run the engine for long periods above 6,500 rpm. Rev the engine freely through the gears, but don't use full throttle.*

c) *300 to 600 miles (500 to 1000 km): Don't use full throttle for prolonged periods and don't cruise at speeds above 8,000 rpm.*

d) *After 600 miles (1,000 km): Full throttle can be used. Don't exceed maximum recommended engine speed (redline).*

3 If a lubrication failure is suspected, stop the engine immediately and try to find the cause. If an engine is run without oil, even for a short period of time, severe damage will occur.

Chapter 3
Fuel and exhaust systems

Contents

Degrees of difficulty

| Easy, suitable for novice with little experience | Fairly easy, suitable for beginner with some experience | Fairly difficult, suitable for competent DIY mechanic | Difficult, suitable for experienced DIY mechanic | Very difficult, suitable for expert DIY or professional |

Specifications

Fuel tank
Fuel grade . . . . Unleaded regular gasoline (petrol)
Tank capacity . . . . 17 litres (4.49 gal, 3.74 Imp gal)
Tank reserve capacity . . . . 3.5 litres (0.9 gal, 0.8 Imp gal)

Carburettor type
US . . . . Mikuni BDS26 (four)
UK (1992-95), Canada . . . . Mikuni BDST28 (four)
UK (1996-on) . . . . Mikuni BDS28 (four)

Jet sizes

US
Main jet	102.5
Jet needle (clip position)	
1992 and 1993	4B10 (fixed)
1994-on	4B10-1 (fixed)
Needle jet	No. 1 and 4, O-4; no. 2 and 3, O-2
Pilot jet	17.5
Pilot screw	
1992 through 1996	Preset
1997-on	2 turns out

UK (1992-95), Canada
Main jet	No. 1 and 4, 105; no. 2 and 3, 102.5
Main air jet	70
Jet needle (clip position)	5CT (3.5)
Needle jet	0.4
Pilot jet	15
Pilot air jet	145
Pilot screw	2 turns out
Valve seat size	1.5
Starter (choke) jet	47.5 (see Note 1)

UK (1996-on)
Main jet	100
Main air jet	1.4
Jet needle (clip position) – 1996 and 1997 models	4BC12 (3)
Jet needle (clip position) – 1998-on models	4BC14 (3)
Needle jet	O-0
Pilot jet – 1996 and 1997 models	17.5
Pilot jet – 1998-on models	15
Pilot air jet – 1996 and 1997 models	140
Pilot air jet – 1998-on models	135
Pilot screw	3 turns out
Starter (choke) jet	20

Carburettor adjustments

US
Float height	7.2 mm (0.28 inch)
Fuel level	4 to 6 mm (0.16 to 0.24 inch)

UK (1992-95), Canada
Float height	11 to 13 mm (0.43 to 0.51 inch)
Fuel level	3 to 5 mm (0.12 to 0.20 inch)

UK (1996-on)
Float height	8.8 to 10.8 mm (0.35 to 0.43 inch)
Fuel level	8.5 to 9.5 mm (0.33 to 0.37 inch)

Torque settings
Exhaust pipe flange nuts	15 Nm (132 in-lbs) (see Note 2)
Exhaust pipe nuts	20 Nm (168 in-lbs)
Muffler/silencer bolts	
M8	20 Nm (168 in-lbs) (see Note 2)
M10	25 Nm (18 ft-lbs) (see Note 2)
Exhaust pipe joint bolts	20 Nm (168 in-lbs) (see Note 2)
Carburettor heater system thermoswitch – 1992-95 models	14 Nm (124 in-lbs)

Notes
1 1993 and early 1994 UK and Canada models may be equipped with a 52.5 starter jet. See Section 7, Step 13.
2 Lubricate the threads with anti-seize compound.

1 General information

The fuel system consists of the fuel tank, the fuel tap, a fuel pump, an in-line filter, the carburettors and the connecting lines, hoses and control cables. A vacuum type fuel tap is fitted to all US models and 1992 to 1995 UK models; all later UK models use an electric fuel pump.

The carburettors used on these motorcycles are four constant vacuum Mikunis with butterfly-type throttle valves. For cold starting, an enrichment circuit is provided. The enrichment circuit is actuated by the choke knob mounted on the carburettor assembly on early models and by a cable controlled by a handlebar lever on later models.

The exhaust system is a four-into-two design.

Many of the fuel system service procedures are considered routine maintenance items and for that reason are included in Chapter 1.

2.3 Remove the screw and detach the fuel tap lever

2.4a Pull the fuel line off the tap stub . . .

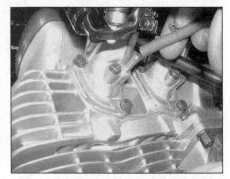

2.4b . . . and the vacuum line off the intake manifold stub

2 Fuel tank and tap –
removal and installation

Warning: Gasoline (petrol) is extremely flammable, so take extra precautions when you work on any part of the fuel system. Don't smoke or allow open flames or bare light bulbs near the work area, and don't work in a garage where a natural gas-type appliance (such as a water heater or clothes dryer) with a pilot light is present. Since gasoline is carcinogenic, wear latex gloves when there's a possibility of being exposed to fuel, and, if you spill any fuel on your skin, rinse it off immediately with soap and water. Mop up any spills immediately and do not store fuel-soaked rags where they could ignite. When you perform any kind of work on the fuel system, wear safety glasses and have a fire extinguisher suitable for a class B type fire (flammable liquids) on hand.

Fuel tank

1 Remove the seat (see Chapter 7).
2 Disconnect the cable from the negative terminal of the battery.
3 Remove the fuel tap lever **(see illustration)**. This is necessary to prevent it from being broken off when the tank is removed.
4 Detach the fuel line from the tank and the

vacuum line from the intake manifold **(see illustrations)**. On all except California models, detach the breather hose **(see illustration)**. On California models, detach the canister hose.
5 The fuel tank is held in place at the forward end by a single bolt that secures it to the frame. The rear of the tank is fastened to a bracket by one bolt and a rubber insulator which fits through a flange projecting from the tank.
6 Remove the tank mounting bolts **(see illustrations)**.
7 Lift the rear of the tank up, then carefully lift it away from the machine.
8 Before installing the tank, check the condition of the rubber mounting damper **(see illustration)** – if it's hardened, cracked, or shows any other signs of deterioration, replace it.
9 When replacing the tank, reverse the above procedure. Make sure the tank seats properly and does not pinch any control cables or wires.

Fuel tap

10 Remove the fuel tank as described above.
11 To detach the tap from the fuel tank, remove the two bolts with washers and carefully withdraw the tap, noting its oval sealing ring.
12 Replacement parts are available for the tap lever assembly. Remove the two screws to detach the lever plate from the front of the

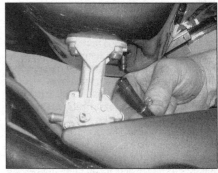

2.4c Pull the breather line off the tank stub

tap and pick out the sealing ring and valve; take careful note of the valve position in the tap body before disturbing it. No parts are available for the diaphragm unit on the rear of the tap.
13 When refitting the tap into the tank, clean its sealing face and install a new oval sealing ring. Inspect the washers on the two mounting bolts and renew them if they are damaged.

3 Fuel tank –
cleaning and repair

1 All repairs to the fuel tank should be carried out by a professional who has experience in this critical and potentially dangerous work.

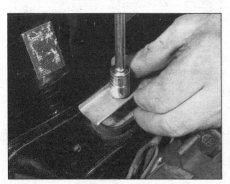

2.6a Remove the mounting bolt at the rear of the tank . . .

2.6b . . . and at the front

2.8 Inspect the rubber mount at the rear of the tank

Even after cleaning and flushing of the fuel system, explosive fumes can remain and ignite during repair of the tank.

2 If the fuel tank is removed from the machine, it should not be placed in an area where sparks or open flames could ignite the fumes coming out of the tank. Be especially careful inside garages where a natural gas-type appliance is located, because the pilot light could cause an explosion.

4 Idle fuel/air mixture adjustment – general information

1 Due to the increased emphasis on controlling motorcycle exhaust emissions, certain governmental regulations have been formulated which directly affect the carburetion of this machine. In order to comply with the regulations, the carburettors on some models have a metal cover over the access hole for the pilot screw (which controls the idle fuel/air mixture) on each carburettor, so they can't be tampered with. These should only be removed in the event of a complete carburettor overhaul, and even then the screws should be returned to their original settings. The pilot screws on other models are accessible, but the use of an exhaust gas analyser is the only accurate way to adjust the idle fuel/air mixture and be sure the machine doesn't exceed the emissions regulations.

2 If the engine runs extremely rough at idle or continually stalls, and if a carburettor overhaul does not cure the problem, take the motorcycle to a Yamaha dealer service department or other repair shop equipped with an exhaust gas analyser. They will be able to properly adjust the idle fuel/air mixture to achieve a smooth idle and restore low speed performance.

5 Carburettor overhaul – general information

1 Poor engine performance, hesitation, hard starting, stalling, flooding and backfiring are all signs that major carburettor maintenance may be required.

2 Keep in mind that many so-called carburettor problems are really not carburettor problems at all, but mechanical problems within the engine or ignition system malfunctions. Try to establish for certain that the carburettors are in need of maintenance before beginning a major overhaul.

3 Check the fuel filter, the fuel lines, the tank breather line (except California models), the intake manifold hose clamps, the vacuum hoses, the air filter element, the cylinder compression, the spark plugs, and the

carburettor synchronisation before assuming that a carburettor overhaul is required.

4 Most carburettor problems are caused by dirt particles, varnish and other deposits which build up in and block the fuel and air passages. Also, in time, gaskets and O-rings shrink or deteriorate and cause fuel and air leaks which lead to poor performance.

5 When the carburettor is overhauled, it is generally disassembled completely and the parts are cleaned thoroughly with a carburettor cleaning solvent and dried with filtered, unlubricated compressed air. The fuel and air passages are also blown through with compressed air to force out any dirt that may have been loosened but not removed by the solvent. Once the cleaning process is complete, the carburettor is reassembled using new gaskets, O-rings and, generally, a new inlet needle valve and seat.

6 Before disassembling the carburettors, make sure you obtain new O-rings, some carburettor cleaner, a supply of rags, some means of blowing out the carburettor passages and a clean place to work. It is recommended that only one carburettor be overhauled at a time to avoid mixing up parts.

6 Carburettors and intake manifolds – removal and installation

⚠ **Warning: Gasoline (petrol) is extremely flammable, so take extra precautions when you work on any part of the fuel system. Don't smoke or allow open flames or bare light bulbs near the work area, and don't work in a garage where a natural gas-type appliance (such as a water heater or clothes dryer) with a pilot light is present. Since gasoline is carcinogenic, wear latex gloves when there's a possibility of being exposed to fuel, and, if you spill any fuel on your skin, rinse it off immediately with soap and water. Mop up any spills immediately and do not store fuel-soaked rags where they could ignite. When you perform any kind of work**

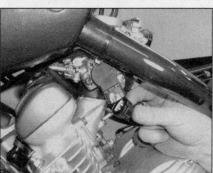

6.3 Disconnecting the TPS on 1996-on UK models

on the fuel system, wear safety glasses and have a fire extinguisher suitable for a class B type fire (flammable liquids) on hand.

Carburettors

Removal

1 Remove the fuel tank (see Section 2). Disconnect the negative cable from the battery.

2 Remove the air cleaner housing and disconnect the throttle cables (see Sections 12 and 10). On 1996-on UK models and 1997-on US models, also disconnect the choke cable from the carburettors (see Section 11).

3 If you're working on a UK 1992 to 1995 model or Canada model, label and disconnect the heater hoses and clamp their ends to prevent oil loss **(see illustration 15.2)**. Also disconnect the wiring from the heater thermoswitch on no. 4 carburettor. On 1996-on UK models, disconnect the wire from each carburettor heater **(see illustration 15.15a)**, including the earth (ground) wire connector, and unplug the wiring connector from the throttle position sensor **(see illustration)**.

4 Lift the rubber heat shield off the carburettor assembly.

5 Loosen the clamping bands on the intake manifolds. Lift the carburettor assembly to disengage the carburettors from the intake manifolds **(see illustration)**, then remove the carburettor assembly.

6 After the carburettors have been removed, stuff clean rags into the intake manifolds to prevent the entry of dirt or other objects.

7 Inspect the rubber clamps. If they're cracked or brittle, replace them.

Installation

8 Installation is the reverse of the removal Steps, with the following additions:

a) When connecting the oil hoses (where applicable), make sure the hoses are primed with engine oil to prevent air locks. Secure each hose with the spring clips.

b) Adjust the throttle grip freeplay (see Chapter 1).

6.5 Loosen the clamping bands and lift the carburettor assembly away from the machine

c) Check and, if necessary, adjust the idle speed and carburettor synchronisation (see Chapter 1).

Intake manifolds

9 Remove the carburettors.

10 Label any vacuum hoses connected to the intake manifolds, then disconnect them. Remove the two bolts which retain each intake manifold to the cylinder head to free the manifolds.

11 Installation is a reverse of the removal procedure, noting that new O-rings should be used at the manifold-to-cylinder head joint. Make sure that the vacuum hoses are a good fit on their unions and secured by the hose clips.

7 Carburettors – disassembly, cleaning and inspection

⚠️ *Warning: Gasoline (petrol) is extremely flammable, so take extra precautions when you work on any part of the fuel system. Don't smoke or allow open flames or bare light bulbs near the work area, and don't work in a garage where a natural gas-type appliance (such as a water heater or clothes dryer) with a pilot light is present. Since gasoline is carcinogenic, wear latex gloves when there's a possibility of being exposed to*

fuel, and, if you spill any fuel on your skin, rinse it off immediately with soap and water. Mop up any spills immediately and do not store fuel-soaked rags where they could ignite. When you perform any kind of work on the fuel system, wear safety glasses and have a fire extinguisher suitable for a class B type fire (flammable liquids) on hand.

Disassembly

1 Remove the carburettors from the machine as described in Section 6. Set the assembly on a clean working surface. **Note:** *Unless the O-rings on the fuel and vent fittings between the carburettors are leaking, don't detach the carburettors from their mounting brackets.*

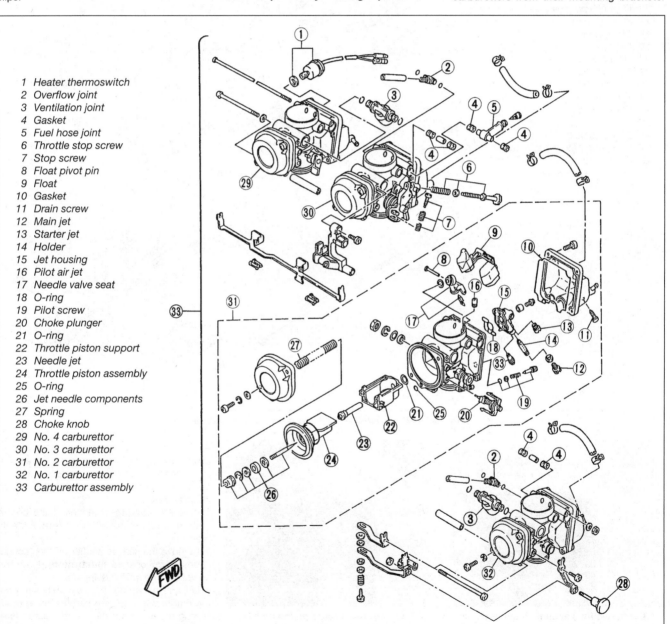

1 Heater thermoswitch
2 Overflow joint
3 Ventilation joint
4 Gasket
5 Fuel hose joint
6 Throttle stop screw
7 Stop screw
8 Float pivot pin
9 Float
10 Gasket
11 Drain screw
12 Main jet
13 Starter jet
14 Holder
15 Jet housing
16 Pilot air jet
17 Needle valve seat
18 O-ring
19 Pilot screw
20 Choke plunger
21 O-ring
22 Throttle piston support
23 Needle jet
24 Throttle piston assembly
25 O-ring
26 Jet needle components
27 Spring
28 Choke knob
29 No. 4 carburettor
30 No. 3 carburettor
31 No. 2 carburettor
32 No. 1 carburettor
33 Carburettor assembly

7.1a Carburettors (UK 1992 to 1995 and Canada models) - exploded view

1   Vacuum chamber cover
2   Spring
3   Jet needle assembly
4   Piston and diaphragm
5   Pilot screw assembly
6   Pilot air jet
7   Heater element
8   Needle jet
9   Washer
10 Plug
11 Gasket
12 Main jet holder
13 Main jet
14 Pilot jet
15 Float needle valve and seat
16 Float chamber gasket
17 Float chamber
18 Drain screw
19 Float
20 Float pivot pin
21 Throttle stop screw
22 Synchronising screw
23 Throttle cable bracket
24 Choke shaft
25 Choke plunger assembly
26 Choke cable bracket
27 Carburettor mounting brackets
28 Carburettor mounting bracket
29 Throttle position sensor

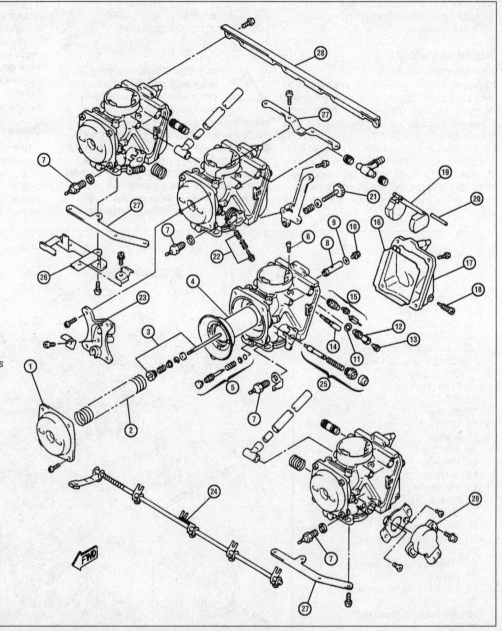

7.1b Carburettors (1996-on UK models) - exploded view

7.3 Remove the vacuum chamber cover screws and lift off the cover and spring; note the location of the diaphragm tab

7.4 Lift out the throttle piston and jet needle

Also, work on one carburettor at a time to avoid getting parts mixed up. It's possible to overhaul the carburettors without removing them from the brackets **(see illustrations).**

2 If you're working on either of the centre carburettors, remove the throttle cable bracket.

3 Remove the screws and lift off the vacuum chamber cover **(see illustration)**. Note the position of the rubber diaphragm.

4 Lift out the spring, then carefully separate the diaphragm from the carburettor without tearing it and lift out the throttle piston **(see illustration)**.

5 Remove the float chamber screws and lift

7.5 Remove the float chamber screws and lift off the float chamber and its O-ring

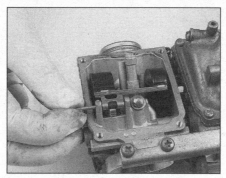

7.6 Remove the float pivot pin

7.7 Lift out the float and unhook the needle valve

off the float chamber **(see illustration)**. On 1992-95 UK models and Canada models disconnect the carburettor warmer system hoses which link the float chambers.

6 Remove the float pivot pin **(see illustration)**. If necessary, push it out with a thin punch.

7 Lift out the float and unhook the needle valve **(see illustration)**.

8 Remove the screw and retainer, then pull out the needle valve seat and remove the filter screen **(see illustrations)**. Remove any dirt build-up on the filter screen.

US models and UK 1996-on models

9 Unscrew the main jet **(see illustration)**. Don't lose the washer.

10 Unscrew the jet holder and remove its gasket **(see illustration)**.

11 Unscrew the pilot jet **(see illustration)**.

12 Remove the plug and washer, then note the position of the pin on the end of the needle jet **(see illustrations)**.

UK 1992 to 1995 models

13 Unscrew the main, pilot and starter jets from the carburettor body **(see illustration 7.1a)**. **Note:** *1993 and early 1994 UK and Canada models may be equipped with a 52.5 starter jet and an S-shaped tube in the carburettor overflow tube. These were installed in cases where the machine was difficult to start after sitting for several days.*

7.8a Remove the screw and retainer . . .

7.8b . . . and pull out the needle valve seat

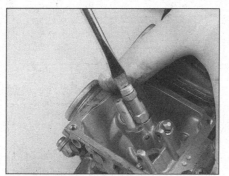

7.9 Unscrew the main jet and lift it out with its washer

7.10 Unscrew the main jet holder and remove its gasket

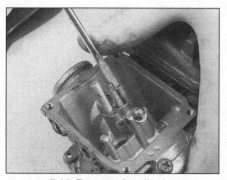

7.11 Remove the pilot jet

7.12a Remove the plug and washer . . .

7.12b . . . and note the position of the needle jet alignment pin

7.15 Removing the needle jet with a pair of needle-nose pliers

7.16a Remove the screw inside the throttle piston . . .

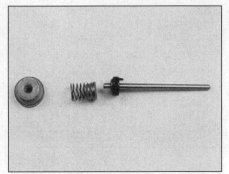

7.16b . . . and lift out the spring and jet needle

14 Remove the jet housing bolt and washer. Take off the jet housing and its gasket.

All models

15 Reach down through the vacuum chamber with needle-nose pliers and lift the needle jet out of its bore **(see illustration)**.
16 Remove the screw from inside the throttle piston and take out the jet needle components **(see illustrations)**. If there's more than one groove on the needle, note which one the clip was fitted to.
17 Unscrew the pilot air jet from the carburettor body **(see illustration)**.
18 On models with the choke operation on

the carburettors (1992-95 UK models and 1992-96 US models) loosen the choke shaft screws and slide the choke shaft out of the brackets **(see illustration)**. Note the detents in the rod used to position the screws in the correct location. Unscrew the choke plungers and pull them out of their bores **(see illustrations)**. On models with the choke operated by cable (1996-on UK models and 1997-on US models), fully slacken the grub screws which clamp the four choke plunger hooks to the choke shaft. Slide the choke shaft out to the right. Unbolt the choke cable bracket from no. 4 carburettor. The individual choke plungers can now be unscrewed from

the carburettor bodies **(see illustration 17.18c)**.
19 The pilot (idle mixture) screw is located in the front of the carburettor body. On US models, this screw may be hidden behind a cover which will have to be removed if the screw is to be taken out. On all models, turn the pilot screw in, counting the number of turns until it bottoms lightly **(see illustration)**. Record that number for use when installing the screw. Now remove the pilot screw along with its spring, washer and O-ring **(see illustration)**.
20 1996-on UK models are fitted with a throttle position sensor on no. 1 carburettor.

7.17 Unscrew the pilot air jet (arrowed)

7.18a Remove the bracket screws for access . . .

7.18b . . . remove the choke rod set screws and slide out the choke rod . . .

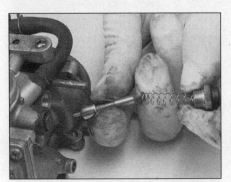

7.18c . . . then unscrew the choke plunger cap and pull out the spring and the choke plunger

7.19a With the cover (if equipped) removed, turn the pilot screw (arrowed) clockwise until it bottoms lightly - count the number of turns and write it down . . .

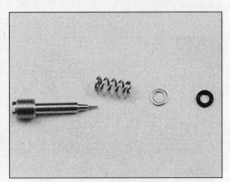

7.19b . . . then remove the screw together with the spring, washer and O-ring

7.26 Lift the throttle piston and make sure it drops smoothly

8.4 Note the position of the springs on the synchroniser screws (arrowed) - they should look like this when installed

Do not disturb the TPS unnecessarily – its exact position requires careful setting up. The TPS is secured to its mounting bracket by two screws; it is advisable to mark the position of the TPS in relation to its mounting bracket before disturbing the screws (see Chapter 4).

Cleaning

Caution: Use only a petroleum-based solvent for carburettor cleaning. Never use caustic cleaners. Be sure that all rubber hoses and plastic fittings are removed before the parts are immersed into the cleaning agent.

21 Submerge the metal components in the solvent for approximately thirty minutes (or longer, if the directions recommend it). After the carburettor has soaked long enough for the cleaner to loosen and dissolve most of the varnish and other deposits, use a brush to remove the stubborn deposits. Rinse it again, then dry it with compressed air. Blow out all of the fuel and air passages in the main and upper body.

Caution: Never clean the jets or passages with a piece of wire or a drill bit, as they will be enlarged, causing the fuel and air metering rates to be upset.

Inspection

22 Check the operation of the choke plunger. If it doesn't move smoothly, replace it, along with the return spring. Inspect the needle on the end of the choke plunger and replace it if it's worn.
23 Check the tapered portion of the pilot screw for wear or damage.
24 Check the carburettor body, float chamber and vacuum chamber cover for cracks, distorted sealing surfaces and other damage. If any defects are found, replace the faulty component, although replacement of the entire carburettor will probably be necessary (check with your parts supplier for the availability of separate components).
25 Check the vacuum diaphragm for splits, holes and general deterioration.

> **HAYNES HiNT** *Holding the diaphragm up to a light will help to reveal problems of this nature.*

26 Insert the throttle piston in the carburettor body and see that it moves up-and-down smoothly **(see illustration)**. Check the surface of the valve for wear. If it's worn excessively or doesn't move smoothly in the bore, replace the carburettor.
27 Check the jet needle for straightness by rolling it on a flat surface (such as a piece of glass). Replace it if it's bent or if the tip is worn.
28 Check the tip of the fuel inlet valve needle. If it has grooves or scratches in it, it must be replaced. Push in on the rod in the other end of the needle, then release it – if it doesn't spring back, replace the valve needle. Inspect the filter screen on the needle valve seat and replace it if it's torn or can't be cleaned.
29 Check the O-ring on the float chamber. Replace it if it's damaged.
30 Operate the throttle shaft to make sure the throttle butterfly valve opens and closes smoothly. If it doesn't, replace the carburettor.
31 Check the floats for damage. This will usually be apparent by the presence of fuel inside one of the floats. If the floats are damaged, they must be replaced.

Reassembly

Caution: When installing the jets, be careful not to overtighten them – they're made of soft material and can strip or shear easily.
Note: When reassembling the carburettors be sure to use new O-rings and gaskets.

32 Install the choke plunger in its bore, followed by its spring and cap. Tighten the cap securely.
33 Install the pilot screw (if removed) along with its spring, washer and O-ring, turning it in until it seats lightly. Now, turn the screw out the number of turns that was previously recorded (or the number listed in this Chapter's Specifications if installing a new screw). On US models install a new metal plug in the hole over the screw. Apply a little bonding agent around the circumference of the plug after it has been seated.
34 The remainder of assembly is the reverse of the disassembly steps, with the following additions:
a) Refer to Section 9 and check the float height.
b) Install the diaphragm and piston in the carburettor body. Be sure the protrusion on the edge of the diaphragm fits into its groove all the way around and the tab on the diaphragm fits into the notch in the carburettor body.

8 Carburettors – separation and joining

1 The carburettors do not need to be separated for normal overhaul. If you need to separate them (to replace a carburettor body, for example), refer to the following procedure.
2 Remove the choke operating shaft and any associated mounting brackets (see Section 7, Step 18); there is no need to unscrew the choke plungers from the carburettor bodies.
3 Remove the bracket screws that hold the carburettors together. You may need an impact driver.
4 Note how the synchronising screws and springs are assembled **(see illustration)**. As you pull the carburettors apart, keep track of the synchroniser screw springs. They should stay with the adjusting screws, but if they don't, find them and install them as shown in the illustrations so they aren't lost.
5 Assembly is the reverse of the disassembly procedure. Use non-permanent thread locking agent on the bracket screws.

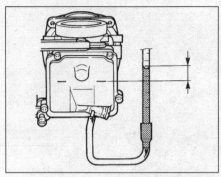

9.4 A gauge like this or a clear tube and ruler can be used to measure fuel level

9 Carburettors – float height and fuel level adjustment

Float height adjustment

1 To check the float height, hold the carburettors upside down (with their float chambers removed), then tilt them back until the float tang contacts the needle valve but the small rod in the end of the needle valve isn't compressed. Work on one carburettor at a time, then go on to check the others.
2 Measure the distance from the carburettor body (without the float chamber gasket) to the top of the float and compare your measurement to the float height listed in this Chapter's Specifications. If it isn't as specified, carefully bend the tang that contacts the needle valve up or down until the float height is correct.

Fuel level adjustment

> ⚠ **Warning:** *Gasoline (petrol) is extremely flammable, so take extra precautions when you work on any part of the fuel system. Don't smoke or allow open flames or bare light bulbs near the work area, and don't work in a garage where a natural gas-type appliance (such as a water heater or clothes dryer) with a pilot light is present. Since gasoline is carcinogenic,*

10.3 Remove the screws (arrowed) and separate the halves of the throttle pulley housing

wear latex gloves when there's a possibility of being exposed to fuel, and, if you spill any fuel on your skin, rinse it off immediately with soap and water. Mop up any spills immediately and do not store fuel-soaked rags where they could ignite. When you perform any kind of work on the fuel system, wear safety glasses and have a fire extinguisher suitable for a class B type fire (flammable liquids) on hand.

3 This procedure is done with the carburettors installed on the motorcycle. Place the bike on its centrestand (if equipped) or support it securely upright. Place a floor jack under the engine and raise it just enough so the carburettors are horizontal.
4 Attach Yamaha service tool no. YM-01312 (US) or 90890-01312 (UK) to the drain fitting on the bottom of one of the carburettor float chambers (all four will be checked). This is a clear plastic tube graduated in millimetres **(see illustration)**. An alternative is to use a length of clear plastic tubing and an accurate ruler. Hold the graduated tube (or the free end of the clear plastic tube) against the carburettor body.
5 With the engine off, unscrew the drain screw at the bottom of the float chamber a couple of turns – fuel will flow into the tube. Wait for the fuel level to stabilise, then note how far the fuel level is below the line where the float chamber joins the carburettor body.
6 Measure the distance between the mark on the float chamber and the top of the fuel level in the tube or gauge **(see illustration 9.4)**.

This distance is the fuel level – write it down on a piece of paper, screw in the drain screw, then move on to the next carburettor and check it the same way.
7 Compare your fuel level readings to the value listed in this Chapter's Specifications. If the fuel level in any carburettor is not correct, remove the float chamber and bend the float tang up or down as necessary, then recheck the fuel level.

10 Throttle cable and grip – removal, installation and adjustment

Removal

1 Remove the fuel tank (see Section 2).
2 Loosen the accelerator cable (see *Throttle operation/grip freeplay – check and adjustment* in Chapter 1).
3 Remove the screws from the throttle pulley housing and separate the halves of the housing **(see illustration)**.
4 Detach the accelerator and decelerator cables from the throttle grip pulley.
5 Detach the other ends of the cables from the bracket and throttle pulley at the carburettors **(see illustrations)**.
6 Remove the cables, noting how they're routed.
7 To remove the throttle grip, unscrew the grip end weight (see Chapter 5) and take the throttle grip off the handlebar.

Installation

8 If the grip was removed, clean the handlebar and apply a light coat of multi-purpose grease. Push the grip onto the handlebar, install the grip end weight and tighten it to the torque listed in the Chapter 5 Specifications.
9 Route the cables into place. Make sure they don't interfere with any other components and aren't kinked or bent sharply.
10 Lubricate the ends of the cables with multi-purpose grease and connect them to the throttle pulleys at the carburettors and at the throttle grip. Assemble the throttle pulley housing and tighten the screws securely.

10.5a Pull the accelerator cable back and out of the slot in the retainer (arrowed)

10.5b Loosen the nut and detach the decelerator cable

10.5c Rotate the cables to align them with the slots in the pulley, then slip the cable ends out

Adjustment

11 Follow the procedure outlined in Chapter 1, Section 5 to adjust the cables.

12 Turn the handlebars back and forth to make sure the cables don't cause the steering to bind. With the engine idling, turn the handlebars back and forth and make sure idle speed doesn't change. If it does, find and fix the cause before riding the motorcycle.

 Warning: Don't ride the bike in this dangerous condition.

13 Install the fuel tank.

11 Choke cable – removal and installation

Removal

1 Remove the two screws from the front of the left handlebar switch and separate the switch halves **(see illustration)**. Ease the choke cable trunnion out of its location in the choke lever **(see illustration)**.

2 Remove the fuel tank (see Section 2) and air cleaner housing (see Section 12) to access the carburetor end of the choke cable. Slacken the clamp screw to release the choke cable outer **(see illustration)**. Release the choke cable end from choke shaft lever on the right side **(see illustration)**. Remove the choke cable having taken note of how it was routed.

Installation

3 Route the cable into place. Make sure it doesn't interfere with any other components and isn't kinked or bent sharply.

4 Lubricate the ends of the cable with multi-purpose grease and connect it to the choke shaft lever at the carburettors and to the choke operating lever at the handlebar. Assemble the switch halves, making sure that the guide elbow is correctly located **(see illustration)** and tighten the screws securely.

11.1a Remove the two screws to separate the switch halves (arrowed)

11.2a Slacken off the cable clamp screw . . .

Position the choke lever so that the choke is OFF. Secure the lower end of the cable outer with the clamp and screw **(see illustration 11.2a)**, noting that the cable must be positioned so that the choke is not activated.

5 The is no specified adjustment setting for the choke cable, but an in-line adjuster is set in the cable to allow small adjustments to be made; it is located under the fuel tank front end, next to the horn **(see illustration)**. The choke adjustment setting is correct if there is a small amount of freeplay just before the choke lever is activated; ie to ensure that the choke plungers in the carburettors are fully OFF when

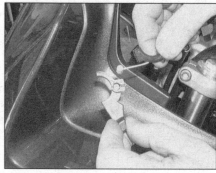

11.1b Separate the cable trunnion from the lever

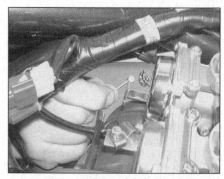

11.2b . . . and disconnect the cable trunnion from the choke shaft

the handlebar lever is in the OFF position. To make adjustment, slacken off the small adjuster lockwheel and rotate the body of the adjuster as required; tighten the lockwheel against the adjuster when complete.

6 Install the air cleaner housing and fuel tank.

12 Air cleaner housing – removal and installation

1 Remove the fuel tank (see Section 2).

2 Disconnect the drain and crankcase

11.4 Locate the guide elbow in the switch channels

11.5 Choke cable in-line adjuster location (arrowed)

12.2a Disconnect the drain hose from the left side of the air cleaner housing . . .

12.2b . . . and from the underside

12.2c Disconnect the large-bore crankcase breather hose from the rear

breather hoses from the air cleaner housing **(see illustrations)**.

3 Remove the mounting bolt **(see illustration)**.

4 Loosen the clamp screws that secure the housing to the carburettor intake joints **(see illustration)**. Lift the air cleaner housing out of the intake joints and away from the bike. If you are going to go on to remove the carburettors or work on the cables, carefully remove the rubber dust shield noting how it fits.

5 If necessary, remove the screws from the underside of the air cleaner housing and separate the top and bottom halves. Check the large O-ring between the halves for brittleness or deterioration and replace it if its condition is in doubt.

6 Assembly and installation are the reverse of the removal steps. Where fitted, ensure that the two carburettor breather tubes locate in the holes in the housing **(see illustration)**.

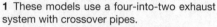

13 Exhaust system – removal and installation

HAYNES HiNT *If the engine has been running the exhaust system will be very hot. Allow the system to cool before carrying out any work.*

1 These models use a four-into-two exhaust system with crossover pipes.

2 Set the machine on the centre stand (if equipped) or prop it securely upright.

3 Remove the lower fairing (if equipped) (see Chapter 7).

4 Support the exhaust system with a floor jack and a piece of wood.

5 Remove the exhaust pipe holder nuts at the cylinder head **(see illustration)** and slide the holders off the mounting studs.

6 Remove the exhaust system mounting fasteners **(see illustrations)**. Pull the exhaust pipes forward to clear the engine, then lower the jack and pull the exhaust system out from under the motorcycle.

7 If necessary, loosen the clamp bolts

12.3 Remove the mounting bolt at the front

12.4 Loosen the clamp screws (arrowed) and slip the air cleaner housing out of the intake joints

12.6 The two breather hoses (arrowed) engage the holes in the base of the housing

13.5 Each exhaust pipe is retained by two nuts at the cylinder head

13.6a Exhaust system is retained by a bolt to the frame . . .

13.6b . . . and a bolt to the footpeg bracket

and separate the exhaust system components.

8 Installation is the reverse of removal, with the following additions:

a) *Use new copper gaskets at the cylinder head.*

b) *Apply a thin coat of anti-seize compound to the studs and nuts before installation.*

c) *Tighten all fasteners to the torque settings listed in this Chapter's Specifications.*

14 Fuel pump –
removal and installation

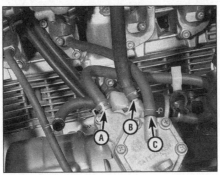

14.3 Fuel pump installation details

A *Inlet line from fuel filter*
B *Outlet line to carburettors*
C *Vacuum hose*

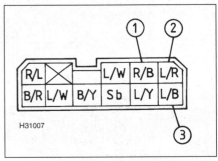

H31007

14.9 Relay unit wire terminal identification for fuel pump relay test

1 *R/B (red/black) wire terminal*
2 *L/R (blue/red) wire terminal*
3 *L/B (blue/black) wire terminal*

Vacuum pump (all US models, 1992-95 UK models)

Note: *On UK models if starting problems are experienced due to fuel evaporation from the carburettor float chambers after the motorcycle has been left standing for a number of days, it is possible to fit the electric fuel pump fitted to 1996-on models; refer to a Yamaha dealer for details.*

1 The fuel pump is operated by vacuum transmitted through a hose connected to the no. 2 cylinder's intake manifold. Yamaha don't provide test procedures or output specifications for the fuel pump, and parts to rebuild the pump aren't available. If insufficient fuel delivery can't be traced to other causes, such as a clogged filter, lines or carburettor passages, low float level, or lack of fuel in the tank, the pump may be at fault.

2 Remove the fuel tank (see Section 2).

3 Disconnect the hoses from the pump **(see illustration)**. Remove its mounting nuts from the underside of the pump bracket and lift it out. **Note:** *You may find it easier to unbolt the bracket from the frame and lift it up for access to the mounting nuts.*

4 Installation is the reverse of the removal steps.

Electric pump (1996-on UK models)

Testing

5 The fuel pump circuit consists of the pump, the pump relay (housed in the relay unit), the igniter, the engine kill switch, the ignition switch, fuses, battery and associated wiring.

6 With the engine kill switch in the RUN position, the fuel pump should start and run for about five seconds after the ignition is switched ON. It should shut off once the carburettor float chambers are full, then run again once the engine is started. If the pump does not operate, first check that the main or ignition circuit fuse is not blown, and make sure that the battery is fully charged. If the fuses and battery are in good order, check the fuel pump circuit in a logical order as described below; be prepared to remove bodywork to access some of the components or wire connectors.

7 To check the ignition switch, first disconnect the battery negative lead, then trace the wiring from the ignition switch to its block connector. Separate the connector and using a continuity tester or ohmmeter, check for continuity between the red wire terminal and brown/blue wire terminal on the switch side of the connector with switch key rotated to the ON position. If continuity is indicated the switch is good, whereas no continuity (infinite resistance) indicates an open-circuit inside the switch. Join the connector halves.

8 To check the engine kill switch, trace the wiring from the right handlebar switch and disconnect the block connector. Separate the connector and using a continuity tester or ohmmeter, check for continuity between the red/wire and red/black wire terminals on the switch side of the connector with the kill switch in the RUN position. If continuity is indicated the switch is good, whereas no continuity (infinite resistance) indicates an open-circuit inside the switch. Join the connector halves.

9 Locate the relay assembly (see Chapter 8),

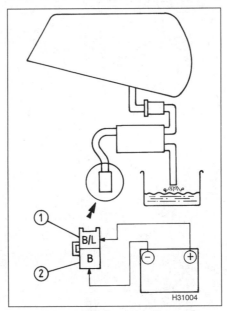

H31004

14.10 Fuel pump operation test

1 *B/L (black/blue) wire terminal*
2 *B (black) wire terminal*

disconnect its connector and move the relay unit to the bench for testing of the fuel pump relay. Using jumper wires connect the positive terminal of a 12 volt battery to the red/black wire terminal and the battery negative terminal to the blue/red wire terminal **(see illustration)**. Now connect an ohmmeter or continuity tester between the red/black wire terminal and blue/black wire terminal. Continuity should be shown. No continuity indicates a faulty fuel pump relay, and thus a new relay unit will be required. Install the relay on the motorcycle when testing is complete.

10 The fuel pump can be checked for correct operation by disconnecting its output hose (the hose between the pump and carburettor) and directing the hose end into a container suitable for the storage of fuel; note that on early models there is a small filter fitted at the hose joint with the carburettor. Trace the 2-pin wire connection from the fuel pump and disconnect it. Using jumper wires and a 12 volt battery, connect the battery positive terminal to the black/blue wire terminal on the pump side of the connector and the battery negative terminal to the black wire terminal on the pump side of the connector **(see illustration)**. If the fuel pump is good it will be heard to operate and fuel will flow out of the hose. If the pump does not operate as described, it is faulty and must be renewed.

11 If all the above components function correctly, yet the pump doesn't operate in circuit, the igniter unit is probably at fault. There are no test specifications for the igniter unit so it can only be tested by substitution of a known good igniter. Note that fuel pump failure could be due to a wire breakage between any of the components in the fuel pump circuit; check each wire and connector block for continuity before condemning the igniter.

12 When testing is complete, reconnect the battery negative lead.

Removal and installation

13 Remove the fuel tank (see Section 2). Detach the fuel line from the carburettors or pump; note that on early models there is a small filter fitted at the hose joint with the carburettor.

14.14 Disconnect the pump's wiring

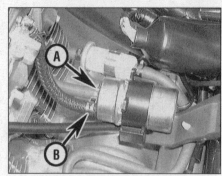

14.15 Pump outlet (B) and inlet (A) line connections

14 Trace the wiring from the fuel pump to the 2-pin connector and disconnect it **(see illustration)**.

15 Take note of the fuel inlet line (from the tank and filter) and outlet line (to the carburettors) locations on the front of the fuel pump so that the lines can be returned to their correct locations on installation **(see illustration)**. Place a rag under the fuel line connections and squeeze the clamp ears together to allow the clamp to be drawn away from the union – the fuel inlet line can be left in place and the pump removed with the fuel filter if desired. Gently ease the fuel pump out of its rubber mounting.

16 Installation is a reverse of the removal procedure. Make sure that you connect the fuel hoses the correct way around and check that there are no fuel leaks.

15 Carburettor heater system – testing

1992-95 models

1 The carburettors are warmed by oil from the engine lubrication system passing through passages in the float chambers. Carburettor temperature is sensed by a thermoswitch in no. 4 carburettor which in turn controls the solenoid valve.

2 If the carburettor heater system is suspected of failure first check the security of the oil hoses which run from the right side of the cylinder head to the solenoid valve, from the solenoid valve to no. 4 carburettor, the link hoses between the float chambers and the hose from no. 1 carburettor to the valve cover **(see illustration)**. The hoses should be secured to their unions with spring clips and there should be no sign of oil leakage.

3 To check the electrical side of the circuit, begin by checking for battery voltage at the thermoswitch red/black wire with the ignition ON. If there is no voltage at this point, refer to the wiring diagram at the end of this manual and check back through the circuit to trace the supply fault.

4 Disconnect the wiring from the thermoswitch on no. 4 carburettor and unscrew the switch **(see illustration 7.1a)**. The thermoswitch is tested by immersing it in water and checking for continuity at specific temperatures. You will need a vessel to hold the water, a heat source, a thermometer and an ohmmeter. Connect the ohmmeter probes to the thermoswitch wires and immerse the sensing portion of the switch in the water. Place the thermometer in the water so that its bulb is close to the switch and not touching the sides of the vessel **(see illustration 15.13b)**.

5 Continuity should be shown with the water cold. Gently heat the water and note the temperature at which the meter indicates no continuity (switch opens); this should be between 30 and 35°C. After this point turn off the heat source and as the water cools note the temperature at which the meter indicates continuity (switch closes); this should be around 23°C. If the thermoswitch does not function as described it must be renewed.

6 When installing the switch, ensure that you install its sealing washer and tighten the thermoswitch to the specified torque setting.

7 The solenoid is held in its bracket by two screws. Disconnect the solenoid black/white wire at the connector and remove the two bolts (noting the ground/earth lead) to free the solenoid from its bracket. Using an ohmmeter, connect its probes to the black/white wire and mounting flange to measure the solenoid resistance; this should be 11 to 15 ohms at 20°C **(see illustration)**. If the ohmmeter

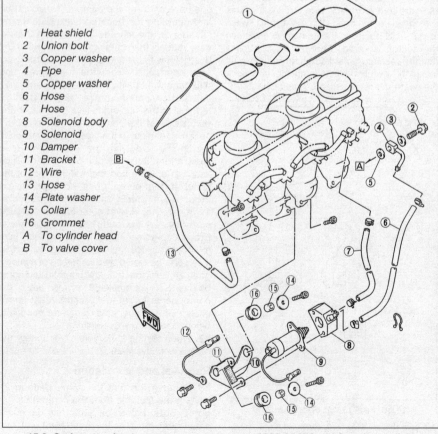

1 Heat shield
2 Union bolt
3 Copper washer
4 Pipe
5 Copper washer
6 Hose
7 Hose
8 Solenoid body
9 Solenoid
10 Damper
11 Bracket
12 Wire
13 Hose
14 Plate washer
15 Collar
16 Grommet
A To cylinder head
B To valve cover

15.2 Carburettor heater system components – 1992-95 UK and Canada models

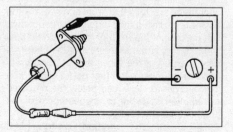

15.7 Measuring the solenoid resistance

15.11a Diode location

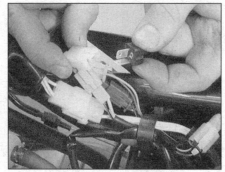

15.11b Unplug the diode . . .

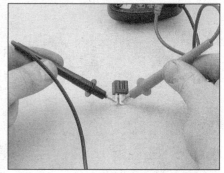

15.11c . . . and test it for continuity

shows an open circuit (very high resistance) the solenoid should be renewed.

1996-on models

8 The carburettor heater system consists of the heater relay, thermoswitch and the carburettor heater unit on each carburettor. The circuit is powered by the battery through the main fuse, ignition main switch and signal fuse. The heaters are energised by a thermoswitch which closes when the temperature drops below a given level. The circuit is further controlled by a relay; when the heaters are operational this relay turns the heaters OFF if the transmission is in neutral, thus preventing the carburettors from overheating when the machine is stationary. For this reason it is important not to allow the engine to idle with the clutch lever pulled in and the transmission in gear.

9 If the carburettor heaters do not come on, first check that the battery is fully charged and that the main fuse and signal fuse are OK. With the ignition ON, use a voltmeter set on the 0 – 20 dc volts scale to check for battery voltage between each brown wire of the heater relay and the frame, then turn the ignition OFF. If no voltage is shown, check the wiring between the relay and battery for continuity.

10 Check the neutral switch by tracing its light blue wire up to the connector. Disconnect it and connect an ohmmeter or continuity tester between the disconnected wire on the switch side and the frame. With the gearbox in neutral continuity should be shown. If no continuity is indicated test the neutral switch further as described in Chapter 8.

11 The neutral switch diode should only allow current to flow in one direction. Locate the diode near the right frame top rail under the fuel tank, under the large plastic sleeve. Remove the insulation tape from its connector **(see illustration)**. Unplug the diode from the connector **(see illustration)**. Using an ohmmeter or continuity tester, connect its probes across the two terminals of the diode **(see illustration)**. Continuity should only be shown in one direction, with no continuity shown when the probes are reversed. If the

15.12a Disconnect the heater relay from its mounting tab (arrowed) and disconnect its wiring

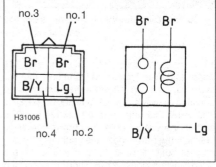

15.12b Heater relay terminal identification and internal circuitry

Br Brown B/Y Black/yellow Lg Light green

diode does not function correctly it must be renewed.

12 To test the heater relay, remove the right side cover (see Chapter 7), disconnect the relay's wiring and remove it from the bike **(see illustration)**. Use as 12 volt battery and two jumper wires, and an ohmmeter or continuity tester to check the relay as follows **(see illustration)**. Connect the meter or tester positive probe to the brown wire terminal (no. 3) and its negative probe to the black/yellow wire terminal (no. 4); no continuity should be indicated. Leaving the meter/tester in place, now connect a jumper wire from the battery positive terminal to the other brown wire terminal (no. 1), then a

jumper wire from the battery negative terminal to the light green wire terminal (no. 2); continuity should now be indicated on the meter. If the relay doesn't function as described it is faulty.

13 The thermoswitch is tested by immersing it in water and checking for continuity at specific temperatures. You will need a vessel to hold the water, a heat source, a thermometer and an ohmmeter. Remove the thermoswitch from its mounting and disconnect its wires **(see illustration)**. Connect the ohmmeter probes to the thermoswitch wires and immerse the switch in the water. Place the thermometer in the water so that its bulb is close to the switch and not touching the sides of the vessel **(see illustration)**.

15.13a Disconnect the thermoswitch from its mounting tab (arrowed) and disconnect its wires

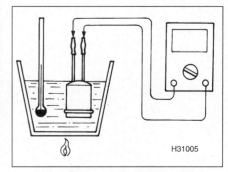

15.13b Thermoswitch test set-up

15.15a Disconnecting the wire from the heater unit on no. 1 carburettor

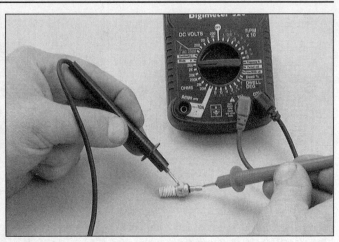

15.15b Heater resistance test

14 Continuity should be shown with the water cold. Gently heat the water and note the temperature at which the meter indicates no continuity (switch opens); this should be 23 ± 3°C. After this point turn off the heat source and as the water cools note the temperature at which the meter indicates continuity (switch closes); this should be 12 ± 4°C. If the thermoswitch does not function as described it must be renewed.

15 Finally, check the individual carburettor heaters. Disconnect the wire connector from each heater element and unscrew the heater from the carburettor body **(see illustration)**. Using an ohmmeter measure the resistance from the wire terminal to the body of the heater **(see illustration)**. Each heater should show a resistance of 6 to 10 ohms at 20°C. If the heater element is faulty it will most likely indicate an open circuit (high resistance) and

should be renewed. Note that the threads of the heaters are coated with a product called 'Heat Sinker'; if this has been removed apply a new coating available from electrical stockists.

16 If the fault cannot be traced to a component in the carburettor heater system, check the wiring between all components for continuity.

Chapter 4
Ignition system

Contents

Degrees of difficulty

Easy, suitable for novice with little experience		Fairly easy, suitable for beginner with some experience		Fairly difficult, suitable for competent DIY mechanic		Difficult, suitable for experienced DIY mechanic		Very difficult, suitable for expert DIY or professional	

Specifications

General
Firing order 1-2-4–3
Ignition timing . . . . Electronic, not adjustable

Ignition coil
Primary resistance (at 20°C/68°F) . . . . 1.92 to 2.88 ohms
Secondary resistance (at 20°C/68°F) . . . . 9.5 to 14.3 K ohms

Spark plug caps and spark plugs
Spark plug cap resistance . . . . 10,000 ohms
Spark plug arcing distance . . . . 6 mm (1/4 inch)
Spark plug type and gap . . . . see Chapter 1

Pickup coil
Resistance (at 20°C/68°F) . . . . 304 to 456 ohms

Torque settings
Pick-up coil plate securing screws . . . . 8 Nm (70 in-lbs)
Timing rotor bolt . . . . 45 Nm (32 ft-lbs)
Signal generator cover screws . . . . 10 Nm (86 in-lbs)

1 General information

This motorcycle is equipped with a battery operated, fully transistorised, breakerless ignition system. The system consists of the following components:

> Pick-up coil
> Igniter unit
> Battery and fuse
> Ignition coils
> Spark plugs
> Ignition (main) and engine kill (stop) switches
> Primary and secondary (HT) circuit wiring

The transistorised ignition system functions on the same principle as a breaker point DC ignition system with the pick-up unit and igniter performing the tasks previously associated with the breaker points and mechanical advance system. As a result, adjustment and maintenance of ignition components is eliminated (with the exception of spark plug replacement).

A microprocessor and a single pick-up coil control ignition timing. As a further aid to ignition timing, a throttle position sensor is fitted to 1996-on UK models.

Because of their nature, the individual ignition system components can be checked but not repaired. If ignition system troubles occur, and the faulty component can be isolated, the only cure for the problem is to replace the part with a new one. Keep in mind that most electrical parts, once purchased, can't be returned. To avoid unnecessary expense, make very sure the faulty component has been positively identified before buying a replacement part.

2 Ignition system – check

 Warning: Because of the very high voltage generated by the ignition system, extreme care should be taken when these checks are performed.

1 If the ignition system is the suspected cause of poor engine performance or failure to start, a number of checks can be made to isolate the problem.

2 Make sure the engine kill switch is in the Run position.

Engine will not start

3 Disconnect one of the spark plug wires, connect the wire to a spare spark plug and lay the plug on the engine with the threads contacting the engine. If necessary, hold the spark plug with an insulated tool. Crank the engine over and make sure a well-defined, blue spark occurs between the spark plug electrodes.

 Warning: Don't remove one of the spark plugs from the engine to perform this check - atomised fuel being pumped out of the open spark plug hole could ignite, causing severe injury!

4 If no spark occurs, the following checks should be made:

5 Unscrew a spark plug cap from a plug wire. Check the cap resistance with an ohmmeter and compare it to the value listed in this Chapter's Specifications. If the resistance is infinite, replace it with a new one. Repeat this check on the remaining plug caps.

6 Make sure all electrical connectors are clean and tight. Check all wires for shorts, opens and correct installation.

7 Check the battery voltage with a voltmeter (see Chapter 8). If the voltage is less than 12-volts, recharge the battery.

8 Check the ignition fuse and the fuse connections. If the fuse is blown, replace it with a new one; if the connections are loose or corroded, clean or repair them.

9 Refer to Chapter 8 and check the ignition switch, engine kill switch, neutral switch, clutch switch and sidestand switch.

10 Refer to Section 3 and check the ignition coil primary and secondary resistance.

11 Refer to Section 4 and check the pick-up coil resistance.

12 If the preceding checks produce positive

2.14 A simple spark gap testing fixture can be made from a block of wood, a large alligator clip, two nails, a screw and a piece of wire

results but there is still no spark at the plug, remove the igniter and have it checked by a Yamaha dealer service department or other repair shop equipped with the special tester required.

Engine starts but misfires

13 If the engine starts but misfires, make the following checks before deciding that the ignition system is at fault.

14 The ignition system must be able to produce a spark across a six millimetre (1/4-inch) gap (minimum). A simple testing fixture **(see illustration)** can be constructed to make sure the minimum spark gap can be jumped. Make sure the fixture electrodes are positioned six millimetres apart.

15 Connect one of the spark plug wires to the protruding test fixture electrode, then attach the fixture's alligator clip to a good engine ground (earth).

16 Crank the engine over (it will probably start and run on the remaining cylinders) and see if well-defined, blue sparks occur between the test fixture electrodes. If the minimum spark gap test is positive, the ignition coil for that cylinder (and its companion cylinder) is functioning properly. Repeat the check on one of the spark plug

wires that is connected to the other coil. If the spark will not jump the gap during either test, or if it is weak (orange coloured), refer to Steps 5 through 11 of this Section and perform the component checks described.

3 Ignition coils – check, removal and installation

Check

1 In order to determine conclusively that the ignition coils are defective, they should be tested by an authorised Yamaha dealer service department which is equipped with the special electrical tester required for this check.

2 However, the coils can be checked visually (for cracks and other damage) and the primary and secondary coil resistances can be measured with an ohmmeter. If the coils are undamaged, and if the resistances are as specified, they are probably capable of proper operation.

3 To check the coils for physical damage, they must be removed (see Step 9). To check the resistances, remove the seat and fuel tank (see Chapters 7 and 3). Unplug the primary circuit electrical connectors from the coil(s) and remove the spark plug wires from the plugs that are connected to the coil being checked. Mark the locations of all wires before disconnecting them.

4 To check the coil primary resistance, first place the ohmmeter selector switch in the ohms (Ω) x 1 position, then attach one ohmmeter lead to one of the primary terminals and the other ohmmeter lead to the other primary terminal **(see illustration)**. Compare the measured resistance to the value listed in this Chapter's Specifications.

5 If the coil primary resistance is as specified, check the coil secondary resistance. Place the ohmmeter selector switch in the K ohms (KΩ) position, then connect the meter leads to the spark plug wire terminals **(see illustration)**.

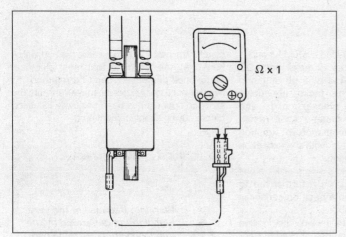

3.4 To test the coil primary resistance, connect the ohmmeter leads between the primary terminals in the coil connector

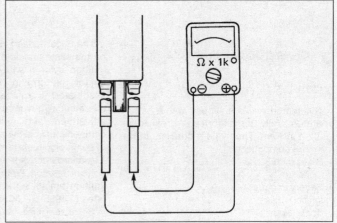

3.5 To test the coil secondary resistance, connect the ohmmeter between the spark plug wires

3.9 To detach the coils, remove the mounting bolts (arrowed) - one bolt head may secure a ground (earth) wire

4.2 Follow the pick-up coil harness (arrowed) to its connector

Compare the measured resistance to the values listed in this Chapter's Specifications.

6 If the resistances are not as specified, the coil is probably defective and should be replaced with a new one.

Removal and installation

7 If you haven't already done so, remove the seat and fuel tank (see Chapters 7 and 3).

8 Look for cylinder number markings on the plug wires and make your own if they aren't visible (number the cylinders one through four, working from the left to the right side of the bike). Disconnect the spark plug wires from the plugs. After labelling them with tape to aid in reinstallation, unplug the coil primary circuit electrical connectors.

9 Support the coil with one hand and remove the coil mounting bolts **(see illustration)**, then withdraw the coil from its bracket.

10 Installation is the reverse of removal. Make sure the primary circuit electrical connectors and plug wires are attached to the proper terminals.

4 Pick-up coil – check, removal and installation

Note: *The pick-up coil is sometimes referred to as the signal generator.*

Check

1 Remove the seat (see Chapter 7).

2 Follow the wiring harness from the pick-up coil on the left side of the engine to the connector, then unplug the connector **(see illustration)**.

3 Probe the terminals in the pick-up coil connector with an ohmmeter and compare the resistance reading with the value listed in this Chapter's Specifications.

4 Set the ohmmeter on the highest resistance range. Measure the resistance between a good ground (earth) and each terminal in the electrical connector. The meter should read infinity.

5 If the pick-up coil fails either of the above tests, it must be replaced.

Removal

6 Remove the pick-up coil cover **(see illustration 25.5 in Chapter 1)**. Remove the pick-up coil mounting screws and detach the pick-up coil from the engine.

7 If necessary, remove the timing rotor bolt and detach the timing rotor from the engine **(see illustration)**. Remove the screws and detach the pick-up coil base. These parts don't have to be removed to remove the pick-up coil.

Installation

8 Installation is the reverse of the removal steps, with the following additions:

a) *Be sure to seat the grommet on the wiring harness into the notch in the crankcase* **(see illustration)** *and route the wiring harness behind the clips on the engine* **(see illustration 4.2)**.

b) *Tighten the pick-up coil screws (and the pick-up coil base screws, if removed) to the torque listed in the Chapter 8 Specifications.*

c) *If the timing rotor was removed, install it, aligning the dowel with the rotor notch* **(see illustration)**, *and tighten the bolt to the torque listed in this Chapter's Specifications.*

4.7 If necessary, remove the timing rotor bolt and the timing plate screws (arrowed)

5 Igniter – check, removal and installation

Check

1 The igniter is checked by process of elimination (when all other possible causes have been checked and eliminated, the igniter is at fault). Because the igniter is expensive and can't be returned once purchased, consider having a Yamaha dealer test the ignition system before you buy a new igniter.

4.8a The pick-up coil harness grommet fits into a notch in the crankcase

4.8b On installation, align the pin with the timing rotor notch (arrowed)

5.3 The igniter is mounted under the seat

6.2 Disconnecting the TPS wire connector

6.4 TPS adjustment screws (arrowed)

Removal and installation

2 Remove the seat.

3 Unplug the electrical connector. Remove the mounting screws and take the igniter out **(see illustration)**.

4 Installation is the reverse of the removal steps.

---

6   Throttle position sensor (1996-on UK models)

---

1 The throttle position sensor is located on the side of the no. 1 carburettor and is keyed to the end of the throttle operating shaft. The sensor provides the igniter unit with information relating to throttle opening and the igniter is thus able to set the ignition timing accordingly to produce the best running conditions and cleaner exhaust emissions. Not surprisingly it is essential that the throttle position sensor should be set up correctly. Do not tamper with the sensor's position unless it has been disturbed during carburettor overhaul or poor running problems have been experienced.

TPS set-up and adjustment

Note: *Before carrying out TPS adjustment ensure that the engine idle speed is correct.*

2 To set up to the throttle position sensor it is first necessary to switch the igniter unit to TPS set up mode. To do this, turn the ignition ON, then disconnect its wiring connector and connect it again **(see illustration)**. If the tachometer reads 5000 rpm the TPS setting is correct and no adjustment is necessary. If the tachometer reads either 10,000 rpm or 1000 rpm the TPS should be adjusted as described below. Turn the ignition OFF.

3 Remove the carburettors from their intake stubs (see Chapter 3); there is no need to disconnect the cables, just position the carburettors so that access is possible to the two TPS screws. Make sure the TPS wire connector is still connected.

4 Loosen the two screws which retain the TPS and turn the ignition ON **(see illustration)**. The angle of the TPS can be read off the tachometer. Rotate the TPS body so that the tachometer reads 5000 rpm and secure the screws to retain this position. Yamaha advise that if the tachometer reads 10,000 rpm the TPS angle is too wide and if it reads 1,000 rpm the angle is too narrow.

5 Following adjustment, install the carburettors and start the engine, or turn the ignition main switch off, then on; this will restore the igniter's TPS function to normal mode.

TPS resistance test

6 If the TPS is suspected of failure, it can be tested as follows. Disconnect the TPS connector **(see illustration 6.2)** and make the following tests on the TPS side of the connector.

7 Using an ohmmeter set to the K ohms scale, connect its probes to the blue wire terminal and the black/blue wire terminal. A resistance of 3.5 to 6.5 K ohms should be shown.

8 Leave one probe connected to the black/blue wire terminal and move the other probe to the yellow wire terminal. Whilst rotating the throttle grip slowly from closed to fully open a resistance of 0 to 5 ± 1.5 K ohms should be shown.

9 If the TPS doesn't produce the specified resistance readings it should be renewed, although it is recommended that your findings are confirmed by a Yamaha dealer before purchasing a new TPS unit.

Chapter 5
Frame, suspension and final drive

Contents

Degrees of difficulty

Easy, suitable for novice with little experience		Fairly easy, suitable for beginner with some experience		Fairly difficult, suitable for competent DIY mechanic		Difficult, suitable for experienced DIY mechanic		Very difficult, suitable for expert DIY or professional	
			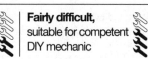						

Specifications

Front forks

Fork spring length – 1992-97 UK models, all US models
  Standard . . . . 476.5 mm (18.8 inches)
  Minimum . . . . 471.5 mm (18.6 inches)
Fork spring length – 1998-on UK models
  Standard . . . . 341 mm (13.4 inches)
  Minimum . . . . 334 mm (13.1 inches)
Fork oil capacity, grade and level . . . . see Chapter 1

Rear suspension

Rear spring free length – 1992-95 UK models, 1992-96 US models
  Standard . . . . 170.5 mm (6.71 inches)
  Minimum . . . . 165 mm (6.51 inches)
Rear spring free length – 1996-on UK models, 1997-on US models
  Standard . . . . 176.5 mm (6.95 inches)
  Minimum . . . . 173 mm (6.81 inches)
Swingarm endplay and side play limits . . . . 1 mm (0.040 inch)

Final drive

Chain size 520
No. of links 110
Chain freeplay and lubricant . . . . see Chapter 1

Torque settings

Front forks
Cap bolt to fork . . . . 23 Nm (17 ft-lbs)
Damper rod bolt* . . . . 30 Nm (22 ft-lbs)
Handlebars and steering stem
Upper triple clamp bolts . . . . 23 Nm (17 ft-lbs)
Lower triple clamp bolts . . . . 38 Nm (27 ft-lbs)
Handlebar bracket bolts . . . . 23 Nm (17 ft-lbs)
Grip end weights . . . . 26 Nm (19 ft-lbs)
Steering stem nut . . . . 110 Nm (80 ft-lbs)
Steering head bearing ring nut . . . . See Chapter 1
Rear shock absorber bolts and nuts . . . . 64 Nm (46 ft-lbs)
Swingarm pivot shaft nut . . . . 91 Nm (66 ft-lbs)
Drive chain front sprocket nut . . . . 110 Nm (80 ft-lbs)
Drive chain rear sprocket nuts . . . . 60 Nm (43 ft-lbs)
Engine sprocket cover bolts . . . . 10 Nm (86 in-lbs)
*Use non-permanent thread locking agent on the threads.

1 General information

All motorcycles covered in this manual use a double cradle frame. The frame is a one-piece unit constructed of round-section tubing.

The front forks are of the conventional coil spring, hydraulically-damped telescopic type.

The rear suspension consists of a steel oval-section swingarm supported by a coil spring/shock absorber unit. Rear spring preload is adjustable.

The final drive uses an endless chain (which means it doesn't have a master link). A rubber damper (often called a 'cush drive') is installed between the rear wheel coupling and the wheel.

2 Frame – inspection and repair

1 The frame shouldn't require attention unless accident damage has occurred. In most cases, frame replacement is the only satisfactory remedy for such damage. A few frame specialists have the jigs and other equipment necessary for straightening the frame to the required standard of accuracy, but even then there is no simple way of assessing to what extent the frame may have been over stressed.
2 After the machine has accumulated a lot of miles, the frame should be examined closely for signs of cracking or splitting at the welded joints. Corrosion can also cause weakness at these joints. Loose engine mount bolts can cause ovaling or fracturing of the mounting tabs. Minor damage can often be repaired by welding, depending on the extent and nature

of the damage. Welding should be performed by an expert in the field.
3 Remember that a frame which is out of alignment will cause handling problems. If misalignment is suspected as the result of an accident, it will be necessary to strip the machine completely so the frame can be thoroughly checked.

3 Side and centrestand – maintenance

1 The centrestand (where fitted) pivots on two bolts attached to the frame. Periodically, remove the pivot bolts and grease them thoroughly to avoid excessive wear.
2 Make sure the return spring is in good condition. A broken or weak spring is an obvious safety hazard.
3 The sidestand is attached to a bracket on the frame (see illustration). A pair of springs anchored to the bracket ensures that the stand is held in the retracted or extended position.

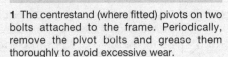
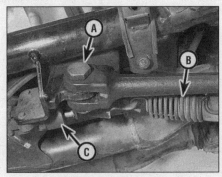

3.3 The sidestand is attached to a bracket on the frame

A Pivot
B Springs
C Sidestand switch

4 Make sure the pivot bolt is tight and the springs are in good condition and not over stretched. An accident is almost certain to occur if the stand extends while the machine is in motion.

4 Handlebars – removal and installation

1 The handlebar is a one-piece unit held in place by light alloy caps.
2 If the handlebar must be removed for access to other components, such as the forks or the steering head, it's not necessary to disconnect the cables, wires or brake hose, but it's a good idea to support the assembly with a piece of wire or rope, to avoid unnecessary strain on the cables, wires and the brake hose.
3 If the handlebar is to be removed completely, refer to Chapter 6 for the master cylinder removal procedures, Chapter 3 for the throttle grip removal procedure and Chapter 8 for the switch removal procedure. If it's necessary to remove the grips, unscrew the grip end weights with an Allen wrench (see illustration).

4.3 Unscrew the grip end weights with an Allen wrench

4.4 Pry or lift the trim caps from the Allen bolts, then remove the bolts and lift off the caps to remove the handlebar; the arrow marks (arrowed) point to the front of the bike when the caps are installed

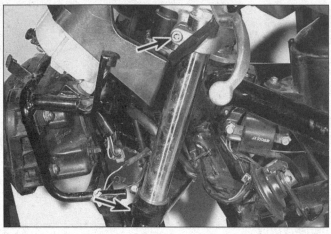

5.6 Loosen the triple clamp bolts (arrowed) and lower the fork out of the triple clamps

4 Pry the trim caps out of the handlebar clamps, then unbolt the clamps and lift off the handlebar **(see illustration)**.

5 Check the handlebars for cracks and distortion and renew them if any undesirable conditions are found.

6 Installation is the reverse of the removal steps, with the following additions:

a) *Align the match mark on the handlebar with the gap between the rear of the right mounting bracket in the upper triple clamp and its cap.*

b) *Position the caps with their arrow marks pointing forward* **(see illustration 4.4)**.

c) *Tighten the front bolts first, then the rear bolts to the torque listed in this Chapter's Specifications. Don't try to close the gaps between the rear of the caps and the upper triple clamp; over-tightening will only break the clamps or strip out the bolt holes.*

d) *Reinstall the trim caps.*

5 Forks –
removal and installation

Removal

1 Set the bike on its centrestand (if equipped) or support it securely upright.

2 Unbolt the brake hose retainer from the fork leg. Remove the caliper mounting bolts and support the caliper out of the way. Don't disconnect the brake hose and don't let the caliper hang by the brake hose.

3 Remove the front wheel (see Chapter 6).

4 Unbolt the front fender.

5 If you're going to remove the fork cap bolts, loosen them now.

6 Loosen the upper and lower triple clamp bolts **(see illustration)**. Slide the fork down out of the triple clamps and remove it from the bike.

1 Cap bolt
2 Cap bolt O-ring
3 Spacer
4 Spring seat
5 Spring
6 Damper rod and rebound spring
7 Oil lock piece
8 Fork tube
9 Seal protector – 1997-on UK
10 Dust seal
11 Retaining clip
12 Oil seal
13 Washer
14 Bushing
15 Fork slider
16 Copper washer
17 Damper rod bolt
18 Oil drain screw and washer – 1992-94 only

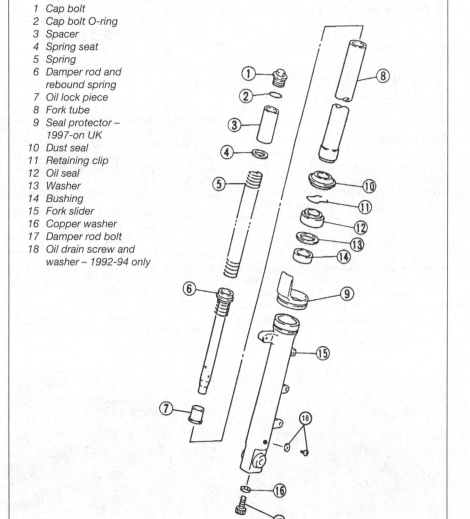

6.2 Front fork – exploded view

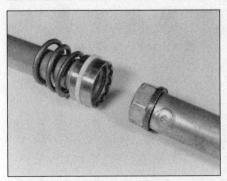

6.4a This is a special tool that's used to hold the damper rod from turning

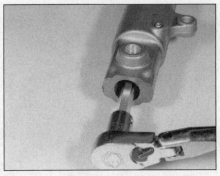

6.4b Loosen the damper rod bolt with an Allen wrench . . .

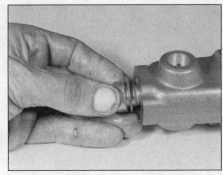

6.4c . . . and remove the bolt and its copper washer – use a new copper washer during reassembly

Installation

7 Installation is the reverse of the removal steps, with the following additions:
  a) Position the ends of the fork tubes flush with the upper triple clamp.
  b) Tighten all fasteners to the torques listed in this Chapter's Specifications.
  c) Pump the front brake lever several times to bring the pads into contact with the discs.

6 Forks – disassembly, inspection and reassembly

Disassembly

1 Remove the forks following the procedure in Section 5. Work on one fork leg at a time to avoid mixing up the parts.
2 Remove the fork cap, spacer, spring seat and spring (the cap should have been loosened before the forks were removed) (see illustration).
3 Invert the fork assembly over a container and pump the fork to expel the oil.
4 Prevent the damper rod from turning using a holding handle and an adapter passed down through the fork inner tube to engage the recessed head of the damper rod. Yamaha service tools are available for this purpose; pt. nos. 90890-01326 and 90890-01328 for 1992 to 1997 models and pt. nos. 90890-01326

You can fabricate your own damper rod holding tool using a bolt with a head that fits inside the top of the damper rod in the fork, two nuts, a socket (to fit on the nuts), a long extension and a ratchet. Thread the two nuts onto the bolt and tighten them against each other (A). Insert the assembly into the socket and tape it into place (B). Now, insert the tool into the fork tube and engage the bolt head into the hex recess in the damper rod.

and 90890-01460 for 1998-on models. On the 1992 to 1997 type fork assembly photographed, we found that a 24 mm hex size adaptor could be fabricated as shown (see Haynes Hint). Unscrew the Allen bolt at the bottom of the outer tube and retrieve the copper washer (see illustrations).
5 Tip out the damper rod and the rebound spring (see illustration). Don't remove the Teflon ring from the damper rod unless a new one will be installed.

6 Pry the dust seal from the outer tube (see illustration).
7 Pry the retaining ring from its groove in the outer tube (see illustration). Remove the ring.
8 Hold the outer tube and yank the inner tube away from it, repeatedly (like a slide-hammer), until the seal and outer tube guide bushing pop loose (see illustration).
9 Slide the seal, washer and bushing from the inner tube (see illustration).

6.5 Remove the damper rod and the Teflon ring – don't separate the ring from the damper rod unless you plan to replace it

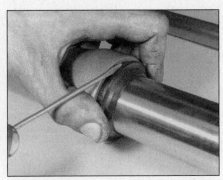

6.6 Pry the dust seal out of the outer tube

6.7 Pry out the retaining ring

6.8 To separate the inner and outer fork tubes, pull them apart firmly several times – the slide hammer effect will pull the tubes apart

6.9 These parts will come out with the inner fork tube

1 Seal
2 Washer
3 Outer tube bushing
4 Inner tube bushing

Inspection

10 Clean all parts in solvent and blow them dry with compressed air, if available. Check the inner and outer fork tubes, the bushings and the damper rod for score marks, scratches, flaking of the chrome and excessive or abnormal wear. Look for dents in the tubes and replace them if any are found. Check the fork seal seat for nicks, gouges and scratches. If damage is evident, leaks will occur around the seal-to-outer tube junction. Replace worn or defective parts with new ones.

11 Check the inner tube for runout with a dial gauge and V-blocks (see illustration). If it's necessary to replace the inner guide bushing (the one that won't come off that's on the bottom of the inner tube), pry it apart at the slit and slide it off. Make sure the new one seats properly.

 Warning: If a tube is bent, it should not be straightened; replace it with a new one.

12 Measure the overall length of the fork spring and check it for cracks and other damage. Compare the length to the minimum

length listed in this Chapter's Specifications. If it's defective or sagged, replace both fork springs with new ones. Never replace only one spring!

13 All UK models from 1997 on have an oil seal protector fitted to the fork slider. If one of these is damaged, ease it out of its retaining groove in the slider and replace it with a new one; install the new seal protector so that its raised shield faces the front of the motorcycle when the fork is installed.

Reassembly

14 Place the rebound spring over the damper rod, then slide the rod assembly into the inner fork tube until it protrudes from the lower end of the tube. Fit the oil lock piece over the end of the damper rod.

15 Insert the inner tube/damper rod assembly into the outer tube until the Allen bolt (with a new copper washer) can be threaded into the damper rod from the lower end of the outer tube. **Note:** Apply a non-permanent thread locking compound to the threads of the bolt. Using the tool described in Step 4, hold the damper rod and tighten the Allen bolt to the torque listed in this Chapter's

Specifications. **Note:** If you didn't use the tool, tighten the damper rod bolt after the fork spring and cap bolt are installed.

16 Slide the outer guide bushing down the inner tube. Using the Yamaha special bushing driver and a used guide bushing placed on top of the guide bushing being installed, drive the bushing into place until it's fully seated (see illustration). If you don't have access to one of these tools, it is highly recommended that you take the assembly to a Yamaha dealer service department or other motorcycle repair shop to have this done. It is possible, however, to drive the bushing into place using a section of pipe and an old guide bushing (see illustration). Wrap tape around the ends of the pipe to prevent it from scratching the fork tube.

17 Slide the washer down the inner tube, into position over the guide bushing.

18 Lubricate the lips and the outer diameter of the fork seal with the recommended fork oil (see Chapter 1) and slide it down the inner tube, with the lip facing down and the seal markings facing upwards. Drive the seal into

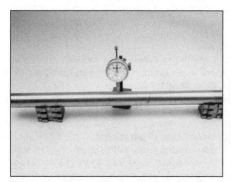

6.11 Check the inner fork tube for runout with a dial gauge and V-blocks

6.16a Drive the bushing into position with a tool like this one if it's available (use the tool like a slide hammer) . . .

6.16b . . . if you don't have the proper tool, a section of pipe can be used the same way the special tool would be used - as a slide hammer (be sure to tape the ends of the pipe so it doesn't scratch the fork tube)

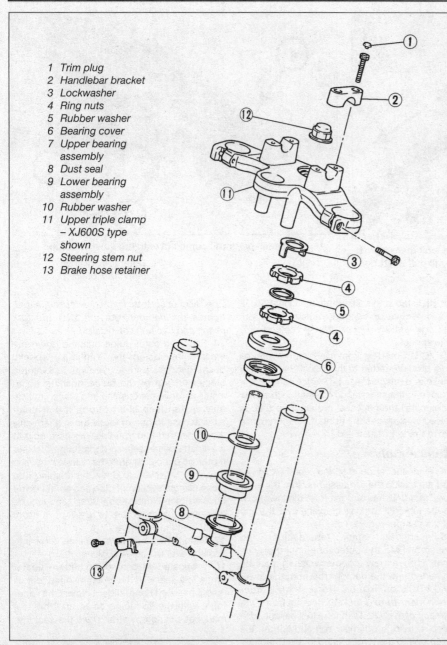

1 Trim plug
2 Handlebar bracket
3 Lockwasher
4 Ring nuts
5 Rubber washer
6 Bearing cover
7 Upper bearing
   assembly
8 Dust seal
9 Lower bearing
   assembly
10 Rubber washer
11 Upper triple clamp
   – XJ600S type
   shown
12 Steering stem nut
13 Brake hose retainer

7.4a Steering head bearings

7.4b Unscrew the steering stem nut

7.5a Lift off the lockwasher . . .

place with the same tools used to drive in the guide bushing. If you don't have access to these, it is recommended that you take the assembly to a Yamaha dealer service department or other motorcycle repair shop to have the seal driven in. If you are very careful, the seal can be driven in with a hammer and a drift punch. Work around the circumference of the seal, tapping gently on the outer edge of the seal until it's seated. Be careful - if you distort the seal, you'll have to disassemble the fork again and end up taking it to a dealer anyway!

19 Install the retaining ring, making sure the ring is completely seated in its groove.
20 Install the dust seal, making sure it seats completely.
21 On 1992-94 models, install the drain screw and a new gasket, if it was removed.
22 Add the recommended type and amount of fork oil (see Chapter 1).
23 Install the fork spring, with the closer-wound coils at the top.
24 Install the spring seat on top of the spring, followed by the spacer.
25 Extend the fork tube and install the fork cap bolt tightening whilst compressing the spring; it will be tightened to the specified torque after the fork is installed.
26 Install the fork by following the procedure outlined in Section 5. If you won't be installing the fork right away, store it in an upright position.
27 Tighten the fork cap bolt to the torque listed in this Chapter's Specifications.

7 Steering head bearings –
replacement

Removal

1 If the steering head bearing check and adjustment (see Chapter 1) does not remedy excessive play or roughness in the steering head bearings, the entire front end must be disassembled and the bearings and races replaced with new ones.
2 Remove the handlebars (see Section 4), the front wheel (see Chapter 6) and the front forks (see Section 5). On XJ600N models, detach the headlamp bracket from the upper triple clamp.
3 Unbolt the brake hose retainer from the lower triple clamp **(see illustration 7.4a or 7.4b in Chapter 6)**.
4 Remove the steering stem nut (with washer – later UK models), then lift off the upper triple clamp (sometimes called the fork bridge, yoke or crown) **(see illustrations)**.
5 Remove the lockwasher, upper ring nut and rubber washer from the steering stem **(see illustrations)**. Use an adjustable spanner **(see illustration 19.7 in Chapter 1)** or the Yamaha service tool, which has a square hole in the handle for measuring torque.

7.5b . . . unscrew the upper ring nut, lift off the rubber washer and unscrew the lower ring nut (arrowed)

7.7a Lift off the bearing cover . . .

7.7b . . . the upper bearing inner race and the bearing

6 Remove the lower ring nut **(see illustration 7.5b)**.

7 Remove the bearing cover, upper bearing inner race and the upper bearing **(see illustrations)**.

8 Lower the steering stem out of the steering head, then remove the rubber washer, lower bearing and dust seal **(see illustration)**. If the steering stem is stuck, gently tap on the top end with a plastic mallet or a hammer and wood block.

Inspection

9 Clean all the parts with solvent and dry them thoroughly, using compressed air, if available. Wipe the old grease out of the bearing outer races in the frame.

10 Examine the outer races in the steering head for cracks, dents, and pits. If even the slightest amount of wear or damage is evident, the races should be replaced with new ones.

11 To remove the bearing outer races from the steering head, drive them out with a hammer and punch **(see illustration)**. A slide-hammer with the proper internal-jaw puller will also work.

12 When installing the outer races, tap them gently into place with a hammer and punch or a large socket. Do not strike the race surface or the race will be damaged.

13 Check the bearings for wear. Look for cracks, dents, and pits in the bearing balls and their cage. Also check for loose balls or for any that may have fallen out of the cage. Replace any defective parts with new ones. If a new bearing is required, replace both bearings and their races as a set.

14 Check the dust seal under the lower bearing and replace it with a new one if necessary.

15 Don't remove the lower bearing inner race unless it must be replaced. To remove the inner race, tap between the race and steering stem with a chisel **(see illustration)**.

16 Inspect the steering stem/lower triple clamp for cracks and other damage. Do not attempt to repair any steering components. Replace them with new parts if defects are found.

Installation

17 Pack the lower bearing with medium weight lithium-based grease and install it on

its inner race on the steering stem. **Note:** *A small hand-operated grease gun will make this job easier.* Coat the top and bottom outer races with grease also.

18 Slip the steering stem/lower triple clamp into the steering head.

19 Pack the upper bearing with grease and install it in its outer race in the top of the steering head.

20 Install the inner race in the upper bearing, then install the bearing cover and lower ring nut (make sure the tapered side of the ring nut faces down). Refer to Chapter 1 and adjust the bearings then install the rubber washer, upper ring nut and lockwasher.

21 Install the upper triple clamp and steering stem nut (with washer, where applicable) and tighten the nut to the specified torque setting. The remainder of installation is the reverse of the removal steps in Steps 2 and 3 of this Section.

8 Rear shock absorber – removal, inspection and installation

Removal

1 Set the bike on its centrestand (if equipped) or support it securely upright.

2 Remove the seat (see Chapter 7) and the fuel tank (see Chapter 3).

> **HAYNES HiNT**
> *Since the outer races are installed with an interference fit in the frame, installation will be easier if the new races are left overnight in a freezer. This will cause them to contract and slip into place in the frame with very little effort.*

7.8 Carefully lower the steering stem out of the steering head and remove the rubber washer, lower bearing and dust seal

7.11 Drive the lower bearing outer race out from above; drive the upper bearing outer race out from below

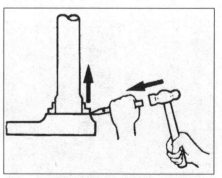

7.15 Tap a chisel between the lower bearing inner race and the lower triple clamp to remove the race

1 Shock absorber
2 Bushing
3 Upper bolt
4 Lower bolt
5 Collar
6 Grease seal
7 Bushing

8.3a Rear shock absorber details

Caution: Wear eye protection to prevent eye damage from escaping gas and/or metal chips.

Installation

8 Installation is the reverse of the removal steps, with the following additions:
   a) Apply multi-purpose lithium grease to the collars and pivot bolt shafts.
   b) Tighten all fasteners to the torques listed in this Chapter's Specifications.

9 Swingarm bearings – check

1 Refer to Chapter 6 and remove the rear wheel, then refer to Section 8 and remove the rear shock absorber.
2 Grasp the rear of the swingarm with one hand and place your other hand at the junction of the swingarm and the frame. Try to move the rear of the swingarm from side-to-side. Any wear (play) in the bearings should be felt as movement between the swingarm and the frame at the front. The swingarm will actually be felt to move forward and backward at the front (not from side-to-side). If any play is noted, the bearings should be replaced with new ones (see Section 11).
3 Next, move the swingarm up and down through its full travel. It should move freely, without any binding or rough spots. If it doesn't move freely, refer to Section 10 for servicing procedures.

10 Swingarm – removal and installation

1 Set the bike on its centrestand (if equipped) or prop it securely upright.
2 Remove the chain guard **(see illustration 1.4a in Chapter 1)** and the rear wheel (see Chapter 6).
3 Remove any support brackets and detach associated wiring, cables, or hoses from the swingarm.

3 Support the rear wheel. Remove the shock absorber lower bolt and its dust seals and collars **(see illustrations)**.
4 Remove the upper mounting bolt and nut. Remove the shock absorber from the motorcycle.

Inspection

5 Check the shock for signs of oil or gas leaks and replace it if you find any.

6 Inspect the pivot hardware at the top and bottom of the shock and replace any worn or damaged parts.
7 Before you discard a worn shock absorber, release the gas pressure by drilling a 2 to 3 mm (0.08 to 0.12 inch) hole through the top of the shock cylinder wall at the specified location **(see illustration)**. You can also take the shock absorber to a Yamaha dealer for safe disposal.

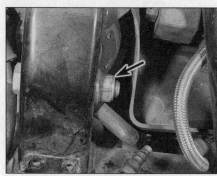

8.3b Remove the upper mounting bolt and nut . . .

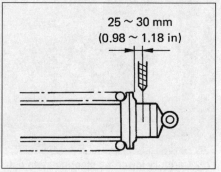

8.3c . . . and the lower mounting bolt and nut and lift the shock absorber out

25 ~ 30 mm
(0.98 ~ 1.18 in)

8.7 Wear eye protection and drill a hole at the point shown to release gas from the shock absorber before discarding it

10.8 Remove the nut (arrowed) from the swingarm pivot shaft

4 Detach the rear brake caliper on models so equipped (see Chapter 6).
5 Detach the brake torque link from the swingarm and position it so that its guide loop does not place any strain on the rear brake hose.
6 Detach the shock absorber from the swingarm (see Section 9).
7 Pry the trim caps from the ends of the swingarm pivot shaft.
8 Remove the swingarm pivot nut **(see illustration)**.
9 Support the swingarm and pull the pivot shaft out **(see illustration)**. Remove the swingarm. If necessary, remove the bolts and detach the suspension linkage relay arm from the swingarm.
10 Check the pivot bearings in the swingarm for dryness or deterioration. If they're in need of lubrication or replacement, refer to Section 11.
11 Installation is the reverse of the removal procedure. Be sure the bearing seals are in position before installing the pivot shaft. Tighten all fasteners to the torques listed in this Chapter's Specifications. Adjust the chain as described in Chapter 1.

11 Swingarm bearings - inspection and replacement

1 Remove the swingarm (see Section 11).

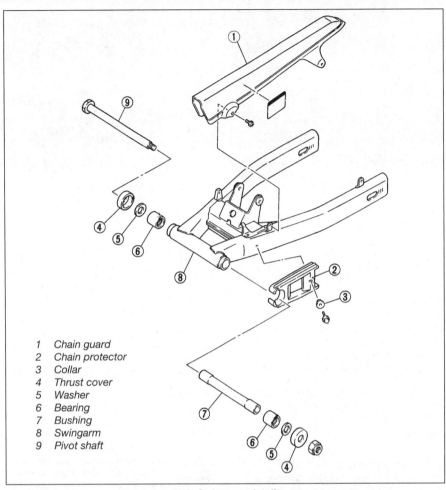

1 Chain guard
2 Chain protector
3 Collar
4 Thrust cover
5 Washer
6 Bearing
7 Bushing
8 Swingarm
9 Pivot shaft

10.9 Swingarm details

2 Remove the dust cap and thrust washer from each side of the swingarm **(see illustration)**.
3 Slide the bushing out **(see illustration)**.
4 Inspect the bearings **(see illustration)**. If they're dry, lubricate them with lithium-based waterproof wheel bearing grease. If they're worn or damaged, take the swingarm to a Yamaha dealer or motorcycle repair shop for bearing replacement.

12 Drive chain – removal, cleaning and installation

Endless type chain

Note: *An endless chain has no riveted (soft) link – all links and pins are the same. The chain fitted as original equipment and supplied as a spare part from Yamaha dealers is of the endless type.*

11.2 Pry off the thrust cover and remove the washer . . .

11.3 . . . then pull out the bushing . . .

11.4 . . . to expose the bearings

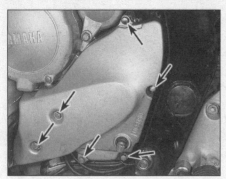

12.2a Remove the bolts (arrowed) . . .

12.2b . . . and take off the engine sprocket cover and bolt spacer

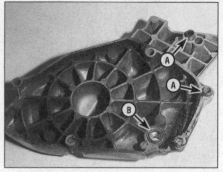

12.2c Note the locations of the dowels (A); replace the seals (B) if they're worn – there are inner and outer seals, with a spacer between them

Removal

1 Disconnect the shift pedal arm from its shaft on the engine (see Chapter 2, Section 21).
2 Remove the bolts securing the engine sprocket cover to the engine case. Take the sprocket cover off (see illustrations).
3 Remove the rear wheel (see Chapter 6).
4 Lift the chain off the engine sprocket.
5 Detach the swingarm from the frame by following the first few Steps of Section 11. Pull the swingarm back far enough to allow the chain to slip between the frame and the front of the swingarm.

Cleaning

6 Soak the chain in kerosene (paraffin) for approximately five or six minutes.
Caution: Don't use gasoline (petrol), solvent or other cleaning fluids. Don't use high-pressure water. Remove the chain, wipe it off, then blow dry it with compressed air immediately. The entire process shouldn't take longer than ten minutes - if it does, the O-rings in the chain rollers could be damaged.

Installation

7 Installation is the reverse of the removal procedure. Tighten the suspension fasteners and the engine sprocket cover bolts to the torque values listed in this Chapter's Specifications. Tighten the rear axle nut to the torque listed in the Chapter 6 Specifications and secure it with a new cotter pin.
8 Lubricate the chain following the procedure described in Chapter 1.

Riveted link type chain

Removal

Note: *The riveted (soft) link can be identified by its identification markings on the side plate and usually slightly different colour. Also the staked ends of the link's two pins look as if they have been deeply centre-punched, instead of peened over as with all other pins.*
9 Locate the joining link in a suitable position to work on by rotating the back wheel; midway between the sprockets is ideal.

10 Slacken the drive chain as described in Chapter 1.
11 Split the chain at the joining link using an approved chain breaker tool intended for motorcycle use. There are a number of types available for motorcycle use and it is important to follow carefully the instructions supplied with the tool – see *Tools and Workshop Tips* in the Reference section for a typical example. Remove the chain from the bike, noting its routing through the swingarm.

Cleaning

12 See Step 6.

Installation

 Warning: NEVER install a drive chain which uses a clip-type master (split) link. If you do not have access to a chain riveting tool, have the chain fitted by a Yamaha dealer.

13 Remove the engine sprocket cover as described in Steps 1 and 2.
14 Thread the chain into position, making sure that it takes the correct route around the swingarm and sprockets and leave the two ends in a convenient place to work on. Obtain a new soft link – never attempt to reuse an old link.
15 Install the new soft link complete with an O-ring on each of its pins through the chain ends from the inside of the chain. Install an O-ring over the pin ends and fit the side plate with its identification marks facing out; use the chain tool to press the side plate into position.
16 Stake the new link pins using the chain riveting tool, following carefully the instructions of both the chain manufacturer and the tool manufacturer. Refer to *Tools and Workshop Tips* in the Reference section for chain riveting details using a typical commercially available tool.
17 After riveting, check the soft link pin ends for any signs of cracking. If there is any evidence of cracking, the soft link, O-rings and side plate must be removed and the procedure repeated with a new soft link.
18 Install the sprocket cover in a reverse of the removal procedure.

13 Sprockets – check and replacement

1 Set the bike on its centrestand (if equipped) or support it securely upright with the rear wheel off the ground.
2 Whenever the drive chain is inspected, the sprockets should be inspected also. If you are renewing the chain, replace the sprockets as well. Likewise, if the sprockets are in need of replacement, install a new chain also.
3 Remove the engine sprocket cover (see Section 12).
4 Check the wear pattern on the sprockets (see Chapter 1). If the sprocket teeth are worn excessively, replace the chain and sprockets.
5 To remove the rear sprocket, remove the rear wheel (see Chapter 6). Unscrew the self-locking nuts holding the sprocket to the wheel coupling and lift it off. Check the condition of the rubber damper under the rear wheel coupling (see Section 14).
6 To remove the engine sprocket, shift the transmission into gear and have an assistant hold the brake on. Bend back the lockwasher and remove the sprocket nut (see illustrations).

13.6a Bend back the lockwasher and remove the nut; the large lockwasher tab goes in one of the sprocket notches (arrowed) on installation . . .

13.6b . . . the recessed side of the nut faces the sprocket

13.7 Slide the sprocket off the splines and disengage it from the chain

14.2 Lift the sprocket/coupling out of the hub

7 Pull the engine sprocket and chain off the shaft, then separate the sprocket from the chain **(see illustration)**.

8 When installing the engine sprocket, engage it with the chain. Install the mounting plate and tighten the nut to the torque listed in this Chapter's Specifications.

9 Install the engine sprocket cover and the shift pedal (see Chapter 2, Section 21).

10 Use new rear sprocket nuts if the self-locking material in the nuts is worn. Tighten the nuts to the torque listed in this Chapter's Specifications.

14 Rear wheel coupling/rubber damper – check and replacement

1 Remove the rear wheel (see Chapter 6).

2 Lift the collar and sprocket/rear wheel coupling from the wheel **(see illustration)**.

3 Lift the rubber damper segments from the wheel and check them for cracks, hardening and general deterioration. Replace the rubber dampers as a set if necessary.

4 Checking and replacement procedures for the coupling bearing are provided in Chapter 6, Section 13.

5 Installation is the reverse of the removal procedure.

15 Suspension – adjustments

1 The rear spring preload can be adjusted for different riding conditions.

2 Adjust rear spring preload by turning the adjuster on the bottom of the shock absorber. Turn the adjuster with the special wrench included in the bike's tool kit.

Notes

Chapter 6
Brakes, wheels and tyres

Contents

Degrees of difficulty

| Easy, suitable for novice with little experience | | Fairly easy, suitable for beginner with some experience | | Fairly difficult, suitable for competent DIY mechanic | | Difficult, suitable for experienced DIY mechanic | | Very difficult, suitable for expert DIY or professional | |

Specifications

Brakes

Brake fluid type	DOT 4 (or as directed on reservoir cap)
Brake pad minimum thickness	see Chapter 1
Brake disc thickness	
Front	
Standard – 1992-97 UK models, all US models	6.0 mm (0.24 inch)
Standard – 1998-on UK models	5.0 mm (0.20 inch)
Minimum	Refer to marks stamped into the disc
Rear	
Standard	5.0 mm (0.20 inch)
Minimum	Refer to marks stamped into the disc
Disc runout limit	
1992-97 UK models, all US models	0.25 mm (0.010 inch)
1998-on UK models	0.15 mm (0.006 inch)

Wheels and tyres

Wheel runout limit – 1992-95 UK models, 1992-96 US models	
Vertical	2.0 mm (0.08 inch)
Lateral	2.0 mm (0.08 inch)
Wheel runout limit – 1996-on UK models, 1997-on US models	
Vertical	1.0 mm (0.04 inch)
Lateral	0.5 mm (0.02 inch)
Tyre pressures and tread depth	see Daily (pre-ride) checks
Tyre sizes**	
Front	110/80-17 57H
Rear	130/70-18 63H

**Refer to the tyre information/fitment label on the motorcycle (it supersedes information printed here).

Torque settings

Caliper bracket mounting bolts
    1992 to 1997 UK models, all US models . . . . 35 Nm (25 ft-lbs)
    1998-on UK models . . . . 40 Nm (30 ft-lbs)
Front caliper bracket Allen bolt . . . . 23 Nm (17 ft-lbs)
Rear caliper pad retaining bolts . . . . 10 Nm (86 in-lbs)
Front axle . . . . 59 Nm (43 ft-lbs)
Front axle pinch bolts . . . . 20 Nm (168 in-lbs)
Brake disc mounting bolts . . . . 20 Nm (168 in-lbs)
Union (banjo fitting) bolts . . . . 30 Nm (22 ft-lbs)
Master cylinder mounting bolts
    Front . . . . 9 Nm (78 in-lbs)
    Rear . . . . 23 Nm (17 ft-lbs)
Rear axle nut . . . . 105 Nm (75 ft-lbs)
Torque link bolts and nuts
    1992-95 UK models, 1992-96 US models . . . . 30 Nm (22 ft-lbs)
    1996-on UK models, 1997-on US models . . . . 23 Nm (17 ft-lbs)

1 General information

All models covered by this manual use a single (dual on 1998-on UK models), pin-slider front caliper with dual pistons and a single, fixed-mount rear caliper with opposed dual pistons.

All models are equipped with cast aluminium wheels, which require very little maintenance and allow tubeless tyres to be used.

2.1a Remove the nut and detach the reflector from the mount . . .

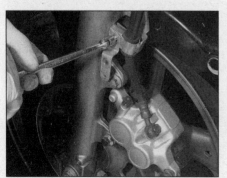

2.1b . . . and unbolt the brake hose bracket from the fork (single disc models . . .

Caution: Disc brake components rarely require disassembly. Do not disassemble components unless absolutely necessary. If any hydraulic brake line connection in the system is loosened, the entire system should be disassembled, drained, cleaned and then properly filled and bled upon reassembly. Do not use solvents on internal brake components. Solvents will cause seals to swell and distort. Use only clean brake fluid, brake system cleaner or alcohol for cleaning. Use care when working with brake fluid as it can injure your eyes and it will damage painted surfaces and plastic parts.

2 Brake pads – replacement

Front caliper

Warning: The dust created by the brake system may contain asbestos, which is harmful to your health. Never blow it out with compressed air and don't inhale any of it. An approved filtering mask should be worn when working on the brakes.

1 Set the bike on its centrestand (if equipped) or prop it securely upright. Remove the nut

2.1c . . . and twin disc models)

and detach the reflector, then unbolt the reflector mount and brake hose bracket **(see illustrations)**.

2 Loosen the caliper lower slider bolt **(see illustrations)**. Remove the caliper mounting bolts, slip the caliper off the disc and remove the lower slider bolt **(see illustration)**.

3 Loosen the caliper bleed valve. Attach a length of hose to the valve and place the free end in a container. This will allow brake fluid to escape when the pistons are pushed into the caliper. Pry the pads apart to make room for the new, thicker pads **(see illustration)**. Push the pistons into the caliper as far as possible, using thumb pressure. If you can't depress the pistons with thumb pressure, try using a G-clamp. If a piston sticks, remove the caliper and overhaul it as described in Section 3. Tighten the bleed valve.

4 Swivel the mounting bracket clear of the caliper and remove the pads **(see illustration)**.

5 Inspect the condition of the pads. If they're worn to the limit listed in the Chapter 1 Specifications (if the wear groove in the pad friction material is worn away), the pads must be replaced. They must also be replaced if

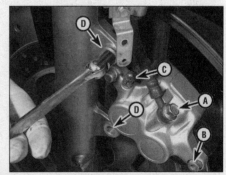

2.2a Loosen the caliper lower slider bolt while the caliper is still installed, then remove the caliper mounting bolts

A Brake hose union bolt
B Caliper lower slider bolt
C Bleed valve
D Mounting bolts (lower bolt removed)

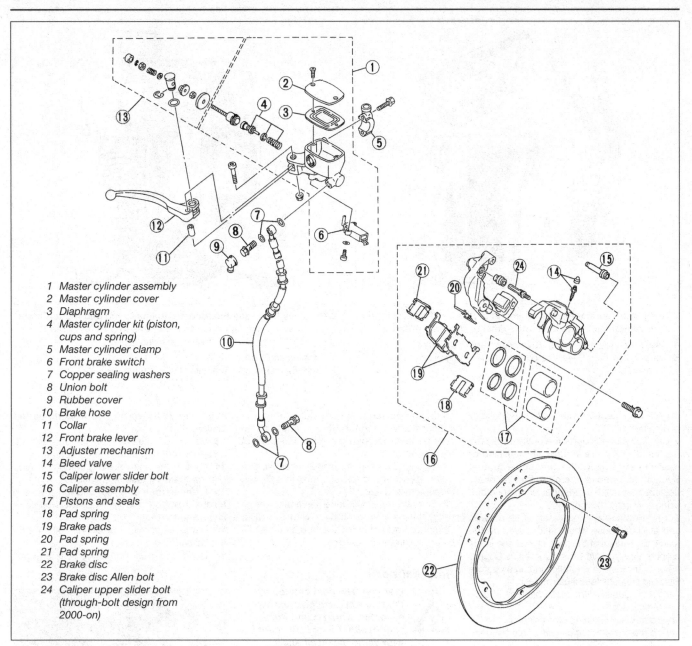

1 Master cylinder assembly
2 Master cylinder cover
3 Diaphragm
4 Master cylinder kit (piston, cups and spring)
5 Master cylinder clamp
6 Front brake switch
7 Copper sealing washers
8 Union bolt
9 Rubber cover
10 Brake hose
11 Collar
12 Front brake lever
13 Adjuster mechanism
14 Bleed valve
15 Caliper lower slider bolt
16 Caliper assembly
17 Pistons and seals
18 Pad spring
19 Brake pads
20 Pad spring
21 Pad spring
22 Brake disc
23 Brake disc Allen bolt
24 Caliper upper slider bolt (through-bolt design from 2000-on)

2.2b Front brake – exploded view

2.2c Remove the caliper lower slider bolt (caliper removed from bike for clarity)

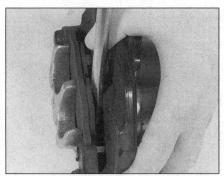

2.3 Pry the pads apart to make room for the new ones (caliper removed from bike for clarity)

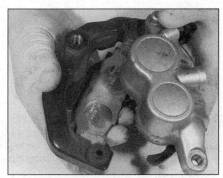

2.4 Remove the pads from the caliper bracket (caliper removed from bike for clarity)

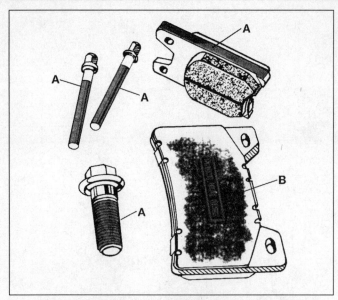

2.7a Special lubricants are required in the UK (and recommended anywhere salt is used on the roads) to prevent corrosion

A   Apply Duckhams Copper 10 or equivalent to the shaded areas
B   Apply Shin-Etsu G-40M or equivalent silicone grease to the shaded areas

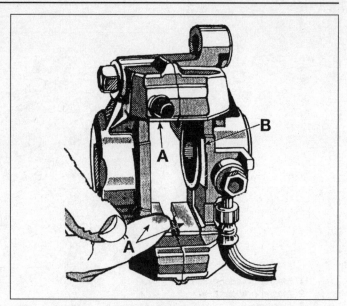

2.7b Apply the recommended lubricants to the pad friction areas inside the caliper and to the exposed portion of the caliper pistons

A   Duckhams Copper 10
B   Shin-Etsu G-40M or equivalent silicone grease

they've been contaminated with oil, grease or brake fluid.

6 Check the condition of the brake discs (see Section 4). If they're in need of machining or replacement, follow the procedure in that Section to remove them. If they're okay, deglaze them with sandpaper or emery cloth, using a swirling motion.

7 The following step is necessary on UK models, and anywhere else where salt is used on the roads, to ensure that the pads move freely in the calipers. Apply a thin film of Duckhams Copper 10 or equivalent to the following areas before installing the pads (see illustrations):

a) To the edges of the metal backing on the brake pads.
b) To the pad retaining pins or bolt(s).
c) To the areas of the caliper where the pads rub.
d) To the threads of the caliper mounting bolts.

Caution: Don't use too much Copper 10 and make sure that none gets on the brake discs or pad friction surfaces.

Apply a thin film of Shin-Etsu G-40M or equivalent silicone grease to the following:

e) Exposed areas of the caliper pistons
f) The areas of the pad backing plates that contact the pistons.

8 Install the pads in the caliper, making sure the pad springs are installed correctly on the caliper and mounting bracket (see illustration 2.2b and the accompanying illustration).

9 Slide the pads into the caliper, making sure the rounded edges of the pads are toward the rear of the motorcycle.

10 If you haven't already lubricated the caliper as described in Step 7, apply a thin coat of multi-purpose grease to the shaft of each slider bolt.

11 Top up the master cylinder reservoir (see Daily (pre-ride) checks) and install the diaphragm and cap.

12 Operate the brake lever several times to bring the pads into contact with the disc. Check the operation of the brakes carefully before riding the motorcycle.

Rear caliper

⚠️ Warning: The dust created by the brake system may contain asbestos, which is harmful to your health. Never blow it out with compressed air and don't inhale any of it. An approved filtering mask should be worn when working on the brakes.

13 Set the bike on its centrestand (if equipped) or support it securely upright.

14 Loosen the pad retaining bolts, but don't remove them yet (see illustrations).

15 Remove the cotter pin and nut from the torque link bolt and pull out the bolt (see illustration 2.14a).

16 Remove the caliper mounting bolts and lift the caliper off the disc.

17 Unscrew the pad retaining bolts and pull

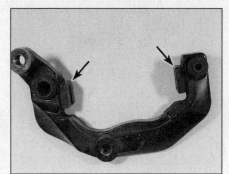

2.8 Make sure the upper and lower springs are installed on the caliper bracket

2.14a Rear caliper mounting details

A   Pad retaining bolts
B   Torque link bolt
C   Mounting bolts
D   Brake hose union bolt
E   Bleed valves

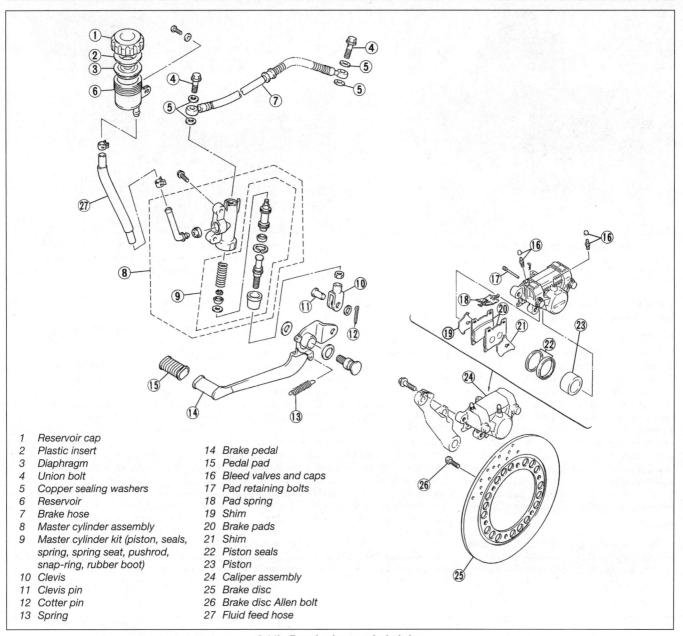

1   Reservoir cap
2   Plastic insert
3   Diaphragm
4   Union bolt
5   Copper sealing washers
6   Reservoir
7   Brake hose
8   Master cylinder assembly
9   Master cylinder kit (piston, seals,
     spring, spring seat, pushrod,
     snap-ring, rubber boot)
10 Clevis
11 Clevis pin
12 Cotter pin
13 Spring

14 Brake pedal
15 Pedal pad
16 Bleed valves and caps
17 Pad retaining bolts
18 Pad spring
19 Shim
20 Brake pads
21 Shim
22 Piston seals
23 Piston
24 Caliper assembly
25 Brake disc
26 Brake disc Allen bolt
27 Fluid feed hose

2.14b Rear brake – exploded view

them out. Remove the pads, shims and pad spring from the caliper **(see illustration)**.

18 Perform Steps 5 through 7 to inspect the pads and disc and prepare the caliper for pad installation.

19 Install the spring, pads and shims in the caliper **(see illustration 2.14b)**. Be sure the spring and shims face in the proper direction.

20 Install the pad retaining bolts and tighten them finger-tight.

21 Install the caliper and tighten its mounting bolts to the torque listed in this Chapter's Specifications. Tighten the pad retaining bolts securely.

22 Install the torque link nut and bolt and tighten them to the torque listed in this

Chapter's Specifications. Secure the nut with a new cotter pin.

3   Brake calipers –
removal, overhaul and
installation

⚠ *Warning: The dust created by the brake system may contain asbestos, which is harmful to your health. Never blow it out with compressed air and don't inhale any of it. An approved filtering mask should be worn when working on the brakes. Do not, under any circumstances, use petroleum-*

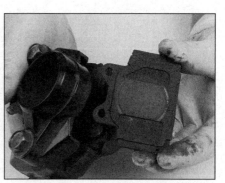

2.17 Slide the pads out of the bottom of the caliper

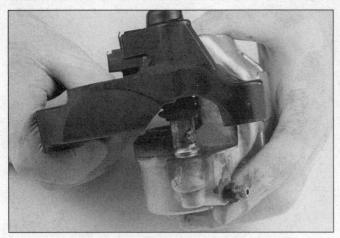

3.4 Separate the caliper bracket from the caliper

3.5 Blow air into the bleed valve hole to force the pistons out, but DO NOT get your fingers in the way; use rags or a piece of wood to catch the pistons

based solvents to clean brake parts. Use brake cleaner or isopropyl alcohol only!

Removal

1 Place the bike on its centrestand (if equipped) or prop it securely upright.
2 Remove the brake hose banjo fitting bolt and separate the hose from the caliper **(see illustration 2.2a or 2.14a)**. Discard the sealing washers. Place the end of the hose in a container and operate the brake lever or pedal to pump out the fluid. Once this is done, wrap a clean shop rag tightly around the hose fitting to soak up any drips and prevent contamination.
3 Refer to the front or rear pad removal procedure in Section 2 to remove the caliper.

Overhaul

4 Clean the exterior of the caliper with brake system cleaner. If you're working on a front caliper, remove the bracket **(see illustration)**.
5 Place a few rags or a piece of wood

between the pistons and the caliper frame to act as a cushion, then use compressed air, directed into the fluid inlet, to remove the pistons **(see illustration)**. Use only enough air pressure to ease the pistons out of the bore. If a piston is blown out, even with the cushion in place, it may be damaged.

 Warning: Never place your fingers in front of the pistons in an attempt to catch or protect them when applying compressed air, as serious injury could occur. If you don't have a compressor, a service station air hose will work. If the pistons won't both come out, push the piston that does come out back into its bore and hold it there with a G-clamp or piece of wood while you blow out the remaining piston.

6 If compressed air isn't available, reconnect the caliper to the brake hose and pump the brake lever or pedal until the pistons are free.
7 Remove the dust seals and piston seals

(see illustrations). Preferably, you should use a wood or plastic tool (such as a toothpick) for this step. If you use a metal tool, be extremely careful not to scratch the bore or nick the grooves.
8 Clean the pistons and the bores with isopropyl alcohol, clean brake fluid or brake system cleaner and blow them dry with filtered, unlubricated compressed air. Inspect the surfaces of the pistons for nicks and burrs and loss of plating. Check the caliper bores, too. If surface defects are present, the caliper must be replaced. If the caliper is in bad shape, the master cylinder should also be checked.
9 Lubricate the piston seals with clean brake fluid and install them in their grooves in the caliper bore. Make sure they aren't twisted and seat completely.
10 Lubricate the dust seals with clean brake fluid and install them in their grooves, making sure they seat correctly.
11 Lubricate the pistons with clean brake

3.7a Remove the dust seal and piston seal from each bore with a pointed tool; this is a front caliper . . .

3.7b . . . and this is a rear caliper

1 Dust seal   2 Piston seal

4.3 Set up a dial gauge to contact the brake disc, then rotate the wheel to check for runout

4.6 Loosen the mounting bolts (arrowed) evenly to detach the brake disc from the wheel

fluid and install them into the caliper bores. Using your thumbs, push the pistons all the way in, making sure they don't get cocked in the bores.

Installation

12 Install the caliper, tightening the mounting bolts to the torque listed in this Chapter's Specifications.

13 Connect the brake hose to the caliper, using new sealing washers on each side of the fitting. Tighten the banjo fitting bolt to the torque listed in this Chapter's Specifications.

14 Fill the master cylinder with the recommended brake fluid (see *Daily (pre-ride) checks*) and bleed the system (see Section 8). Check for leaks.

15 Check the operation of the brakes carefully before riding the motorcycle.

4 Brake discs – inspection, removal and installation

Inspection

1 Set the bike on its centrestand (if equipped) or prop it securely upright.

2 Visually inspect the surface of the disc(s) for score marks and other damage. Light scratches are normal after use and won't affect brake operation, but deep grooves and heavy score marks will reduce braking efficiency and accelerate pad wear. If the discs are badly grooved they must be machined or replaced.

3 To check disc runout, mount a dial gauge to the fork leg or the swingarm, with the plunger touching the surface of the disc near the outer edge **(see illustration)**. Support the wheel being checked off the ground and slowly turn the wheel (if you're checking the front disc on a model equipped with a centrestand, have an assistant sit on the seat to raise the front

wheel off the ground) and watch the gauge needle, comparing your reading with the limit listed in this Chapter's Specifications. If the runout is greater than listed, check the hub bearings for play (see Chapter 1). If the bearings are worn, replace them and repeat this check. If the disc runout is still excessive, it will have to be replaced.

4 The disc must not be machined or allowed to wear down to a thickness less than the minimum allowable thickness, stamped on the disc itself. The thickness of the disc can be checked with a micrometer. If the thickness of the disc is less than the minimum allowable, it must be replaced.

Removal

5 Remove the wheel (see Section 12 for front wheel removal or Section 13 for rear wheel removal).

Caution: Don't lay the wheel down and allow it to rest on the disc – the disc could become warped.

6 Mark the relationship of the disc to the wheel, so it can be installed in the same position. Remove the Allen bolts that retain the disc to the wheel **(see illustration)**. Loosen the bolts a little at a time, in a criss-cross pattern, to avoid distorting the disc.

Caution: The bolts are secured with thread locking agent and can be very difficult to remove. Be careful not to round out the bolt sockets.

7 Take note of any paper shims that may be present where the disc mates to the wheel. If there are any, mark their position and be sure to include them when installing the disc.

Installation

8 Position the disc on the wheel, aligning the previously applied matchmarks (if you're reinstalling the original disc). Make sure the arrow (stamped on the disc) marking the direction of rotation is pointing in the proper direction.

9 Apply a non-hardening thread locking compound to the threads of the bolts. Install the bolts, tightening them a little at a time, in a criss-cross pattern, until the torque listed in this Chapter's Specifications is reached. Clean off all grease from the brake disc using acetone or brake system cleaner.

10 Install the wheel.

11 Operate the brake lever or pedal several times to bring the pads into contact with the disc. Check the operation of the brakes carefully before riding the motorcycle.

5 Front brake master cylinder – removal, overhaul and installation

1 If the master cylinder is leaking fluid, or if the lever does not produce a firm feel when the brake is applied, and bleeding the brakes does not help, master cylinder overhaul is recommended. Before disassembling the master cylinder, read through the entire procedure and make sure that you have the correct rebuild kit. Also, you will need some new, clean brake fluid of the recommended type, some clean rags and internal snap-ring pliers. **Note:** *To prevent damage to the paint from spilled brake fluid, always cover the fuel tank when working on the master cylinder.*

2 Disassembly, overhaul and reassembly of the brake master cylinder must be done in a spotlessly clean work area to avoid contamination and possible failure of the brake hydraulic system components.

Removal

3 Loosen, but do not remove, the screws holding the reservoir cover in place (see *Daily (pre-ride) checks*).

4 Disconnect the electrical connectors from the brake light switch.

5 Pull back the rubber boot, loosen the union bolt and separate the brake hose from the

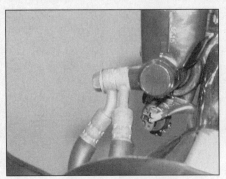

5.5a Pull back the rubber cover, place rags under the fitting to catch brake fluid spills and remove the union bolt . . .

5.5b . . . note that there are two hoses on 1988-on UK models

5.6 Remove the master cylinder mounting bolts (arrowed)

master cylinder (see illustration). On 1998-on UK models (with twin disc brakes) there will be two hoses connected to the master cylinder (see illustration). Wrap the end of the hose in a clean rag and suspend the hose in an upright position or bend it down carefully and place the open end in a clean container. The objective is to prevent excessive loss of brake fluid, fluid spills and system contamination.

6 Remove the master cylinder mounting bolts (see illustration) and separate the master cylinder from the handlebar.

Caution: Do not tip the master cylinder upside down or brake fluid will run out.

Overhaul

7 Remove the locknut and lever pivot bolt, then remove the brake lever (see illustration). Remove the small snap-ring and take the adjuster components off the master cylinder pushrod.

8 Detach the reservoir cover and the rubber diaphragm, then drain the brake fluid into a suitable container. Remove the splash plate

from the bottom of the reservoir (if equipped) (see illustration), then wipe any remaining fluid out of the reservoir with a clean rag.

9 Prevent the pushrod from turning by holding it with a wrench, then unscrew the pushrod nut and remove the washer (see illustration). Carefully remove the rubber dust boot from the end of the piston (see illustration).

10 Using snap-ring pliers, remove the snap-ring and master cylinder pushrod (see illustrations).

11 Slide out the piston assembly, spring seat

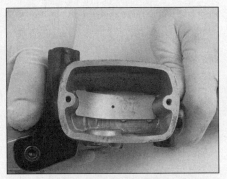

5.7 Remove the snap-ring (left arrow); undo the locknut (right arrow) and unscrew the pivot bolt

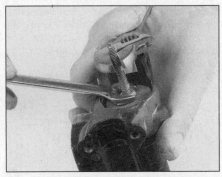

5.8 Lift the splash plate (if equipped) out of the cylinder body so you can clean the fluid ports in the bottom

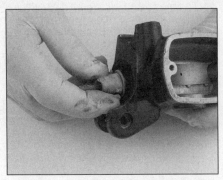

5.9a Hold the pushrod and remove the nut and washer . . .

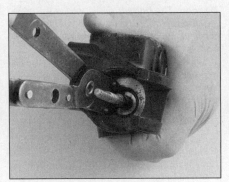

5.9b . . . and remove the rubber boot

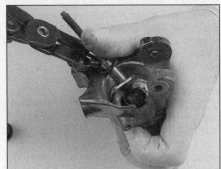

5.10a Remove the snap-ring from the cylinder bore . . .

5.10b . . . then pull out the pushrod . . .

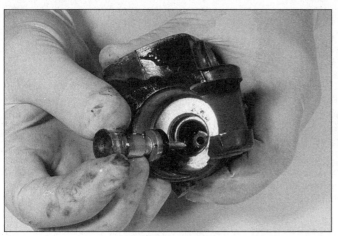

5.11a . . . the piston assembly . . .

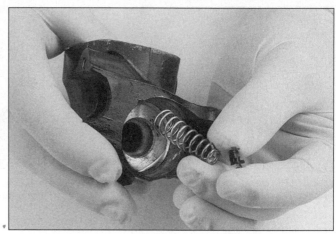

5.11b . . . the spring and spring seat

and spring **(see illustrations)**. Lay the parts out in the proper order to prevent confusion during reassembly.

12 Clean all of the parts with brake system cleaner (available at auto parts stores), isopropyl alcohol or clean brake fluid. *Caution: Do not, under any circumstances, use a petroleum-based solvent to clean brake parts. If compressed air is available, use it to dry the parts thoroughly (make sure it's filtered and unlubricated). Check the master cylinder bore for corrosion, scratches, nicks and score marks. If damage is evident, the master cylinder must be replaced with a new one. If the master cylinder is in poor condition, then the caliper should be checked as well.*

13 Use all of the new parts in the rebuild kit, regardless of the apparent condition of the old ones.

14 Before reassembling the master cylinder, soak the piston and the rubber cup seals in clean brake fluid for ten or fifteen minutes. Lubricate the master cylinder bore with the lubricant supplied in the rebuild kit or with clean brake fluid, then carefully insert the piston and related parts in the reverse order of disassembly. Make sure the lips on the cup seals do not turn inside out when they are slipped into the bore.

15 Depress the piston, then install the snap-ring (make sure the snap-ring is properly seated in the groove). Install the rubber dust boot (make sure the lip is seated properly in the piston groove).

Installation

16 Attach the master cylinder to the handlebar and tighten the bolts to the torque listed in this Chapter's Specifications. Tighten the upper bolt first, then the lower bolt, and don't try to close the gap between the lower end of the bracket and the master cylinder. Overtightening will only break the master cylinder or bracket casting.

17 Connect the brake hose to the master cylinder, using new sealing washers on each side of the union; on 1988-on UK models also use a new sealing washer between the two unions. Tighten the banjo fitting bolt to the torque listed in this Chapter's Specifications. Refer to Section 8 and bleed the air from the system.

6 Rear brake master cylinder – removal, overhaul and installation

1 If the master cylinder is leaking fluid, or if the pedal does not produce a firm feel when the brake is applied, and bleeding the brakes does not help, master cylinder overhaul is recommended. Before disassembling the master cylinder, read through the entire procedure and make sure that you have the correct rebuild kit. Also, you will need some new, clean brake fluid of the recommended type, some clean rags and internal snap-ring pliers.

2 Disassembly, overhaul and reassembly of the brake master cylinder must be done in a spotlessly clean work area to avoid contamination and possible failure of the brake hydraulic system components.

Removal

3 Set the bike on its centrestand (if equipped) or prop it securely upright.

4 Remove the cotter pin from the clevis pin on the master cylinder pushrod **(see illustration 2.14b and the accompanying illustration)**. Remove the clevis pin and washer.

5 Loosen the brake hose union bolt, then remove the Allen bolts that secure the master cylinder to the footpeg bracket **(see illustration)**.

6 If you plan to remove the reservoir, remove its mounting screw.

7 If you don't plan to remove the reservoir, have a container and some rags ready to catch spilling brake fluid. Using a pair of pliers, slide the clamp up the fluid feed hose and detach the hose from the master cylinder. Direct the end of the hose into the container,

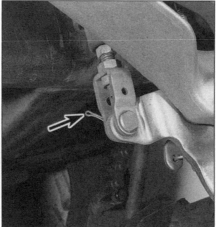

6.4 Pull out the cotter pin (arrowed) and remove the washer and clevis pin

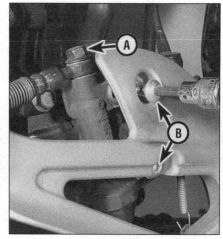

6.5 Loosen the union bolt (A) and remove the mounting bolts (B)

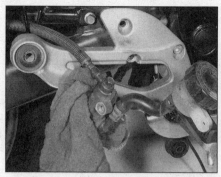

6.8 Lift the master cylinder up and over the footpeg bracket, then undo the union bolt

6.10a Pry the fluid feed hose fitting out of the grommet . . .

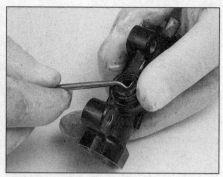

6.10b . . . and pry the grommet out of the master cylinder bore

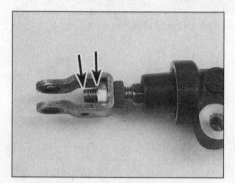

6.11a Measure the length of exposed threads (arrowed) and write it down for use on assembly; this affects brake pedal height

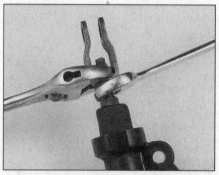

6.11b Hold the clevis, loosen the locknut and unscrew the clevis and nuts from the pushrod . . .

6.11c . . . then remove the rubber boot

unscrew the cap on the master cylinder reservoir and allow the fluid to drain.

8 Lift the master cylinder up to clear the footpeg bracket, then lift it away from the motorcycle (together with the reservoir if it's being removed) **(see illustration)**. Unscrew the union bolt from the master cylinder and discard the sealing washers on each side of the fitting.

9 Remove the master cylinder from the motorcycle.

Overhaul

10 Check for brake fluid leaks at the fluid inlet fitting. If there are signs of leakage, the inlet seal must be replaced. The seal isn't included in the rebuild kit and is not especially easy to replace. To do so, carefully pry the inlet fitting from the master cylinder body, then remove the seal from the fitting bore **(see illustration 2.14b and the accompanying illustrations)**. Install the new seal after the master cylinder body has been cleaned.

11 Note how far onto the pushrod the clevis is threaded **(see illustration)**. This affects brake pedal height adjustment. Hold the clevis with a wrench and loosen the locknut **(see illustration)**. Unscrew the clevis and locknut from the pushrod and carefully remove the rubber dust boot **(see illustration)**.

12 Depress the pushrod and, using snap-ring pliers, remove the snap-ring. Slide out the piston assembly and spring **(see illustrations)**. Lay the parts out in the proper

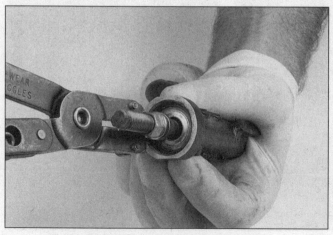

6.12a Remove the snap-ring from the bore . . .

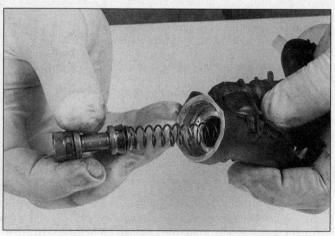

6.12b . . . then remove the piston and spring

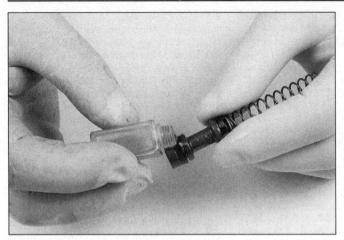

6.15 Lubricate the piston cups with brake fluid or the lubricant supplied in the rebuild kit

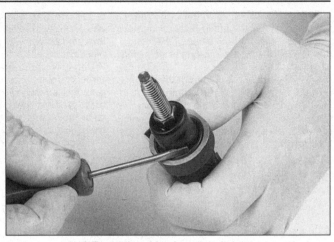

6.16 Push the rubber boot into its groove

order to prevent confusion during reassembly.
13 Clean all of the parts with brake system cleaner (available at auto parts stores), isopropyl alcohol or clean brake fluid. *Caution: Do not, under any circumstances, use a petroleum-based solvent to clean brake parts. If compressed air is available, use it to dry the parts thoroughly (make sure it's filtered and unlubricated). Check the master cylinder bore for corrosion, scratches, nicks and score marks. If damage is evident, the master cylinder must be replaced with a new one. If the master cylinder is in poor condition, then the caliper should be checked as well.*
14 A new piston and spring are included in the rebuild kit. Use them regardless of the condition of the old ones.
15 Before reassembling the master cylinder, soak the piston and the rubber cup seals in clean brake fluid for ten or fifteen minutes. Lubricate the master cylinder bore and the piston seals with the lubricant supplied in the rebuild kit **(see illustration)** or with clean brake fluid, then carefully insert the parts in the reverse order of disassembly. Make sure the lips on the cup seals do not turn inside-out when they are slipped into the bore.
16 Depress the pushrod, then install the snap-ring (make sure the snap-ring is properly seated in the groove). Install the rubber dust boot (make sure the lip is seated properly in the groove) **(see illustration)**.
17 Install the clevis to the end of the pushrod, threading it on the same distance as it was before removal, then tighten the locknut.
18 If the fluid inlet seal was removed, coat a new one with the lubricant supplied in the rebuild kit or with clean brake fluid. Install the seal in the bore, wide end first. Push the inlet fitting into the seal, making sure it seats securely.

Installation

19 Position the master cylinder on the footpeg bracket and tighten its mounting bolts.

20 Connect the banjo fitting to the top of the master cylinder, using a new sealing washer on each side of the fitting. Tighten the banjo fitting bolt to the torque listed in this Chapter's Specifications.
21 Connect the fluid feed hose to the inlet fitting and install the hose clamp.
22 Connect the clevis to the brake pedal and secure the clevis pin with a new cotter pin.
23 Attach the reservoir and tighten its mounting screw (if it was removed). Fill the fluid reservoir with the specified fluid (see *Daily (pre-ride) checks*) and bleed the system following the procedure in Section 8.
24 Check the position of the brake pedal (see Chapter 1) and adjust it if necessary. Check the operation of the brakes carefully before riding the motorcycle.

7 Brake hoses – inspection and replacement

Inspection

1 Once a week, or if the motorcycle is used less frequently, before every ride, check the condition of the brake hoses.
2 Twist and flex the rubber hoses while looking for cracks, bulges and seeping fluid. Check extra carefully around the areas where the hoses connect with the banjo fittings, as these are common areas for hose failure.
3 Inspect the metal banjo fittings connected to brake hoses. If the plating on the metal tubes is chipped or scratched, the lines may rust. If the fittings are rusted, scratched or cracked, replace them.

Replacement

4 The brake hoses have banjo fittings on each end of the hose. Cover the surrounding area with plenty of rags and unscrew the banjo bolt on each end of the hose. If you're working on the front brake hose, detach the hose bracket from the lower triple clamp **(see illustrations)**, as well as from the retainer on the front fork. Note that the rear brake hose passes through a guide on the brake torque link.
5 Position the new hose, making sure it isn't twisted or otherwise strained, between the two components, routing it through any guides provided. Make sure the metal tube portion of the banjo fitting is located between the protrusions on the component it's connected to, if equipped. In some cases, there's a cast lug (on caliper bodies, for example) that keeps the brake hose from

7.4a Unbolt the brake hose retainer from the lower triple clamp (single disc models . . .

7.4b . . . and twin disc models)

spinning clockwise as the banjo bolt is tightened. Install the banjo bolts, using new sealing washers on both sides of the fittings, and tighten them to the torque listed in this Chapter's Specifications.

6 Flush the old brake fluid from the system, refill the system with the recommended fluid (see Specifications) and bleed the air from the system (see Section 8). Check the operation of the brakes carefully before riding the motorcycle.

8 Brake system - bleeding

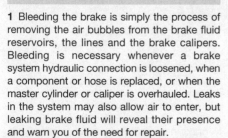

1 Bleeding the brake is simply the process of removing the air bubbles from the brake fluid reservoirs, the lines and the brake calipers. Bleeding is necessary whenever a brake system hydraulic connection is loosened, when a component or hose is replaced, or when the master cylinder or caliper is overhauled. Leaks in the system may also allow air to enter, but leaking brake fluid will reveal their presence and warn you of the need for repair.

2 To bleed the brakes, you will need some new, clean brake fluid of the recommended type (see Specifications), a length of clear vinyl or plastic tubing, a small container partially filled with clean brake fluid, some rags and a wrench to fit the brake caliper bleeder valves.

3 Cover the fuel tank and other painted components to prevent damage in the event that brake fluid is spilled.

4 Remove the reservoir cap or cover and *slowly* pump the brake lever or pedal a few times, until no air bubbles can be seen floating up from the holes at the bottom of the reservoir.

5 Slip a box-end wrench (ring spanner) over the caliper bleed valve. Attach one end of the clear vinyl or plastic tubing to the bleeder valve and submerge the other end in the brake fluid in the container **(see illustration)**.

6 Remove the reservoir cap or cover and check the fluid level. Do not allow the fluid level to drop below the lower mark during the bleeding process.

7 Carefully pump the brake lever or pedal three or four times and hold it. Open the caliper bleed valve. When the valve is opened, brake fluid will flow out of the caliper into the clear tubing and the lever will move toward the handlebar or the pedal will move down.

8 Retighten the bleeder valve, then release the brake lever or pedal gradually. Repeat the process until no air bubbles are visible in the brake fluid leaving the caliper and the lever or pedal is firm when applied. **Note:** *On rear calipers with two bleed valves or dual front brake calipers, air must be bled from both, one after the other. Remember to add fluid to the reservoir as the level drops. Use only new, clean brake fluid of the recommended type. Never reuse the fluid lost during bleeding.*

9 Replace the reservoir cover or cap, wipe up any spilled brake fluid and check the entire system for leaks.

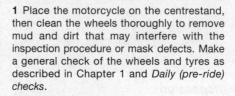

HAYNES HiNT *If bleeding is difficult, it may be necessary to let the brake fluid in the system stabilise for a few hours (it may be aerated). Repeat the bleeding procedure when the tiny bubbles in the system have floated out.*

9 Wheels - inspection and repair

1 Place the motorcycle on the centrestand, then clean the wheels thoroughly to remove mud and dirt that may interfere with the inspection procedure or mask defects. Make a general check of the wheels and tyres as described in Chapter 1 and *Daily (pre-ride) checks*.

2 With the motorcycle on the centrestand (if equipped) or supported securely upright and the wheel in the air, attach a dial gauge to the fork slider or the swingarm and position the stem against the side of the rim **(see illustration)**. Spin the wheel slowly and check the side-to-side (lateral) runout of the rim, then compare your readings with the value listed in this Chapter's Specifications. In order to accurately check radial runout with the dial gauge, the wheel would have to be removed from the machine and the tyre removed from the wheel. With the axle clamped in a vice, the wheel can be rotated to check the runout.

3 An easier, though slightly less accurate, method is to attach a stiff wire pointer to the fork slider or the swingarm and position the end a fraction of an inch from the wheel (where the wheel and tyre join). If the wheel is true, the distance from the pointer to the rim will be constant as the wheel is rotated. Repeat the procedure to check the runout of the rear wheel. **Note:** *If wheel runout is excessive, check the wheel bearings very carefully before replacing the wheel*.

4 The wheels should also be visually inspected for cracks, flat spots on the rim and other damage. Since tubeless tyres are fitted, look very closely for dents in the area where the tyre bead contacts the rim. Dents in this area may prevent complete sealing of the tyre against the rim, which leads to deflation of the tyre over a period of time.

5 If damage is evident, or if runout in either direction is excessive, the wheel will have to be replaced with a new one. Never attempt to repair a damaged cast aluminium wheel.

10 Wheels - alignment check

1 Misalignment of the wheels, which may be due to a cocked rear wheel or a bent frame or triple clamps, can cause strange and possibly

8.5 Loosen the bleed valve to release fluid

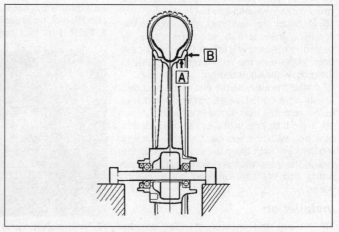

9.2 Check the wheel for out-of-round (A) and lateral movement (B)

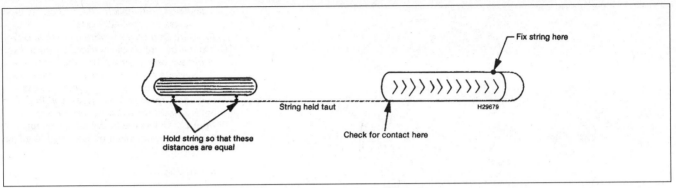

10.5 Wheel alignment check using string

serious handling problems. If the frame or triple clamps are at fault, repair by a frame specialist or replacement with new parts are the only alternatives.

2 To check the alignment you will need an assistant, a length of string or a perfectly straight piece of wood and a ruler graduated

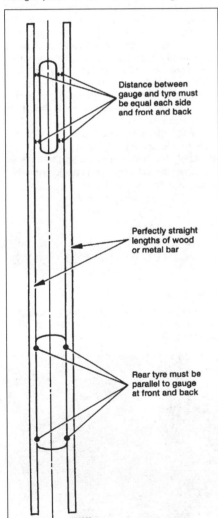

Distance between gauge and tyre must be equal each side and front and back

Perfectly straight lengths of wood or metal bar

Rear tyre must be parallel to gauge at front and back

10.7 Wheel alignment check using a straight-edge

in 1/64 inch increments. A plumb bob or other suitable weight will also be required.

3 Place the motorcycle on the centrestand, then measure the width of both tyres at their widest points. Subtract the smaller measurement from the larger measurement, then divide the difference by two. The result is the amount of offset that should exist between the front and rear tyres on both sides.

4 If a string is used, have your assistant hold one end of it about half way between the floor and the rear axle, touching the rear sidewall of the tyre.

5 Run the other end of the string forward and pull it tight so that it is roughly parallel to the floor. Slowly bring the string into contact with the front sidewall of the rear tyre, then turn the front wheel until it is parallel with the string. Measure the distance from the front tyre sidewall to the string (see illustration).

6 Repeat the procedure on the other side of the motorcycle. The distance from the front tyre sidewall to the string should be equal on both sides.

7 As was previously pointed out, a perfectly straight length of wood may be substituted for the string (see illustration). The procedure is the same.

8 If the distance between the string and tyre is greater on one side, or if the rear wheel appears to be cocked, refer to Chapter 5, Swingarm bearings – check, and make sure the swingarm is tight.

9 If the front-to-back alignment is correct, the

wheels still may be out of alignment vertically.

10 Using the plumb bob, or other suitable weight, and a length of string, check the rear wheel to make sure it is vertical. To do this, hold the string against the tyre upper sidewall and allow the weight to settle just off the floor. When the string touches both the upper and lower tyre sidewalls and is perfectly straight, the wheel is vertical. If it isn't, place thin spacers under one leg of the centrestand.

11 Once the rear wheel is vertical, check the front wheel in the same manner. If both wheels are not perfectly vertical, the frame and/or major suspension components are bent.

11 Front wheel – removal and installation

Removal

1 Place the motorcycle on the centrestand (if equipped) or support it securely upright, then raise the front wheel off the ground by placing a floor jack, with a wood block on the jack head, under the engine.

2 Disconnect the speedometer cable from the drive unit (see Chapter 8).

3 Remove the brake caliper(s) and support it with a piece of wire. Don't disconnect the brake hose from the caliper.

4 Remove the axle clamp bolts (see illustrations). On 1992 to 1997 UK models

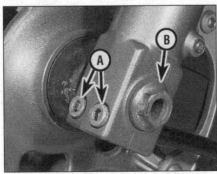

11.4a Axle clamp bolts (A) and axle head (B) – 1992-97 UK models and all US models

11.4b Axle clamp bolt and axle head – 1998-on UK models

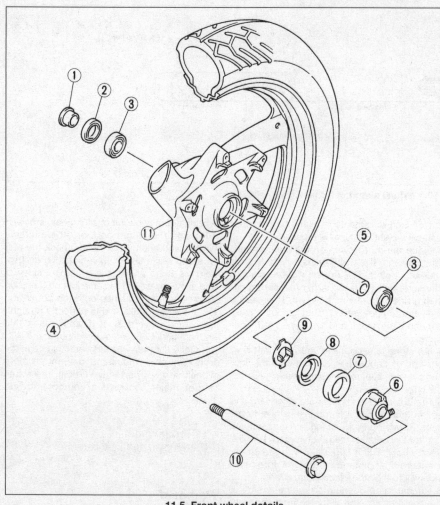

11.5 Front wheel details

1	Collar	7	Grease seal
2	Grease seal	8	Speedometer clutch
3	Wheel bearing		retainer
4	Tire	9	Speedometer clutch
5	Spacer	10	Axle*
6	Speedometer drive unit	11	Front wheel

*Note that the axle passes through the hub from the other side on 1998-on UK models

unscrewed from the left side, and on 1998-on UK models from the right side.

Caution: Don't lay the wheel down and allow it to rest on the brake disc – the disc could become warped. Roll the axle on a flat surface such as a piece of plate glass. If it's bent at all, replace it. If the axle is corroded, remove the corrosion with fine emery cloth. Note: Do not operate the front brake lever with the wheel removed.

6 Check the condition of the wheel bearings (see Section 13).

Installation

7 Installation is the reverse of removal. Be sure the collar is in place on the right side of the wheel **(see illustration)**. Apply a thin coat of grease to the seal lip, then slide the axle into the hub. Position the speedometer drive unit in the left side of the hub (if it was removed), then slide the wheel into place. Make sure the lugs in the speedometer drive clutch line up with the notches in the speedometer drive unit **(see illustration)**. Make sure the protrusion on the inner side of the left fork fits into the notch in the speedometer drive unit **(see illustration)**. If the disc won't slide between the brake pads, carefully pry them apart with a piece of wood.

8 Slip the axle into place from the left side (1992 to 1997 UK models and all US models) or right side (1998-on UK models) and tighten it to the torque listed in this Chapter's Specifications.

9 Tighten the axle pinch bolts to the torque listed in this Chapter's Specifications.

10 Apply the front brake, pump the forks up and down several times and check for binding and proper brake operation.

12 Rear wheel – removal and installation

Removal

1 Set the bike on its centrestand (if equipped) or prop it securely upright with the rear wheel off the ground.

and all US models, there are two axle clamp bolts in the left fork leg; 1998-on UK models have a single clamp bolt in the right fork leg.

5 Support the wheel, then unscrew the axle and pull it out and carefully lower the wheel **(see illustration)**. On 1992 to 1997 UK models and all US models the axle is

11.7a There's a collar in the right side grease seal

11.7b Align the lugs on the speedometer clutch with the slots in the drive unit (arrowed)

11.7c Align the fork leg protrusion with the notch in the speedometer drive unit (arrowed)

2 Remove the chain guard (see Chapter 1 if necessary).

3 Remove the cotter pin from the axle nut and loosen the nut (see the chain adjustment section of Chapter 1).

4 Fully loosen both drive chain adjusters.

5 Push the rear wheel as far forward as possible. Lift the top of the chain up off the rear sprocket and pull it to the left while rotating the wheel backwards. This will disengage the chain from the sprocket.

 Warning: Don't let your fingers slip between the chain and the sprocket.

6 Unscrew the axle nut **(see illustration)**.

7 Support the wheel and slide the axle out. Lower the wheel and remove it from the swingarm, being careful not to lose the spacers on either side of the hub. Slide the disc out from between the brake pads.

Caution: Don't lay the wheel down and allow it to rest on the disc or the sprocket – they could become warped. Set the wheel on wood blocks so the disc or the sprocket doesn't support the weight of the wheel. Don't operate the brake pedal with the wheel removed.

8 Before installing the wheel, check the axle for straightness by rolling it on a flat surface such as a piece of plate glass (if the axle is corroded, first remove the corrosion with fine emery cloth). If the axle is bent at all, replace it.

9 Check the condition of the wheel bearings and renew them if necessary (see Section 13).

Installation

10 Apply a thin coat of grease to the seal lips, then slide the spacers into their proper positions on the sides of the hub.

11 Slide the wheel into place, making sure the brake disc slides between the brake pads. If it doesn't, spread the pads apart with a piece of wood.

12 Pull the chain up over the sprocket, raise the wheel and install the axle and axle nut. Don't tighten the axle nut yet.

13 Adjust the chain slack (see Chapter 1) and tighten the adjuster locknuts.

14 Tighten the axle nut to the torque listed in this Chapter's Specifications. Install a new cotter pin, tightening the axle nut an additional amount, if necessary, to align the hole in the axle with the castellations on the nut. Be sure to bend the cotter pin correctly (see *Drive chain and sprockets – check, adjustment and lubrication* in Chapter 1).

15 Check the operation of the rear brake carefully before riding the motorcycle.

13 Wheel bearings – inspection and maintenance

1 Remove the wheel. See Section 11 (front wheel) or Section 12 (rear wheel).

2 Set the wheel down on wood blocks so it doesn't rest on the brake disc(s) or sprocket.

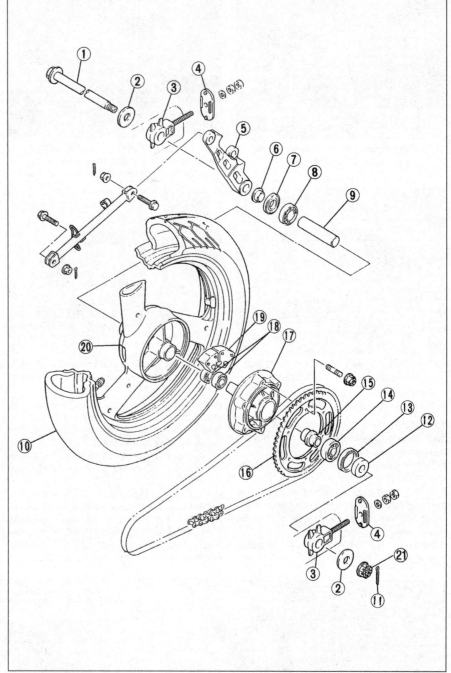

12.6 Rear wheel details

1 Axle	12 Collar
2 Plate washer	13 Grease seal
3 Chain adjuster	14 Coupling bearing
4 End plate	15 Collar
5 Caliper bracket	16 Rear sprocket
6 Collar	17 Rear wheel coupling
7 Grease seal	18 Rear wheel bearings (left side)
8 Rear wheel bearing (right side)	19 Damper segments
9 Spacer	20 Rear wheel
10 Tire	21 Axle nut
11 Cotter pin	

13.3 Pry out the grease seal on the right side of the wheel

13.5 Pry out the seal on the left side of the wheel and remove the speedometer clutch retainer and the speedometer clutch

13.6a Tap out the bearing on the opposite side with a drift

13.6b Pull out the spacer (arrowed) and drive out the remaining bearing

13.9 Fill the bearing with grease, working it into the spaces between the bearing balls

13.10a Place the bearing in position with the sealed side facing out . . .

Front wheel bearings

3 From the right side of the wheel, lift out the collar (see illustration 11.7a) and pry out the grease seal (see illustration).

4 From the left side of the wheel, lift out the speedometer drive unit.

5 From the left side of the wheel, pry out the grease seal, then lift out the speedometer clutch retainer and speedometer clutch (see illustration).

6 Using a metal rod (preferably a brass drift punch) inserted through the centre of the hub bearing, tap evenly around the inner race of the opposite bearing to drive it from the hub (see illustration). The bearing spacer will also come out (see illustration).

7 Lay the wheel on its other side and remove the remaining bearing using the same technique.

8 Clean the bearings with a high flash-point solvent (one which won't leave any residue) and blow them dry with compressed air (don't let the bearings spin as you dry them). Apply a few drops of oil to the bearing. Hold the outer race of the bearing and rotate the inner race – if the bearing doesn't turn smoothly, has rough spots or is noisy, replace it with a new assembly.

9 If the bearing checks out okay and will be reused, wash it in solvent once again and dry it, then pack the bearing with high-quality bearing grease (see illustration).

10 Thoroughly clean the hub area of the wheel. Install one of the bearings into the recess in the hub, with the marked or sealed side facing out (see illustration). Using a bearing driver or a socket large enough to contact the outer race of the bearing, drive it in until it's completely seated (see illustration).

13.10b . . . and drive it in with a socket or bearing driver the same diameter as the bearing outer race; if pressure is applied to the sealed area or inner race, the bearing will be ruined

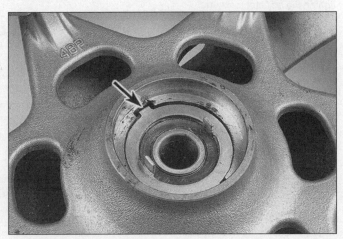

13.11 Position the speedometer clutch inner tab in the slot of the wheel (arrowed)

13.15a Remove the collar from the coupling . . .

13.15b . . . and pry out the grease seal

13.16 Remove the coupling collar; don't forget to install it later or the bearings will be ruined

13.17a Tap the old bearing out of the coupling . . .

13.17b . . . place the new bearing in the coupling . . .

13.17c . . . and install the bearing with a bearing driver or a socket the same diameter as the bearing outer race

11 Turn the wheel over and install the bearing spacer and bearing, driving the bearing into place as described in Step 10. Install the speedometer clutch and retainer on the left side of the wheel **(see illustration)**.

12 Install new grease seals, using a seal driver, large socket or a flat piece of wood to drive them into place.

13 Install the speedometer drive unit, making sure the lugs in the speedometer clutch align with the notches in the gear **(see illustration 11.7b)**.

14 Clean off all grease from the brake disc(s) using acetone or brake system cleaner. Install the wheel.

Rear coupling bearing

15 Lift the collar from the coupling on the sprocket side of the wheel **(see illustration 12.6 and the accompanying illustration)**. Pry out the grease seal **(see illustration)**.

16 Lift the sprocket and coupling out of the wheel and turn them over. Remove the coupling collar (tap it out if necessary) **(see illustration)**.

17 Spin the coupling bearing inner race. If It's rough, loose or noisy, drive the bearing out with a drift **(see illustration)**. Drive a new one in with a bearing driver or socket that bears against the outer race, then drive in a new grease seal **(see illustrations)**.

Rear wheel bearings

18 If you haven't already done so, remove the collar from the right side of the wheel **(see illustration)** and the sprocket and coupling from the left side. Pry the grease seal out of the right side **(see illustration 13.3)**.

19 Insert a drift through the right bearing and tap out the bearings on the left side **(see illustrations)**. There are two bearings on the left side of the wheel and one on the right. Remove the spacer. **Note:** *There's just enough room to tilt the drift far enough to catch the edge of the inner left bearing when you're driving the bearings out. If the drift keeps glancing off the edge of the bearing, try*

13.18 Lift the collar out of the brake disc side of the wheel

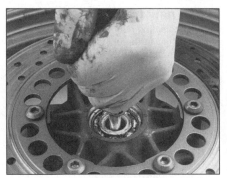

13.19a Drive out the bearings with a drift . . .

13.19b . . . and take out the spacer

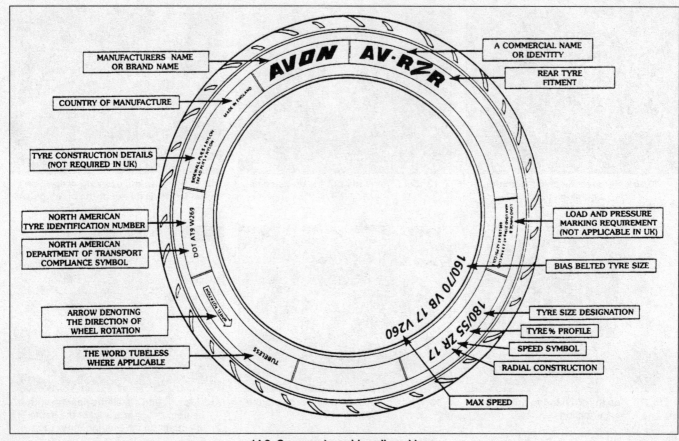

14.3 Common tyre sidewall markings

grinding its end so it has sharp corners. Another method is to use a slide-hammer with blind hole puller to pull the bearings out.

20 Turn the wheel over and tap out the bearing(s) on the opposite side.

21 Perform Steps 8 and 9 to inspect the bearings.

22 Install the bearings with their sealed sides facing out. Use a bearing driver or socket the same diameter as the outer race of the bearing.

23 Install the grease seals and collars.

24 Install the coupling to the wheel, making sure the coupling collar is in place.

Caution: If the coupling collar is left out, the rear wheel bearings will be damaged when the axle nut is tightened.

14 Tyres –
general information and fitting

General information

1 The wheels fitted to all models are designed to take tubeless tyres.

2 Refer to the 'Daily (pre-ride) checks' at the beginning of this manual, and to the scheduled checks in Chapter 1 for tyre and wheel maintenance. Tyre sizes are given in the Specifications at the beginning of this Chapter.

Fitting new tyres

3 When selecting new tyres, refer to the tyre options listed in the owners handbook or on tyre information sticker on the motorcycle.

Ensure that front and rear tyre types are compatible, the correct size and correct speed rating; if necessary seek advice from a Yamaha dealer or tyre fitting specialist **(see illustration)**.

4 It is recommended that tyres are fitted by a motorcycle tyre specialist rather than attempted in the home workshop. The force required to break the seal between the wheel rim and tyre bead is substantial, and is usually beyond the capabilities of an individual working with normal tyre levers. Additionally, the specialist will be able to balance the wheels after tyre fitting and provide new valves.

5 Only certain types of puncture repair are suitable for tubeless motorcycle tyres. Refer to a tyre fitting specialist for advice and to your owner's manual for details of the reduced speeds advised for a repaired tyre.

Chapter 7
Fairings and bodywork

Contents

Degrees of difficulty

Easy, suitable for novice with little experience		**Fairly easy,** suitable for beginner with some experience		**Fairly difficult,** suitable for competent DIY mechanic		**Difficult,** suitable for experienced DIY mechanic		**Very difficult,** suitable for expert DIY or professional	

1 General information

This Chapter covers the procedures necessary to remove and install the fairings and other body parts for service access. Since many service and repair operations on these motorcycles require removal of the fairings or other body parts, the procedures are grouped here and referred to from other Chapters.

In the event of damage to the fairings or other body parts, it is usually necessary to remove the broken component and replace it with a new (or used) one. The material that the fairings are composed of doesn't lend itself to conventional repair techniques. There are, however, some shops that specialise in 'plastic welding', so it would be advantageous to check around first before throwing the damaged part away.

2 Seat - removal and installation

1 Turn the seat lock counterclockwise (anti-clockwise) with the key.
2 Pull the seat back and up to disengage its mounting tabs **(see illustration)**. Lift the seat out.
3 Installation is the reverse of the removal steps.

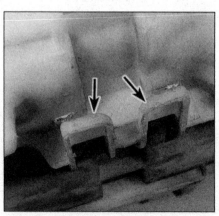

2.2 Pull the seat back and up to disengage the tab at the front of the seat

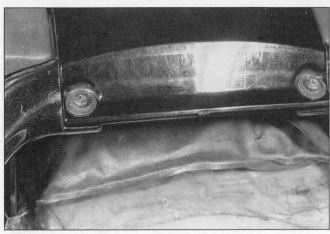

3.3a Remove the tail cover screws . . .

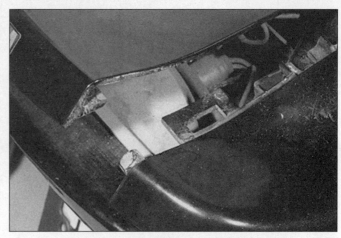

3.3b . . . and disengage the tabs at the rear

3 Tail cover, grab bars and side covers - removal and installation

1992-95 UK models, 1992-96 US models

1 Set the bike on its centrestand (if equipped) or prop it securely upright.
2 Remove the seat (see Section 2).
3 Remove the tail cover screws (see illustration). Lift the tail cover slightly up at the front and pull it back to remove it (see illustration).
4 Unbolt the grab bars (see illustration). Remove the screw from each side which retains the side covers to the frame.
5 Lift the lower edges of the side covers to disengage the tabs and pull gently to disengage the post from the grommet (see illustrations), then remove the side cover.
6 Installation is the reverse of the removal steps.

1996-on UK models, 1997-on US models

7 Set the bike on its stand.
8 Remove the seat (see Section 2).
9 Remove its two screws and detach the tail cover, disengaging its tabs with the side covers and easing it rearwards (see illustrations).
10 At this point either side cover can be removed independently from the other. Unbolt the grab bars (see illustrations).

3.4 Remove the grab bar bolts

3.5a Disengage the side cover tabs . . .

3.5b . . . and posts (arrowed)

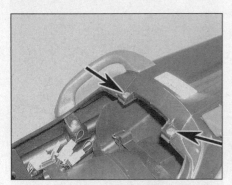

3.9a The tail cover is retained by two screws (arrowed)

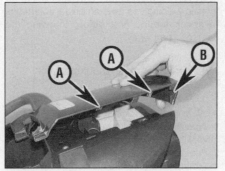

3.9b The hooks (A) engage the side cover slots and the cutout (B) engages the screw head

3.10a Remove the grab bar two screws (arrowed) . . .

3.10b . . . and remove it from the side cover

3.11a Side cover retaining screws (arrowed)

3.11b Front fillet is held by two grommets (arrowed) . . .

11 Each side cover is retained by two screws **(see illustration)**. The side cover front fillets are retained by two grommets and a hook **(see illustrations)**.
12 Installation is the reverse of the removal steps.

3 Remove the fairing mounting screws and rubber washers **(see illustrations)**. Lower the fairing away from the motorcycle.
4 Installation is the reverse of the removal steps.

one below the headlight assembly and two on each side of the fairing **(see illustrations)**. Note the positions of the mounting grommets. If you're working on a 1993-95 UK model, remove the windscreen and the inner fairing.
2 Installation is the reverse of the removal steps.

4 Lower fairing (belly pan) - removal and installation (XJ600S)

Note: A lower fairing is optional on XJ600S models.
1 Support the motorcycle securely upright.
2 Support the fairing from below so it won't fall on the ground and be scratched.

5 Upper fairing - removal and installation (XJ600S)

1992-95 UK models, 1992-96 US models

1 Remove the fairing fasteners; there are two that also secure the base of the windshield,

1996-on UK models, 1997-on US models

3 Remove the fuel tank (see Chapter 3). Although fuel tank removal is not absolutely necessary, it is advised in case of damage to its paintwork.
4 Remove the six screws retaining the

3.11c . . . and a hook on the inside

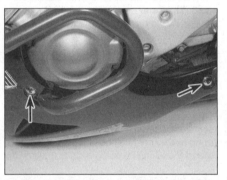

4.3a With the fairing supported from below, remove the mounting fasteners on each side (arrowed) . . .

4.3b . . . and remove the rubber washers

5.1a Remove the two screws below the windshield . . .

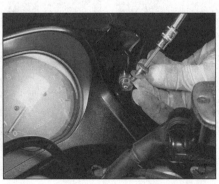

5.1b . . . an Allen bolt at each side of the fairing near the front . . .

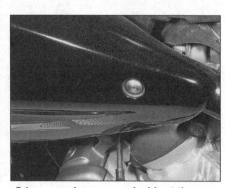

5.1c . . . and one on each side at the rear

5.4a Remove the six screws (arrowed) . . .

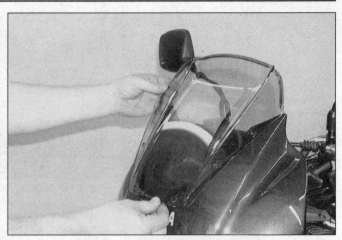

5.4b . . . and remove the windshield

5.5a Ease the rubber expanders out of the fairing

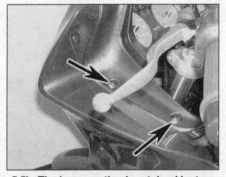

5.5b The inner section is retained by two screws (arrowed) on each side

5.5c Remove the inner section from the fairing

windshield and carefully lift the windshield off the fairing **(see illustrations)**.
5 Ease the six rubber expanders out of the windshield mounting points in the fairing **(see illustration)**. Remove the four bolts which retain the fairing inner section (two on each side) and manoeuvre the inner section free from the fairing **(see illustrations)**.
6 Reach inside the fairing and trace the turn

signal wiring to the bullet connectors. Disconnect them and unscrew the nuts which retains the turn signals to the fairing. Thread the nut off the wires and remove each turn signal assembly **(see illustrations)**.
7 The fairing is retained to its stay by six bolts **(see illustrations)**. Have an assistant hold the fairing as the mounting bolts are removed, then extend the fairing forwards slightly to allow the

wiring from the headlight and parking light (UK models) to be disconnected **(see illustration)**.
8 Installation is the reverse of the removal steps.
9 If required, the fairing stay can be detached from the frame after the instruments have been removed. It is retained to the headstock by two bolts and to the frame top tube by a bolt on each side **(see illustrations)**.

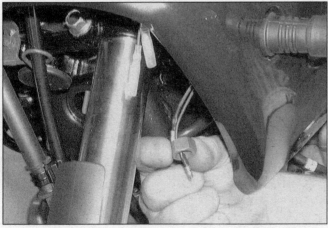

5.6a Thread the nut off the turn signal wiring . . .

5.6b . . . and withdraw the turn signal from the fairing

5.7a The fairing is retained at the front by two screws (arrowed) . . .

5.7b . . . a screw on each side (arrowed) . . .

5.7c . . . and a screw on each top edge (arrowed)

5.7d Manoeuvre the fairing forwards, splaying its sides out to clear the turn signal mounts

5.9a Fairing stay is mounted by two bolts at the headstock (arrowed) . . .

5.9b . . . and by a bolt to the frame top tube on each side (arrowed)

Notes

Chapter 8
Electrical system

Contents

Degrees of difficulty

Easy, suitable for novice with little experience	**Fairly easy,** suitable for beginner with some experience	**Fairly difficult,** suitable for competent DIY mechanic 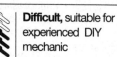	**Difficult,** suitable for experienced DIY mechanic	**Very difficult,** suitable for expert DIY or professional

Specifications

Battery
Type .... Maintenance free
Capacity 12V, 8Ah

Fuses
Main .... 30 amps
Headlight .... 15 amps
Signal .... 15 amps (1992-96 UK, all US), 10 amp (1997-on UK)
Hazard (1997-on UK models) .... 10 amps
Ignition .... 10 amps
Spares .... one 30-amp, one 15-amp, one 10-amp

Starter motor
Starter commutator diameter
    Standard .... 28 mm (1.1 inch)
    Minimum .... 27 mm (1.06 inch)
Starter brush length
    Standard .... 12.5 mm (0.49 inch)
    Minimum .... 4.0 mm (0.16 inch)
Starter relay resistance .... 3.9 to 4.7 ohms at 20°C (68°F)

Alternator

No-load regulated voltage
1992-95 UK models, all US models	14.3 to 15.3 volts at 5000 rpm
1996-97 UK models	14.2 to 15.2 volts at 5000 rpm
1998-on UK models	14.1 to 14.9 volts at 5000 rpm

Nominal output
1992-95 UK models, all US models	14 volts, 21 amps at 5000 rpm
1996-on UK models	14 volts, 20 amps at 5000 rpm

Stator coil resistance
1992-95 UK models, all US models	0.32 to 0.48 ohms at 20°C (68°F)
1996-on UK models	0.24 to 0.36 ohms at 20°C (68°F)

Bulbs

Headlight	60/55W
Parking (auxiliary) light – UK only	4W
Tail/stop light	5/21W
Licence plate light – UK only	5W

Turn signal lights
US	
Front (with running light)	27/8W
Rear	27W
UK	21W
Meter lights	1.7W
Neutral, oil level, turn signal and high beam lights	3.4W

Torque settings

Neutral switch screws	3.5 Nm (35 in-lbs)*
Alternator	
Rotor bolt	80 Nm (58 ft-lbs)
Cover Allen bolts	10 Nm (86 in-lbs)
Starter mounting bolts	10 Nm (86 in-lbs)
Regulator/rectifier Allen bolts	7 Nm (61 in-lbs)

Apply non-permanent thread locking agent to the threads.

1 General information

The machines covered by this manual are equipped with a 12-volt electrical system.

The regulator/rectifier maintains the charging system output within the specified range to prevent overcharging and converts the AC (alternating current) output of the alternator to DC (direct current) to power the lights and other components and to charge the battery.

The alternator uses permanent magnets mounted in the rotor; the rotor, mounted at the top of the engine case, is turned by the starter clutch shaft.

An electric starter mounted to the engine case behind the cylinders is standard equipment. The starting system includes the motor, the battery, the solenoid and the various wires and switches. On models equipped with a sidestand switch and clutch switch, if the engine kill switch and the main key switch are both in the On position, the circuit relay allows the starter motor to operate only if the transmission is in Neutral (Neutral switch on) or the clutch lever is pulled to the handlebar (clutch switch on) and the sidestand is up (sidestand switch on).

Note: *Keep in mind that electrical parts, once purchased, can't be returned. To avoid unnecessary expense, make very sure the faulty component has been positively identified before buying a replacement part.*

2 Electrical fault finding

Warning: To prevent the risk of short circuits, the ignition (main) switch must always be 'OFF' and the battery negative (-ve) terminal should be disconnected before any of the bike's other electrical components are disturbed. Don't forget to reconnect the terminal securely once work is finished or if battery power is needed for circuit testing.

A typical electrical circuit consists of an electrical component, the switches, relays, etc. related to that component and the wiring and connectors that hook the component to both the battery and the frame. To aid in locating a problem in any electrical circuit, complete wiring diagrams of each model are included at the end of this Chapter.

Before tackling any troublesome electrical circuit, first study the appropriate diagrams thoroughly to get a complete picture of what makes up that individual circuit. Trouble spots, for instance, can often be narrowed down by noting if other components related to that circuit are operating properly or not. If several components or circuits fail at one time, chances are the fault lies in the fuse or ground (earth) connection, as several circuits often are routed through the same fuse and ground (earth) connections.

Electrical problems often stem from simple causes, such as loose or corroded connections or a blown fuse. Prior to any electrical troubleshooting, always visually check the condition of the fuse, wires and connections in the problem circuit. Intermittent failures can be especially frustrating, since you can't always duplicate the failure when it's convenient to test. In such situations, a good practice is to clean all connections in the affected circuit, whether or not they appear to be good. All of the connections and wires should also be wiggled to check for looseness which can cause intermittent failure.

If testing instruments are going to be utilised, use the diagrams to plan where you will make the necessary connections in order to accurately pinpoint the trouble spot.

The basic tools needed for electrical fault finding include a battery and bulb test circuit, a continuity tester, a test light, and a jumper wire. A multimeter capable of reading volts, ohms and amps is also very useful as an alternative to the above, and is necessary for performing more extensive tests and checks.

 HAYNES HiNT *Refer to Fault Finding Equipment in the Reference section for details of how to use electrical test equipment.*

3 Battery – inspection and maintenance

1 Most battery damage is caused by heat, vibration, and/or low electrolyte levels. The battery used on these vehicles is a maintenance free (sealed) type and therefore doesn't require the addition of water. However, the following checks should still be regularly performed.

 Warning: Always disconnect the negative cable first and connect it last to prevent sparks which could lead the battery to explode.

2 Check around the base inside of the battery for sediment, which is the result of sulphation caused by low electrolyte levels. These deposits will cause internal short circuits, which can quickly discharge the battery. Look for cracks in the case and replace the battery if either of these conditions is found.

3 Check the battery terminals and cable ends for tightness and corrosion. If corrosion is evident, disconnect the cables from the battery, disconnecting the negative (–) terminal first, and clean the terminals and cable ends with a wire brush or knife and emery paper. Reconnect the cables, connecting the negative cable last, and apply

a thin coat of petroleum jelly to the cables to slow further corrosion.

4 The battery case should be kept clean to prevent current leakage, which can discharge the battery over a period of time (especially when it sits unused). Wash the outside of the case with a solution of baking soda and water. Do not get any baking soda solution in the battery cells. Rinse the battery thoroughly, then dry it.

5 If acid has been spilled on the frame or battery box, neutralise it with a baking soda and water solution, then touch up any damaged paint.

6 If the motorcycle sits unused for long periods of time, disconnect the cables from the battery terminals. Refer to Section 4 and charge the battery approximately once every month.

4 Battery – charging

1 If the motorcycle sits idle for extended periods or if the charging system malfunctions, the battery can be charged from an external source.

2 Do not allow the battery to be subjected to a so-called quick charge (high rate of charge over a short period of time) unless you are prepared to buy a new battery. When charging the battery, always remove it from the machine.

3 Yamaha recommends different charging techniques, depending on the type of battery charger. Since a hydrometer can't be used to check battery condition (there's no way to insert it into the cells), a voltmeter is used instead to measure the voltage between the positive and negative terminals (open-circuit voltage). Before taking the measurement, wait at least 30 minutes after any charging has taken place (including running the engine).

4 To check open-circuit voltage, disconnect

the negative cable from the battery, then the positive cable. Make sure the battery terminals are clean, then connect the positive terminal of the voltmeter to the battery positive terminal and the negative terminal to the voltmeter to the battery negative terminal. If battery voltage reads 12.8V no charging is necessary. If voltage is below this figure, charge time can be established by reference to the graph **(see illustration)**.

Variable current (adjustable voltage) charger

5 Connect the charger to the battery. If the charger doesn't have an ammeter built in, connect one in series with the charger **(see illustration)**.

6 Plug in the charger, set the voltage at 16 to 17 volts and note the charging current. If it's less than the standard charging current printed on the battery, go to Step 7. If it's more than the standard charging current, skip to Step 8.

7 Set the charging voltage at 20 to 25 volts then watch the charging current for three to five minutes. If it reaches one amp or more, reset the voltage at 16 to 17 volts and continue charging. If the current isn't higher than the standard charging current after five minutes, replace the battery.

8 Adjust the voltage so the charging current is at the standard charging level. Set the timer on the charger according to the charging time determined in Step 4.

9 After the battery has charged, unplug the charger and disconnect it from the battery. Wait 30 minutes, then connect a voltmeter between the battery terminals and measure the open-circuit voltage (the battery needs this time to stabilise).

a) If the reading is 12.8 volts or more, the battery is charged.

b) If the reading is 12.0 to 12.7 volts, continue charging the battery.

c) If the reading is less than 12.0 volts, replace the battery.

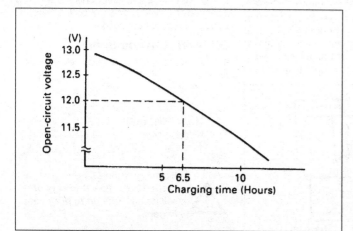

4.4 Battery open-circuit voltage and charge time relationship
Figures apply to an ambient temperature of 20°C (68°F) and a battery which is in good condition

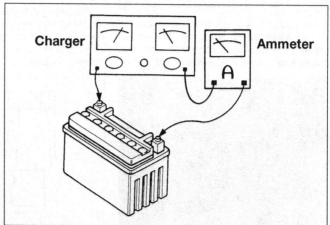

4.5 If the charger doesn't have an ammeter built in, connect one in series with the charger like this; DO NOT connect the ammeter between the battery terminals or it will be ruined

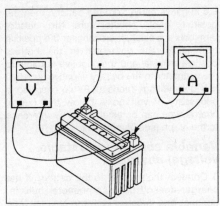

4.10 Connect the charger, ammeter and voltmeter to the battery like this; DO NOT connect the ammeter between the battery terminals or it will be ruined

Constant voltage charger

10 Connect the charger, a voltmeter and an ammeter to the battery **(see illustration)**.

11 Plug in the charger and check the ammeter reading.

a) *If it's less than the standard charging current printed on the battery, the charger won't work with a maintenance free battery. Use a variable voltage charger instead.*

b) *If the current flow is at the standard charging current, set charging time to a maximum of 20 hours and continue charging until charging voltage reaches 15 volts.*

12 Once charging voltage has reached 15 volts, unplug the charger. Disconnect the charger from the battery and refer to Step 9 to check open-circuit voltage.

5 Fuses –
check and replacement

1 All models have one fuse block located under the seat **(see illustration)**. They include the main, headlight, signal, ignition and hazard fuses, as well as spares. Fuse ratings

are listed in this Chapter's Specifications and inside the fuse block cover. Lift the cover from the fuse block for access to the fuses.

2 If you have a test light, all of the fuses can be checked without removing them. Turn the ignition to the ON position, connect one end of the test light to a good ground (earth), then probe each terminal on top of the fuse. If the fuse is good, there will be voltage available at both terminals. If the fuse is blown, there will only be voltage present at one of the terminals.

3 The fuses can also be tested with an ohmmeter or self-powered test light. Remove the fuse and connect the tester to the ends of the fuse. If the ohmmeter shows continuity or the test lamp lights, the fuse is good. If the ohmmeter shows infinite resistance or the test lamp stays out, the fuse is blown.

4 The fuses can be checked visually. A blown fuse is easily identified by a break in the element **(see illustration)**.

5 If a fuse blows, be sure to check the wiring harnesses very carefully for evidence of a short-circuit. Look for bare wires and chafed, melted or burned insulation. If a fuse is replaced before the cause is located, the new fuse will blow immediately.

Caution: Never, under any circumstances, use a higher rated fuse or bridge the fuse block terminals, as damage to the electrical system could result.

6 Occasionally a fuse will blow or cause an open-circuit for no obvious reason. Corrosion of the fuse ends and fuse block terminals may occur and cause poor fuse contact. If this happens, remove the corrosion with a wire brush or emery paper, then spray the fuse end and terminals with electrical contact cleaner.

6 Lighting system – check

1 The battery provides power for operation of the headlight, tail light, brake light, licence plate light and instrument cluster lights. If none of the lights operate, always check battery voltage before proceeding. Low

battery voltage indicates either a faulty battery or a defective charging system. Refer to Section 4 for the battery open-circuit check and Sections 26 and 27 for charging system tests. Also, check the condition of the fuses and replace any blown fuses with new ones.

Headlight

2 If the headlight is out when the engine is running (US models) or it won't switch on (UK models), check the fuse first with the key On (see Section 5), then unplug the electrical connector for the headlight and use jumper wires to connect the bulb directly to the battery terminals. If the light comes on, the problem lies in the wiring or one of the switches in the circuit. Refer to Section 15 or 16 for the switch testing procedures, and also the wiring diagrams at the end of this Chapter.

Tail light/licence plate light

3 If the tail light fails to work, check the bulb and the bulb terminals first, then check for battery voltage at the tail light electrical connector. If voltage is present, check the ground (earth) circuit for an open or poor connection.

4 If no voltage is indicated, check the wiring between the tail light and the ignition switch, then check the switch. On UK models, check the lighting switch as well.

Brake light

5 See Section 11 for the brake light switch checking procedure.

Neutral indicator light

6 If the neutral light fails to operate when the transmission is in Neutral, check the fuses and the bulb (see Section 13 for bulb removal procedures). If the bulb and fuses are in good condition, check for battery voltage at the connector attached to the neutral switch on the left side of the engine. If battery voltage is present, refer to Section 18 for the neutral switch check and replacement procedures.

7 If no voltage is indicated, check the wiring between the switch and the bulb for open-circuits and poor connections.

Oil level warning light

8 See Section 14 for the oil level sender check.

7 Headlight bulb –
replacement

 Warning: If the bulb has just burned out, allow it to cool. It will be hot enough to burn your fingers.

Headlight bulb

XJ600S models

1 Reach inside the fairing, disconnect the

5.1 The fuse block is located under the seat; lift the cover for access to the fuses

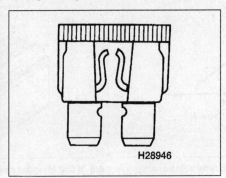

H28946

5.4 A blown fuse can be identified by a break in its element

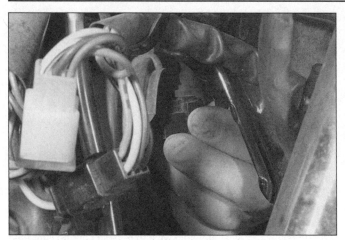

7.1a Disconnect the electrical connector from the headlight . . .

7.1b . . . and pull the cover off; the TOP mark must be up on installation

electrical connector and pull off the headlight cover **(see illustrations)**.

2 Unhook the retainer spring and remove the bulb **(see illustrations)**. If you find bulb removal too difficult due to limited access remove the fairing as described in Chapter 7.

3 Installation is the reverse of the removal steps, with the following additions:

a) *Be sure not to touch the glass portion of the bulb with your fingers – oil from your skin will cause the bulb to overheat and*

fail prematurely. If you do touch the bulb, wipe it off with a clean rag dampened with rubbing alcohol.

b) *Be sure the TOP mark on the headlight cover is up.*

XJ600N models

4 Remove the headlight assembly securing screws and pull the assembly out of the housing **(see illustration)**.

5 Disconnect the headlight electrical

connectors and remove the cover **(see illustration)**.

6 Turn the bulb retainer counterclockwise (anti-clockwise) and pull the bulb out of the of the headlight assembly **(see illustration)**.

7 Refer to Step 3 for installation procedures.

Parking light bulb (UK models)
XJ600S models

8 Reach inside the fairing and disconnect the electrical connector from the parking light.

7.2a Lift the retaining clip to free the bulb . . .

7.2b . . . and pull the bulb out; be careful not to touch the bulb glass with your fingers

7.4 Remove the headlight assembly retaining screws (1) . . .

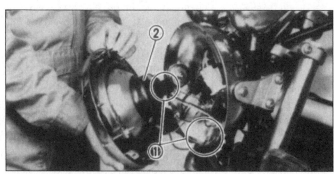

7.5 . . . disconnect the electrical connectors (1), remove the bulb cover (2) . . .

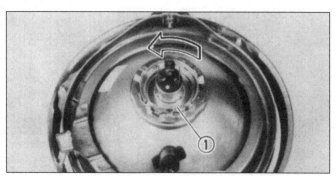

7.6 . . . and rotate the retainer ring (1) counterclockwise to free the bulb

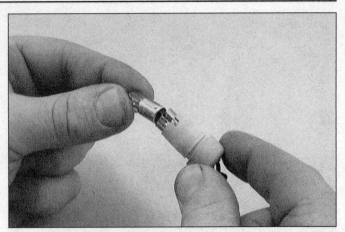

7.8a Parking light bulbholder is a push fit in headlight unit

7.8b Press in and twist anticlockwise to release parking light bulb

8.3a Beam adjuster screws – 1992-95 (UK) and 1992-96 (US) XJ600S models (arrowed)

Left arrow – vertical adjuster   Right arrow – horizontal adjuster

8.3b Beam adjuster screws – 1996-on (UK) and 1997-on (US) XJ600S models (arrowed)

Gently ease the bulbholder from the base of the headlight unit **(see illustration)**. Press the bulb in and twist it anticlockwise to remove it from the bulbholder **(see illustration)**.

9 Installation is the reverse of the removal steps.

XJ600N models

10 Remove the headlight assembly securing screws and pull the assembly out of the

9.1 To replace a turn signal bulb, remove the screws and take off the lens

housing **(see illustration 7.4)**. Disconnect the headlight and parking light electrical connectors.

11 Ease the parking light bulbholder out of its location in the base of the headlight. Press the bulb in and twist it anticlockwise to remove it from the bulbholder.

12 Installation is the reverse of the removal steps.

---

8 Headlight aim – check and adjustment

1 An improperly adjusted headlight may cause problems for oncoming traffic or provide poor, unsafe illumination of the road ahead. Before adjusting the headlight, be sure to consult with local traffic laws and regulations. In the UK refer to *MOT Test Checks* in the Reference section.

2 The headlight beam can be adjusted both vertically and horizontally. Before performing the adjustment, make sure the fuel tank is at

least half full, and have an assistant sit on the seat.

XJ600S models

3 To make vertical and horizontal adjustments, reach inside the fairing and turn the adjusting screws **(see illustrations)**.

XJ600N models

4 Horizontal adjustment is carried out by turning the single adjusting screw. Vertical adjustment is made by loosening the headlight mounting bolts and moving the light up or down, as necessary.

---

9 Turn signal and tail light bulbs – replacement

Turn signal bulbs

1 The turn signals are contained in stalks attached to the body panels or the frame. To replace a bulb, remove the lens securing screw(s) on the back of the assembly **(see illustration)**.

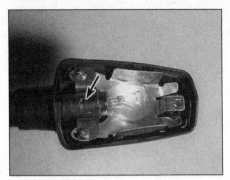

9.2 Press the bulb into its socket, turn counterclockwise (anti-clockwise) to release the pins (arrowed) and pull it out

9.3 To replace tail light bulb, remove the lens securing screws (arrowed) . . .

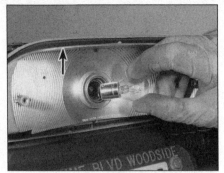

9.4 . . . turn the bulb socket counterclockwise (anti-clockwise) and pull it out; replace the lens gasket (arrowed) if it's brittle or cracked

2 Push the bulb in and turn it counterclockwise (anti-clockwise) to remove it **(see illustration)**. Check the socket terminals for corrosion and clean them if necessary. Line up the pins on the new bulb with the slots in the socket, push in and turn the bulb clockwise until it locks in place. **Note:** *The front turn signal bulbs on certain US models double as running lights and therefore have offset pins – take care to fit them correctly..*

Tail/brake light bulbs

3 Remove the lens securing screws **(see illustration)** and take off the lens.
4 Press the bulb into its socket and turn it counterclockwise (anti-clockwise) to disengage the pins, then pull it out **(see illustration)**. Check the socket terminals for corrosion and clean them if necessary. Replace the lens gasket if it's brittle or cracked.
5 Line up the pins on the new bulb with the slots in the socket, push in and turn the bulb clockwise until it locks in place. **Note:** *The pins on the bulb are offset so it can only be installed one way. It is a good idea to use a paper towel or dry cloth when handling the new bulb to prevent injury if the bulb should break and to increase bulb life.*
6 Install the lens and tighten the screws securely, but not tight enough to crack the lens.

10.3 The flasher relay (arrowed) is mounted on the left side of the bike forward of the battery on early models

10 Turn signal circuit – check

1 The battery provides power for operation of the signal lights, so if they do not operate, always check the battery open-circuit voltage first. Low battery voltage indicates either a faulty battery or a defective charging system. Refer to Section 4 for the battery open-circuit check and charging procedures and Sections 26 and 27 for charging system tests. Also, check the fuses (see Section 5) and the switch (see Section 16).
2 Most turn signal problems are the result of a burned out bulb or corroded socket. This is especially true when the turn signals function properly in one direction, but fail to flash in the other direction. Check the bulbs and the sockets (see Section 9).

Flasher relay

3 The flasher relay is mounted just in front of the battery on the left side on early models (1992 to 1996 US, 1992 to 1995 UK) **(see illustration)**; remove the seat for access. On later models, the flasher relay is mounted on the rear of the frame, behind the right side cover **(see illustrations 30.2b, c or d)**.
4 If the bulbs and sockets check out okay, turn the ignition switch ON and check for voltage at the brown (brown/red on 1997-on UK models) wire terminal on the relay assembly (connect the voltmeter positive lead to the brown wire terminal and the negative lead to the black wire terminal). If there's no voltage at the terminal, check the wiring from the signal fuse to the flasher relay terminal for a break or bad connection. On 1997-on UK models, if there's no voltage check the hazard relay as described below.
5 If there's voltage at the brown wire terminal, move the voltmeter positive lead to the brown/white wire terminal at the relay assembly and check for voltage again (the ignition switch should still be ON). If there's no voltage, the flasher relay is probably defective and should be renewed.

6 If there's voltage when there should be in Steps 4 and 5, and if the turn signal switch tested OK, the most likely problem is a poor contact in a turn signal bulb socket. Check the sockets for corrosion or damage. Another possible cause is a worn contact at the base of the bulb. Try a known good bulb in the socket that won't work.
7 If the flasher is okay, check the wiring between the turn signal flasher and the turn signal light sockets (see the *Wiring diagrams* at the end of this Chapter).

Hazard relay (1997-on UK models)

8 The hazard relay is mounted on the rear of the frame, behind the right side cover **(see illustration 30.2c)**.
9 If there's no voltage at the flasher relay brown/red wire (see Step 4) check for voltage at the hazard relay brown wires. If no voltage is shown check the signal fuse and the wiring between the fuse and hazard relay for a break or bad connection. Also check for voltage at the blue/red wire; if no voltage is shown check the hazard fuse and the wiring between hazard fuse and hazard relay. Finally check the brown/red wire from the hazard relay to the flasher relay for a break or bad connection. If the fault still exists, renew the hazard relay.

11 Brake light switches – check and replacement

Circuit check

1 Before checking any electrical circuit, check the fuses (see Section 5).
2 Using a test light connected to a good ground (earth), check for voltage at the brake light switch. If there's no voltage present, check the wire between the switch and the fuse block (see the *Wiring diagrams* at the end of this Chapter).
3 If voltage is available, touch the probe of the test light to the other terminal of the

11.5 Disconnect the wires and remove the screws (arrowed) to remove the front brake light switch

12.3 Unscrew the knurled nut and pull the speedometer cable out of the speedometer

12.6a Instrument cluster mounting nuts and washers (arrowed) – 1992-95 (UK), 1992-96 (US) models . . .

12.6b . . . and 1996-on (UK), 1997-on (US) models (arrowed)

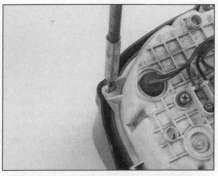

12.8a Remove the four screws (one from each corner) . . .

12.8b . . . and detach the instrument casing

switch, then pull the brake lever or depress the brake pedal – if the test light doesn't light up, replace the switch.

4 If the test light does light, check the wiring between the switch and the brake lights (see the *Wiring diagrams* at the end of this Chapter).

Switch replacement

Front brake lever switch

5 Remove the mounting screws and unplug the electrical connector from the switch (see illustration).
6 Detach the switch from the brake lever bracket/front master cylinder.
7 Installation is the reverse of the removal procedure. The brake lever switch isn't adjustable.

Rear brake pedal switch

8 Follow the wiring harness from the switch to the connector and disconnect it.
9 Disconnect the lower end of the switch spring from the brake pedal.
10 Hold the plastic nut to prevent it from turning with a small screwdriver or similar tool (the nut is recessed into the casting of the brake pedal bracket). Rotate the switch body until the switch threads separate from the plastic nut. Pull the spring through the nut and lift the switch out.
11 Install the switch by reversing the removal procedure, then adjust the switch by following the procedure described in Chapter 1.

12 Instruments and speedometer cable – removal, cluster disassembly and installation

1 This section describes removal, disassembly and installation procedures for the XJ600S instrument cluster. The XJ600N uses separate gauges.

Instruments

Removal

2 Remove the upper fairing (see Chapter 7).
3 Detach the speedometer cable from the speedometer (see illustration).
4 Disconnect the left and right turn signal connectors. Label the wires for left and right sides to make connection easier.

12.8c Carefully pry back the clips and lift off the cluster lens

5 Follow the wiring harness down from the instrument cluster to the two cluster connectors and disconnect them.
6 Remove the cluster mounting nuts and washers and lift the cluster out (see illustrations).

Disassembly and reassembly

7 The cluster can be disassembled as far as the speedometer/tachometer sub-assembly. The speedometer and tachometer aren't available separately.
8 To disassemble the XJ600S cluster, refer to the accompanying photographs (see illus-

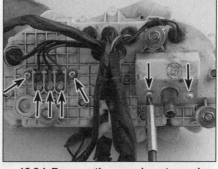

12.8d Remove the speedometer and tachometer mounting screws and the wiring screws (arrowed) (label the wires for reconnection if the wire colours or the colour codes cast in the cluster housing aren't visible) . . .

trations). For the XJ600N refer to the line drawing **(see illustration)**.

9 Assembly is the reverse of the disassembly steps. Tighten the screws securely, but not tightly enough to crack the plastic.

Speedometer cable

Removal

10 Disconnect the speedometer cable from the speedometer **(see illustration 12.3)**.

11 Note how it's routed, then disconnect the speedometer cable from the drive unit at the left front fork.

Installation

12 Installation is the reverse of the removal procedure. Be sure the speedometer cable is routed through the retainers on the fender and left fork leg. Be sure it doesn't cause the steering to bind or interfere with other components.

13 Instrument and warning light bulbs – replacement

1 If you're working on an XJ600S, remove the upper fairing (see Chapter 7). If you need to access the instrument illumination bulbs on the XJ600N, remove the single screw from the base of the chrome pod and withdraw the pod.

2 Pull the appropriate rubber socket out of the back of the instrument cluster or gauge,

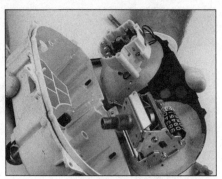

12.8e . . . and lift the speedometer/ tachometer subassembly out of the cluster housing; don't try to remove the speedometer or tachometer from the subassembly

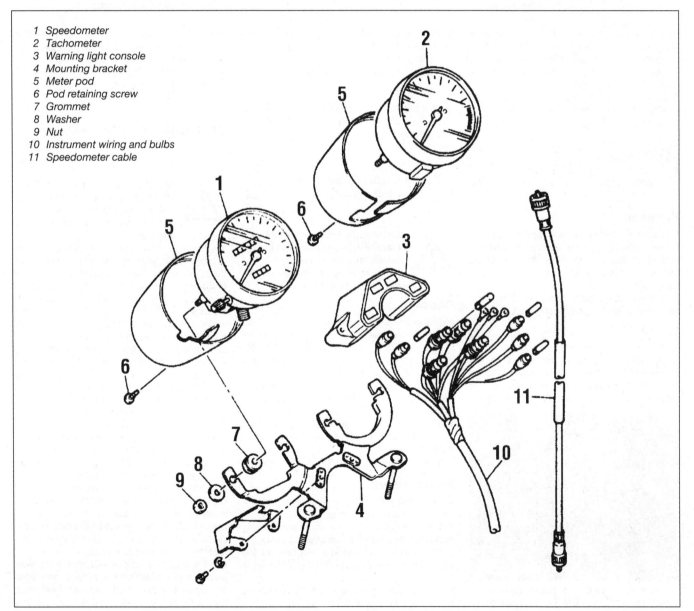

1 Speedometer
2 Tachometer
3 Warning light console
4 Mounting bracket
5 Meter pod
6 Pod retaining screw
7 Grommet
8 Washer
9 Nut
10 Instrument wiring and bulbs
11 Speedometer cable

12.8f Instrument assembly – XJ600N

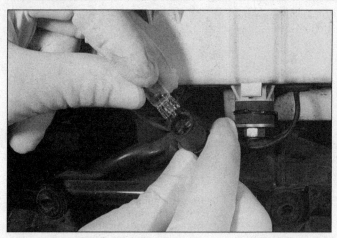

13.2 Pull the bulb socket out of the cluster, then pull the bulb out of the socket

14.3 Remove the bolts and pull the oil level sender out of the oil pan; use a new O-ring on installation

then pull the bulb out of the socket **(see illustration)**. If the socket contacts are dirty or corroded, they should be scraped clean and sprayed with electrical contact cleaner before new bulbs are installed.

3 Carefully push the new bulb into position, then push the socket into the cluster housing.

14 Oil level sender – removal, check and installation

Removal

1 Drain the engine oil (see Chapter 1).
2 The oil level sender is mounted in the bottom of the oil pan. Note how its wiring harness is routed, then unplug the electrical connector.
3 Remove the sender mounting bolts and remove the sender **(see illustration)**.

Check

4 Connect an ohmmeter between the terminals of the sender harness. With the sender in its normal installed position (flange and wiring harness at the bottom), the ohmmeter should indicate infinite resistance.

15.5 Remove the mounting screws (arrowed) to detach the ignition main (key) switch

5 Turn the sender upside down. The ohmmeter should now read zero ohms.
6 If the ohmmeter doesn't give the correct indication in Step 4 or 5, replace the sender.

Installation

7 Installation is the reverse of the removal steps. Use a new O-ring on the sender body and tighten the sender mounting bolts securely.

15 Ignition main (key) switch – check and replacement

⚠ **Warning: To prevent the risk of short-circuits, disconnect the battery negative (-ve) lead before making any ignition main (key) switch checks.**

Check

1 Follow the wiring harness from the ignition switch to the electrical connector. Remove fairing (XJ600S) and instrument cluster components as necessary for access and disconnect the connector.
2 Using an ohmmeter, check the continuity of the terminal pairs indicated in the wiring diagram at the end of the book. Continuity should exist between the terminals connected by a solid line when the switch is in the indicated position.
3 If the switch fails any of the tests, replace it.

Replacement

4 Unplug the switch electrical connector if you haven't already done so.
5 The switch is held to the upper triple clamp with two screws **(see illustration)**. Unlock the switch with the ignition key and remove the bolts. Detach the switch from the upper triple clamp.
6 If necessary, remove the Phillips screws and separate the switch from the bracket.
7 Attach the new switch to the bracket with

the Phillips screws (if it was removed). Tighten the screws securely. Hold the new switch in position and install the bolts.
8 The remainder of installation is the reverse of the removal procedure.

16 Handlebar switches – check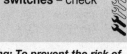

⚠ **Warning: To prevent the risk of short-circuits, disconnect the battery negative (-ve) lead before making any switch checks.**

1 Generally speaking, the switches are reliable and trouble-free. Most troubles, when they do occur, are caused by dirty or corroded contacts, but wear and breakage of internal parts is a possibility that should not be overlooked. If breakage does occur, the entire switch and related wiring harness will have to be replaced with a new one, since individual parts are not usually available.
2 The switches can be checked for continuity with an ohmmeter or a continuity test light. Always disconnect the battery negative cable, which will prevent the possibility of a short circuit, before making the checks.
3 Trace the wiring harness of the switch in question and unplug the electrical connectors.
4 Find the continuity diagram for the switch being checked in the appropriate wiring diagram at the end of this Chapter.
5 Using the ohmmeter or test light, check for continuity between the terminals of the switch harness with the switch in the various positions. Continuity should exist between the terminals connected by a solid line when the switch is in the indicated position.
6 If the continuity check indicates a problem exists, refer to Section 17, remove the switch and spray the switch contacts with electrical contact cleaner. If they are accessible, the contacts can be scraped clean with a knife or

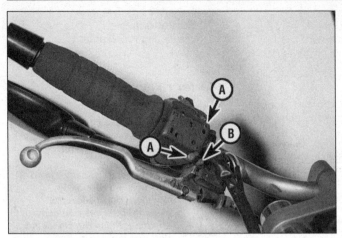

17.1a Left handlebar switch screws (A) and clutch switch screw (B) – early models

17.1b Right handlebar switch screws (arrowed) – early models

polished with crocus cloth. If switch components are damaged or broken, it will be obvious when the switch is disassembled.

17 Handlebar switches – removal and installation

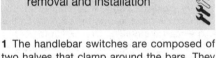

1 The handlebar switches are composed of two halves that clamp around the bars. They are easily removed for cleaning or inspection by taking out the clamp screws and pulling the switch halves away from the handlebars **(see illustrations)**.

2 To completely remove the switches, the electrical connectors in the wiring harness must be unplugged.

3 When installing the switches, make sure the wiring harnesses are properly routed to avoid pinching or stretching the wires. Align the protrusion on the switch with the corresponding hole in the handlebar. On later

models, with a handlebar-mounted choke control, make sure the choke lever assembly is positioned correctly when the left switch is installed (see Chapter 3, Section 11 if required).

18 Neutral switch – check and replacement

Check

1 Make sure the transmission is in neutral.
2 Follow the switch harness (it comes from behind the engine sprocket cover on the left side of the engine) to its connector, then unplug the connector.
3 Locate the sky blue wire's terminal in the harness side of the connector (not the side of the connector that goes to the neutral switch). Connect the terminal to ground (earth) (bare

metal on the motorcycle frame) with a short length of wire. Turn the ignition switch On.
  a) If the light stays out, check the bulb and the wiring between the ignition switch and neutral switch.
  b) If the neutral indicator light comes on, the neutral switch may be bad. Connect an ohmmeter between the sky blue terminal in the switch side of the connector and ground (earth). Shift through the gears. The ohmmeter should indicate continuity in neutral and infinite resistance in all other gears. If not, replace the neutral switch.

Replacement

4 Remove the engine sprocket cover (see Chapter 6).
5 Unplug the electrical connector (if you haven't already done so). Unbolt the wiring harness retainers from the crankcase and oil pan.
6 Loosen the screw and disconnect the wire

17.1c Left handlebar switch screws (arrowed) – later models

17.1d Right handlebar switch screws (arrowed) – later models

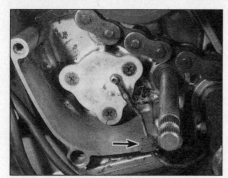

18.6 Remove the small screw to disconnect the switch wire and remove the three mounting screws; the grommet (arrowed) fits into a notch in the crankcase

from the switch **(see illustration)**. Remove the switch mounting screws and detach the switch from the crankcase.

7 Installation is the reverse of the removal steps. Be sure to install a new O-ring and/or gasket when you reinstall the switch.

19 Sidestand switch – check and replacement

Check

1 Follow the wiring harness from the switch to the connector, then unplug the connector. Connect the leads of an ohmmeter to the wire terminals. With the sidestand in the up position, there should be continuity through the switch (0 ohms).
2 With the sidestand in the down position, the meter should indicate infinite resistance.
3 If the switch fails either of these tests, replace it.

Replacement

4 With the sidestand in the up position, unscrew the two screws and remove the switch **(see illustration)**. Disconnect the switch electrical connector.
5 Installation is the reverse of the removal procedure.

20 Clutch switch – check and replacement

Check

1 Disconnect the electrical connector from the clutch switch **(see illustration 17.1a)**.
2 Connect an ohmmeter between the terminals in the clutch switch. With the clutch lever pulled in, the ohmmeter should show continuity (little or no resistance). With the lever out, the ohmmeter should show infinite resistance.
3 If the switch doesn't check out as described, replace it.

Replacement

4 If you haven't already done so, unplug the wiring connector. Remove the mounting screw and take the switch off **(see illustration 17.1a)**.
5 Installation is the reverse of removal.

21 Horn – check and replacement

Check

1 Unplug the electrical connectors from the horn **(see illustration)**. Using two jumper wires, apply battery voltage directly to the terminals on the horn. If the horn sounds, check the switch and the wiring between the switch and the horn (see the *Wiring diagrams* at the end of this Chapter).
2 If the horn doesn't sound, replace it.

Replacement

3 Unbolt the horn bracket from the lower triple clamp **(see illustration 21.1)** and detach the electrical connectors.
4 Installation is the reverse of removal.

22 Starter relays – check and replacement

Starter relay

Check

1 Remove the seat (see Chapter 7) and the fuel tank (see Chapter 3). Remove the side cover on the right side of the motorcycle (see Chapter 7).
2 Disconnect the starter cable from the starter motor **(see illustration 23.2)**.

⚠️ *Warning: Don't allow the disconnected cable to contact anything. Raise the sidestand. With the ignition switch ON, the engine kill switch in RUN and the transmission in neutral, press the starter switch. The relay should be heard to click.*

3 If the relay doesn't click, disconnect the negative cable from the battery, then disconnect the positive cable from the battery and the relay. Disconnect the thin wire and remove the relay. Connect one lead of an ohmmeter to the terminal stud that the battery positive cable was connected to. Connect the other lead to the terminal on the thin wire. If the reading isn't within the range listed in this Chapter's Specifications, replace the relay.

Replacement

4 Disconnect the cable from the negative terminal of the battery.
5 Detach the battery positive cable, the starter cable and electrical connector from the relay **(see illustration)**.
6 Slide the relay off its mounting tabs.
7 Remove the relay from its rubber mounting.
8 Installation is the reverse of removal. Reconnect the negative battery cable after all the other electrical connections are made.

Starter cut-off relay

Check

9 Remove the relay assembly from the bike

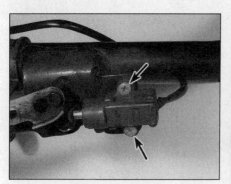

19.4 The sidestand switch is secured by two screws (arrowed)

21.1 Disconnect the wires and remove the mounting nut (arrowed) to detach the horn

22.5 Detach the wires from the starter relay

and conduct the following test on the bench (see Section 30). Connector an ohmmeter or continuity tester between the two blue/white wire terminals of the relay. Using a 12 volt battery and two jumper leads, connect the positive lead to the red/black wire terminal on the relay and the negative lead to the black/yellow relay terminal; continuity should be shown. Now transfer the battery negative lead to the light blue wire terminal and check whether continuity is shown.

10 If no continuity is indicated in either test, the starter cut-off relay is faulty and the relay assembly should be renewed.

Removal and installation

11 The starter cut-off relay is contained within the relay assembly. Refer to Section 30.

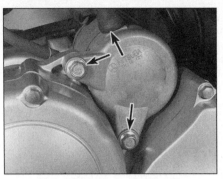

23.2 Starter mounting details

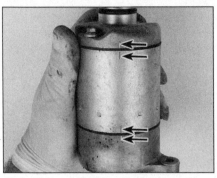

24.1a There should be alignment marks on the housing and end covers (arrowed)

23 Starter motor – removal and installation

Removal

1 Remove the seat (see Chapter 7). Disconnect the cable from the negative terminal of the battery.

2 Pull back the rubber boot from the nut retaining the starter cable to the starter **(see illustration)**. Remove the nut and the starter mounting bolts.

3 Pull the starter up slightly and slide it out of the engine case.

4 Check the condition of the O-ring on the end of the starter and replace it if necessary.

Installation

5 Apply a little engine oil to the O-ring and install the starter by reversing the removal procedure. Tighten the two mounting bolts to the torque listed in this Chapter's Specifications.

24 Starter motor – disassembly, inspection and reassembly

Disassembly

1 Look for marks indicating the position of the housing to each end cover; if they aren't visible, make your own **(see illustration)**. Remove the two long screws and detach both end covers, noting the location and number of the shims on each end of the armature **(see illustration)**.

2 Pull the armature out of the housing.

3 Carefully note how the washers are arranged on the terminal bolt. Remove the nut and washers and push the terminal bolt through the starter housing, then reinstall the washers and nut on the bolt so you don't

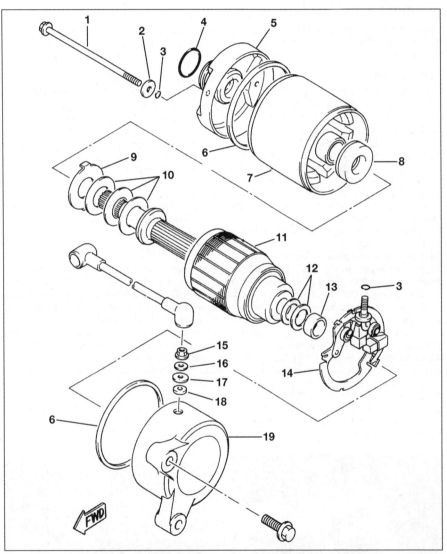

24.1b Starter motor - exploded view

1 Through-bolt	8 Bearing and seal	14 Brush plate
2 Washer	9 Seal retainer	15 Nut
3 O-ring	10 Shims	16 Metal washer
4 O-ring	11 Armature	17 Washer
5 End cover	12 Shims	18 Rubber washer
6 O-ring	13 Bushing	19 Brush end cover
7 Starter housing		

24.3a Remove the nut and washers from the terminal bolt

24.3b Push the terminal bolt through its hole and remove the brush plate from the housing

24.4 Measure the length of the brushes

forget how they go **(see illustration)**. Remove the brush plate from the housing **(see illustration)**.

Inspection

4 The parts of the starter motor that most likely will require attention are the brushes. Measure the length of the brushes and compare the results to the brush length listed in this Chapter's Specifications **(see illustration)**. If either of the brushes is worn beyond the specified limits, replace the brush holder assembly with a new one. If the brushes are not worn excessively, nor cracked, chipped, or otherwise damaged, they may be reused.

5 Inspect the commutator **(see illustration)** for scoring, scratches and discoloration. The commutator can be cleaned and polished with crocus cloth, but do not use sandpaper or emery paper. After cleaning, wipe away any residue with a cloth soaked in an electrical system cleaner or denatured alcohol. Measure the commutator diameter and compare it to the diameter listed in this Chapter's Specifications. If it is less than the service limit, the motor must be replaced with a new one.

6 Using an ohmmeter or a continuity test light, check for continuity between the commutator bars **(see illustration)**. Continuity should exist between each bar and all of the others. Also, check for continuity between the commutator bars and the armature shaft **(see**

illustration). There should be no continuity between the commutator and the shaft. If the checks indicate otherwise, the armature is defective.

7 Check for continuity between the brush plate and the brushes. The meter should read close to 0 ohms. If it doesn't, the brush plate has an open and must be replaced.

8 Using the highest range on the ohmmeter, measure the resistance between the insulated brush holder and the brush plate. The reading should be infinite. If there is any reading at all, replace the brush plate.

9 Check the starter pinion gear for worn, cracked, chipped and broken teeth. If the gear is damaged or worn, replace the starter motor.

Reassembly

10 Install the brush plate in the housing. Make sure the terminal bolt and washers are assembled in their original order. Tighten the terminal nut loosely at this point to hold the washers on the terminal bolt.

11 Install any washers that were present on the ends of the armature shaft. Install the armature in the starter housing and install the end cover on the pinion gear end. Align the cover and housing marks.

12 Install the end cover and brush holder over the commutator, pushing back the brushes to make room for the commutator. Align the end cover matchmarks.

13 Install the two long screws with their washers and O-rings and tighten them securely.

25 Charging system testing – general information and precautions

1 If the performance of the charging system is suspect, the system as a whole should be checked first, followed by testing of the individual components (the alternator and the voltage regulator/rectifier). **Note:** *Before beginning the checks, make sure the battery is fully charged and that all system connections are clean and tight.*

2 Checking the output of the charging system and the performance of the various components within the charging system requires the use of special electrical test equipment. A voltmeter or a multimeter are the absolute minimum tools required. In addition, an ohmmeter is required for checking the remainder of the system.

3 When making the checks, follow the procedures carefully to prevent incorrect connections or short circuits, as irreparable damage to electrical system components may result if short circuits occur. Because of the special tools and expertise required, it is recommended that the job of checking the

24.5 Check the commutator for cracks and discolouring, then measure its diameter

24.6a Continuity should exist between the commutator bars

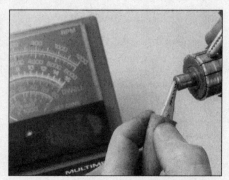

24.6b There should be no continuity between the commutator bars and the armature shaft

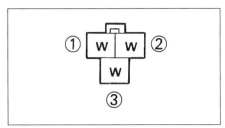

27.2 Connect the ohmmeter between all three pairs of terminals (connect it between terminal 1 and terminals 2 and 3 in turn, then between terminals 2 and 3)

charging system be left to a dealer service department or other reputable motorcycle repair shop.

26 Charging system – output test

Caution: Never disconnect the battery cables from the battery while the engine is running. If the battery is disconnected, the alternator and regulator/rectifier will be damaged.

1 To check the charging system output, you will need a voltmeter or a multimeter with a voltmeter function.
2 The battery must be fully charged (charge it from an external source if necessary) and the engine must be at normal operating temperature to obtain an accurate reading.
3 Attach the positive (red) voltmeter lead to the positive (+) battery terminal and the negative (black) lead to the battery negative (–) terminal. The voltmeter selector switch (if equipped) must be in the 0 to 20 dc volt range.
4 Start the engine.
5 The charging system output should be within the no-load regulated voltage range listed in this Chapter's Specifications.
6 If the output is as specified, the alternator is functioning properly. If the charging system as

a whole is not performing as it should, refer to Section 27 and test the system further.
7 Low voltage output may be the result of wiring problems or of damaged windings in the alternator stator coils. Make sure all electrical connections are clean and tight, then refer to Section 27 for stator coil tests.
8 High voltage output (above the specified range) indicates a defective voltage regulator/rectifier.

27 Charging system – stator coil test

Note: *This test is made with the ignition OFF and the battery negative (–) lead disconnected.*
1 Follow the stator coil wiring harness (three white wires) from the alternator on the left side of the engine to the connector and unplug the connector.
2 Connect an ohmmeter to all three pairs of terminals in the connector (the alternator side of the connector, not the wiring harness side) and compare the resistance readings to those listed in this Chapter's Specifications **(see illustration)**. If the readings are not within specifications, the stator coil is defective. Replace it.

28 Alternator – removal and installation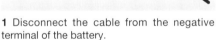

1 Disconnect the cable from the negative terminal of the battery.
2 Remove the seat and left side cover for access (see Chapter 7).
3 Remove the alternator wiring harness retainers on the left side of the engine. Remove the alternator cover bolts and remove the alternator cover, together with the stator coil **(see illustration).**
4 Place the transmission in gear and have an assistant hold the rear brake on to keep the engine from turning. Loosen the rotor bolt, then remove the bolt and washer. **Note:** *You*

can also hold the rotor with a strap wrench of the type used for removing large oil filters.
5 Thread a rotor puller into the rotor and remove the rotor from the end of the crankshaft **(see illustration)**. The rotor used on these models doesn't have a Woodruff key. **Note:** *If you use an aftermarket rotor puller with multiple thread sizes, there may not be enough room to rotate it and thread it into the rotor because the engine case is in the way. In this case, hold the puller against the rotor and turn the rotor, either with a strap wrench or by turning the back wheel with the transmission in gear.*

⚠ *Warning: Make sure the ignition (main key) switch is OFF when turning the engine.*

6 To remove the stator coil, remove the screws and detach the coil from the alternator cover.
7 Installation is the reverse of the removal steps, with the following additions:
a) *Make sure no metal objects have stuck to the magnets inside the rotor* **(see illustration)**.
b) *Tighten the rotor bolt to the torque listed in this Chapter's Specifications.*
c) *Apply non-permanent thread locking agent to the threads of the stator coil Allen bolts (if they were removed). Tighten the bolts securely, but be careful not to strip out the threads.*
d) *Tighten the cover bolts to the torque listed in this Chapter's Specifications.*

29 Regulator/rectifier – removal and installation

1 The regulator is mounted on the left side of the motorcycle under the side cover.
2 To remove the regulator/rectifier, remove the side cover (see Chapter 7). Disconnect the electrical connector, remove the mounting screws and take the unit out **(see**

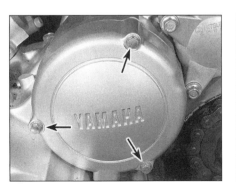

28.3 Remove the alternator cover bolts (arrowed) and take off the cover together with the stator coil

28.5 Remove the rotor bolt (arrowed) and use a tool like this one to separate the rotor from the crankshaft

28.7 Be sure there aren't any metal objects stuck to the rotor magnets; an inconspicuous item like this screw (arrowed) can ruin the rotor and stator if the engine is run

29.2a Regulator/rectifier unit – early models

29.2b Regulator/rectifier unit – later models

illustrations). Note that a different regulator/rectifier unit was fitted from 1997 in the US and from 1996 in the UK.

3 Installation is the reverse of the removal steps.

30 Relay assembly and diode

Relay assembly

1 The relay assembly houses the starter circuit cut-off relay and diodes, and on 1996-on UK models it also houses the fuel pump relay. Refer to the wiring diagrams at the end of this Chapter for details of the relay's internal connections. Where test procedures are possible these are included with the starter relay check in this Chapter or the fuel pump circuit checks in Chapter 3.

2 On 1992 to 1996 US models and 1992 to 1995 UK models, the relay assembly is located under the seat on the left side (behind the regulator/rectifier unit) **(see illustration)**. On all later models the relay assembly is located under the right side cover **(see illustrations)**.

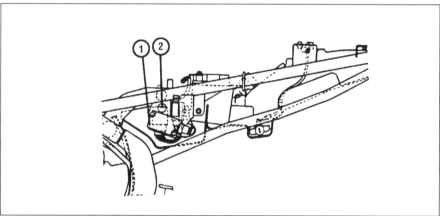

30.2a Relay assembly location on 1992-95 UK models and 1992-96 US models

1 Regulator/rectifier   2 Relay assembly

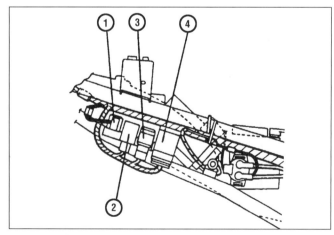

30.2b Relay assembly location on 1996 UK models

1	Themoswitch	3	Heater relay
2	Flasher relay	4	Relay assembly

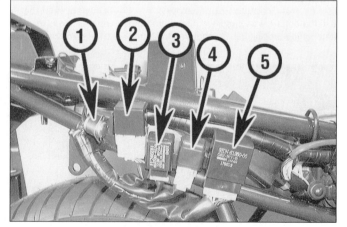

30.2c Relay assembly location on 1997-on UK models

1	Themoswitch	3	Flasher relay	5	Relay assembly
2	Hazard relay	4	Heater relay		

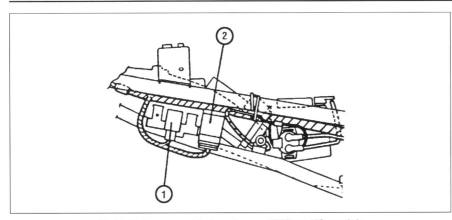

30.2d Relay assembly location on 1997-on US models

1 Flasher relay   2 Relay assembly

remove the insulation tape from its connector **(see illustration)**. Unplug the diode from the connector **(see illustration)**. Using an ohmmeter or continuity tester, connect its probes across the two terminals on the diode side of the connector **(see illustration)**. Continuity should only be shown in one direction, with no continuity shown when the probes are reversed. If the diode does not function correctly it must be renewed.

31 Wiring diagrams

Prior to troubleshooting a circuit, check the fuses to make sure they're in good condition. Make sure the battery is fully charged and check the cable connections.

When checking a circuit, make sure all connectors are clean, with no broken or loose terminals or wires. When unplugging a connector, don't pull on the wires – pull only on the connector housings themselves.

Diode

3 1996-on UK models are equipped with a diode in the neutral switch wiring. The diode should only allow current to flow in one direction and can be tested as follows.

4 Locate the diode on the left side of the frame top rail, under the large plastic sleeve

30.3a Diode location

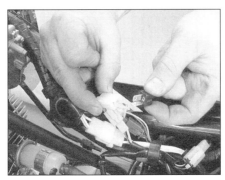

30.3b Unplug the diode . . .

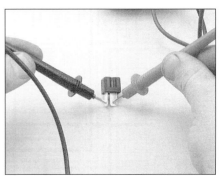

30.3c . . . and test it for continuity

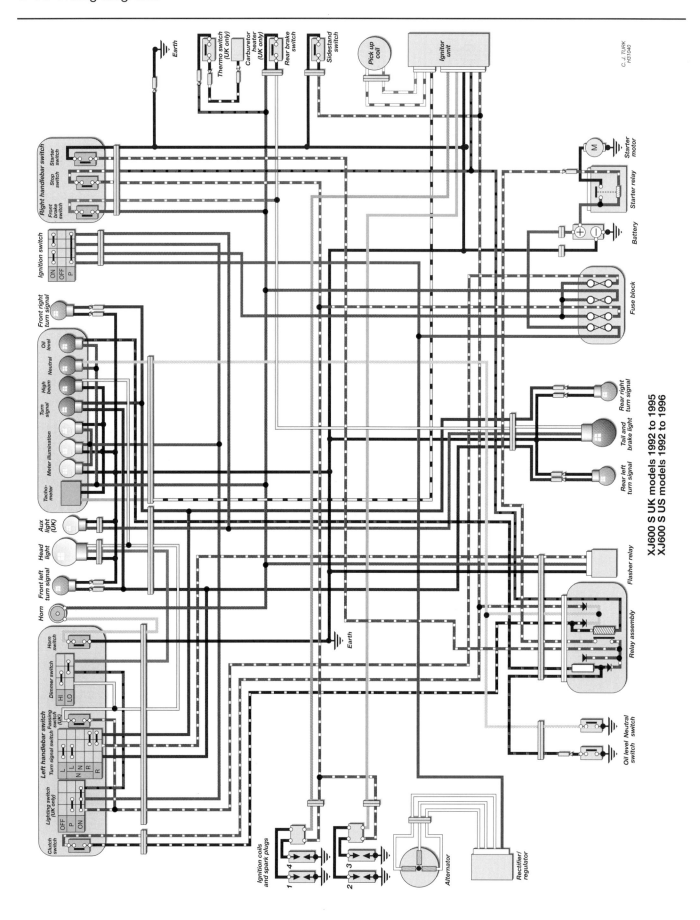

C. J. TURK
H31040

XJ600 S UK models 1992 to 1995
XJ600 S US models 1992 to 1996

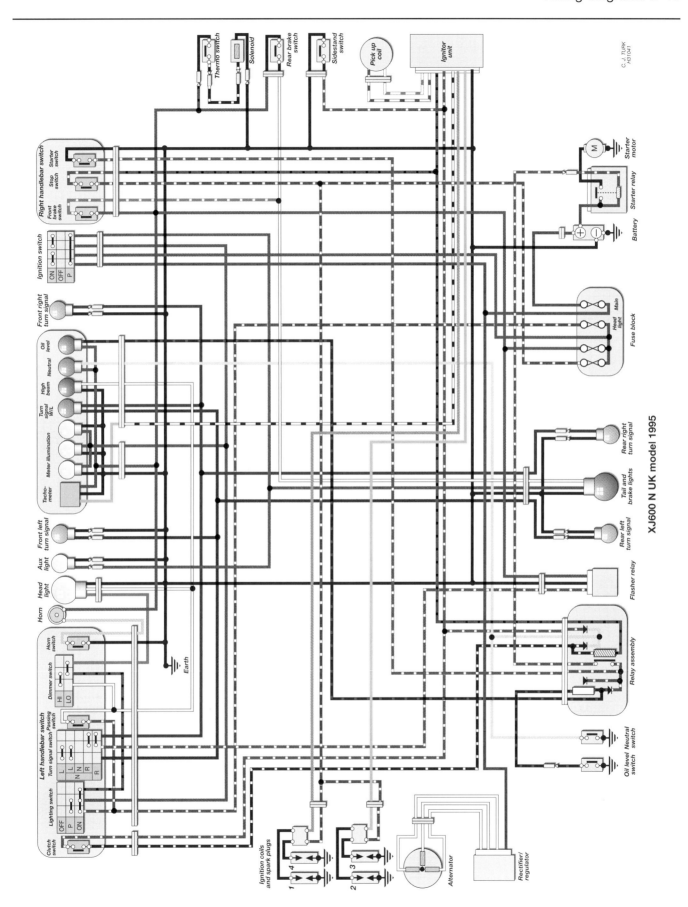

C.J. TURK
H31041

Thermo switch
Solenoid
Rear brake switch
Sidestand switch
Pick up coil
Ignitor unit

Starter motor
Starter relay
Battery

Right handlebar switch
Starter switch
Stop switch
Front brake switch

Ignition switch
ON
OFF
P

Main
Head light
Fuse block

Front right turn signal
Oil level
Neutral
High beam
Turn signal W/L
Meter illumination
Tacho-meter

Rear right turn signal
Tail and brake lights
Rear left turn signal

Front left turn signal
Aux light
Head light
Horn

Flasher relay

Relay assembly

Horn switch
Dimmer switch
HI
LO
Left handlebar switch
Passing switch
Turn signal switch
L
L
N
R
R
Lighting switch
OFF
P
ON
Clutch switch

Earth

Oil level Neutral switch

Ignition coils and spark plugs
1
4
2
3
Alternator
Rectifier/ regulator

XJ600 N UK model 1995

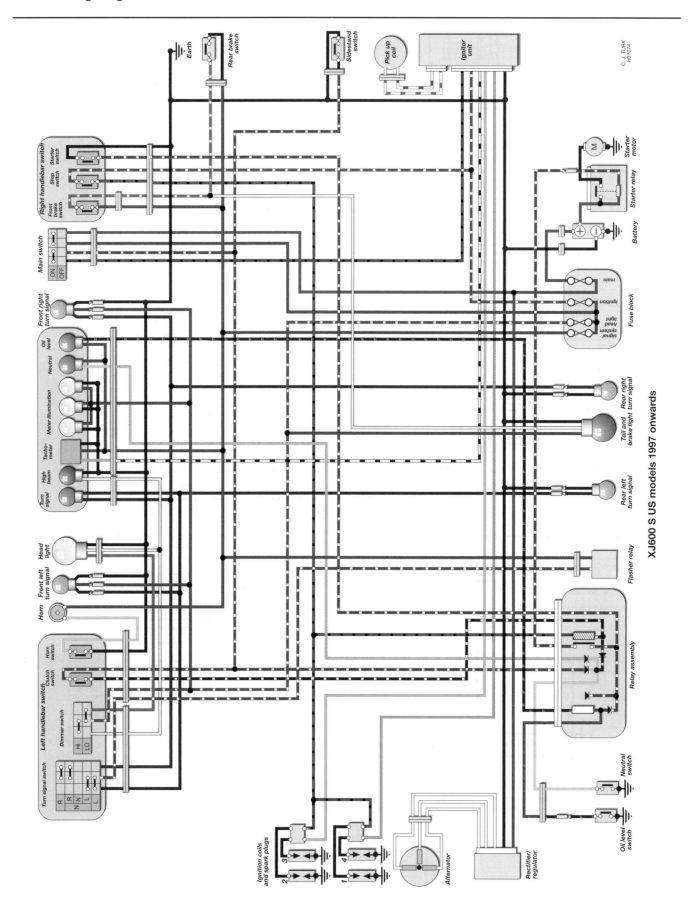

XJ600 S US models 1997 onwards

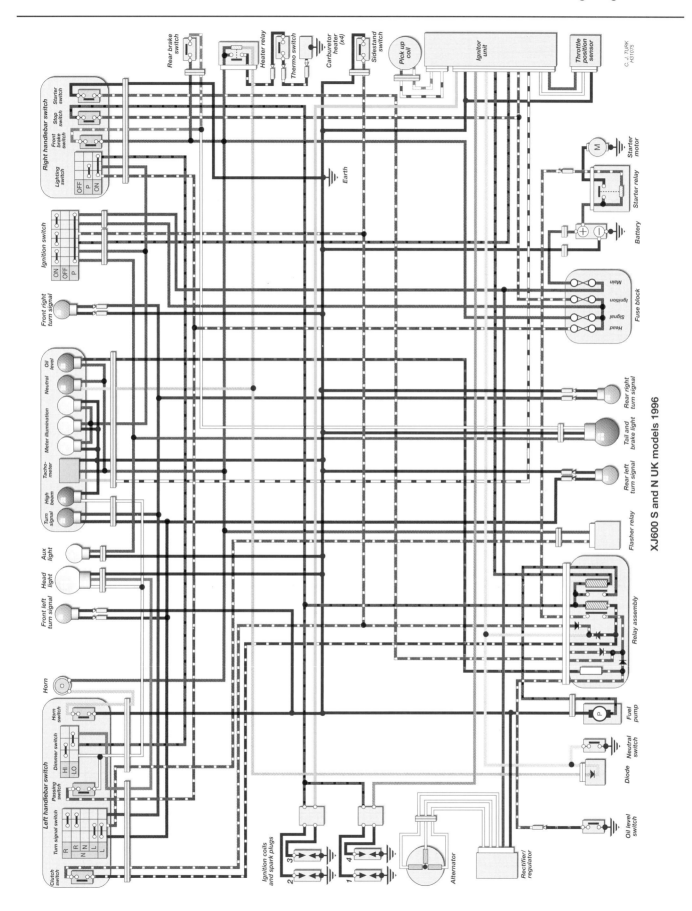

XJ600 S and N UK models 1996

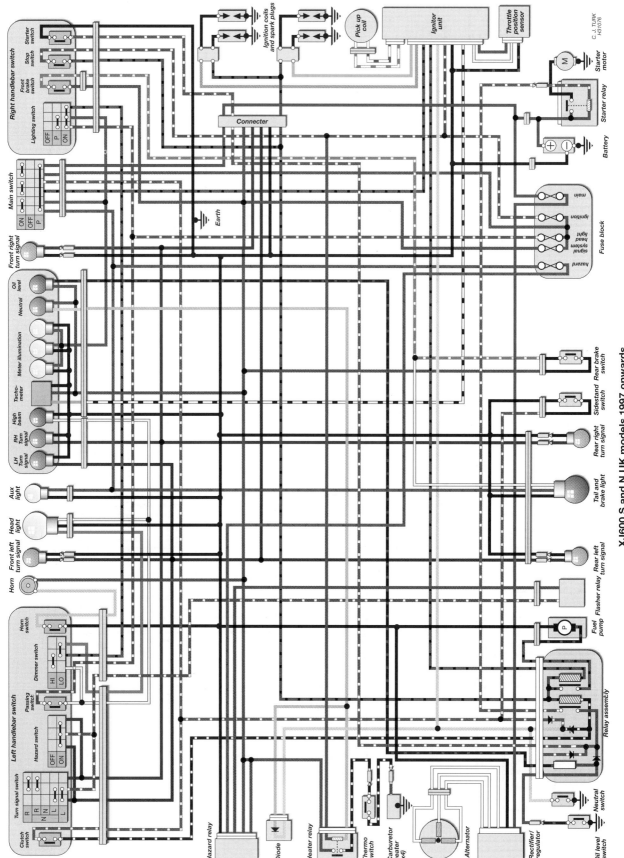

XJ600 S and N UK models 1997 onwards

Dimensions and Weights

Wheelbase
All models . . . . 1445 mm (56.9 inches)

Overall length
XJ600S
  US models . . . . 2095 mm (82.5 inches)
  UK models . . . . 2170 mm (84.5 inches)
XJ600N . . . . 2170 mm (84.5 inches)

Overall width
US 1992-96 models, UK 1992-95 models . . . . 750 mm (29.5 inches)
US 1997-on models, UK 1996-on models . . . . 735 mm (28.9 inches)

Overall height
XJ600S
  US 1992-93 models . . . . 1170 mm (46.1 inches)
  US 1994-96 models, UK 1992-95 models . . . . 1220 mm (48.0 inches)
  US 1997-on models, UK 1996-on models . . . . 1205 mm (47.4 inches)
XJ600N . . . . 1090 mm (42.9 inches)

Seat height
All models . . . . 770 mm (30.3 inches)

Ground clearance (minimum)
All models . . . . 150 mm (5.9 inches)

Weight (with oil and full fuel tank)
XJ600S
    US 1992-93 models* . . . . 197 kg (434 lbs)
    US 1994-96 models* . . . . 200 kg (441 lbs)
    US 1997-on models* . . . . 205 kg (452 lbs)
    UK 1992-95 models . . . . 202 kg (445 lbs)
    UK 1996-97 models . . . . 208 kg (459 lbs)
    UK 1998-on models . . . . 213 kg (470 lbs)
XJ600N
    1995 models . . . . 202 kg (445 lbs)
    1996-on models . . . . 205 kg (452 lbs)
*Add 1 kg for California models

Length (distance)

Inches (in)	x 25.4	= Millimetres (mm)	x 0.0394	= Inches (in)
Feet (ft)	x 0.305	= Metres (m)	x 3.281	= Feet (ft)
Miles	x 1.609	= Kilometres (km)	x 0.621	= Miles

Volume (capacity)

Cubic inches (cu in; in^3)	x 16.387	= Cubic centimetres (cc; cm^3)	x 0.061	= Cubic inches (cu in; in^3)
Imperial pints (Imp pt)	x 0.568	= Litres (l)	x 1.76	= Imperial pints (Imp pt)
Imperial quarts (Imp qt)	x 1.137	= Litres (l)	x 0.88	= Imperial quarts (Imp qt)
Imperial quarts (Imp qt)	x 1.201	= US quarts (US qt)	x 0.833	= Imperial quarts (Imp qt)
US quarts (US qt)	x 0.946	= Litres (l)	x 1.057	= US quarts (US qt)
Imperial gallons (Imp gal)	x 4.546	= Litres (l)	x 0.22	= Imperial gallons (Imp gal)
Imperial gallons (Imp gal)	x 1.201	= US gallons (US gal)	x 0.833	= Imperial gallons (Imp gal)
US gallons (US gal)	x 3.785	= Litres (l)	x 0.264	= US gallons (US gal)

Mass (weight)

Ounces (oz)	x 28.35	= Grams (g)	x 0.035	= Ounces (oz)
Pounds (lb)	x 0.454	= Kilograms (kg)	x 2.205	= Pounds (lb)

Force

Ounces-force (ozf; oz)	x 0.278	= Newtons (N)	x 3.6	= Ounces-force (ozf; oz)
Pounds-force (lbf; lb)	x 4.448	= Newtons (N)	x 0.225	= Pounds-force (lbf; lb)
Newtons (N)	x 0.1	= Kilograms-force (kgf; kg)	x 9.81	= Newtons (N)

Pressure

Pounds-force per square inch (psi; lbf/in^2; lb/in^2)	x 0.070	= Kilograms-force per square centimetre (kgf/cm^2; kg/cm^2)	x 14.223	= Pounds-force per square inch (psi; lbf/in^2; lb/in^2)
Pounds-force per square inch (psi; lbf/in^2; lb/in^2)	x 0.068	= Atmospheres (atm)	x 14.696	= Pounds-force per square inch (psi; lbf/in^2; lb/in^2)
Pounds-force per square inch (psi; lbf/in^2; lb/in^2)	x 0.069	= Bars	x 14.5	= Pounds-force per square inch (psi; lbf/in^2; lb/in^2)
Pounds-force per square inch (psi; lbf/in^2; lb/in^2)	x 6.895	= Kilopascals (kPa)	x 0.145	= Pounds-force per square inch (psi; lbf/in^2; lb/in^2)
Kilopascals (kPa)	x 0.01	= Kilograms-force per square centimetre (kgf/cm^2; kg/cm^2)	x 98.1	= Kilopascals (kPa)
Millibar (mbar)	x 100	= Pascals (Pa)	x 0.01	= Millibar (mbar)
Millibar (mbar)	x 0.0145	= Pounds-force per square inch (psi; lbf/in^2; lb/in^2)	x 68.947	= Millibar (mbar)
Millibar (mbar)	x 0.75	= Millimetres of mercury (mmHg)	x 1.333	= Millibar (mbar)
Millibar (mbar)	x 0.401	= Inches of water (inH$_2$O)	x 2.491	= Millibar (mbar)
Millimetres of mercury (mmHg)	x 0.535	= Inches of water (inH$_2$O)	x 1.868	= Millimetres of mercury (mmHg)
Inches of water (inH$_2$O)	x 0.036	= Pounds-force per square inch (psi; lbf/in^2; lb/in^2)	x 27.68	= Inches of water (inH$_2$O)

Torque (moment of force)

Pounds-force inches (lbf in; lb in)	x 1.152	= Kilograms-force centimetre (kgf cm; kg cm)	x 0.868	= Pounds-force inches (lbf in; lb in)
Pounds-force inches (lbf in; lb in)	x 0.113	= Newton metres (Nm)	x 8.85	= Pounds-force inches (lbf in; lb in)
Pounds-force inches (lbf in; lb in)	x 0.083	= Pounds-force feet (lbf ft; lb ft)	x 12	= Pounds-force inches (lbf in; lb in)
Pounds-force feet (lbf ft; lb ft)	x 0.138	= Kilograms-force metres (kgf m; kg m)	x 7.233	= Pounds-force feet (lbf ft; lb ft)
Pounds-force feet (lbf ft; lb ft)	x 1.356	= Newton metres (Nm)	x 0.738	= Pounds-force feet (lbf ft; lb ft)
Newton metres (Nm)	x 0.102	= Kilograms-force metres (kgf m; kg m)	x 9.804	= Newton metres (Nm)

Power

Horsepower (hp)	x 745.7	= Watts (W)	x 0.0013	= Horsepower (hp)

Velocity (speed)

Miles per hour (miles/hr; mph)	x 1.609	= Kilometres per hour (km/hr; kph)	x 0.621	= Miles per hour (miles/hr; mph)

Fuel consumption*

Miles per gallon (mpg)	x 0.354	= Kilometres per litre (km/l)	x 2.825	= Miles per gallon (mpg)

Temperature

Degrees Fahrenheit = (°C x 1.8) + 32   Degrees Celsius (Degrees Centigrade; °C) = (°F - 32) x 0.56

It is common practice to convert from miles per gallon (mpg) to litres/100 kilometres (l/100km), where mpg x l/100 km = 282

Buying tools

A toolkit is a fundamental requirement for servicing and repairing a motorcycle. Although there will be an initial expense in building up enough tools for servicing, this will soon be offset by the savings made by doing the job yourself. As experience and confidence grow, additional tools can be added to enable the repair and overhaul of the motorcycle. Many of the specialist tools are expensive and not often used so it may be preferable to hire them, or for a group of friends or motorcycle club to join in the purchase.

As a rule, it is better to buy more expensive, good quality tools. Cheaper tools are likely to wear out faster and need to be renewed more often, nullifying the original saving.

> **Warning: To avoid the risk of a poor quality tool breaking in use, causing injury or damage to the component being worked on, always aim to purchase tools which meet the relevant national safety standards.**

The following lists of tools do not represent the manufacturer's service tools, but serve as a guide to help the owner decide which tools are needed for this level of work. In addition, items such as an electric drill, hacksaw, files, soldering iron and a workbench equipped with a vice, may be needed. Although not classed as tools, a selection of bolts, screws, nuts, washers and pieces of tubing always come in useful.

For more information about tools, refer to the Haynes *Motorcycle Workshop Practice TechBook* (Bk. No. 3470).

Manufacturer's service tools

Inevitably certain tasks require the use of a service tool. Where possible an alternative tool or method of approach is recommended, but sometimes there is no option if personal injury or damage to the component is to be avoided. Where required, service tools are referred to in the relevant procedure.

Service tools can usually only be purchased from a motorcycle dealer and are identified by a part number. Some of the commonly-used tools, such as rotor pullers, are available in aftermarket form from mail-order motorcycle tool and accessory suppliers.

Maintenance and minor repair tools

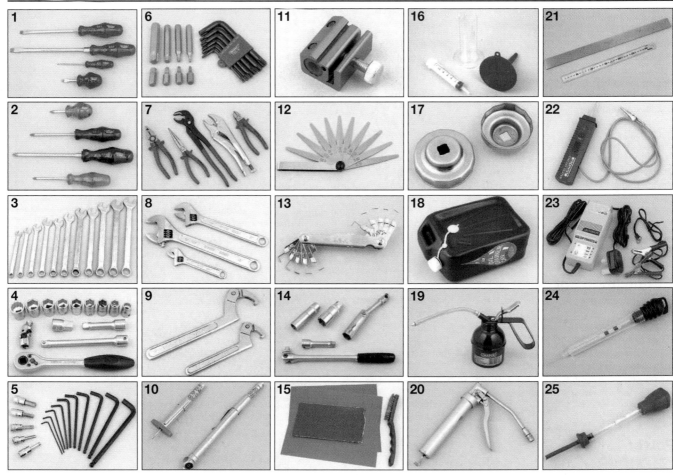

1 Set of flat-bladed screwdrivers
2 Set of Phillips head screwdrivers
3 Combination open-end and ring spanners
4 Socket set (3/8 inch or 1/2 inch drive)
5 Set of Allen keys or bits

6 Set of Torx keys or bits
7 Pliers, cutters and self-locking grips (Mole grips)
8 Adjustable spanners
9 C-spanners
10 Tread depth gauge and tyre pressure gauge

11 Cable oiler clamp
12 Feeler gauges
13 Spark plug gap measuring tool
14 Spark plug spanner or deep plug sockets
15 Wire brush and emery paper

16 Calibrated syringe, measuring vessel and funnel
17 Oil filter adapters
18 Oil drainer can or tray
19 Pump type oil can
20 Grease gun

21 Straight-edge and steel rule
22 Continuity tester
23 Battery charger
24 Hydrometer (for battery specific gravity check)
25 Anti-freeze tester (for liquid-cooled engines)

Repair and overhaul tools

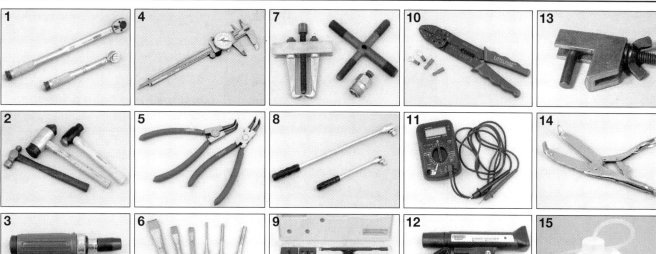

1   Torque wrench
    (small and mid-ranges)
2   Conventional, plastic or
    soft-faced hammers
3   Impact driver set

4   Vernier gauge
5   Circlip pliers (internal and
    external, or combination)
6   Set of cold chisels
    and punches

7   Selection of pullers
8   Breaker bars
9   Chain breaking/
    riveting tool set

10 Wire stripper and
    crimper tool
11 Multimeter (measures
    amps, volts and ohms)
12 Stroboscope (for
    dynamic timing checks)

13 Hose clamp
    (wingnut type shown)
14 Clutch holding tool
15 One-man brake/clutch
    bleeder kit

Specialist tools

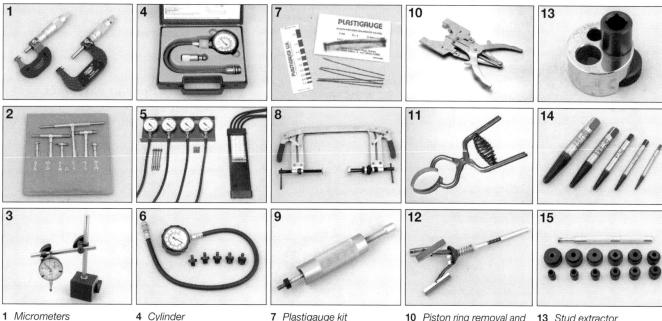

1   Micrometers
    (external type)
2   Telescoping gauges
3   Dial gauge

4   Cylinder
    compression gauge
5   Vacuum gauges (left) or
    manometer (right)
6   Oil pressure gauge

7   Plastigauge kit
8   Valve spring compressor
    (4-stroke engines)
9   Piston pin drawbolt tool

10 Piston ring removal and
    installation tool
11 Piston ring clamp
12 Cylinder bore hone
    (stone type shown)

13 Stud extractor
14 Screw extractor set
15 Bearing driver set

1 Workshop equipment and facilities

The workbench

● Work is made much easier by raising the bike up on a ramp - components are much more accessible if raised to waist level. The hydraulic or pneumatic types seen in the dealer's workshop are a sound investment if you undertake a lot of repairs or overhauls **(see illustration 1.1)**.

1.1 Hydraulic motorcycle ramp

● If raised off ground level, the bike must be supported on the ramp to avoid it falling. Most ramps incorporate a front wheel locating clamp which can be adjusted to suit different diameter wheels. When tightening the clamp, take care not to mark the wheel rim or damage the tyre - use wood blocks on each side to prevent this.
● Secure the bike to the ramp using tie-downs **(see illustration 1.2)**. If the bike has only a sidestand, and hence leans at a dangerous angle when raised, support the bike on an auxiliary stand.

1.2 Tie-downs are used around the passenger footrests to secure the bike

● Auxiliary (paddock) stands are widely available from mail order companies or motorcycle dealers and attach either to the wheel axle or swingarm pivot **(see illustration 1.3)**. If the motorcycle has a centrestand, you can support it under the crankcase to prevent it toppling whilst either wheel is removed **(see illustration 1.4)**.

1.3 This auxiliary stand attaches to the swingarm pivot

1.4 Always use a block of wood between the engine and jack head when supporting the engine in this way

Fumes and fire

● Refer to the Safety first! page at the beginning of the manual for full details. Make sure your workshop is equipped with a fire extinguisher suitable for fuel-related fires (Class B fire - flammable liquids) - it is not sufficient to have a water-filled extinguisher.
● Always ensure adequate ventilation is available. Unless an exhaust gas extraction system is available for use, ensure that the engine is run outside of the workshop.
● If working on the fuel system, make sure the workshop is ventilated to avoid a build-up of fumes. This applies equally to fume build-up when charging a battery. Do not smoke or allow anyone else to smoke in the workshop.

Fluids

● If you need to drain fuel from the tank, store it in an approved container marked as suitable for the storage of petrol (gasoline) **(see illustration 1.5)**. Do not store fuel in glass jars or bottles.

1.5 Use an approved can only for storing petrol (gasoline)

● Use proprietary engine degreasers or solvents which have a high flash-point, such as paraffin (kerosene), for cleaning off oil, grease and dirt - never use petrol (gasoline) for cleaning. Wear rubber gloves when handling solvent and engine degreaser. The fumes from certain solvents can be dangerous - always work in a well-ventilated area.

Dust, eye and hand protection

● Protect your lungs from inhalation of dust particles by wearing a filtering mask over the nose and mouth. Many frictional materials still contain asbestos which is dangerous to your health. Protect your eyes from spouts of liquid and sprung components by wearing a pair of protective goggles **(see illustration 1.6)**.

1.6 A fire extinguisher, goggles, mask and protective gloves should be at hand in the workshop

● Protect your hands from contact with solvents, fuel and oils by wearing rubber gloves. Alternatively apply a barrier cream to your hands before starting work. If handling hot components or fluids, wear suitable gloves to protect your hands from scalding and burns.

What to do with old fluids

● Old cleaning solvent, fuel, coolant and oils should not be poured down domestic drains or onto the ground. Package the fluid up in old oil containers, label it accordingly, and take it to a garage or disposal facility. Contact your local authority for location of such sites or ring the oil care hotline.

OIL CARE
FOLLOW THE CODE
OIL BANK LINE
0800 66 33 66

Note: It is antisocial and illegal to dump oil down the drain. To find the location of your local oil recycling bank, call this number free.

In the USA, note that any oil supplier must accept used oil for recycling.

2 Fasteners - screws, bolts and nuts

Fastener types and applications

Bolts and screws

● Fastener head types are either of hexagonal, Torx or splined design, with internal and external versions of each type **(see illustrations 2.1 and 2.2)**; splined head fasteners are not in common use on motorcycles. The conventional slotted or Phillips head design is used for certain screws. Bolt or screw length is always measured from the underside of the head to the end of the item **(see illustration 2.11)**.

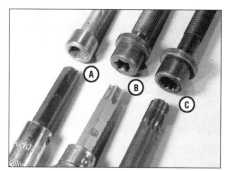

2.1 Internal hexagon/Allen (A), Torx (B) and splined (C) fasteners, with corresponding bits

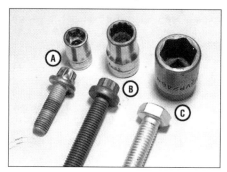

2.2 External Torx (A), splined (B) and hexagon (C) fasteners, with corresponding sockets

● Certain fasteners on the motorcycle have a tensile marking on their heads, the higher the marking the stronger the fastener. High tensile fasteners generally carry a 10 or higher marking. Never replace a high tensile fastener with one of a lower tensile strength.

Washers (see illustration 2.3)

● Plain washers are used between a fastener head and a component to prevent damage to the component or to spread the load when torque is applied. Plain washers can also be used as spacers or shims in certain assemblies. Copper or aluminium plain washers are often used as sealing washers on drain plugs.

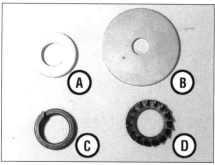

2.3 Plain washer (A), penny washer (B), spring washer (C) and serrated washer (D)

● The split-ring spring washer works by applying axial tension between the fastener head and component. If flattened, it is fatigued and must be renewed. If a plain (flat) washer is used on the fastener, position the spring washer between the fastener and the plain washer.
● Serrated star type washers dig into the fastener and component faces, preventing loosening. They are often used on electrical earth (ground) connections to the frame.
● Cone type washers (sometimes called Belleville) are conical and when tightened apply axial tension between the fastener head and component. They must be installed with the dished side against the component and often carry an OUTSIDE marking on their outer face. If flattened, they are fatigued and must be renewed.
● Tab washers are used to lock plain nuts or bolts on a shaft. A portion of the tab washer is bent up hard against one flat of the nut or bolt to prevent it loosening. Due to the tab washer being deformed in use, a new tab washer should be used every time it is disturbed.
● Wave washers are used to take up endfloat on a shaft. They provide light springing and prevent excessive side-to-side play of a component. Can be found on rocker arm shafts.

Nuts and split pins

● Conventional plain nuts are usually six-sided **(see illustration 2.4)**. They are sized by thread diameter and pitch. High tensile nuts carry a number on one end to denote their tensile strength.

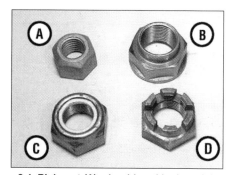

2.4 Plain nut (A), shouldered locknut (B), nylon insert nut (C) and castellated nut (D)

● Self-locking nuts either have a nylon insert, or two spring metal tabs, or a shoulder which is staked into a groove in the shaft - their advantage over conventional plain nuts is a resistance to loosening due to vibration. The nylon insert type can be used a number of times, but must be renewed when the friction of the nylon insert is reduced, ie when the nut spins freely on the shaft. The spring tab type can be reused unless the tabs are damaged. The shouldered type must be renewed every time it is disturbed.
● Split pins (cotter pins) are used to lock a castellated nut to a shaft or to prevent slackening of a plain nut. Common applications are wheel axles and brake torque arms. Because the split pin arms are deformed to lock around the nut a new split pin must always be used on installation - always fit the correct size split pin which will fit snugly in the shaft hole. Make sure the split pin arms are correctly located around the nut **(see illustrations 2.5 and 2.6)**.

2.5 Bend split pin (cotter pin) arms as shown (arrows) to secure a castellated nut

2.6 Bend split pin (cotter pin) arms as shown to secure a plain nut

Caution: If the castellated nut slots do not align with the shaft hole after tightening to the torque setting, tighten the nut until the next slot aligns with the hole - never slacken the nut to align its slot.

● R-pins (shaped like the letter R), or slip pins as they are sometimes called, are sprung and can be reused if they are otherwise in good condition. Always install R-pins with their closed end facing forwards **(see illustration 2.7)**.

2.7 Correct fitting of R-pin. Arrow indicates forward direction

Circlips (see illustration 2.8)

● Circlips (sometimes called snap-rings) are used to retain components on a shaft or in a housing and have corresponding external or internal ears to permit removal. Parallel-sided (machined) circlips can be installed either way round in their groove, whereas stamped circlips (which have a chamfered edge on one face) must be installed with the chamfer facing away from the direction of thrust load **(see illustration 2.9)**.

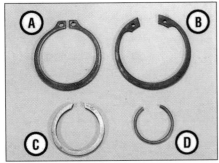

2.8 External stamped circlip (A), internal stamped circlip (B), machined circlip (C) and wire circlip (D)

● Always use circlip pliers to remove and install circlips; expand or compress them just enough to remove them. After installation, rotate the circlip in its groove to ensure it is securely seated. If installing a circlip on a splined shaft, always align its opening with a shaft channel to ensure the circlip ends are well supported and unlikely to catch **(see illustration 2.10)**.

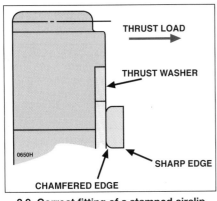

THRUST LOAD

THRUST WASHER

0650H

SHARP EDGE

CHAMFERED EDGE

2.9 Correct fitting of a stamped circlip

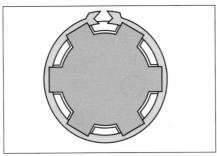

2.10 Align circlip opening with shaft channel

● Circlips can wear due to the thrust of components and become loose in their grooves, with the subsequent danger of becoming dislodged in operation. For this reason, renewal is advised every time a circlip is disturbed.
● Wire circlips are commonly used as piston pin retaining clips. If a removal tang is provided, long-nosed pliers can be used to dislodge them, otherwise careful use of a small flat-bladed screwdriver is necessary. Wire circlips should be renewed every time they are disturbed.

Thread diameter and pitch

● Diameter of a male thread (screw, bolt or stud) is the outside diameter of the threaded portion **(see illustration 2.11)**. Most motorcycle manufacturers use the ISO (International Standards Organisation) metric system expressed in millimetres, eg M6 refers to a 6 mm diameter thread. Sizing is the same for nuts, except that the thread diameter is measured across the valleys of the nut.
● Pitch is the distance between the peaks of the thread **(see illustration 2.11)**. It is expressed in millimetres, thus a common bolt size may be expressed as 6.0 x 1.0 mm (6 mm thread diameter and 1 mm pitch). Generally pitch increases in proportion to thread diameter, although there are always exceptions.
● Thread diameter and pitch are related for conventional fastener applications and the accompanying table can be used as a guide. Additionally, the AF (Across Flats), spanner or socket size dimension of the bolt or nut **(see illustration 2.11)** is linked to thread and pitch specification. Thread pitch can be measured with a thread gauge **(see illustration 2.12)**.

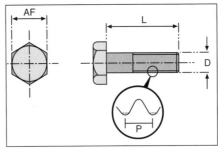

2.11 Fastener length (L), thread diameter (D), thread pitch (P) and head size (AF)

2.12 Using a thread gauge to measure pitch

AF size	Thread diameter x pitch (mm)
8 mm	M5 x 0.8
8 mm	M6 x 1.0
10 mm	M6 x 1.0
12 mm	M8 x 1.25
14 mm	M10 x 1.25
17 mm	M12 x 1.25

● The threads of most fasteners are of the right-hand type, ie they are turned clockwise to tighten and anti-clockwise to loosen. The reverse situation applies to left-hand thread fasteners, which are turned anti-clockwise to tighten and clockwise to loosen. Left-hand threads are used where rotation of a component might loosen a conventional right-hand thread fastener.

Seized fasteners

● Corrosion of external fasteners due to water or reaction between two dissimilar metals can occur over a period of time. It will build up sooner in wet conditions or in countries where salt is used on the roads during the winter. If a fastener is severely corroded it is likely that normal methods of removal will fail and result in its head being ruined. When you attempt removal, the fastener thread should be heard to crack free and unscrew easily - if it doesn't, stop there before damaging something.
● A smart tap on the head of the fastener will often succeed in breaking free corrosion which has occurred in the threads **(see illustration 2.13)**.
● An aerosol penetrating fluid (such as WD-40) applied the night beforehand may work its way down into the thread and ease removal. Depending on the location, you may be able to make up a Plasticine well around the fastener head and fill it with penetrating fluid.

2.13 A sharp tap on the head of a fastener will often break free a corroded thread

● If you are working on an engine internal component, corrosion will most likely not be a problem due to the well lubricated environment. However, components can be very tight and an impact driver is a useful tool in freeing them **(see illustration 2.14)**.

2.14 Using an impact driver to free a fastener

● Where corrosion has occurred between dissimilar metals (eg steel and aluminium alloy), the application of heat to the fastener head will create a disproportionate expansion rate between the two metals and break the seizure caused by the corrosion. Whether heat can be applied depends on the location of the fastener - any surrounding components likely to be damaged must first be removed **(see illustration 2.15)**. Heat can be applied using a paint stripper heat gun or clothes iron, or by immersing the component in boiling water - wear protective gloves to prevent scalding or burns to the hands.

2.15 Using heat to free a seized fastener

● As a last resort, it is possible to use a hammer and cold chisel to work the fastener head unscrewed **(see illustration 2.16)**. This will damage the fastener, but more importantly extreme care must be taken not to damage the surrounding component.

Caution: Remember that the component being secured is generally of more value than the bolt, nut or screw - when the fastener is freed, do not unscrew it with force, instead work the fastener back and forth when resistance is felt to prevent thread damage.

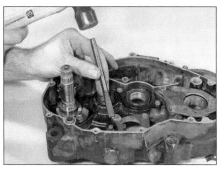

2.16 Using a hammer and chisel to free a seized fastener

Broken fasteners and damaged heads

● If the shank of a broken bolt or screw is accessible you can grip it with self-locking grips. The knurled wheel type stud extractor tool or self-gripping stud puller tool is particularly useful for removing the long studs which screw into the cylinder mouth surface of the crankcase or bolts and screws from which the head has broken off **(see illustration 2.17)**. Studs can also be removed by locking two nuts together on the threaded end of the stud and using a spanner on the lower nut **(see illustration 2.18)**.

2.17 Using a stud extractor tool to remove a broken crankcase stud

2.18 Two nuts can be locked together to unscrew a stud from a component

● A bolt or screw which has broken off below or level with the casing must be extracted using a screw extractor set. Centre punch the fastener to centralise the drill bit, then drill a hole in the fastener **(see illustration 2.19)**. Select a drill bit which is approximately half to three-quarters the

2.19 When using a screw extractor, first drill a hole in the fastener . . .

diameter of the fastener and drill to a depth which will accommodate the extractor. Use the largest size extractor possible, but avoid leaving too small a wall thickness otherwise the extractor will merely force the fastener walls outwards wedging it in the casing thread.

● If a spiral type extractor is used, thread it anti-clockwise into the fastener. As it is screwed in, it will grip the fastener and unscrew it from the casing **(see illustration 2.20)**.

2.20 . . . then thread the extractor anti-clockwise into the fastener

● If a taper type extractor is used, tap it into the fastener so that it is firmly wedged in place. Unscrew the extractor (anti-clockwise) to draw the fastener out.

⚠ *Warning: Stud extractors are very hard and may break off in the fastener if care is not taken - ask an engineer about spark erosion if this happens.*

● Alternatively, the broken bolt/screw can be drilled out and the hole retapped for an oversize bolt/screw or a diamond-section thread insert. It is essential that the drilling is carried out squarely and to the correct depth, otherwise the casing may be ruined - if in doubt, entrust the work to an engineer.

● Bolts and nuts with rounded corners cause the correct size spanner or socket to slip when force is applied. Of the types of spanner/socket available always use a six-point type rather than an eight or twelve-point type - better grip

2.21 Comparison of surface drive ring spanner (left) with 12-point type (right)

is obtained. Surface drive spanners grip the middle of the hex flats, rather than the corners, and are thus good in cases of damaged heads **(see illustration 2.21)**.

● Slotted-head or Phillips-head screws are often damaged by the use of the wrong size screwdriver. Allen-head and Torx-head screws are much less likely to sustain damage. If enough of the screw head is exposed you can use a hacksaw to cut a slot in its head and then use a conventional flat-bladed screwdriver to remove it. Alternatively use a hammer and cold chisel to tap the head of the fastener around to slacken it. Always replace damaged fasteners with new ones, preferably Torx or Allen-head type.

HAYNES
HiNT

A dab of valve grinding compound between the screw head and screw-driver tip will often give a good grip.

Thread repair

● Threads (particularly those in aluminium alloy components) can be damaged by overtightening, being assembled with dirt in the threads, or from a component working loose and vibrating. Eventually the thread will fail completely, and it will be impossible to tighten the fastener.

● If a thread is damaged or clogged with old locking compound it can be renovated with a thread repair tool (thread chaser) **(see illustrations 2.22 and 2.23)**; special thread

2.22 A thread repair tool being used to correct an internal thread

2.23 A thread repair tool being used to correct an external thread

chasers are available for spark plug hole threads. The tool will not cut a new thread, but clean and true the original thread. Make sure that you use the correct diameter and pitch tool. Similarly, external threads can be cleaned up with a die or a thread restorer file **(see illustration 2.24)**.

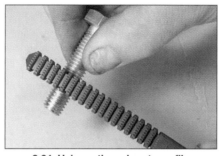

2.24 Using a thread restorer file

● It is possible to drill out the old thread and retap the component to the next thread size. This will work where there is enough surrounding material and a new bolt or screw can be obtained. Sometimes, however, this is not possible - such as where the bolt/screw passes through another component which must also be suitably modified, also in cases where a spark plug or oil drain plug cannot be obtained in a larger diameter thread size.

● The diamond-section thread insert (often known by its popular trade name of Heli-Coil) is a simple and effective method of renewing the thread and retaining the original size. A kit can be purchased which contains the tap, insert and installing tool **(see illustration 2.25)**. Drill out the damaged thread with the size drill specified **(see illustration 2.26)**. Carefully retap the thread **(see illustration 2.27)**. Install the

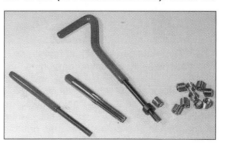

2.25 Obtain a thread insert kit to suit the thread diameter and pitch required

2.26 To install a thread insert, first drill out the original thread . . .

2.27 . . . tap a new thread . . .

2.28 . . . fit insert on the installing tool . . .

2.29 . . . and thread into the component . . .

2.30 . . . break off the tang when complete

insert on the installing tool and thread it slowly into place using a light downward pressure **(see illustrations 2.28 and 2.29)**. When positioned between a 1/4 and 1/2 turn below the surface withdraw the installing tool and use the break-off tool to press down on the tang, breaking it off **(see illustration 2.30)**.

● There are epoxy thread repair kits on the market which can rebuild stripped internal threads, although this repair should not be used on high load-bearing components.

Thread locking and sealing compounds

● Locking compounds are used in locations where the fastener is prone to loosening due to vibration or on important safety-related items which might cause loss of control of the motorcycle if they fail. It is also used where important fasteners cannot be secured by other means such as lockwashers or split pins.

● Before applying locking compound, make sure that the threads (internal and external) are clean and dry with all old compound removed. Select a compound to suit the component being secured - a non-permanent general locking and sealing type is suitable for most applications, but a high strength type is needed for permanent fixing of studs in castings. Apply a drop or two of the compound to the first few threads of the fastener, then thread it into place and tighten to the specified torque. Do not apply excessive thread locking compound otherwise the thread may be damaged on subsequent removal.

● Certain fasteners are impregnated with a dry film type coating of locking compound on their threads. Always renew this type of fastener if disturbed.

● Anti-seize compounds, such as copper-based greases, can be applied to protect threads from seizure due to extreme heat and corrosion. A common instance is spark plug threads and exhaust system fasteners.

3 Measuring tools and gauges

Feeler gauges

● Feeler gauges (or blades) are used for measuring small gaps and clearances (see illustration 3.1). They can also be used to measure endfloat (sideplay) of a component on a shaft where access is not possible with a dial gauge.

● Feeler gauge sets should be treated with care and not bent or damaged. They are etched with their size on one face. Keep them clean and very lightly oiled to prevent corrosion build-up.

3.1 Feeler gauges are used for measuring small gaps and clearances - thickness is marked on one face of gauge

● When measuring a clearance, select a gauge which is a light sliding fit between the two components. You may need to use two gauges together to measure the clearance accurately.

Micrometers

● A micrometer is a precision tool capable of measuring to 0.01 or 0.001 of a millimetre. It should always be stored in its case and not in the general toolbox. It must be kept clean and never dropped, otherwise its frame or measuring anvils could be distorted resulting in inaccurate readings.

● External micrometers are used for measuring outside diameters of components and have many more applications than internal micrometers. Micrometers are available in different size ranges, eg 0 to 25 mm, 25 to 50 mm, and upwards in 25 mm steps; some large micrometers have interchangeable anvils to allow a range of measurements to be taken. Generally the largest precision measurement you are likely to take on a motorcycle is the piston diameter.

● Internal micrometers (or bore micrometers) are used for measuring inside diameters, such as valve guides and cylinder bores. Telescoping gauges and small hole gauges are used in conjunction with an external micrometer, whereas the more expensive internal micrometers have their own measuring device.

External micrometer

Note: *The conventional analogue type instrument is described. Although much easier to read, digital micrometers are considerably more expensive.*

● Always check the calibration of the micrometer before use. With the anvils closed (0 to 25 mm type) or set over a test gauge (for

3.2 Check micrometer calibration before use

the larger types) the scale should read zero **(see illustration 3.2)**; make sure that the anvils (and test piece) are clean first. Any discrepancy can be adjusted by referring to the instructions supplied with the tool. Remember that the micrometer is a precision measuring tool - don't force the anvils closed, use the ratchet (4) on the end of the micrometer to close it. In this way, a measured force is always applied.

● To use, first make sure that the item being measured is clean. Place the anvil of the micrometer (1) against the item and use the thimble (2) to bring the spindle (3) lightly into contact with the other side of the item **(see illustration 3.3)**. Don't tighten the thimble down because this will damage the micrometer - instead use the ratchet (4) on the end of the micrometer. The ratchet mechanism applies a measured force preventing damage to the instrument.

● The micrometer is read by referring to the linear scale on the sleeve and the annular scale on the thimble. Read off the sleeve first to obtain the base measurement, then add the fine measurement from the thimble to obtain the overall reading. The linear scale on the sleeve represents the measuring range of the micrometer (eg 0 to 25 mm). The annular scale

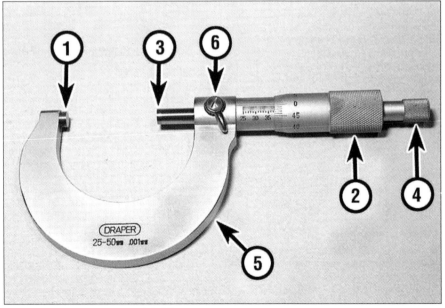

3.3 Micrometer component parts

1 Anvil	3 Spindle	5 Frame
2 Thimble	4 Ratchet	6 Locking lever

on the thimble will be in graduations of 0.01 mm (or as marked on the frame) - one full revolution of the thimble will move 0.5 mm on the linear scale. Take the reading where the datum line on the sleeve intersects the thimble's scale. Always position the eye directly above the scale otherwise an inaccurate reading will result.

In the example shown the item measures 2.95 mm **(see illustration 3.4)**:

Linear scale	2.00 mm
Linear scale	0.50 mm
Annular scale	0.45 mm
Total figure	**2.95 mm**

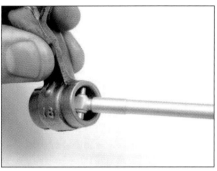

3.7 Expand the telescoping gauge in the bore, lock its position . . .

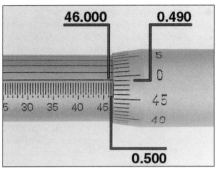

3.5 Micrometer reading of 46.99 mm on linear and annular scales . . .

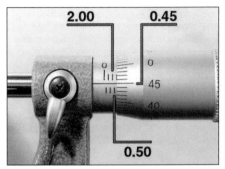

3.4 Micrometer reading of 2.95 mm

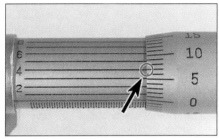

3.6 . . . and 0.004 mm on vernier scale

3.8 . . . then measure the gauge with a micrometer

Most micrometers have a locking lever (6) on the frame to hold the setting in place, allowing the item to be removed from the micrometer.
● Some micrometers have a vernier scale on their sleeve, providing an even finer measurement to be taken, in 0.001 increments of a millimetre. Take the sleeve and thimble measurement as described above, then check which graduation on the vernier scale aligns with that of the annular scale on the thimble **Note:** *The eye must be perpendicular to the scale when taking the vernier reading - if necessary rotate the body of the micrometer to ensure this.* Multiply the vernier scale figure by 0.001 and add it to the base and fine measurement figures.

In the example shown the item measures 46.994 mm **(see illustrations 3.5 and 3.6)**:

Linear scale (base)	46.000 mm
Linear scale (base)	00.500 mm
Annular scale (fine)	00.490 mm
Vernier scale	00.004 mm
Total figure	**46.994 mm**

Internal micrometer

● Internal micrometers are available for measuring bore diameters, but are expensive and unlikely to be available for home use. It is suggested that a set of telescoping gauges and small hole gauges, both of which must be used with an external micrometer, will suffice for taking internal measurements on a motorcycle.
● Telescoping gauges can be used to

measure internal diameters of components. Select a gauge with the correct size range, make sure its ends are clean and insert it into the bore. Expand the gauge, then lock its position and withdraw it from the bore **(see illustration 3.7)**. Measure across the gauge ends with a micrometer **(see illustration 3.8)**.
● Very small diameter bores (such as valve guides) are measured with a small hole gauge. Once adjusted to a slip-fit inside the component, its position is locked and the gauge withdrawn for measurement with a micrometer **(see illustrations 3.9 and 3.10)**.

Vernier caliper

Note: *The conventional linear and dial gauge type instruments are described. Digital types are easier to read, but are far more expensive.*
● The vernier caliper does not provide the precision of a micrometer, but is versatile in being able to measure internal and external diameters. Some types also incorporate a depth gauge. It is ideal for measuring clutch plate friction material and spring free lengths.
● To use the conventional linear scale vernier, slacken off the vernier clamp screws (1) and set its jaws over (2), or inside (3), the item to be measured **(see illustration 3.11)**. Slide the jaw into contact, using the thumbwheel (4) for fine movement of the sliding scale (5) then tighten the clamp screws (1). Read off the main scale (6) where the zero on the sliding scale (5) intersects it, taking the whole number to the left of the zero; this provides the base measurement. View along the sliding scale and select the division which

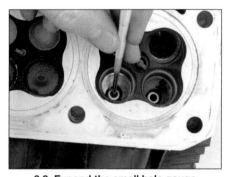

3.9 Expand the small hole gauge in the bore, lock its position . . .

3.10 . . . then measure the gauge with a micrometer

lines up exactly with any of the divisions on the main scale, noting that the divisions usually represents 0.02 of a millimetre. Add this fine measurement to the base measurement to obtain the total reading.

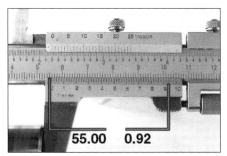

3.11 Vernier component parts (linear gauge)

1	Clamp screws	3	Internal jaws	5	Sliding scale	7	Depth gauge
2	External jaws	4	Thumbwheel	6	Main scale		

In the example shown the item measures 55.92 mm **(see illustration 3.12)**:

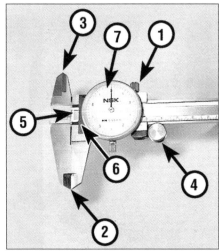

3.12 Vernier gauge reading of 55.92 mm

3.13 Vernier component parts (dial gauge)

1	Clamp screw	5	Main scale
2	External jaws	6	Sliding scale
3	Internal jaws	7	Dial gauge
4	Thumbwheel		

Base measurement	55.00 mm
Fine measurement	00.92 mm
Total figure	**55.92 mm**

● Some vernier calipers are equipped with a dial gauge for fine measurement. Before use, check that the jaws are clean, then close them fully and check that the dial gauge reads zero. If necessary adjust the gauge ring accordingly. Slacken the vernier clamp screw (1) and set its jaws over (2), or inside (3), the item to be measured **(see illustration 3.13)**. Slide the jaws into contact, using the thumbwheel (4) for fine movement. Read off the main scale (5) where the edge of the sliding scale (6) intersects it, taking the whole number to the left of the zero; this provides the base measurement. Read off the needle position on the dial gauge (7) scale to provide the fine measurement; each division represents 0.05 of a millimetre. Add this fine measurement to the base measurement to obtain the total reading.

In the example shown the item measures 55.95 mm **(see illustration 3.14)**:

Base measurement	55.00 mm
Fine measurement	00.95 mm
Total figure	**55.95 mm**

3.14 Vernier gauge reading of 55.95 mm

Plastigauge

● Plastigauge is a plastic material which can be compressed between two surfaces to measure the oil clearance between them. The width of the compressed Plastigauge is measured against a calibrated scale to determine the clearance.

● Common uses of Plastigauge are for measuring the clearance between crankshaft journal and main bearing inserts, between crankshaft journal and big-end bearing inserts, and between camshaft and bearing surfaces. The following example describes big-end oil clearance measurement.

● Handle the Plastigauge material carefully to prevent distortion. Using a sharp knife, cut a length which corresponds with the width of the bearing being measured and place it carefully across the journal so that it is parallel with the shaft **(see illustration 3.15)**. Carefully install both bearing shells and the connecting rod. Without rotating the rod on the journal tighten its bolts or nuts (as applicable) to the specified torque. The connecting rod and bearings are then disassembled and the crushed Plastigauge examined.

3.15 Plastigauge placed across shaft journal

● Using the scale provided in the Plastigauge kit, measure the width of the material to determine the oil clearance **(see illustration 3.16)**. Always remove all traces of Plastigauge after use using your fingernails.

> **Caution: Arriving at the correct clearance demands that the assembly is torqued correctly, according to the settings and sequence (where applicable) provided by the motorcycle manufacturer.**

3.16 Measuring the width of the crushed Plastigauge

Dial gauge or DTI (Dial Test Indicator)

● A dial gauge can be used to accurately measure small amounts of movement. Typical uses are measuring shaft runout or shaft endfloat (sideplay) and setting piston position for ignition timing on two-strokes. A dial gauge set usually comes with a range of different probes and adapters and mounting equipment.
● The gauge needle must point to zero when at rest. Rotate the ring around its periphery to zero the gauge.
● Check that the gauge is capable of reading the extent of movement in the work. Most gauges have a small dial set in the face which records whole millimetres of movement as well as the fine scale around the face periphery which is calibrated in 0.01 mm divisions. Read off the small dial first to obtain the base measurement, then add the measurement from the fine scale to obtain the total reading.

In the example shown the gauge reads 1.48 mm **(see illustration 3.17)**:

Base measurement	1.00 mm
Fine measurement	0.48 mm
Total figure	**1.48 mm**

3.17 Dial gauge reading of 1.48 mm

● If measuring shaft runout, the shaft must be supported in vee-blocks and the gauge mounted on a stand perpendicular to the shaft. Rest the tip of the gauge against the centre of the shaft and rotate the shaft slowly whilst watching the gauge reading **(see illustration 3.18)**. Take several measurements along the length of the shaft and record the

3.18 Using a dial gauge to measure shaft runout

maximum gauge reading as the amount of runout in the shaft. **Note:** *The reading obtained will be total runout at that point - some manufacturers specify that the runout figure is halved to compare with their specified runout limit.*
● Endfloat (sideplay) measurement requires that the gauge is mounted securely to the surrounding component with its probe touching the end of the shaft. Using hand pressure, push and pull on the shaft noting the maximum endfloat recorded on the gauge **(see illustration 3.19)**.

3.19 Using a dial gauge to measure shaft endfloat

● A dial gauge with suitable adapters can be used to determine piston position BTDC on two-stroke engines for the purposes of ignition timing. The gauge, adapter and suitable length probe are installed in the place of the spark plug and the gauge zeroed at TDC. If the piston position is specified as 1.14 mm BTDC, rotate the engine back to 2.00 mm BTDC, then slowly forwards to 1.14 mm BTDC.

Cylinder compression gauges

● A compression gauge is used for measuring cylinder compression. Either the rubber-cone type or the threaded adapter type can be used. The latter is preferred to ensure a perfect seal against the cylinder head. A 0 to 300 psi (0 to 20 Bar) type gauge (for petrol/gasoline engines) will be suitable for motorcycles.
● The spark plug is removed and the gauge either held hard against the cylinder head (cone type) or the gauge adapter screwed into the cylinder head (threaded type) **(see illustration 3.20)**. Cylinder compression is measured with the engine turning over, but not running - carry out the compression test as described in

3.20 Using a rubber-cone type cylinder compression gauge

Fault Finding Equipment. The gauge will hold the reading until manually released.

Oil pressure gauge

● An oil pressure gauge is used for measuring engine oil pressure. Most gauges come with a set of adapters to fit the thread of the take-off point **(see illustration 3.21)**. If the take-off point specified by the motorcycle manufacturer is an external oil pipe union, make sure that the specified replacement union is used to prevent oil starvation.

3.21 Oil pressure gauge and take-off point adapter (arrow)

● Oil pressure is measured with the engine running (at a specific rpm) and often the manufacturer will specify pressure limits for a cold and hot engine.

Straight-edge and surface plate

● If checking the gasket face of a component for warpage, place a steel rule or precision straight-edge across the gasket face and measure any gap between the straight-edge and component with feeler gauges **(see illustration 3.22)**. Check diagonally across the component and between mounting holes **(see illustration 3.23)**.

3.22 Use a straight-edge and feeler gauges to check for warpage

3.23 Check for warpage in these directions

- Checking individual components for warpage, such as clutch plain (metal) plates, requires a perfectly flat plate or piece or plate glass and feeler gauges.

4 Torque and leverage

What is torque?

- Torque describes the twisting force about a shaft. The amount of torque applied is determined by the distance from the centre of the shaft to the end of the lever and the amount of force being applied to the end of the lever; distance multiplied by force equals torque.
- The manufacturer applies a measured torque to a bolt or nut to ensure that it will not slacken in use and to hold two components securely together without movement in the joint. The actual torque setting depends on the thread size, bolt or nut material and the composition of the components being held.
- Too little torque may cause the fastener to loosen due to vibration, whereas too much torque will distort the joint faces of the component or cause the fastener to shear off. Always stick to the specified torque setting.

Using a torque wrench

- Check the calibration of the torque wrench and make sure it has a suitable range for the job. Torque wrenches are available in Nm (Newton-metres), kgf m (kilograms-force metre), lbf ft (pounds-feet), lbf in (inch-pounds). Do not confuse lbf ft with lbf in.
- Adjust the tool to the desired torque on the scale **(see illustration 4.1)**. If your torque wrench is not calibrated in the units specified, carefully convert the figure (see *Conversion Factors*). A manufacturer sometimes gives a torque setting as a range (8 to 10 Nm) rather than a single figure - in this case set the tool midway between the two settings. The same torque may be expressed as 9 Nm ± 1 Nm. Some torque wrenches have a method of locking the setting so that it isn't inadvertently altered during use.

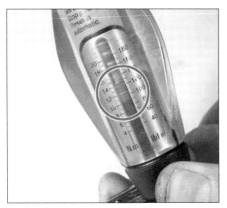

4.1 Set the torque wrench index mark to the setting required, in this case 12 Nm

- Install the bolts/nuts in their correct location and secure them lightly. Their threads must be clean and free of any old locking compound. Unless specified the threads and flange should be dry - oiled threads are necessary in certain circumstances and the manufacturer will take this into account in the specified torque figure. Similarly, the manufacturer may also specify the application of thread-locking compound.
- Tighten the fasteners in the specified sequence until the torque wrench clicks, indicating that the torque setting has been reached. Apply the torque again to double-check the setting. Where different thread diameter fasteners secure the component, as a rule tighten the larger diameter ones first.
- When the torque wrench has been finished with, release the lock (where applicable) and fully back off its setting to zero - do not leave the torque wrench tensioned. Also, do not use a torque wrench for slackening a fastener.

Angle-tightening

- Manufacturers often specify a figure in degrees for final tightening of a fastener. This usually follows tightening to a specific torque setting.
- A degree disc can be set and attached to the socket **(see illustration 4.2)** or a protractor can be used to mark the angle of movement on the bolt/nut head and the surrounding casting **(see illustration 4.3)**.

4.2 Angle tightening can be accomplished with a torque-angle gauge . . .

4.3 . . . or by marking the angle on the surrounding component

Loosening sequences

- Where more than one bolt/nut secures a component, loosen each fastener evenly a little at a time. In this way, not all the stress of the joint is held by one fastener and the components are not likely to distort.
- If a tightening sequence is provided, work in the REVERSE of this, but if not, work from the outside in, in a criss-cross sequence **(see illustration 4.4)**.

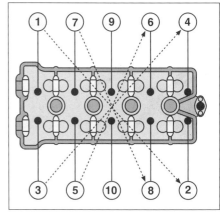

4.4 When slackening, work from the outside inwards

Tightening sequences

- If a component is held by more than one fastener it is important that the retaining bolts/nuts are tightened evenly to prevent uneven stress build-up and distortion of sealing faces. This is especially important on high-compression joints such as the cylinder head.
- A sequence is usually provided by the manufacturer, either in a diagram or actually marked in the casting. If not, always start in the centre and work outwards in a criss-cross pattern **(see illustration 4.5)**. Start off by securing all bolts/nuts finger-tight, then set the torque wrench and tighten each fastener by a small amount in sequence until the final torque is reached. By following this practice,

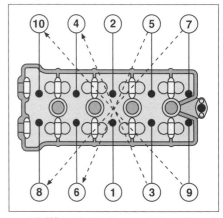

4.5 When tightening, work from the inside outwards

the joint will be held evenly and will not be distorted. Important joints, such as the cylinder head and big-end fasteners often have two- or three-stage torque settings.

Applying leverage

● Use tools at the correct angle. Position a socket wrench or spanner on the bolt/nut so that you pull it towards you when loosening. If this can't be done, push the spanner without curling your fingers around it **(see illustration 4.6)** - the spanner may slip or the fastener loosen suddenly, resulting in your fingers being crushed against a component.

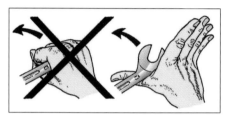

4.6 If you can't pull on the spanner to loosen a fastener, push with your hand open

● Additional leverage is gained by extending the length of the lever. The best way to do this is to use a breaker bar instead of the regular length tool, or to slip a length of tubing over the end of the spanner or socket wrench.
● If additional leverage will not work, the fastener head is either damaged or firmly corroded in place (see *Fasteners*).

5 Bearings

Bearing removal and installation

Drivers and sockets

● Before removing a bearing, always inspect the casing to see which way it must be driven out - some casings will have retaining plates or a cast step. Also check for any identifying markings on the bearing and if installed to a certain depth, measure this at this stage. Some roller bearings are sealed on one side - take note of the original fitted position.
● Bearings can be driven out of a casing using a bearing driver tool (with the correct size head) or a socket of the correct diameter. Select the driver head or socket so that it contacts the outer race of the bearing, not the balls/rollers or inner race. Always support the casing around the bearing housing with wood blocks, otherwise there is a risk of fracture. The bearing is driven out with a few blows on the driver or socket from a heavy mallet. Unless access is severely restricted (as with wheel bearings), a pin-punch is not recommended unless it is moved around the bearing to keep it square in its housing.

● The same equipment can be used to install bearings. Make sure the bearing housing is supported on wood blocks and line up the bearing in its housing. Fit the bearing as noted on removal - generally they are installed with their marked side facing outwards. Tap the bearing squarely into its housing using a driver or socket which bears only on the bearing's outer race - contact with the bearing balls/rollers or inner race will destroy it **(see illustrations 5.1 and 5.2)**.
● Check that the bearing inner race and balls/rollers rotate freely.

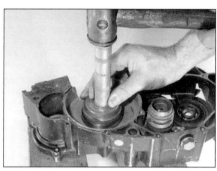

5.1 Using a bearing driver against the bearing's outer race

5.2 Using a large socket against the bearing's outer race

Pullers and slide-hammers

● Where a bearing is pressed on a shaft a puller will be required to extract it **(see illustration 5.3)**. Make sure that the puller clamp or legs fit securely behind the bearing and are unlikely to slip out. If pulling a bearing

5.3 This bearing puller clamps behind the bearing and pressure is applied to the shaft end to draw the bearing off

off a gear shaft for example, you may have to locate the puller behind a gear pinion if there is no access to the race and draw the gear pinion off the shaft as well **(see illustration 5.4)**.

> *Caution: Ensure that the puller's centre bolt locates securely against the end of the shaft and will not slip when pressure is applied. Also ensure that puller does not damage the shaft end.*

5.4 Where no access is available to the rear of the bearing, it is sometimes possible to draw off the adjacent component

● Operate the puller so that its centre bolt exerts pressure on the shaft end and draws the bearing off the shaft.
● When installing the bearing on the shaft, tap only on the bearing's inner race - contact with the balls/rollers or outer race with destroy the bearing. Use a socket or length of tubing as a drift which fits over the shaft end **(see illustration 5.5)**.

5.5 When installing a bearing on a shaft use a piece of tubing which bears only on the bearing's inner race

● Where a bearing locates in a blind hole in a casing, it cannot be driven or pulled out as described above. A slide-hammer with knife-edged bearing puller attachment will be required. The puller attachment passes through the bearing and when tightened expands to fit firmly behind the bearing **(see illustration 5.6)**. By operating the slide-hammer part of the tool the bearing is jarred out of its housing **(see illustration 5.7)**.
● It is possible, if the bearing is of reasonable weight, for it to drop out of its housing if the casing is heated as described opposite. If this

5.6 Expand the bearing puller so that it locks behind the bearing . . .

5.7 . . . attach the slide hammer to the bearing puller

method is attempted, first prepare a work surface which will enable the casing to be tapped face down to help dislodge the bearing - a wood surface is ideal since it will not damage the casing's gasket surface. Wearing protective gloves, tap the heated casing several times against the work surface to dislodge the bearing under its own weight **(see illustration 5.8)**.

5.8 Tapping a casing face down on wood blocks can often dislodge a bearing

● Bearings can be installed in blind holes using the driver or socket method described above.

Drawbolts

● Where a bearing or bush is set in the eye of a component, such as a suspension linkage arm or connecting rod small-end, removal by drift may damage the component. Furthermore, a rubber bushing in a shock absorber eye cannot successfully be driven out of position. If access is available to a engineering press, the task is straightforward. If not, a drawbolt can be fabricated to extract the bearing or bush.

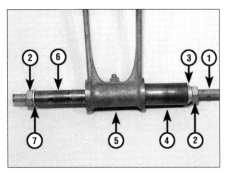

5.9 Drawbolt component parts assembled on a suspension arm

1 Bolt or length of threaded bar
2 Nuts
3 Washer (external diameter greater than tubing internal diameter)
4 Tubing (internal diameter sufficient to accommodate bearing)
5 Suspension arm with bearing
6 Tubing (external diameter slightly smaller than bearing)
7 Washer (external diameter slightly smaller than bearing)

5.10 Drawing the bearing out of the suspension arm

● To extract the bearing/bush you will need a long bolt with nut (or piece of threaded bar with two nuts), a piece of tubing which has an internal diameter larger than the bearing/bush, another piece of tubing which has an external diameter slightly smaller than the bearing/bush, and a selection of washers **(see illustrations 5.9 and 5.10)**. Note that the pieces of tubing must be of the same length, or longer, than the bearing/bush.
● The same kit (without the pieces of tubing) can be used to draw the new bearing/bush back into place **(see illustration 5.11)**.

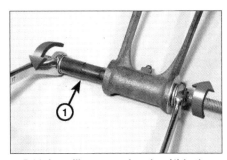

5.11 Installing a new bearing (1) in the suspension arm

Temperature change

● If the bearing's outer race is a tight fit in the casing, the aluminium casing can be heated to release its grip on the bearing. Aluminium will expand at a greater rate than the steel bearing outer race. There are several ways to do this, but avoid any localised extreme heat (such as a blow torch) - aluminium alloy has a low melting point.
● Approved methods of heating a casing are using a domestic oven (heated to 100°C) or immersing the casing in boiling water **(see illustration 5.12)**. Low temperature range localised heat sources such as a paint stripper heat gun or clothes iron can also be used **(see illustration 5.13)**. Alternatively, soak a rag in boiling water, wring it out and wrap it around the bearing housing.

> ⚠ **Warning: All of these methods require care in use to prevent scalding and burns to the hands. Wear protective gloves when handling hot components.**

5.12 A casing can be immersed in a sink of boiling water to aid bearing removal

5.13 Using a localised heat source to aid bearing removal

● If heating the whole casing note that plastic components, such as the neutral switch, may suffer - remove them beforehand.
● After heating, remove the bearing as described above. You may find that the expansion is sufficient for the bearing to fall out of the casing under its own weight or with a light tap on the driver or socket.
● If necessary, the casing can be heated to aid bearing installation, and this is sometimes the recommended procedure if the motorcycle manufacturer has designed the housing and bearing fit with this intention.

● Installation of bearings can be eased by placing them in a freezer the night before installation. The steel bearing will contract slightly, allowing easy insertion in its housing. This is often useful when installing steering head outer races in the frame.

Bearing types and markings

● Plain shell bearings, ball bearings, needle roller bearings and tapered roller bearings will all be found on motorcycles **(see illustrations 5.14 and 5.15)**. The ball and roller types are usually caged between an inner and outer race, but uncaged variations may be found.

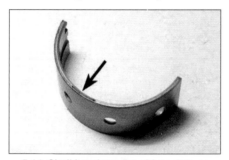

5.14 Shell bearings are either plain or grooved. They are usually identified by colour code (arrow)

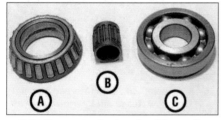

5.15 Tapered roller bearing (A), needle roller bearing (B) and ball journal bearing (C)

● Shell bearings (often called inserts) are usually found at the crankshaft main and connecting rod big-end where they are good at coping with high loads. They are made of a phosphor-bronze material and are impregnated with self-lubricating properties.
● Ball bearings and needle roller bearings consist of a steel inner and outer race with the balls or rollers between the races. They require constant lubrication by oil or grease and are good at coping with axial loads. Taper roller bearings consist of rollers set in a tapered cage set on the inner race; the outer race is separate. They are good at coping with axial loads and prevent movement along the shaft - a typical application is in the steering head.
● Bearing manufacturers produce bearings to ISO size standards and stamp one face of the bearing to indicate its internal and external diameter, load capacity and type **(see illustration 5.16)**.
● Metal bushes are usually of phosphor-bronze material. Rubber bushes are used in suspension mounting eyes. Fibre bushes have also been used in suspension pivots.

5.16 Typical bearing marking

Bearing fault finding

● If a bearing outer race has spun in its housing, the housing material will be damaged. You can use a bearing locking compound to bond the outer race in place if damage is not too severe.
● Shell bearings will fail due to damage of their working surface, as a result of lack of lubrication, corrosion or abrasive particles in the oil **(see illustration 5.17)**. Small particles of dirt in the oil may embed in the bearing material whereas larger particles will score the bearing and shaft journal. If a number of short journeys are made, insufficient heat will be generated to drive off condensation which has built up on the bearings.

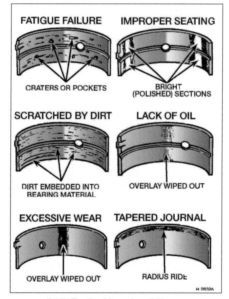

5.17 Typical bearing failures

● Ball and roller bearings will fail due to lack of lubrication or damage to the balls or rollers. Tapered-roller bearings can be damaged by overloading them. Unless the bearing is sealed on both sides, wash it in paraffin (kerosene) to remove all old grease then allow it to dry. Make a visual inspection looking to dented balls or rollers, damaged cages and worn or pitted races **(see illustration 5.18)**.
● A ball bearing can be checked for wear by listening to it when spun. Apply a film of light oil to the bearing and hold it close to the ear - hold the outer race with one hand and spin the inner

5.18 Example of ball journal bearing with damaged balls and cages

5.19 Hold outer race and listen to inner race when spun

race with the other hand **(see illustration 5.19)**. The bearing should be almost silent when spun; if it grates or rattles it is worn.

6 Oil seals

Oil seal removal and installation

● Oil seals should be renewed every time a component is dismantled. This is because the seal lips will become set to the sealing surface and will not necessarily reseal.
● Oil seals can be prised out of position using a large flat-bladed screwdriver **(see illustration 6.1)**. In the case of crankcase seals, check first that the seal is not lipped on the inside, preventing its removal with the crankcases joined.

6.1 Prise out oil seals with a large flat-bladed screwdriver

● New seals are usually installed with their marked face (containing the seal reference code) outwards and the spring side towards the fluid being retained. In certain cases, such as a two-stroke engine crankshaft seal, a double lipped seal may be used due to there being fluid or gas on each side of the joint.

● Use a bearing driver or socket which bears only on the outer hard edge of the seal to install it in the casing - tapping on the inner edge will damage the sealing lip.

Oil seal types and markings

● Oil seals are usually of the single-lipped type. Double-lipped seals are found where a liquid or gas is on both sides of the joint.
● Oil seals can harden and lose their sealing ability if the motorcycle has been in storage for a long period - renewal is the only solution.
● Oil seal manufacturers also conform to the ISO markings for seal size - these are moulded into the outer face of the seal (see illustration 6.2).

6.2 These oil seal markings indicate inside diameter, outside diameter and seal thickness

7 Gaskets and sealants

Types of gasket and sealant

● Gaskets are used to seal the mating surfaces between components and keep lubricants, fluids, vacuum or pressure contained within the assembly. Aluminium gaskets are sometimes found at the cylinder joints, but most gaskets are paper-based. If the mating surfaces of the components being joined are undamaged the gasket can be installed dry, although a dab of sealant or grease will be useful to hold it in place during assembly.
● RTV (Room Temperature Vulcanising) silicone rubber sealants cure when exposed to moisture in the atmosphere. These sealants are good at filling pits or irregular gasket faces, but will tend to be forced out of the joint under very high torque. They can be used to replace a paper gasket, but first make sure that the width of the paper gasket is not essential to the shimming of internal components. RTV sealants should not be used on components containing petrol (gasoline).
● Non-hardening, semi-hardening and hard setting liquid gasket compounds can be used with a gasket or between a metal-to-metal joint. Select the sealant to suit the application: universal non-hardening sealant can be used on virtually all joints; semi-hardening on joint faces which are rough or damaged; hard setting sealant on joints which require a permanent bond and are subjected to high temperature and pressure. Note: Check first if the paper gasket has a bead of sealant

impregnated in its surface before applying additional sealant.
● When choosing a sealant, make sure it is suitable for the application, particularly if being applied in a high-temperature area or in the vicinity of fuel. Certain manufacturers produce sealants in either clear, silver or black colours to match the finish of the engine. This has a particular application on motorcycles where much of the engine is exposed.
● Do not over-apply sealant. That which is squeezed out on the outside of the joint can be wiped off, whereas an excess of sealant on the inside can break off and clog oilways.

Breaking a sealed joint

● Age, heat, pressure and the use of hard setting sealant can cause two components to stick together so tightly that they are difficult to separate using finger pressure alone. Do not resort to using levers unless there is a pry point provided for this purpose (see illustration 7.1) or else the gasket surfaces will be damaged.
● Use a soft-faced hammer (see illustration 7.2) or a wood block and conventional hammer to strike the component near the mating surface. Avoid hammering against cast extremities since they may break off. If this method fails, try using a wood wedge between the two components.

Caution: If the joint will not separate, double-check that you have removed all the fasteners.

7.1 If a pry point is provided, apply gently pressure with a flat-bladed screwdriver

7.2 Tap around the joint with a soft-faced mallet if necessary - don't strike cooling fins

Removal of old gasket and sealant

● Paper gaskets will most likely come away complete, leaving only a few traces stuck on

Most components have one or two hollow locating dowels between the two gasket faces. If a dowel cannot be removed, do not resort to gripping it with pliers - it will almost certainly be distorted. Install a close-fitting socket or Phillips screwdriver into the dowel and then grip the outer edge of the dowel to free it.

the sealing faces of the components. It is imperative that all traces are removed to ensure correct sealing of the new gasket.
● Very carefully scrape all traces of gasket away making sure that the sealing surfaces are not gouged or scored by the scraper (see illustrations 7.3, 7.4 and 7.5). Stubborn deposits can be removed by spraying with an aerosol gasket remover. Final preparation of

7.3 Paper gaskets can be scraped off with a gasket scraper tool . . .

7.4 . . . a knife blade . . .

7.5 . . . or a household scraper

7.6 Fine abrasive paper is wrapped around a flat file to clean up the gasket face

7.7 A kitchen scourer can be used on stubborn deposits

the gasket surface can be made with very fine abrasive paper or a plastic kitchen scourer (see illustrations 7.6 and 7.7).
● Old sealant can be scraped or peeled off components, depending on the type originally used. Note that gasket removal compounds are available to avoid scraping the components clean; make sure the gasket remover suits the type of sealant used.

8 Chains

Breaking and joining final drive chains

● Drive chains for all but small bikes are continuous and do not have a clip-type connecting link. The chain must be broken using a chain breaker tool and the new chain securely riveted together using a new soft rivet-type link. Never use a clip-type connecting link instead of a rivet-type link, except in an emergency. Various chain breaking and riveting tools are available, either as separate tools or combined as illustrated in the accompanying photographs - read the instructions supplied with the tool carefully.

 Warning: The need to rivet the new link pins correctly cannot be overstressed - loss of control of the motorcycle is very likely to result if the chain breaks in use.

● Rotate the chain and look for the soft link. The soft link pins look like they have been

8.1 Tighten the chain breaker to push the pin out of the link . . .

8.2 . . . withdraw the pin, remove the tool . . .

8.3 . . . and separate the chain link

deeply centre-punched instead of peened over like all the other pins (see illustration 8.9) and its sideplate may be a different colour. Position the soft link midway between the sprockets and assemble the chain breaker tool over one of the soft link pins (see illustration 8.1). Operate the tool to push the pin out through the chain (see illustration 8.2). On an O-ring chain, remove the O-rings (see illustration 8.3). Carry out the same procedure on the other soft link pin.

Caution: Certain soft link pins (particularly on the larger chains) may require their ends to be filed or ground off before they can be pressed out using the tool.

● Check that you have the correct size and strength (standard or heavy duty) new soft link - do not reuse the old link. Look for the size marking on the chain sideplates (see illustration 8.10).
● Position the chain ends so that they are engaged over the rear sprocket. On an O-ring

8.4 Insert the new soft link, with O-rings, through the chain ends . . .

8.5 . . . install the O-rings over the pin ends . . .

8.6 . . . followed by the sideplate

chain, install a new O-ring over each pin of the link and insert the link through the two chain ends (see illustration 8.4). Install a new O-ring over the end of each pin, followed by the sideplate (with the chain manufacturer's marking facing outwards) (see illustrations 8.5 and 8.6). On an unsealed chain, insert the link through the two chain ends, then install the sideplate with the chain manufacturer's marking facing outwards.
● Note that it may not be possible to install the sideplate using finger pressure alone. If using a joining tool, assemble it so that the plates of the tool clamp the link and press the sideplate over the pins (see illustration 8.7). Otherwise, use two small sockets placed over

8.7 Push the sideplate into position using a clamp

8.8 Assemble the chain riveting tool over one pin at a time and tighten it fully

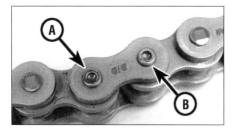

8.9 Pin end correctly riveted (A), pin end unriveted (B)

the rivet ends and two pieces of the wood between a G-clamp. Operate the clamp to press the sideplate over the pins.

● Assemble the joining tool over one pin (following the maker's instructions) and tighten the tool down to spread the pin end securely **(see illustrations 8.8 and 8.9)**. Do the same on the other pin.

 Warning: Check that the pin ends are secure and that there is no danger of the sideplate coming loose. If the pin ends are cracked the soft link must be renewed.

Final drive chain sizing

● Chains are sized using a three digit number, followed by a suffix to denote the chain type **(see illustration 8.10)**. Chain type is either standard or heavy duty (thicker sideplates), and also unsealed or O-ring/X-ring type.

● The first digit of the number relates to the pitch of the chain, ie the distance from the centre of one pin to the centre of the next pin **(see illustration 8.11)**. Pitch is expressed in eighths of an inch, as follows:

8.10 Typical chain size and type marking

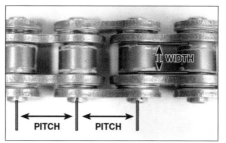

8.11 Chain dimensions

> Sizes commencing with a 4 (eg 428) have a pitch of 1/2 inch (12.7 mm)
>
> Sizes commencing with a 5 (eg 520) have a pitch of 5/8 inch (15.9 mm)
>
> Sizes commencing with a 6 (eg 630) have a pitch of 3/4 inch (19.1 mm)

● The second and third digits of the chain size relate to the width of the rollers, again in imperial units, eg the 525 shown has 5/16 inch (7.94 mm) rollers **(see illustration 8.11)**.

9 Hoses

Clamping to prevent flow

● Small-bore flexible hoses can be clamped to prevent fluid flow whilst a component is worked on. Whichever method is used, ensure that the hose material is not permanently distorted or damaged by the clamp.

a) A brake hose clamp available from auto accessory shops **(see illustration 9.1)**.
b) A wingnut type hose clamp **(see illustration 9.2)**.

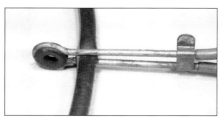

9.1 Hoses can be clamped with an automotive brake hose clamp . . .

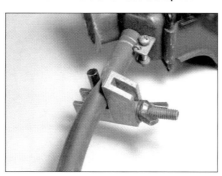

9.2 . . . a wingnut type hose clamp . . .

c) Two sockets placed each side of the hose and held with straight-jawed self-locking grips **(see illustration 9.3)**.
d) Thick card each side of the hose held between straight-jawed self-locking grips **(see illustration 9.4)**.

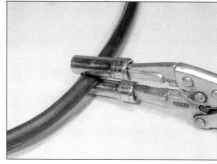

9.3 . . . two sockets and a pair of self-locking grips . . .

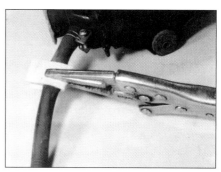

9.4 . . . or thick card and self-locking grips

Freeing and fitting hoses

● Always make sure the hose clamp is moved well clear of the hose end. Grip the hose with your hand and rotate it whilst pulling it off the union. If the hose has hardened due to age and will not move, slit it with a sharp knife and peel its ends off the union **(see illustration 9.5)**.

● Resist the temptation to use grease or soap on the unions to aid installation; although it helps the hose slip over the union it will equally aid the escape of fluid from the joint. It is preferable to soften the hose ends in hot water and wet the inside surface of the hose with water or a fluid which will evaporate.

9.5 Cutting a coolant hose free with a sharp knife

About the MOT Test

In the UK, all vehicles more than three years old are subject to an annual test to ensure that they meet minimum safety requirements. A current test certificate must be issued before a machine can be used on public roads, and is required before a road fund licence can be issued. Riding without a current test certificate will also invalidate your insurance.

For most owners, the MOT test is an annual cause for anxiety, and this is largely due to owners not being sure what needs to be checked prior to submitting the motorcycle for testing. The simple answer is that a fully roadworthy motorcycle will have no difficulty in passing the test.

This is a guide to getting your motorcycle through the MOT test. Obviously it will not be possible to examine the motorcycle to the same standard as the professional MOT tester, particularly in view of the equipment required for some of the checks. However, working through the following procedures will enable you to identify any problem areas before submitting the motorcycle for the test.

It has only been possible to summarise the test requirements here, based on the regulations in force at the time of printing. Test standards are becoming increasingly stringent, although there are some exemptions for older vehicles. More information about the MOT test can be obtained from the TSO publications, *How Safe is your Motorcycle* and *The MOT Inspection Manual for Motorcycle Testing*.

Many of the checks require that one of the wheels is raised off the ground. If the motorcycle doesn't have a centre stand, note that an auxiliary stand will be required. Additionally, the help of an assistant may prove useful.

Certain exceptions apply to machines under 50 cc, machines without a lighting system, and Classic bikes - if in doubt about any of the requirements listed below seek confirmation from an MOT tester prior to submitting the motorcycle for the test.

Check that the frame number is clearly visible.

> **HAYNES HiNT** *If a component is in borderline condition, the tester has discretion in deciding whether to pass or fail it. If the motorcycle presented is clean and evidently well cared for, the tester may be more inclined to pass a borderline component than if the motorcycle is scruffy and apparently neglected.*

Electrical System

Lights, turn signals, horn and reflector

✔ With the ignition on, check the operation of the following electrical components. **Note:** *The electrical components on certain small-capacity machines are powered by the generator, requiring that the engine is run for this check.*

a) *Headlight and tail light. Check that both illuminate in the low and high beam switch positions.*

b) *Position lights. Check that the front position (or sidelight) and tail light illuminate in this switch position.*

c) *Turn signals. Check that all flash at the correct rate, and that the warning light(s) function correctly. Check that the turn signal switch works correctly.*

d) *Hazard warning system (where fitted). Check that all four turn signals flash in this switch position.*

e) *Brake stop light. Check that the light comes on when the front and rear brakes are independently applied. Models first used on or after 1st April 1986 must have a brake light switch on each brake.*

f) *Horn. Check that the sound is continuous and of reasonable volume.*

✔ Check that there is a red reflector on the rear of the machine, either mounted separately or as part of the tail light lens.

✔ Check the condition of the headlight, tail light and turn signal lenses.

Headlight beam height

✔ The MOT tester will perform a headlight beam height check using specialised beam setting equipment **(see illustration 1)**. This equipment will not be available to the home mechanic, but if you suspect that the headlight is incorrectly set or may have been maladjusted in the past, you can perform a rough test as follows.

✔ Position the bike in a straight line facing a brick wall. The bike must be off its stand, upright and with a rider seated. Measure the height from the ground to the centre of the headlight and mark a horizontal line on the wall at this height. Position the motorcycle 3.8 metres from the wall and draw a vertical

Headlight beam height checking equipment

line up the wall central to the centreline of the motorcycle. Switch to dipped beam and check that the beam pattern falls slightly lower than the horizontal line and to the left of the vertical line **(see illustration 2)**.

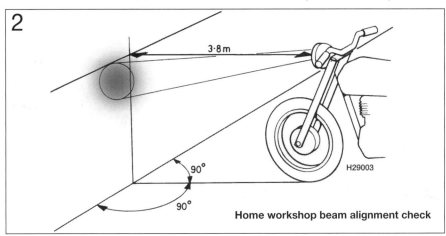

Home workshop beam alignment check

Exhaust System and Final Drive

Exhaust

✔ Check that the exhaust mountings are secure and that the system does not foul any of the rear suspension components.

✔ Start the motorcycle. When the revs are increased, check that the exhaust is neither holed nor leaking from any of its joints. On a linked system, check that the collector box is not leaking due to corrosion.

✔ Note that the exhaust decibel level ("loudness" of the exhaust) is assessed at the discretion of the tester. If the motorcycle was first used on or after 1st January 1985 the silencer must carry the BSAU 193 stamp, or a marking relating to its make and model, or be of OE (original equipment) manufacture. If the silencer is marked NOT FOR ROAD USE, RACING USE ONLY or similar, it will fail the MOT.

Final drive

✔ On chain or belt drive machines, check that the chain/belt is in good condition and does not have excessive slack. Also check that the sprocket is securely mounted on the rear wheel hub. Check that the chain/belt guard is in place.

✔ On shaft drive bikes, check for oil leaking from the drive unit and fouling the rear tyre.

Steering and Suspension

Steering

✔ With the front wheel raised off the ground, rotate the steering from lock to lock. The handlebar or switches must not contact the fuel tank or be close enough to trap the rider's hand. Problems can be caused by damaged lock stops on the lower yoke and frame, or by the fitting of non-standard handlebars.

✔ When performing the lock to lock check, also ensure that the steering moves freely without drag or notchiness. Steering movement can be impaired by poorly routed cables, or by overtight head bearings or worn bearings. The tester will perform a check of the steering head bearing lower race by mounting the front wheel on a surface plate, then performing a lock to

lock check with the weight of the machine on the lower bearing (see illustration 3).

✔ Grasp the fork sliders (lower legs) and attempt to push and pull on the forks (see

Front wheel mounted on a surface plate for steering head bearing lower race check

illustration 4). Any play in the steering head bearings will be felt. Note that in extreme cases, wear of the front fork bushes can be misinterpreted for head bearing play.

✔ Check that the handlebars are securely mounted.

✔ Check that the handlebar grip rubbers are secure. They should by bonded to the bar left end and to the throttle cable pulley on the right end.

Front suspension

✔ With the motorcycle off the stand, hold the front brake on and pump the front forks up and down (see illustration 5). Check that they are adequately damped.

Checking the steering head bearings for freeplay

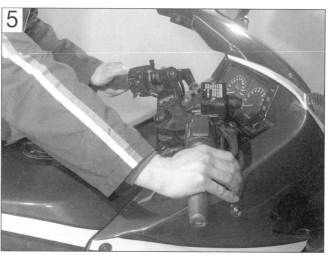

Hold the front brake on and pump the front forks up and down to check operation

Inspect the area around the fork dust seal for oil leakage (arrow)

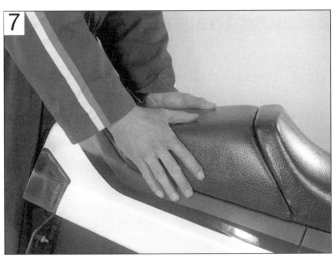

Bounce the rear of the motorcycle to check rear suspension operation

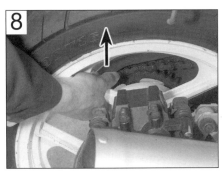

Checking for rear suspension linkage play

✔ Inspect the area above and around the front fork oil seals **(see illustration 6)**. There should be no sign of oil on the fork tube (stanchion) nor leaking down the slider (lower leg). On models so equipped, check that there is no oil leaking from the anti-dive units.

✔ On models with swingarm front suspension, check that there is no freeplay in the linkage when moved from side to side.

Rear suspension

✔ With the motorcycle off the stand and an assistant supporting the motorcycle by its handlebars, bounce the rear suspension **(see illustration 7)**. Check that the suspension components do not foul on any of the cycle parts and check that the shock absorber(s) provide adequate damping.

✔ Visually inspect the shock absorber(s) and check that there is no sign of oil leakage from its damper. This is somewhat restricted on certain single shock models due to the location of the shock absorber.

✔ With the rear wheel raised off the ground, grasp the wheel at the highest point and attempt to pull it up **(see illustration 8)**. Any play in the swingarm pivot or suspension linkage bearings will be felt as movement. **Note:** *Do not confuse play with actual suspension movement.* Failure to lubricate suspension linkage bearings can lead to bearing failure **(see illustration 9)**.

✔ With the rear wheel raised off the ground, grasp the swingarm ends and attempt to move the swingarm from side to side and forwards and backwards - any play indicates wear of the swingarm pivot bearings **(see illustration 10)**.

Worn suspension linkage pivots (arrows) are usually the cause of play in the rear suspension

Grasp the swingarm at the ends to check for play in its pivot bearings

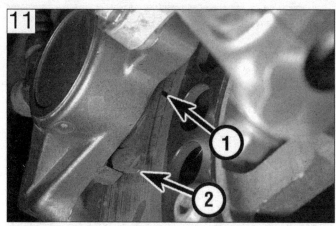

Brake pad wear can usually be viewed without removing the caliper. Most pads have wear indicator grooves (1) and some also have indicator tangs (2)

On drum brakes, check the angle of the operating lever with the brake fully applied. Most drum brakes have a wear indicator pointer and scale.

Brakes, Wheels and Tyres

Brakes

✔ With the wheel raised off the ground, apply the brake then free it off, and check that the wheel is about to revolve freely without brake drag.

✔ On disc brakes, examine the disc itself. Check that it is securely mounted and not cracked.

✔ On disc brakes, view the pad material through the caliper mouth and check that the pads are not worn down beyond the limit (see illustration 11).

✔ On drum brakes, check that when the brake is applied the angle between the operating lever and cable or rod is not too great (see illustration 12). Check also that the operating lever doesn't foul any other components.

✔ On disc brakes, examine the flexible hoses from top to bottom. Have an assistant hold the brake on so that the fluid in the hose is under pressure, and check that there is no sign of fluid leakage, bulges or cracking. If there are any metal brake pipes or unions, check that these are free from corrosion and damage. Where a brake-linked anti-dive system is fitted, check the hoses to the anti-dive in a similar manner.

✔ Check that the rear brake torque arm is secure and that its fasteners are secured by self-locking nuts or castellated nuts with split-pins or R-pins (see illustration 13).

✔ On models with ABS, check that the self-check warning light in the instrument panel works.

✔ The MOT tester will perform a test of the motorcycle's braking efficiency based on a calculation of rider and motorcycle weight. Although this cannot be carried out at home, you can at least ensure that the braking systems are properly maintained. For hydraulic disc brakes, check the fluid level, lever/pedal feel (bleed of air if its spongy) and pad material. For drum brakes, check adjustment, cable or rod operation and shoe lining thickness.

Wheels and tyres

✔ Check the wheel condition. Cast wheels should be free from cracks and if of the built-up design, all fasteners should be secure. Spoked wheels should be checked for broken, corroded, loose or bent spokes.

✔ With the wheel raised off the ground, spin the wheel and visually check that the tyre and wheel run true. Check that the tyre does not foul the suspension or mudguards.

✔ With the wheel raised off the ground, grasp the wheel and attempt to move it about the axle (spindle) (see illustration 14). Any play felt here indicates wheel bearing failure.

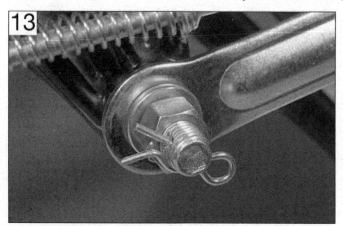

Brake torque arm must be properly secured at both ends

Check for wheel bearing play by trying to move the wheel about the axle (spindle)

Checking the tyre tread depth

Tyre direction of rotation arrow can be found on tyre sidewall

Castellated type wheel axle (spindle) nut must be secured by a split pin or R-pin

Two straightedges are used to check wheel alignment

✔ If the tyre sidewall carries a direction of rotation arrow, this must be pointing in the direction of normal wheel rotation (see illustration 16).

✔ Check that the wheel axle (spindle) nuts (where applicable) are properly secured. A self-locking nut or castellated nut with a split-pin or R-pin can be used (see illustration 17).

✔ Wheel alignment is checked with the motorcycle off the stand and a rider seated. With the front wheel pointing straight ahead, two perfectly straight lengths of metal or wood and placed against the sidewalls of both tyres (see illustration 18). The gap each side of the front tyre must be equidistant on both sides. Incorrect wheel alignment may be due to a cocked rear wheel (often as the result of poor chain adjustment) or in extreme cases, a bent frame.

✔ Check the tyre tread depth, tread condition and sidewall condition (see illustration 15).

✔ Check the tyre type. Front and rear tyre types must be compatible and be suitable for road use. Tyres marked NOT FOR ROAD USE, COMPETITION USE ONLY or similar, will fail the MOT.

General checks and condition

✔ Check the security of all major fasteners, bodypanels, seat, fairings (where fitted) and mudguards.

✔ Check that the rider and pillion footrests, handlebar levers and brake pedal are securely mounted.

✔ Check for corrosion on the frame or any load-bearing components. If severe, this may affect the structure, particularly under stress.

Sidecars

A motorcycle fitted with a sidecar requires additional checks relating to the stability of the machine and security of attachment and swivel joints, plus specific wheel alignment (toe-in) requirements. Additionally, tyre and lighting requirements differ from conventional motorcycle use. Owners are advised to check MOT test requirements with an official test centre.

Preparing for storage

Before you start

If repairs or an overhaul is needed, see that this is carried out now rather than left until you want to ride the bike again.

Give the bike a good wash and scrub all dirt from its underside. Make sure the bike dries completely before preparing for storage.

Engine

● Remove the spark plug(s) and lubricate the cylinder bores with approximately a teaspoon of motor oil using a spout-type oil can **(see illustration 1)**. Reinstall the spark plug(s). Crank the engine over a couple of times to coat the piston rings and bores with oil. If the bike has a kickstart, use this to turn the engine over. If not, flick the kill switch to the OFF position and crank the engine over on the starter **(see illustration 2)**. If the nature on the ignition system prevents the starter operating with the kill switch in the OFF position,

remove the spark plugs and fit them back in their caps; ensure that the plugs are earthed (grounded) against the cylinder head when the starter is operated **(see illustration 3)**.

⚠️ *Warning: It is important that the plugs are earthed (grounded) away from the spark plug holes otherwise there is a risk of atomised fuel from the cylinders igniting.*

HAYNES HiNT *On a single cylinder four-stroke engine, you can seal the combustion chamber completely by positioning the piston at TDC on the compression stroke.*

● Drain the carburettor(s) otherwise there is a risk of jets becoming blocked by gum deposits from the fuel **(see illustration 4)**.

● If the bike is going into long-term storage, consider adding a fuel stabiliser to the fuel in the tank. If the tank is drained completely, corrosion of its internal surfaces may occur if left unprotected for a long period. The tank can be treated with a rust preventative especially for this purpose. Alternatively, remove the tank and pour half a litre of motor oil into it, install the filler cap and shake the tank to coat its internals with oil before draining off the excess. The same effect can also be achieved by spraying WD40 or a similar water-dispersant around the inside of the tank via its flexible nozzle.

● Make sure the cooling system contains the correct mix of antifreeze. Antifreeze also contains important corrosion inhibitors.

● The air intakes and exhaust can be sealed off by covering or plugging the openings. Ensure that you do not seal in any condensation; run the engine until it is hot,

Squirt a drop of motor oil into each cylinder

Flick the kill switch to OFF . . .

. . . and ensure that the metal bodies of the plugs (arrows) are earthed against the cylinder head

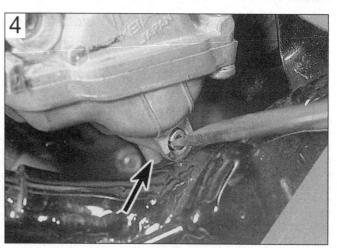

Connect a hose to the carburettor float chamber drain stub (arrow) and unscrew the drain screw

Exhausts can be sealed off with a plastic bag

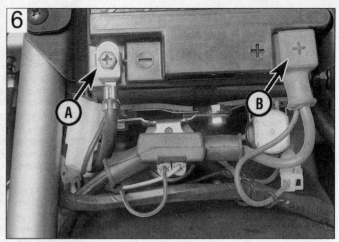

Disconnect the negative lead (A) first, followed by the positive lead (B)

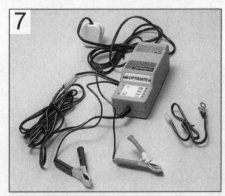

Use a suitable battery charger - this kit also assess battery condition

then switch off and allow to cool. Tape a piece of thick plastic over the silencer end(s) **(see illustration 5)**. Note that some advocate pouring a tablespoon of motor oil into the silencer(s) before sealing them off.

Battery

● Remove it from the bike - in extreme cases of cold the battery may freeze and crack its case **(see illustration 6)**.

● Check the electrolyte level and top up if necessary (conventional refillable batteries). Clean the terminals.
● Store the battery off the motorcycle and away from any sources of fire. Position a wooden block under the battery if it is to sit on the ground.
● Give the battery a trickle charge for a few hours every month **(see illustration 7)**.

Tyres

● Place the bike on its centrestand or an auxiliary stand which will support the motorcycle in an upright position. Position wood blocks under the tyres to keep them off the ground and to provide insulation from damp. If the bike is being put into long-term storage, ideally both tyres should be off the ground; not only will this protect the tyres, but will also ensure that no load is placed on the steering head or wheel bearings.
● Deflate each tyre by 5 to 10 psi, no more or the beads may unseat from the rim, making subsequent inflation difficult on tubeless tyres.

Pivots and controls

● Lubricate all lever, pedal, stand and footrest pivot points. If grease nipples are fitted to the rear suspension components, apply lubricant to the pivots.
● Lubricate all control cables.

Cycle components

● Apply a wax protectant to all painted and plastic components. Wipe off any excess, but don't polish to a shine. Where fitted, clean the screen with soap and water.
● Coat metal parts with Vaseline (petroleum jelly). When applying this to the fork tubes, do not compress the forks otherwise the seals will rot from contact with the Vaseline.
● Apply a vinyl cleaner to the seat.

Storage conditions

● Aim to store the bike in a shed or garage which does not leak and is free from damp.
● Drape an old blanket or bedspread over the bike to protect it from dust and direct contact with sunlight (which will fade paint). This also hides the bike from prying eyes. Beware of tight-fitting plastic covers which may allow condensation to form and settle on the bike.

Getting back on the road

Engine and transmission

● Change the oil and replace the oil filter. If this was done prior to storage, check that the oil hasn't emulsified - a thick whitish substance which occurs through condensation.
● Remove the spark plugs. Using a spout-type oil can, squirt a few drops of oil into the cylinder(s). This will provide initial lubrication as the piston rings and bores comes back into contact. Service the spark plugs, or fit new ones, and install them in the engine.

● Check that the clutch isn't stuck on. The plates can stick together if left standing for some time, preventing clutch operation. Engage a gear and try rocking the bike back and forth with the clutch lever held against the handlebar. If this doesn't work on cable-operated clutches, hold the clutch lever back against the handlebar with a strong elastic band or cable tie for a couple of hours **(see illustration 8)**.
● If the air intakes or silencer end(s) were blocked off, remove the bung or cover used.
● If the fuel tank was coated with a rust

Hold clutch lever back against the handlebar with elastic bands or a cable tie

preventative, oil or a stabiliser added to the fuel, drain and flush the tank and dispose of the fuel sensibly. If no action was taken with the fuel tank prior to storage, it is advised that the old fuel is disposed of since it will go off over a period of time. Refill the fuel tank with fresh fuel.

Frame and running gear

● Oil all pivot points and cables.

● Check the tyre pressures. They will definitely need inflating if pressures were reduced for storage.

● Lubricate the final drive chain (where applicable).

● Remove any protective coating applied to the fork tubes (stanchions) since this may well destroy the fork seals. If the fork tubes weren't protected and have picked up rust spots, remove them with very fine abrasive paper and refinish with metal polish.

● Check that both brakes operate correctly. Apply each brake hard and check that it's not possible to move the motorcycle forwards, then check that the brake frees off again once released. Brake caliper pistons can stick due to corrosion around the piston head, or on the sliding caliper types, due to corrosion of the slider pins. If the brake doesn't free after repeated operation, take the caliper off for examination. Similarly drum brakes can stick

due to a seized operating cam, cable or rod linkage.

● If the motorcycle has been in long-term storage, renew the brake fluid and clutch fluid (where applicable).

● Depending on where the bike has been stored, the wiring, cables and hoses may have been nibbled by rodents. Make a visual check and investigate disturbed wiring loom tape.

Battery

● If the battery has been previously removal and given top up charges it can simply be reconnected. Remember to connect the positive cable first and the negative cable last.

● On conventional refillable batteries, if the battery has not received any attention, remove it from the motorcycle and check its electrolyte level. Top up if necessary then charge the battery. If the battery fails to hold a charge and a visual checks show heavy white sulphation of the plates, the battery is probably defective and must be renewed. This is particularly likely if the battery is old. Confirm battery condition with a specific gravity check.

● On sealed (MF) batteries, if the battery has not received any attention, remove it from the motorcycle and charge it according to the information on the battery case - if the battery fails to hold a charge it must be renewed.

Starting procedure

● If a kickstart is fitted, turn the engine over a couple of times with the ignition OFF to distribute oil around the engine. If no kickstart is fitted, flick the engine kill switch OFF and the ignition ON and crank the engine over a couple of times to work oil around the upper cylinder components. If the nature of the ignition system is such that the starter won't work with the kill switch OFF, remove the spark plugs, fit them back into their caps and earth (ground) their bodies on the cylinder head. Reinstall the spark plugs afterwards.

● Switch the kill switch to RUN, operate the choke and start the engine. If the engine won't start don't continue cranking the engine - not only will this flatten the battery, but the starter motor will overheat. Switch the ignition off and try again later. If the engine refuses to start, go through the fault finding procedures in this manual. **Note:** *If the bike has been in storage for a long time, old fuel or a carburettor blockage may be the problem. Gum deposits in carburettors can block jets - if a carburettor cleaner doesn't prove successful the carburettors must be dismantled for cleaning.*

● Once the engine has started, check that the lights, turn signals and horn work properly.

● Treat the bike gently for the first ride and check all fluid levels on completion. Settle the bike back into the maintenance schedule.

A number of chemicals and lubricants are available for use in motorcycle maintenance and repair. They include a wide variety of products ranging from cleaning solvents and degreasers to lubricants and protective sprays for rubber, plastic and vinyl.

● **Contact point/spark plug cleaner** is a solvent used to clean oily film and dirt from points, grime from electrical connectors and oil deposits from spark plugs. It is oil free and leaves no residue. It can also be used to remove gum and varnish from carburettor jets and other orifices.

● **Carburettor cleaner** is similar to contact point/spark plug cleaner but it usually has a stronger solvent and may leave a slight oily reside. It is not recommended for cleaning electrical components or connections.

● **Brake system cleaner** is used to remove grease or brake fluid from brake system components (where clean surfaces are absolutely necessary and petroleum-based solvents cannot be used); it also leaves no residue.

● **Silicone-based lubricants** are used to protect rubber parts such as hoses and grommets, and are used as lubricants for hinges and locks.

● **Multi-purpose grease** is an all purpose lubricant used wherever grease is more practical than a liquid lubricant such as oil. Some multi-purpose grease is coloured white and specially formulated to be more resistant to water than ordinary grease.

● **Gear oil** (sometimes called gear lube) is a specially designed oil used in transmissions and final drive units, as well as other areas where high friction, high temperature lubrication is required. It is available in a number of viscosities (weights) for various applications.

● **Motor oil**, of course, is the lubricant specially formulated for use in the engine. It normally contains a wide variety of additives to prevent corrosion and reduce foaming and wear. Motor oil comes in various weights (viscosity ratings) of from 5 to 80. The recommended weight of the oil depends on the seasonal temperature and the demands on the engine. Light oil is used in cold climates and under light load conditions; heavy oil is used in hot climates and where high loads are encountered. Multi-viscosity oils are designed to have characteristics of both light and heavy oils and are available in a number of weights from 5W-20 to 20W-50.

● **Petrol additives** perform several functions, depending on their chemical makeup. They usually contain solvents that help dissolve gum and varnish that build up on carburettor and inlet parts. They also serve to break down carbon deposits that form on the inside surfaces of the combustion chambers. Some additives contain upper cylinder lubricants for valves and piston rings.

● **Brake and clutch fluid** is a specially formulated hydraulic fluid that can withstand the heat and pressure encountered in brake/clutch systems. Care must be taken that this fluid does not come in contact with painted surfaces or plastics. An opened container should always be resealed to prevent contamination by water or dirt.

● **Chain lubricants** are formulated especially for use on motorcycle final drive chains. A good chain lube should adhere well and have good penetrating qualities to be effective as a lubricant inside the chain and on the side plates, pins and rollers. Most chain lubes are either the foaming type or quick drying type and are usually marketed as sprays. Take care to use a lubricant marked as being suitable for O-ring chains.

● **Degreasers** are heavy duty solvents used to remove grease and grime that may accumulate on engine and frame components. They can be sprayed or brushed on and, depending on the type, are rinsed with either water or solvent.

● **Solvents** are used alone or in combination with degreasers to clean parts and assemblies during repair and overhaul. The home mechanic should use only solvents that are non-flammable and that do not produce irritating fumes.

● **Gasket sealing compounds** may be used in conjunction with gaskets, to improve their sealing capabilities, or alone, to seal metal-to-metal joints. Many gasket sealers can withstand extreme heat, some are impervious to petrol and lubricants, while others are capable of filling and sealing large cavities. Depending on the intended use, gasket sealers either dry hard or stay relatively soft and pliable. They are usually applied by hand, with a brush, or are sprayed on the gasket sealing surfaces.

● **Thread locking compound** is an adhesive locking compound that prevents threaded fasteners from loosening because of vibration. It is available in a variety of types for different applications.

● **Moisture dispersants** are usually sprays that can be used to dry out electrical components such as the fuse block and wiring connectors. Some types can also be used as treatment for rubber and as a lubricant for hinges, cables and locks.

● **Waxes and polishes** are used to help protect painted and plated surfaces from the weather. Different types of paint may require the use of different types of wax polish. Some polishes utilise a chemical or abrasive cleaner to help remove the top layer of oxidised (dull) paint on older vehicles. In recent years, many non-wax polishes (that contain a wide variety of chemicals such as polymers and silicones) have been introduced. These non-wax polishes are usually easier to apply and last longer than conventional waxes and polishes.

This Section provides an easy reference-guide to the more common faults that are likely to afflict your machine. Obviously, the opportunities are almost limitless for faults to occur as a result of obscure failures, and to try and cover all eventualities would require a book. Indeed, a number have been written on the subject.

Successful troubleshooting is not a mysterious 'black art' but the application of a bit of knowledge combined with a systematic and logical approach to the problem. Approach any troubleshooting by first accurately identifying the symptom and then checking through the list of possible causes, starting with the simplest or most obvious and progressing in stages to the most complex.

Take nothing for granted, but above all apply liberal quantities of common sense.

The main symptom of a fault is given in the text as a major heading below which are listed the various systems or areas which may contain the fault. Details of each possible cause for a fault and the remedial action to be taken are given, in brief, in the paragraphs below each heading. Further information should be sought in the relevant Chapter.

1 Engine doesn't start or is difficult to start

- ☐ Starter motor doesn't rotate
- ☐ Starter motor rotates but engine does not turn over
- ☐ Starter works but engine won't turn over (seized)
- ☐ No fuel flow
- ☐ Engine flooded
- ☐ No spark or weak spark
- ☐ Compression low
- ☐ Stalls after starting
- ☐ Rough idle

2 Poor running at low speeds

- ☐ Spark weak
- ☐ Fuel/air mixture incorrect
- ☐ Compression low
- ☐ Poor acceleration

3 Poor running or no power at high speed

- ☐ Firing incorrect
- ☐ Fuel/air mixture incorrect
- ☐ Compression low
- ☐ Knocking or pinking
- ☐ Miscellaneous causes

4 Overheating

- ☐ Engine overheats
- ☐ Firing incorrect
- ☐ Fuel/air mixture incorrect
- ☐ Compression too high
- ☐ Engine load excessive
- ☐ Lubrication inadequate
- ☐ Miscellaneous causes

5 Clutch problems

- ☐ Clutch slipping
- ☐ Clutch not disengaging completely

6 Gear shifting problems

- ☐ Doesn't go into gear, or lever doesn't return
- ☐ Jumps out of gear
- ☐ Overshifts

7 Abnormal engine noise

- ☐ Knocking or pinking
- ☐ Piston slap or rattling
- ☐ Valve noise
- ☐ Other noise

8 Abnormal driveline noise

- ☐ Clutch noise
- ☐ Transmission noise
- ☐ Final drive noise

9 Abnormal frame and suspension noise

- ☐ Front end noise
- ☐ Shock absorber noise
- ☐ Brake noise

10 Oil level indicator light comes on

- ☐ Engine lubrication system
- ☐ Electrical system

11 Excessive exhaust smoke

- ☐ White smoke
- ☐ Black smoke
- ☐ Brown smoke

12 Poor handling or stability

- ☐ Handlebar hard to turn
- ☐ Handlebar shakes or vibrates excessively
- ☐ Handlebar pulls to one side
- ☐ Poor shock absorbing qualities

13 Braking problems

- ☐ Brakes are spongy, don't hold
- ☐ Brake lever or pedal pulsates
- ☐ Brakes drag

14 Electrical problems

- ☐ Battery dead or weak
- ☐ Battery overcharged

1 Engine doesn't start or is difficult to start

Starter motor does not rotate

☐ Engine kill switch Off.
☐ Fuse blown. Check fuse block (Chapter 8).
☐ Battery voltage low. Check and recharge battery (Chapter 8).
☐ Starter motor defective. Make sure the wiring to the starter is secure. Make sure the starter relay clicks when the start button is pushed. If the relay clicks, then the fault is in the wiring or motor.
☐ Starter relay faulty. Check it according to the procedure in Chapter 8.
☐ Starter button not contacting. The contacts could be wet, corroded or dirty. Disassemble and clean the switch (Chapter 8).
☐ Wiring open or shorted. Check all wiring connections and harnesses to make sure that they are dry, tight and not corroded. Also check for broken or frayed wires that can cause a short to ground (see wiring diagrams, Chapter 8).
☐ Ignition switch defective. Check the switch according to the procedure in Chapter 8. Replace the switch with a new one if it is defective.
☐ Engine kill switch defective. Check for wet, dirty or corroded contacts. Clean or replace the switch as necessary (Chapter 8).
☐ Faulty sidestand or clutch switch. Check the wiring to the switch and the switch itself according to the procedures in Chapter 8.

Starter motor rotates but engine does not turn over

☐ Starter motor clutch defective. Inspect and repair or replace (Chapter 2).
☐ Damaged idler or starter gears. Inspect and replace the damaged parts (Chapter 2).

Starter works but engine won't turn over (seized)

☐ Seized engine caused by one or more internally damaged components. Failure due to wear, abuse or lack of lubrication. Damage can include seized valves, valve lifters, camshaft, pistons, crankshaft, connecting rod bearings, or transmission gears or bearings. Refer to Chapter 2 for engine disassembly.

No fuel flow

☐ No fuel in tank.
☐ Inline fuel filter clogged (see Chapter 1).
☐ Tank cap air vent obstructed (except California models). Usually caused by dirt or water. Remove it and clean the cap vent hole.
☐ Fuel tap clogged. Remove the tap and clean it (Chapter 3).
☐ Fuel pump failure. Test the pump (Chapter 3).
☐ Fuel line clogged. Pull the fuel line loose and carefully blow through it.
☐ Inlet needle valve clogged. For all of the valves to be clogged, either a very bad batch of fuel with an unusual additive has been used, or some other foreign material has entered the tank. Many times after a machine has been stored for many months without running, the fuel turns to a varnish-like liquid and forms deposits on the inlet needle valves and jets. The carburettors should be removed and overhauled if draining the float bowls doesn't solve the problem.

Engine flooded

☐ Float level too high. Check and adjust as described in Chapter 3.
☐ Inlet needle valve worn or stuck open. A piece of dirt, rust or other debris can cause the inlet needle to seat improperly, causing excess fuel to be admitted to the float bowl. In this case, the float chamber should be cleaned and the needle and seat inspected. If the needle and seat are worn, then the leaking will persist and the parts should be replaced with new ones (Chapter 3).
☐ Starting technique incorrect. Under normal circumstances (ie, if all the carburettor functions are sound) the machine should start with little or no throttle. When the engine is cold, the choke should be operated and the engine started without opening the throttle. When the engine is at operating temperature, only a very slight amount of throttle should be necessary. If the engine is flooded, turn the fuel tap off and hold the throttle open while cranking the engine. This will allow additional air to reach the cylinders. Remember to turn the fuel tap back on after the engine starts.

No spark or weak spark

☐ Ignition switch Off.
☐ Engine kill switch turned to the Off position.
☐ Battery voltage low. Check and recharge battery as necessary (Chapter 8).
☐ Spark plug dirty, defective or worn out. Locate reason for fouled plug(s) using spark plug condition chart on the inside rear cover and follow the plug maintenance procedures in Chapter 1.
☐ Spark plug cap or secondary (HT) wiring faulty. Check condition. Replace either or both components if cracks or deterioration are evident (Chapter 4).
☐ Spark plug cap not making good contact. Make sure that the plug cap fits snugly over the plug end.
☐ Igniter defective. Check the unit, referring to Chapter 4 for details.
☐ Pick-up coil defective. Check the unit, referring to Chapter 4 for details.
☐ Ignition coil(s) defective. Check the coils, referring to Chapter 4.
☐ Ignition or kill switch shorted. This is usually caused by water, corrosion, damage or excessive wear. The switches can be disassembled and cleaned with electrical contact cleaner. If cleaning does not help, replace the switches (Chapter 8).
☐ Wiring shorted or broken between:
   a) Ignition switch and engine kill switch (or blown fuse)
   b) Igniter and engine kill switch
   c) Igniter and ignition coil
   d) Ignition coil and plug
   e) Igniter and pick-up coil
☐ Make sure that all wiring connections are clean, dry and tight. Look for chafed and broken wires (Chapters 4 and 8).

Compression low

☐ Spark plug loose. Remove the plug and inspect the threads. Reinstall and tighten to the specified torque (Chapter 1).
☐ Cylinder head not sufficiently tightened down. If the cylinder head is suspected of being loose, then there's a chance that the gasket or head is damaged if the problem has persisted for any length of time. The head nuts should be tightened to the proper torque in the correct sequence (Chapter 2).
☐ Improper valve clearance. This means that the valve is not closing completely and compression pressure is leaking past the valve. Check and adjust the valve clearances (Chapter 1).
☐ Cylinder and/or piston worn. Excessive wear will cause compression pressure to leak past the rings. This is usually accompanied by worn rings as well. A top end overhaul is necessary (Chapter 2).
☐ Piston rings worn, weak, broken, or sticking. Broken or sticking piston rings usually indicate a lubrication or carburetion problem that causes excess carbon deposits or seizures to form on the pistons and rings. Top end overhaul is necessary (Chapter 2).
☐ Piston ring-to-groove clearance excessive. This is caused by excessive wear of the piston ring lands. Piston replacement is necessary (Chapter 2).
☐ Cylinder head gasket damaged. If the head is allowed to become loose, or if excessive carbon build-up on the piston crown and combustion chamber causes extremely high compression, the head gasket may leak. Retorquing the head is not always sufficient to restore the seal, so gasket replacement is necessary (Chapter 2).

- ☐ Cylinder head warped. This is caused by overheating or improperly tightened head nuts. Machine shop resurfacing or head replacement is necessary (Chapter 2).
- ☐ Valve spring broken or weak. Caused by component failure or wear; the spring(s) must be replaced (Chapter 2).
- ☐ Valve not seating properly. This is caused by a bent valve (from over-revving or improper valve adjustment), burned valve or seat (improper carburetion) or an accumulation of carbon deposits on the seat (from carburetion or lubrication problems). The valves must be cleaned and/or replaced and the seats serviced if possible (Chapter 2).

Stalls after starting

- ☐ Improper choke action. Make sure the choke rod is getting a full stroke and staying in the out position. On later models make sure that the choke cable is correctly adjusted. (Chapter 3).
- ☐ Ignition malfunction. See Chapter 4.
- ☐ Carburettor malfunction. See Chapter 3.
- ☐ Fuel contaminated. The fuel can be contaminated with either dirt or water, or can change chemically if the machine is allowed to sit for several months or more. Drain the tank and float chambers (Chapter 3).

- ☐ Intake air leak. Check for loose carburettor-to-intake manifold connections, loose or missing vacuum gauge access port plug or hose, or loose carburettor top (Chapter 3).
- ☐ Engine idle speed incorrect. Turn throttle stop screw until the engine idles at the specified rpm (Chapters 1 and 3).

Rough idle

- ☐ Ignition malfunction. See Chapter 4.
- ☐ Idle speed incorrect. See Chapter 1.
- ☐ Carburettors not synchronised. Adjust carburettors with vacuum gauge or manometer set as described in Chapter 1.
- ☐ Carburettor malfunction. See Chapter 3.
- ☐ Fuel contaminated. The fuel can be contaminated with either dirt or water, or can change chemically if the machine is allowed to sit for several months or more. Drain the tank and float chambers (Chapter 3).
- ☐ Intake air leak. Check for loose carburettor-to-intake manifold connections, loose or missing vacuum gauge access port cap or hose, or loose carburettor top (Chapter 3).
- ☐ Air cleaner clogged. Service or replace air filter element (Chapter 1).

2 Poor running at low speeds

Spark weak

- ☐ Battery voltage low. Check and recharge battery (Chapter 8).
- ☐ Spark plug fouled, defective or worn out. Refer to Chapter 1 for spark plug maintenance.
- ☐ Spark plug cap or high tension wiring defective. Refer to Chapters 1 and 5 for details of the ignition system.
- ☐ Spark plug cap not making contact.
- ☐ Incorrect spark plug. Wrong type, heat range or cap configuration. Check and install correct plugs listed in Chapter 1. A cold plug or one with a recessed firing electrode will not operate at low speeds without fouling.
- ☐ Igniter defective. See Chapter 4.
- ☐ Signal generator defective. See Chapter 4.
- ☐ Ignition coil(s) defective. See Chapter 4.

Fuel/air mixture incorrect

- ☐ Pilot screw(s) out of adjustment (Chapter 3).
- ☐ Pilot jet or air passage clogged. Remove and overhaul the carburettors (Chapter 3).
- ☐ Air bleed holes clogged. Remove carburettor and blow out all passages (Chapter 3).
- ☐ Air cleaner clogged, poorly sealed or missing.
- ☐ Air cleaner-to-carburettor boot poorly sealed. Look for cracks, holes or loose clamps and replace or repair defective parts.
- ☐ Fuel level too high or too low. Adjust the floats (Chapter 3).
- ☐ Fuel tank air vent obstructed. Make sure that the air vent passage in the filler cap is open.
- ☐ Carburettor intake manifolds loose. Check for cracks, breaks, tears or loose clamps or bolts. Repair or replace the rubber boots.

Compression low

- ☐ Spark plug loose. Remove the plugs and inspect their threads. Reinstall and tighten to the specified torque (Chapter 1).
- ☐ Cylinder head not sufficiently tightened down. If the cylinder head is suspected of being loose, then there's a chance that the gasket and head are damaged if the problem has persisted for any length of time. The head nuts should be tightened to the proper torque in the correct sequence (Chapter 2).
- ☐ Improper valve clearance. This means that the valve is not closing completely and compression pressure is leaking past the valve. Check and adjust the valve clearances (Chapter 1).

- ☐ Cylinder and/or piston worn. Excessive wear will cause compression pressure to leak past the rings. This is usually accompanied by worn rings as well. A top end overhaul is necessary (Chapter 2).
- ☐ Piston rings worn, weak, broken, or sticking. Broken or sticking piston rings usually indicate a lubrication or carburetion problem that causes excess carbon deposits or seizures to form on the pistons and rings. Top end overhaul is necessary (Chapter 2).
- ☐ Piston ring-to-groove clearance excessive. This is caused by excessive wear of the piston ring lands. Piston replacement is necessary (Chapter 2).
- ☐ Cylinder head gasket damaged. If the head is allowed to become loose, or if excessive carbon build-up on the piston crown and combustion chamber causes extremely high compression, the head gasket may leak. Retorquing the head is not always sufficient to restore the seal, so gasket replacement is necessary (Chapter 2).
- ☐ Cylinder head warped. This is caused by overheating or improperly tightened head nuts. Machine shop resurfacing or head replacement is necessary (Chapter 2).
- ☐ Valve spring broken or weak. Caused by component failure or wear; the spring(s) must be replaced (Chapter 2).
- ☐ Valve not seating properly. This is caused by a bent valve (from over-revving or improper valve adjustment), burned valve or seat (improper carburetion) or an accumulation of carbon deposits on the seat (from carburetion, lubrication problems). The valves must be cleaned and/or replaced and the seats serviced if possible (Chapter 2).

Poor acceleration

- ☐ Carburettors leaking or dirty. Overhaul the carburettors (Chapter 3).
- ☐ Timing not advancing. The pick-up coil(s) or the igniter may be defective. If so, they must be replaced with new ones, as they can't be repaired.
- ☐ Carburettors not synchronised. Adjust them with a vacuum gauge set or manometer (Chapter 1).
- ☐ Engine oil viscosity too high. Using a heavier oil than that recommended in Chapter 1 can damage the oil pump or lubrication system and cause drag on the engine.
- ☐ Brakes dragging. Usually caused by debris which has entered the brake piston sealing boot (disc brakes) or from a warped disc or bent axle. Repair as necessary (Chapter 6).

3 Poor running or no power at high speed

Firing incorrect

☐ Air filter restricted. Clean or replace filter (Chapter 1).
☐ Spark plug fouled, defective or worn out. See Chapter 1 for spark plug maintenance.
☐ Spark plug cap or secondary (HT) wiring defective. See Chapters 1 and 4 for details of the ignition system.
☐ Spark plug cap not in good contact. See Chapter 4.
☐ Incorrect spark plug. Wrong type, heat range or cap configuration. Check and install correct plugs listed in Chapter 1. A cold plug or one with a recessed firing electrode will not operate at low speeds without fouling.
☐ Igniter defective. See Chapter 4.
☐ Ignition coil(s) defective. See Chapter 4.
☐ Spark plug wires crossed (see Chapters 1 and 4).

Fuel/air mixture incorrect

☐ Main jet clogged. Dirt, water or other contaminants can clog the main jets. Clean the fuel tap filter, the float chamber area, and the jets and carburettor orifices (Chapter 3).
☐ Main jet wrong size. The standard jetting is for sea level atmospheric pressure and oxygen content.
☐ Throttle shaft-to-carburettor body clearance excessive. Refer to Chapter 3 for inspection and part replacement procedures.
☐ Air bleed holes clogged. Remove and overhaul carburettors (Chapter 3).
☐ Air cleaner clogged, poorly sealed, or missing.
☐ Air cleaner-to-carburettor boot poorly sealed. Look for cracks, holes or loose clamps, and replace or repair defective parts.
☐ Fuel level too high or too low. Adjust the float(s) (Chapter 3).
☐ Fuel tank air vent obstructed. Make sure the air vent passage in the filler cap is open.
☐ Carburettor intake manifolds loose. Check for cracks, breaks, tears or loose clamps or bolts. Repair or replace the rubber boots (Chapter 2).
☐ Fuel filter clogged. Renew the in-line fuel filter (Chapter 1) and clean the fuel tap filter (Chapter 3).
☐ Fuel line clogged. Pull the fuel line loose and carefully blow through it.

Compression low

☐ Spark plug loose. Remove the plugs and inspect their threads. Reinstall and tighten to the specified torque (Chapter 1).
☐ Cylinder head not sufficiently tightened down. If the cylinder head is suspected of being loose, then there's a chance that the gasket and head are damaged if the problem has persisted for any length of time. The head nuts should be tightened to the proper torque in the correct sequence (Chapter 2).
☐ Improper valve clearance. This means that the valve is not closing completely and compression pressure is leaking past the valve. Check and adjust the valve clearances (Chapter 1).
☐ Cylinder and/or piston worn. Excessive wear will cause compression pressure to leak past the rings. This is usually accompanied by worn rings as well. A top end overhaul is necessary (Chapter 2).
☐ Piston rings worn, weak, broken, or sticking. Broken or sticking piston rings usually indicate a lubrication or carburetion problem that causes excess carbon deposits or seizures to form on the pistons and rings. Top end overhaul is necessary (Chapter 2).
☐ Piston ring-to-groove clearance excessive. This is caused by excessive wear of the piston ring lands. Piston replacement is necessary (Chapter 2).
☐ Cylinder head gasket damaged. If the head is allowed to become loose, or if excessive carbon build-up on the piston crown and combustion chamber causes extremely high compression, the head gasket may leak. Retorquing the head is not always sufficient to restore the seal, so gasket replacement is necessary (Chapter 2).
☐ Cylinder head warped. This is caused by overheating or improperly tightened head nuts. Machine shop resurfacing or head replacement is necessary (Chapter 2).
☐ Valve spring broken or weak. Caused by component failure or wear; the spring(s) must be replaced (Chapter 2).
☐ Valve not seating properly. This is caused by a bent valve (from over-revving or improper valve adjustment), burned valve or seat (improper carburetion) or an accumulation of carbon deposits on the seat (from carburetion or lubrication problems). The valves must be cleaned and/or replaced and the seats serviced if possible (Chapter 2).

Knocking or pinking

☐ Carbon build-up in combustion chamber. Use of a fuel additive that will dissolve the adhesive bonding the carbon particles to the crown and chamber is the easiest way to remove the build-up. Otherwise, the cylinder head will have to be removed and decarbonised (Chapter 2).
☐ Incorrect or poor quality fuel. Old or improper grades of fuel can cause detonation. This causes the piston to rattle, thus the knocking or pinking sound. Drain old fuel and always use the recommended fuel grade.
☐ Spark plug heat range incorrect. Uncontrolled detonation indicates the plug heat range is too hot. The plug in effect becomes a glow plug, raising cylinder temperatures. Install the proper heat range plug (Chapter 1).
☐ Improper air/fuel mixture. This will cause the cylinder to run hot, which leads to detonation. Clogged jets or an air leak can cause this imbalance. See Chapter 3.

Miscellaneous causes

☐ Throttle valve doesn't open fully. Adjust the cable slack (Chapter 1).
☐ Maladjusted throttle position sensor – later models (Chapter 4).
☐ Clutch slipping. May be caused by loose or worn clutch components. Refer to Chapter 2 for clutch overhaul procedures.
☐ Timing not advancing.
☐ Engine oil viscosity too high. Using a heavier oil than the one recommended in Chapter 1 can damage the oil pump or lubrication system and cause drag on the engine.
☐ Brakes dragging. Usually caused by debris which has entered the brake piston sealing boot, or from a warped disc or bent axle. Repair as necessary.

4 Overheating

Engine overheats

☐ Engine oil level low. Check and add oil (Daily (pre-ride) checks).
☐ Wrong type of oil. If you're not sure what type of oil is in the engine, drain it and fill with the correct type (Chapter 1).
☐ Air leak at carburettor intake boots. Check and tighten or replace as necessary (Chapter 3).
☐ Fuel level low. Check and adjust if necessary (Chapter 3).
☐ Worn oil pump or clogged oil passages. Check oil pressure (Chapter 2). Replace pump or clean passages as necessary.
☐ Carbon build-up in combustion chambers. Use of a fuel additive that will dissolve the adhesive bonding the carbon particles to the piston crowns and chambers is the easiest way to remove the build-up. Otherwise, the cylinder head will have to be removed and decarbonised (Chapter 2).

Firing incorrect

☐ Spark plugs fouled, defective or worn out. See Chapter 1 for spark plug maintenance.
☐ Incorrect spark plugs.
☐ Faulty ignition coil(s) (Chapter 4).

Fuel/air mixture incorrect

☐ Main jet clogged. Dirt, water and other contaminants can clog the main jets. Clean the fuel tap filter, the float chamber area and the jets and carburettor orifices (Chapter 3). Renew the in-line fuel filter (Chapter 1).
☐ Main jet wrong size. The standard jetting is for sea level atmospheric pressure and oxygen content.
☐ Air cleaner poorly sealed or missing.
☐ Air cleaner-to-carburettor boot poorly sealed. Look for cracks, holes or loose clamps and replace or repair.
☐ Fuel level too low. Adjust the float(s) (Chapter 3).
☐ Fuel tank air vent obstructed. Make sure that the air vent passage in the filler cap is open.
☐ Carburettor intake manifolds loose. Check for cracks, breaks, tears or loose clamps or bolts. Repair or replace the rubber boots (Chapter 3). Remove the manifolds and inspect the O-rings (see Chapter 3).

Compression too high

☐ Carbon build-up in combustion chamber. Use of a fuel additive that will dissolve the adhesive bonding the carbon particles to the piston crown and chamber is the easiest way to remove the build-up. Otherwise, the cylinder head will have to be removed and decarbonised (Chapter 2).
☐ Improperly machined head surface or installation of incorrect gasket during engine assembly. Check Specifications (Chapter 2).

Engine load excessive

☐ Clutch slipping. Can be caused by damaged, loose or worn clutch components. Refer to Chapter 2 for overhaul procedures.
☐ Engine oil level too high. The addition of too much oil will cause pressurisation of the crankcase and inefficient engine operation. Check Specifications and drain to proper level (Daily (pre-ride) checks).
☐ Engine oil viscosity too high. Using a heavier oil than the one recommended in Chapter 1 can damage the oil pump or lubrication system as well as cause drag on the engine.
☐ Brakes dragging. Usually caused by debris which has entered the brake piston sealing boot, or from a warped disc or bent axle. Repair as necessary.

Lubrication inadequate

☐ Engine oil level too low. Friction caused by intermittent lack of lubrication or from oil that is overworked can cause overheating. The oil provides a definite cooling function in the engine. Check the oil level (Daily (pre-ride) checks).

Miscellaneous causes

☐ Modification to exhaust system. Most aftermarket exhaust systems cause the engine to run leaner, which makes it run hotter. When installing an accessory exhaust system, always reject the carburettors.

5 Clutch problems

Clutch slipping

☐ Friction plates worn or warped. Overhaul the clutch assembly (Chapter 2).
☐ Steel plates worn or warped (Chapter 2).
☐ Clutch springs broken or weak. Old or heat-damaged (from slipping clutch) springs should be replaced with new ones (Chapter 2).
☐ Worn or warped clutch plates. Replace (Chapter 2).
☐ Clutch release mechanism defective. Replace any defective parts (Chapter 2).
☐ Clutch hub or housing unevenly worn. This causes improper engagement of the discs. Replace the damaged or worn parts (Chapter 2).

Clutch not disengaging completely

☐ Sticking cable. Inspect and lubricate or replace (Chapter 2).
☐ Clutch plates warped or damaged. This will cause clutch drag, which in turn will cause the machine to creep. Overhaul the clutch assembly (Chapter 2).

☐ Clutch spring tension uneven. Usually caused by a sagged or broken spring. Check and replace the spring (Chapter 2).
☐ Engine oil deteriorated. Old, thin, worn out oil will not provide proper lubrication for the discs, causing the clutch to drag. Replace the oil and filter (Chapter 1).
☐ Engine oil viscosity too high. Using a heavier oil than recommended in Chapter 1 can cause the plates to stick together, putting a drag on the engine. Change to the correct weight oil (Chapter 1).
☐ Clutch housing seized on shaft. Lack of lubrication, severe wear or damage can cause the housing to seize on the shaft. Overhaul of the clutch, and perhaps transmission, may be necessary to repair the damage (Chapter 2).
☐ Clutch release mechanism defective. Worn or damaged release mechanism parts can stick and fail to apply force to the pressure plate. Overhaul the release mechanism components (Chapter 2).
☐ Loose clutch hub nut. Causes housing and hub misalignment putting a drag on the engine. Engagement adjustment continually varies. Overhaul the clutch assembly (Chapter 2).

6 Gear shifting problems

Doesn't go into gear or lever doesn't return

- ☐ Clutch not disengaging. See Section 5.
- ☐ Shift fork(s) bent or seized. Often caused by dropping the machine or from lack of lubrication. Overhaul the transmission (Chapter 2).
- ☐ Gear(s) stuck on shaft. Most often caused by a lack of lubrication or excessive wear in transmission bearings and bushings. Overhaul the transmission (Chapter 2).
- ☐ Shift cam binding. Caused by lubrication failure or excessive wear. Replace the cam and bearings (Chapter 2).
- ☐ Shift lever return spring weak or broken (Chapter 2).
- ☐ Shift lever broken. Splines stripped out of lever or shaft, caused by allowing the lever to get loose or from dropping the machine. Replace necessary parts (Chapter 2).
- ☐ Shift mechanism pawl broken or worn. Full engagement and rotary movement of shift cam results. Replace shaft assembly (Chapter 2).

- ☐ Pawl spring broken. Allows pawl to float, causing sporadic shift operation. Replace spring (Chapter 2).

Jumps out of gear

- ☐ Shift fork(s) worn. Overhaul the transmission (Chapter 2).
- ☐ Gear groove(s) worn. Overhaul the transmission (Chapter 2).
- ☐ Gear dogs or dog slots worn or damaged. The gears should be inspected and replaced. No attempt should be made to service the worn parts.

Overshifts

- ☐ Pawl spring weak or broken (Chapter 2).
- ☐ Shift cam stopper lever not functioning (Chapter 2).
- ☐ Overshift limiter broken or distorted (Chapter 2).

7 Abnormal engine noise

Knocking or pinking

- ☐ Carbon build-up in combustion chamber. Use of a fuel additive that will dissolve the adhesive bonding the carbon particles to the piston crown and chamber is the easiest way to remove the build-up. Otherwise, the cylinder head will have to be removed and decarbonised (Chapter 2).
- ☐ Incorrect or poor quality fuel. Old or improper fuel can cause detonation. This causes the pistons to rattle, thus the knocking or pinking sound. Drain the old fuel and always use the recommended grade fuel (Chapter 3).
- ☐ Spark plug heat range incorrect. Uncontrolled detonation indicates that the plug heat range is too hot. The plug in effect becomes a glow plug, raising cylinder temperatures. Install the proper heat range plug (Chapter 1).
- ☐ Improper air/fuel mixture. This will cause the cylinders to run hot and lead to detonation. Clogged jets or an air leak can cause this imbalance. See Chapter 3.

Piston slap or rattling

- ☐ Cylinder-to-piston clearance excessive. Caused by improper assembly. Inspect and overhaul top end parts (Chapter 2).
- ☐ Connecting rod bent. Caused by over-revving, trying to start a badly flooded engine or from ingesting a foreign object into the combustion chamber. Replace the damaged parts (Chapter 2).
- ☐ Piston pin or piston pin bore worn or seized from wear or lack of lubrication. Replace damaged parts (Chapter 2).
- ☐ Piston ring(s) worn, broken or sticking. Overhaul the top end (Chapter 2).
- ☐ Piston seizure damage. Usually from lack of lubrication or overheating. Replace the pistons and bore the cylinders, as necessary (Chapter 2).

- ☐ Connecting rod upper or lower end clearance excessive. Caused by excessive wear or lack of lubrication. Replace worn parts.

Valve noise

- ☐ Incorrect valve clearances. Adjust the clearances by referring to Chapter 1.
- ☐ Valve spring broken or weak. Check and replace weak valve springs (Chapter 2).
- ☐ Camshaft or cylinder head worn or damaged. Lack of lubrication at high rpm is usually the cause of damage. Insufficient oil or failure to change the oil at the recommended intervals are the chief causes. Since there are no replaceable bearings in the head, the head itself will have to be replaced if there is excessive wear or damage (Chapter 2).

Other noise

- ☐ Cylinder head gasket leaking.
- ☐ Exhaust pipe leaking at cylinder head connection. Caused by improper fit of pipe(s) or loose exhaust flange. All exhaust fasteners should be tightened evenly and carefully. Failure to do this will lead to a leak.
- ☐ Crankshaft runout excessive. Caused by a bent crankshaft (from over-revving) or damage from an upper cylinder component failure. Can also be attributed to dropping the machine on either of the crankshaft ends.
- ☐ Engine mounting bolts loose. Tighten all engine mount bolts to the specified torque (Chapter 2).
- ☐ Crankshaft bearings worn (Chapter 2).
- ☐ Camshaft chain tensioner defective. Inspect and replace as necessary (Chapter 2).
- ☐ Camshaft chain, sprockets or guides worn (Chapter 2).

8 Abnormal driveline noise

Clutch noise

- ☐ Clutch housing/friction plate clearance excessive (Chapter 2).
- ☐ Loose or damaged clutch pressure plate and/or bolts (Chapter 2).

Transmission noise

- ☐ Bearings worn. Also includes the possibility that the shafts are worn. Overhaul the transmission (Chapter 2).
- ☐ Gears worn or chipped (Chapter 2).
- ☐ Metal chips jammed in gear teeth. Probably pieces from a broken clutch, gear or shift mechanism that were picked up by the gears. This will cause early bearing failure (Chapter 2).

- ☐ Engine oil level too low. Causes a howl from transmission. Also affects engine power and clutch operation (Daily (pre-ride) checks).

Final drive noise

- ☐ Chain not adjusted properly (Chapter 1).
- ☐ Engine sprocket or rear sprocket loose. Tighten fasteners (Chapters 2 and 5).
- ☐ Sprocket(s) worn. Replace sprocket(s). (Chapter 5).
- ☐ Rear sprocket warped. Replace (Chapter 5).
- ☐ Wheel coupling (cush drive) worn. Replace coupling (Chapter 5).

9 Abnormal frame and suspension noise

Front end noise

☐ Low fluid level or improper viscosity oil in forks. This can sound like spurting and is usually accompanied by irregular fork action (Chapter 5).

☐ Spring weak or broken. Makes a clicking or scraping sound. Fork oil, when drained, will have a lot of metal particles in it (Chapter 5).

☐ Steering head bearings loose or damaged. Clicks when braking. Check and adjust or replace as necessary (Chapters 1 and 5).

☐ Fork clamps loose. Make sure all fork clamp pinch bolts are tight (Chapter 5).

☐ Fork tube bent. Good possibility if machine has been dropped. Replace tube with a new one (Chapter 5).

☐ Front axle or axle clamp bolt loose. Tighten them to the specified torque (Chapter 6).

Shock absorber noise

☐ Fluid level incorrect. Indicates a leak caused by defective seal. Shock will be covered with oil. Replace shock (Chapter 5).

☐ Defective shock absorber with internal damage. This is in the body of the shock and can't be remedied. The shock must be replaced with a new one (Chapter 5).

☐ Bent or damaged shock body. Replace the shock with a new one (Chapter 5).

Brake noise

☐ Squeal caused by pad shim not installed or positioned correctly (Chapter 6).

☐ Squeal caused by dust on brake pads. Usually found in combination with glazed pads. Clean using brake cleaning solvent (Chapter 6).

☐ Contamination of brake pads. Oil, brake fluid or dirt causing brake to chatter or squeal. Clean or renew pads (Chapter 6).

☐ Pads glazed. Caused by excessive heat from prolonged use or from contamination. Do not use sandpaper, emery cloth, carborundum cloth or any other abrasive to roughen the pad surfaces as abrasives will stay in the pad material and damage the disc. A very fine flat file can be used, but pad replacement is suggested as a cure (Chapter 6).

☐ Disc warped. Can cause a chattering, clicking or intermittent squeal. Usually accompanied by a pulsating lever and uneven braking. Replace the disc (Chapter 6).

☐ Loose or worn wheel bearings. Check and replace as needed (Chapter 6).

10 Oil level indicator light comes on

Engine lubrication system

☐ These models use an oil level light rather than an oil pressure light.

☐ Engine oil level low. Inspect for leak or other problem causing low oil level and add recommended oil (Daily (pre-ride) checks).

Electrical system

☐ Oil level switch defective. Check the switch according to the procedure in Chapter 8. Replace it if it's defective.

☐ Oil level indicator light circuit defective. Check for pinched, shorted, disconnected or damaged wiring (Chapter 8).

11 Excessive exhaust smoke

White smoke

☐ Piston oil ring worn. The ring may be broken or damaged, causing oil from the crankcase to be pulled past the piston into the combustion chamber. Replace the rings with new ones (Chapter 2).

☐ Cylinders worn, cracked, or scored. Caused by overheating or oil starvation. The cylinders will have to be rebored and new pistons installed.

☐ Valve oil seal damaged or worn. Replace oil seals with new ones (Chapter 2).

☐ Valve guide worn. Perform a complete valve job (Chapter 2).

☐ Engine oil level too high, which causes the oil to be forced past the rings. Drain oil to the proper level (Daily (pre-ride) checks).

☐ Head gasket broken between oil return and cylinder. Causes oil to be pulled into the combustion chamber. Replace the head gasket and check the head for warpage (Chapter 2).

☐ Abnormal crankcase pressurisation, which forces oil past the rings. Clogged breather or hoses usually the cause (Chapter 3).

Black smoke

☐ Air cleaner clogged. Clean or replace the element (Chapter 1).

☐ Main jet too large or loose. Compare the jet size to the Specifications (Chapter 3).

☐ Choke stuck, causing fuel to be pulled through choke circuit (Chapter 3).

☐ Fuel level too high. Check and adjust the float level as necessary (Chapter 3).

☐ Inlet needle held off needle seat. Clean the float chambers and fuel line and replace the needles and seats if necessary (Chapter 3).

Brown smoke

☐ Main jet too small or clogged. Lean condition caused by wrong size main jet or by a restricted orifice. Clean float chamber and jets and compare jet size to Specifications (Chapter 3).

☐ Fuel flow insufficient. Fuel inlet needle valve stuck closed due to chemical reaction with old fuel. Fuel level incorrect. Restricted fuel line. Clean line and float chamber and adjust floats if necessary.

☐ Carburettor intake manifolds loose (Chapter 3).

☐ Air cleaner poorly sealed or not installed (Chapter 1).

12 Poor handling or stability

Handlebar hard to turn

☐ Steering stem locknut too tight (Chapter 5).
☐ Bearings damaged. Roughness can be felt as the bars are turned from side-to-side. Replace bearings and races (Chapter 5).
☐ Races dented or worn. Denting results from wear in only one position (eg, straight ahead), from a collision or hitting a pothole or from dropping the machine. Replace races and bearings (Chapter 5).
☐ Steering stem lubrication inadequate. Causes are grease getting hard from age or being washed out by high pressure car washes. Disassemble steering head and repack bearings (Chapter 5).
☐ Steering stem bent. Caused by a collision, hitting a pothole or by dropping the machine. Replace damaged part. Don't try to straighten the steering stem (Chapter 5).
☐ Front tyre air pressure too low (Chapter 1).

Handlebar shakes or vibrates excessively

☐ Tyres worn or out of balance (Chapter 6).
☐ Swingarm bearings worn. Replace worn bearings by referring to Chapter 6.
☐ Rim(s) warped or damaged. Inspect wheels for runout (Chapter 6).
☐ Wheel bearings worn. Worn front or rear wheel bearings can cause poor tracking. Worn front bearings will cause wobble (Chapter 6).
☐ Handlebar clamp bolts loose (Chapter 5).
☐ Steering stem or fork clamps loose. Tighten them to the specified torque (Chapter 5).
☐ Engine mounting bolts loose. Will cause excessive vibration with increased engine rpm (Chapter 2).

Handlebar pulls to one side

☐ Frame bent. Definitely suspect this if the machine has been dropped. May or may not be accompanied by cracking near the bend. Replace the frame (Chapter 5).
☐ Wheel out of alignment. Caused by improper location of axle spacers or from bent steering stem or frame (Chapter 5).
☐ Swingarm bent or twisted. Caused by age (metal fatigue) or impact damage. Replace the arm (Chapter 5).
☐ Steering stem bent. Caused by impact damage or by dropping the motorcycle. Replace the steering stem (Chapter 5).
☐ Fork leg bent. Disassemble the forks and replace the damaged parts (Chapter 6).
☐ Fork oil level uneven. Check and add or drain as necessary (Chapter 1).

Poor shock absorbing qualities

☐ Too hard:
  a) Fork oil level excessive (Chapter 5).
  b) Fork oil viscosity too high.
  c) Fork tube bent. Causes a harsh, sticking feeling (Chapter 5).
  d) Shock shaft or body bent or damaged (Chapter 5).
  e) Fork internal damage (Chapter 5).
  f) Shock internal damage.
  g) Tyre pressure too high (Chapters 1 and 6).
☐ Too soft:
  a) Fork or shock oil insufficient and/or leaking (Chapter 5).
  b) Fork oil level too low (Chapter 5).
  c) Fork oil viscosity too light (Chapter 5).
  d) Fork springs weak or broken (Chapter 5).

13 Braking problems

Brakes are spongy, don't hold

☐ Air in brake line. Caused by inattention to master cylinder fluid level or by leakage. Locate problem and bleed brakes (Chapter 6).
☐ Pad or disc worn (Chapters 1 and 6).
☐ Brake fluid leak. See paragraph 1.
☐ Contaminated pads. Caused by contamination with oil, grease, brake fluid, etc. Clean or replace pads. Clean disc thoroughly with brake cleaner (Chapter 6).
☐ Brake fluid deteriorated. Fluid is old or contaminated. Drain system, replenish with new fluid and bleed the system (Chapter 6).
☐ Master cylinder internal parts worn or damaged causing fluid to bypass (Chapter 6).
☐ Master cylinder bore scratched by foreign material or broken spring. Repair or replace master cylinder (Chapter 6).
☐ Disc warped. Replace disc (Chapter 6).

Brake lever or pedal pulsates

☐ Disc warped. Replace disc (Chapter 6).
☐ Axle bent. Replace axle (Chapter 5).
☐ Brake caliper bolts loose (Chapter 6).

☐ Brake caliper shafts damaged or sticking, causing caliper to bind. Lube the shafts or replace them if they are corroded or bent (Chapter 6).
☐ Wheel warped or otherwise damaged (Chapter 6).
☐ Wheel bearings damaged or worn (Chapter 6).

Brakes drag

☐ Master cylinder piston seized. Caused by wear or damage to piston or cylinder bore (Chapter 6).
☐ Lever balky or stuck. Check pivot and lubricate (Chapter 6).
☐ Brake caliper binds (rear caliper). Caused by inadequate lubrication or damage to caliper slider pins (Chapter 6).
☐ Brake caliper piston seized in bore. Caused by wear or ingestion of dirt past deteriorated seal (Chapter 6).
☐ Brake pad damaged. Pad material separated from backing plate. Usually caused by faulty manufacturing process or from contact with chemicals. Replace pads (Chapter 6).
☐ Pads improperly installed (Chapter 6).
☐ Rear brake pedal freeplay insufficient (Chapter 1).
☐ Corrosion in brake pad cavities. On UK models, refer to the pad replacement procedure in Chapter 6 and apply special lubricants to the recommended areas.

14 Electrical problems

Battery dead or weak

☐ Battery faulty. Caused by sulphated plates which are shorted through sedimentation or low electrolyte level. Also, broken battery terminal making only occasional contact (Chapter 8).

☐ Battery cables making poor contact (Chapter 8).

☐ Load excessive. Caused by addition of high wattage lights or other electrical accessories.

☐ Ignition switch defective. Switch either grounds internally or fails to shut off system. Replace the switch (Chapter 8).

☐ Regulator/rectifier defective (Chapter 8).

☐ Alternator stator coil open or shorted (Chapter 8).

☐ Wiring faulty. Wiring grounded or connections loose in ignition, charging or lighting circuits (Chapter 8).

Battery overcharged

☐ Regulator/rectifier defective. Overcharging is noticed when battery gets excessively warm or boils over (Chapter 8).

☐ Battery defective. Replace battery with a new one (Chapter 8).

☐ Battery amperage too low, wrong type or size. Install manufacturer's specified amp-hour battery to handle charging load (Chapter 8).

Checking engine compression

● Low compression will result in exhaust smoke, heavy oil consumption, poor starting and poor performance. A compression test will provide useful information about an engine's condition and if performed regularly, can give warning of trouble before any other symptoms become apparent.

● A compression gauge will be required, along with an adapter to suit the spark plug hole thread size. Note that the screw-in type gauge/adapter set up is preferable to the rubber cone type.

● Before carrying out the test, first check the valve clearances as described in Chapter 1.

1 Run the engine until it reaches normal operating temperature, then stop it and remove the spark plug(s), taking care not to scald your hands on the hot components.

2 Install the gauge adapter and compression gauge in No. 1 cylinder spark plug hole (see illustration 1).

Screw the compression gauge adapter into the spark plug hole, then screw the gauge into the adapter

3 On kickstart-equipped motorcycles, make sure the ignition switch is OFF, then open the throttle fully and kick the engine over a couple of times until the gauge reading stabilises.

4 On motorcycles with electric start only, the procedure will differ depending on the nature of the ignition system. Flick the engine kill switch (engine stop switch) to OFF and turn the ignition switch ON; open the throttle fully and crank the engine over on the starter motor for a couple of revolutions until the gauge reading stabilises. If the starter will not operate with the kill switch OFF, turn the ignition switch OFF and refer to the next paragraph.

5 Install the spark plugs back into their suppressor caps and arrange the plug electrodes so that their metal bodies are earthed (grounded) against the cylinder head; this is essential to prevent damage to the ignition system as the engine is spun over (see illustration 2). Position the plugs well

All spark plugs must be earthed (grounded) against the cylinder head

away from the plug holes otherwise there is a risk of atomised fuel escaping from the combustion chambers and igniting. As a safety precaution, cover the top of the valve cover with rag. Now turn the ignition switch ON and kill switch ON, open the throttle fully and crank the engine over on the starter motor for a couple of revolutions until the gauge reading stabilises.

6 After one or two revolutions the pressure should build up to a maximum figure and then stabilise. Take a note of this reading and on multi-cylinder engines repeat the test on the remaining cylinders.

7 The correct pressures are given in Chapter 2 Specifications. If the results fall within the specified range and on multi-cylinder engines all are relatively equal, the engine is in good condition. If there is a marked difference between the readings, or if the readings are

lower than specified, inspection of the top-end components will be required.

8 Low compression pressure may be due to worn cylinder bores, pistons or rings, failure of the cylinder head gasket, worn valve seals, or poor valve seating.

9 To distinguish between cylinder/piston wear and valve leakage, pour a small quantity of oil into the bore to temporarily seal the piston rings, then repeat the compression tests (see illustration 3). If the readings show

Bores can be temporarily sealed with a squirt of motor oil

a noticeable increase in pressure this confirms that the cylinder bore, piston, or rings are worn. If, however, no change is indicated, the cylinder head gasket or valves should be examined.

10 High compression pressure indicates excessive carbon build-up in the combustion chamber and on the piston crown. If this is the case the cylinder head should be removed and the deposits removed. Note that excessive carbon build-up is less likely with the used on modern fuels.

Checking battery open-circuit voltage

 Warning: The gases produced by the battery are explosive - never smoke or create any sparks in the vicinity of the battery. Never allow the electrolyte to contact your skin or clothing - if it does, wash it off and seek immediate medical attention.

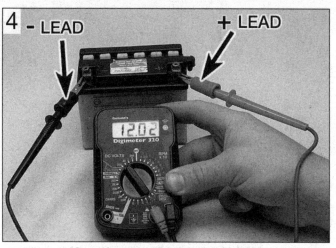

Measuring open-circuit battery voltage

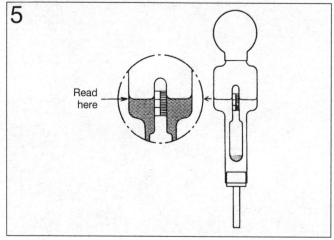

Float-type hydrometer for measuring battery specific gravity

● Before any electrical fault is investigated the battery should be checked.

● You'll need a dc voltmeter or multimeter to check battery voltage. Check that the leads are inserted in the correct terminals on the meter, red lead to positive (+ve), black lead to negative (-ve). Incorrect connections can damage the meter.

● A sound fully-charged 12 volt battery should produce between 12.3 and 12.6 volts across its terminals (12.8 volts for a maintenance-free battery). On machines with a 6 volt battery, voltage should be between 6.1 and 6.3 volts.

1 Set a multimeter to the 0 to 20 volts dc range and connect its probes across the battery terminals. Connect the meter's positive (+ve) probe, usually red, to the battery positive (+ve) terminal, followed by the meter's negative (-ve) probe, usually black, to the battery negative terminal (-ve) **(see illustration 4)**.

2 If battery voltage is low (below 10 volts on a 12 volt battery or below 4 volts on a six volt battery), charge the battery and test the voltage again. If the battery repeatedly goes flat, investigate the motorcycle's charging system.

Checking battery specific gravity (SG)

⚠ *Warning: The gases produced by the battery are explosive - never smoke or create any sparks in the vicinity of the battery. Never allow the electrolyte to contact your skin or clothing - if it does, wash it off and seek immediate medical attention.*

● The specific gravity check gives an indication of a battery's state of charge.

● A hydrometer is used for measuring specific gravity. Make sure you purchase one which has a small enough hose to insert in the aperture of a motorcycle battery.

● Specific gravity is simply a measure of the electrolyte's density compared with that of water. Water has an SG of 1.000 and fully-charged battery electrolyte is about 26% heavier, at 1.260.

● Specific gravity checks are not possible on maintenance-free batteries. Testing the open-circuit voltage is the only means of determining their state of charge.

1 To measure SG, remove the battery from the motorcycle and remove the first cell cap. Draw

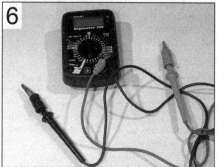

Digital multimeter can be used for all electrical tests

some electrolyte into the hydrometer and note the reading **(see illustration 5)**. Return the electrolyte to the cell and install the cap.

2 The reading should be in the region of 1.260 to 1.280. If SG is below 1.200 the battery needs charging. Note that SG will vary with temperature; it should be measured at 20°C (68°F). Add 0.007 to the reading for every 10°C above 20°C, and subtract 0.007 from the reading for every 10°C below 20°C. Add 0.004 to the reading for every 10°F above 68°F, and subtract 0.004 from the reading for every 10°F below 68°F.

3 When the check is complete, rinse the hydrometer thoroughly with clean water.

Checking for continuity

● The term continuity describes the uninterrupted flow of electricity through an electrical circuit. A continuity check will determine whether an **open-circuit** situation exists.

● Continuity can be checked with an ohmmeter, multimeter, continuity tester or battery and bulb test circuit **(see illustrations 6, 7 and 8)**.

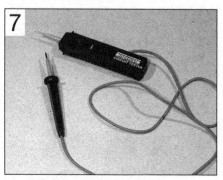

Battery-powered continuity tester

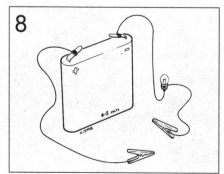

Battery and bulb test circuit

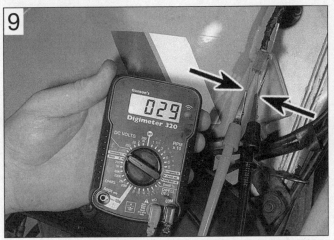

Continuity check of front brake light switch using a meter - note split pins used to access connector terminals

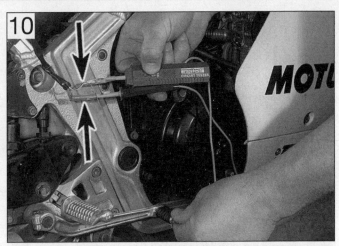

Continuity check of rear brake light switch using a continuity tester

● All of these instruments are self-powered by a battery, therefore the checks are made with the ignition OFF.

● As a safety precaution, always disconnect the battery negative (-ve) lead before making checks, particularly if ignition switch checks are being made.

● If using a meter, select the appropriate ohms scale and check that the meter reads infinity (∞). Touch the meter probes together and check that meter reads zero; where necessary adjust the meter so that it reads zero.

● After using a meter, always switch it OFF to conserve its battery.

Switch checks

1 If a switch is at fault, trace its wiring up to the wiring connectors. Separate the wire connectors and inspect them for security and condition. A build-up of dirt or corrosion here will most likely be the cause of the problem - clean up and apply a water dispersant such as WD40.

2 If using a test meter, set the meter to the ohms x 10 scale and connect its probes across the wires from the switch (see illustration 9). Simple ON/OFF type switches, such as brake light switches, only have two wires whereas combination switches, like the

ignition switch, have many internal links. Study the wiring diagram to ensure that you are connecting across the correct pair of wires. Continuity (low or no measurable resistance - 0 ohms) should be indicated with the switch ON and no continuity (high resistance) with it OFF.

3 Note that the polarity of the test probes doesn't matter for continuity checks, although care should be taken to follow specific test procedures if a diode or solid-state component is being checked.

4 A continuity tester or battery and bulb circuit can be used in the same way. Connect its probes as described above (see illustration 10). The light should come on to indicate continuity in the ON switch position, but should extinguish in the OFF position.

Wiring checks

● Many electrical faults are caused by damaged wiring, often due to incorrect routing or chaffing on frame components.

● Loose, wet or corroded wire connectors can also be the cause of electrical problems, especially in exposed locations.

1 A continuity check can be made on a single length of wire by disconnecting it at each end and connecting a meter or continuity tester

across both ends of the wire (see illustration 11).

2 Continuity (low or no resistance - 0 ohms) should be indicated if the wire is good. If no continuity (high resistance) is shown, suspect a broken wire.

Checking for voltage

● A voltage check can determine whether current is reaching a component.

● Voltage can be checked with a dc voltmeter, multimeter set on the dc volts scale, test light or buzzer (see illustrations 12 and 13). A meter has the advantage of being able to measure actual voltage.

● When using a meter, check that its leads are inserted in the correct terminals on the meter, red to positive (+ve), black to negative (-ve). Incorrect connections can damage the meter.

● A voltmeter (or multimeter set to the dc volts scale) should always be connected in parallel (across the load). Connecting it in series will not harm the meter, but the reading will not be meaningful.

● Voltage checks are made with the ignition ON.

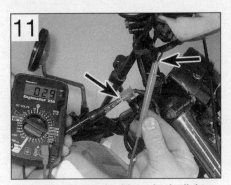

Continuity check of front brake light switch sub-harness

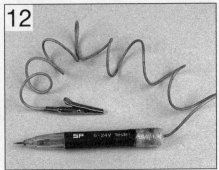

A simple test light can be used for voltage checks

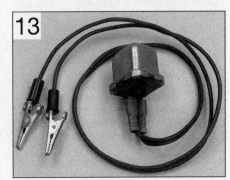

A buzzer is useful for voltage checks

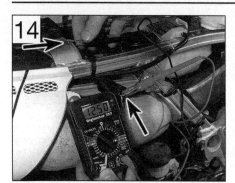

Checking for voltage at the rear brake light power supply wire using a meter . . .

1 First identify the relevant wiring circuit by referring to the wiring diagram at the end of this manual. If other electrical components share the same power supply (ie are fed from the same fuse), take note whether they are working correctly - this is useful information in deciding where to start checking the circuit.
2 If using a meter, check first that the meter leads are plugged into the correct terminals on the meter (see above). Set the meter to the dc volts function, at a range suitable for the battery voltage. Connect the meter red probe (+ve) to the power supply wire and the black probe to a good metal earth (ground) on the motorcycle's frame or directly to the battery negative (-ve) terminal **(see illustration 14)**. Battery voltage should be shown on the meter

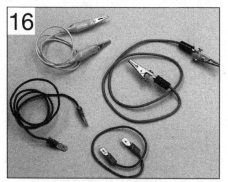

A selection of jumper wires for making earth (ground) checks

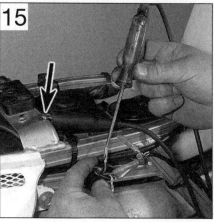

. . . or a test light - note the earth connection to the frame (arrow)

with the ignition switched ON.
3 If using a test light or buzzer, connect its positive (+ve) probe to the power supply terminal and its negative (-ve) probe to a good earth (ground) on the motorcycle's frame or directly to the battery negative (-ve) terminal **(see illustration 15)**. With the ignition ON, the test light should illuminate or the buzzer sound.
4 If no voltage is indicated, work back towards the fuse continuing to check for voltage. When you reach a point where there is voltage, you know the problem lies between that point and your last check point.

Checking the earth (ground)

● Earth connections are made either directly to the engine or frame (such as sensors, neutral switch etc. which only have a positive feed) or by a separate wire into the earth circuit of the wiring harness. Alternatively a short earth wire is sometimes run directly from the component to the motorcycle's frame.
● Corrosion is often the cause of a poor earth connection.
● If total failure is experienced, check the security of the main earth lead from the

negative (-ve) terminal of the battery and also the main earth (ground) point on the wiring harness. If corroded, dismantle the connection and clean all surfaces back to bare metal.
1 To check the earth on a component, use an insulated jumper wire to temporarily bypass its earth connection **(see illustration 16)**. Connect one end of the jumper wire between the earth terminal or metal body of the component and the other end to the motorcycle's frame.
2 If the circuit works with the jumper wire installed, the original earth circuit is faulty. Check the wiring for open-circuits or poor connections. Clean up direct earth connections, removing all traces of corrosion and remake the joint. Apply petroleum jelly to the joint to prevent future corrosion.

Tracing a short-circuit

● A short-circuit occurs where current shorts to earth (ground) bypassing the circuit components. This usually results in a blown fuse.

● A short-circuit is most likely to occur where the insulation has worn through due to wiring chafing on a component, allowing a direct path to earth (ground) on the frame.

1 Remove any bodypanels necessary to access the circuit wiring.
2 Check that all electrical switches in the circuit are OFF, then remove the circuit fuse and connect a test light, buzzer or voltmeter (set to the dc scale) across the fuse terminals. No voltage should be shown.
3 Move the wiring from side to side whilst observing the test light or meter. When the test light comes on, buzzer sounds or meter shows voltage, you have found the cause of the short. It will usually shown up as damaged or burned insulation.
4 Note that the same test can be performed on each component in the circuit, even the switch.

A

ABS (Anti-lock braking system) A system, usually electronically controlled, that senses incipient wheel lockup during braking and relieves hydraulic pressure at wheel which is about to skid.

Aftermarket Components suitable for the motorcycle, but not produced by the motorcycle manufacturer.

Allen key A hexagonal wrench which fits into a recessed hexagonal hole.

Alternating current (ac) Current produced by an alternator. Requires converting to direct current by a rectifier for charging purposes.

Alternator Converts mechanical energy from the engine into electrical energy to charge the battery and power the electrical system.

Ampere (amp) A unit of measurement for the flow of electrical current. Current = Volts ÷ Ohms.

Ampere-hour (Ah) Measure of battery capacity.

Angle-tightening A torque expressed in degrees. Often follows a conventional tightening torque for cylinder head or main bearing fasteners **(see illustration)**.

Angle-tightening cylinder head bolts

Antifreeze A substance (usually ethylene glycol) mixed with water, and added to the cooling system, to prevent freezing of the coolant in winter. Antifreeze also contains chemicals to inhibit corrosion and the formation of rust and other deposits that would tend to clog the radiator and coolant passages and reduce cooling efficiency.

Anti-dive System attached to the fork lower leg (slider) to prevent fork dive when braking hard.

Anti-seize compound A coating that reduces the risk of seizing on fasteners that are subjected to high temperatures, such as exhaust clamp bolts and nuts.

API American Petroleum Institute. A quality standard for 4-stroke motor oils.

Asbestos A natural fibrous mineral with great heat resistance, commonly used in the composition of brake friction materials. Asbestos is a health hazard and the dust created by brake systems should never be inhaled or ingested.

ATF Automatic Transmission Fluid. Often used in front forks.

ATU Automatic Timing Unit. Mechanical device for advancing the ignition timing on early engines.

ATV All Terrain Vehicle. Often called a Quad.

Axial play Side-to-side movement.

Axle A shaft on which a wheel revolves. Also known as a spindle.

B

Backlash The amount of movement between meshed components when one component is held still. Usually applies to gear teeth.

Ball bearing A bearing consisting of a hardened inner and outer race with hardened steel balls between the two races.

Bearings Used between two working surfaces to prevent wear of the components and a build-up of heat. Four types of bearing are commonly used on motorcycles: plain shell bearings, ball bearings, tapered roller bearings and needle roller bearings.

Bevel gears Used to turn the drive through 90°. Typical applications are shaft final drive and camshaft drive **(see illustration)**.

Bevel gears are used to turn the drive through 90°

BHP Brake Horsepower. The British measurement for engine power output. Power output is now usually expressed in kilowatts (kW).

Bias-belted tyre Similar construction to radial tyre, but with outer belt running at an angle to the wheel rim.

Big-end bearing The bearing in the end of the connecting rod that's attached to the crankshaft.

Bleeding The process of removing air from an hydraulic system via a bleed nipple or bleed screw.

Bottom-end A description of an engine's crankcase components and all components contained there-in.

BTDC Before Top Dead Centre in terms of piston position. Ignition timing is often expressed in terms of degrees or millimetres BTDC.

Bush A cylindrical metal or rubber component used between two moving parts.

Burr Rough edge left on a component after machining or as a result of excessive wear.

C

Cam chain The chain which takes drive from the crankshaft to the camshaft(s).

Canister The main component in an evaporative emission control system (California market only); contains activated charcoal granules to trap vapours from the fuel system rather than allowing them to vent to the atmosphere.

Castellated Resembling the parapets along the top of a castle wall. For example, a castellated wheel axle or spindle nut.

Catalytic converter A device in the exhaust system of some machines which converts certain pollutants in the exhaust gases into less harmful substances.

Charging system Description of the components which charge the battery, ie the alternator, rectifier and regulator.

Circlip A ring-shaped clip used to prevent endwise movement of cylindrical parts and shafts. An internal circlip is installed in a groove in a housing; an external circlip fits into a groove on the outside of a cylindrical piece such as a shaft. Also known as a snap-ring.

Clearance The amount of space between two parts. For example, between a piston and a cylinder, between a bearing and a journal, etc.

Coil spring A spiral of elastic steel found in various sizes throughout a vehicle, for example as a springing medium in the suspension and in the valve train.

Compression Reduction in volume, and increase in pressure and temperature, of a gas, caused by squeezing it into a smaller space.

Compression damping Controls the speed the suspension compresses when hitting a bump.

Compression ratio The relationship between cylinder volume when the piston is at top dead centre and cylinder volume when the piston is at bottom dead centre.

Continuity The uninterrupted path in the flow of electricity. Little or no measurable resistance.

Continuity tester Self-powered bleeper or test light which indicates continuity.

Cp Candlepower. Bulb rating commonly found on US motorcycles.

Crossply tyre Tyre plies arranged in a criss-cross pattern. Usually four or six plies used, hence 4PR or 6PR in tyre size codes.

Cush drive Rubber damper segments fitted between the rear wheel and final drive sprocket to absorb transmission shocks **(see illustration)**.

Cush drive rubbers dampen out transmission shocks

D

Degree disc Calibrated disc for measuring piston position. Expressed in degrees.

Dial gauge Clock-type gauge with adapters for measuring runout and piston position. Expressed in mm or inches.

Diaphragm The rubber membrane in a master cylinder or carburettor which seals the upper chamber.

Diaphragm spring A single sprung plate often used in clutches.

Direct current (dc) Current produced by a dc generator.

Decarbonisation The process of removing carbon deposits - typically from the combustion chamber, valves and exhaust port/system.

Detonation Destructive and damaging explosion of fuel/air mixture in combustion chamber instead of controlled burning.

Diode An electrical valve which only allows current to flow in one direction. Commonly used in rectifiers and starter interlock systems.

Disc valve (or rotary valve) A induction system used on some two-stroke engines.

Double-overhead camshaft (DOHC) An engine that uses two overhead camshafts, one for the intake valves and one for the exhaust valves.

Drivebelt A toothed belt used to transmit drive to the rear wheel on some motorcycles. A drivebelt has also been used to drive the camshafts. Drivebelts are usually made of Kevlar.

Driveshaft Any shaft used to transmit motion. Commonly used when referring to the final driveshaft on shaft drive motorcycles.

E

Earth return The return path of an electrical circuit, utilising the motorcycle's frame.

ECU (Electronic Control Unit) A computer which controls (for instance) an ignition system, or an anti-lock braking system.

EGO Exhaust Gas Oxygen sensor. Sometimes called a Lambda sensor.

Electrolyte The fluid in a lead-acid battery.

EMS (Engine Management System) A computer controlled system which manages the fuel injection and the ignition systems in an integrated fashion.

Endfloat The amount of lengthways movement between two parts. As applied to a crankshaft, the distance that the crankshaft can move side-to-side in the crankcase.

Endless chain A chain having no joining link. Common use for cam chains and final drive chains.

EP (Extreme Pressure) Oil type used in locations where high loads are applied, such as between gear teeth.

Evaporative emission control system Describes a charcoal filled canister which stores fuel vapours from the tank rather than allowing them to vent to the atmosphere. Usually only fitted to California models and referred to as an EVAP system.

Expansion chamber Section of two-stroke engine exhaust system so designed to improve engine efficiency and boost power.

F

Feeler blade or gauge A thin strip or blade of hardened steel, ground to an exact thickness, used to check or measure clearances between parts.

Final drive Description of the drive from the transmission to the rear wheel. Usually by chain or shaft, but sometimes by belt.

Firing order The order in which the engine cylinders fire, or deliver their power strokes, beginning with the number one cylinder.

Flooding Term used to describe a high fuel level in the carburettor float chambers, leading to fuel overflow. Also refers to excess fuel in the combustion chamber due to incorrect starting technique.

Free length The no-load state of a component when measured. Clutch, valve and fork spring lengths are measured at rest, without any preload.

Freeplay The amount of travel before any action takes place. The looseness in a linkage, or an assembly of parts, between the initial application of force and actual movement. For example, the distance the rear brake pedal moves before the rear brake is actuated.

Fuel injection The fuel/air mixture is metered electronically and directed into the engine intake ports (indirect injection) or into the cylinders (direct injection). Sensors supply information on engine speed and conditions.

Fuel/air mixture The charge of fuel and air going into the engine. See **Stoichiometric ratio**.

Fuse An electrical device which protects a circuit against accidental overload. The typical fuse contains a soft piece of metal which is calibrated to melt at a predetermined current flow (expressed as amps) and break the circuit.

G

Gap The distance the spark must travel in jumping from the centre electrode to the side electrode in a spark plug. Also refers to the distance between the ignition rotor and the pickup coil in an electronic ignition system.

Gasket Any thin, soft material - usually cork, cardboard, asbestos or soft metal - installed between two metal surfaces to ensure a good seal. For instance, the cylinder head gasket seals the joint between the block and the cylinder head.

Gauge An instrument panel display used to monitor engine conditions. A gauge with a movable pointer on a dial or a fixed scale is an analogue gauge. A gauge with a numerical readout is called a digital gauge.

Gear ratios The drive ratio of a pair of gears in a gearbox, calculated on their number of teeth.

Glaze-busting see **Honing**

Grinding Process for renovating the valve face and valve seat contact area in the cylinder head.

Gudgeon pin The shaft which connects the connecting rod small-end with the piston. Often called a piston pin or wrist pin.

H

Helical gears Gear teeth are slightly curved and produce less gear noise that straight-cut gears. Often used for primary drives.

Installing a Helicoil thread insert in a cylinder head

Helicoil A thread insert repair system. Commonly used as a repair for stripped spark plug threads **(see illustration)**.

Honing A process used to break down the glaze on a cylinder bore (also called glaze-busting). Can also be carried out to roughen a rebored cylinder to aid ring bedding-in.

HT (High Tension) Description of the electrical circuit from the secondary winding of the ignition coil to the spark plug.

Hydraulic A liquid filled system used to transmit pressure from one component to another. Common uses on motorcycles are brakes and clutches.

Hydrometer An instrument for measuring the specific gravity of a lead-acid battery.

Hygroscopic Water absorbing. In motorcycle applications, braking efficiency will be reduced if DOT 3 or 4 hydraulic fluid absorbs water from the air - care must be taken to keep new brake fluid in tightly sealed containers.

I

Ibf ft Pounds-force feet. An imperial unit of torque. Sometimes written as ft-lbs.

Ibf in Pound-force inch. An imperial unit of torque, applied to components where a very low torque is required. Sometimes written as in-lbs.

IC Abbreviation for Integrated Circuit.

Ignition advance Means of increasing the timing of the spark at higher engine speeds. Done by mechanical means (ATU) on early engines or electronically by the ignition control unit on later engines.

Ignition timing The moment at which the spark plug fires, expressed in the number of crankshaft degrees before the piston reaches the top of its stroke, or in the number of millimetres before the piston reaches the top of its stroke.

Infinity (∞) Description of an open-circuit electrical state, where no continuity exists.

Inverted forks (upside down forks) The sliders or lower legs are held in the yokes and the fork tubes or stanchions are connected to the wheel axle (spindle). Less unsprung weight and stiffer construction than conventional forks.

J

JASO Quality standard for 2-stroke oils.

Joule The unit of electrical energy.

Journal The bearing surface of a shaft.

K

Kickstart Mechanical means of turning the engine over for starting purposes. Only usually fitted to mopeds, small capacity motorcycles and off-road motorcycles.

Kill switch Handebar-mounted switch for emergency ignition cut-out. Cuts the ignition circuit on all models, and additionally prevent starter motor operation on others.

km Symbol for kilometre.

kmh Abbreviation for kilometres per hour.

L

Lambda (λ) sensor A sensor fitted in the exhaust system to measure the exhaust gas oxygen content (excess air factor).

Lapping see **Grinding**.
LCD Abbreviation for Liquid Crystal Display.
LED Abbreviation for Light Emitting Diode.
Liner A steel cylinder liner inserted in a aluminium alloy cylinder block.
Locknut A nut used to lock an adjustment nut, or other threaded component, in place.
Lockstops The lugs on the lower triple clamp (yoke) which abut those on the frame, preventing handlebar-to-fuel tank contact.
Lockwasher A form of washer designed to prevent an attaching nut from working loose.
LT Low Tension Description of the electrical circuit from the power supply to the primary winding of the ignition coil.

M

Main bearings The bearings between the crankshaft and crankcase.
Maintenance-free (MF) battery A sealed battery which cannot be topped up.
Manometer Mercury-filled calibrated tubes used to measure intake tract vacuum. Used to synchronise carburettors on multi-cylinder engines.
Micrometer A precision measuring instrument that measures component outside diameters **(see illustration)**.

Tappet shims are measured with a micrometer

MON (Motor Octane Number) A measure of a fuel's resistance to knock.
Monograde oil An oil with a single viscosity, eg SAE80W.
Monoshock A single suspension unit linking the swingarm or suspension linkage to the frame.
mph Abbreviation for miles per hour.
Multigrade oil Having a wide viscosity range (eg 10W40). The W stands for Winter, thus the viscosity ranges from SAE10 when cold to SAE40 when hot.
Multimeter An electrical test instrument with the capability to measure voltage, current and resistance. Some meters also incorporate a continuity tester and buzzer.

N

Needle roller bearing Inner race of caged needle rollers and hardened outer race. Examples of uncaged needle rollers can be found on some engines. Commonly used in rear suspension applications and in two-stroke engines.
Nm Newton metres.
NOx Oxides of Nitrogen. A common toxic pollutant emitted by petrol engines at higher temperatures.

O

Octane The measure of a fuel's resistance to knock.
OE (Original Equipment) Relates to components fitted to a motorcycle as standard or replacement parts supplied by the motorcycle manufacturer.
Ohm The unit of electrical resistance. Ohms = Volts ÷ Current.
Ohmmeter An instrument for measuring electrical resistance.
Oil cooler System for diverting engine oil outside of the engine to a radiator for cooling purposes.
Oil injection A system of two-stroke engine lubrication where oil is pump-fed to the engine in accordance with throttle position.
Open-circuit An electrical condition where there is a break in the flow of electricity - no continuity (high resistance).
O-ring A type of sealing ring made of a special rubber-like material; in use, the O-ring is compressed into a groove to provide the sealing action.
Oversize (OS) Term used for piston and ring size options fitted to a rebored cylinder.
Overhead cam (sohc) engine An engine with single camshaft located on top of the cylinder head.
Overhead valve (ohv) engine An engine with the valves located in the cylinder head, but with the camshaft located in the engine block or crankcase.
Oxygen sensor A device installed in the exhaust system which senses the oxygen content in the exhaust and converts this information into an electric current. Also called a Lambda sensor.

P

Plastigauge A thin strip of plastic thread, available in different sizes, used for measuring clearances. For example, a strip of Plastigauge is laid across a bearing journal. The parts are assembled and dismantled; the width of the crushed strip indicates the clearance between journal and bearing.
Polarity Either negative or positive earth (ground), determined by which battery lead is connected to the frame (earth return). Modern motorcycles are usually negative earth.
Pre-ignition A situation where the fuel/air mixture ignites before the spark plug fires. Often due to a hot spot in the combustion chamber caused by carbon build-up. Engine has a tendency to 'run-on'.
Pre-load (suspension) The amount a spring is compressed when in the unloaded state. Preload can be applied by gas, spacer or mechanical adjuster.
Premix The method of engine lubrication on older two-stroke engines. Engine oil is mixed with the petrol in the fuel tank in a specific ratio. The fuel/oil mix is sometimes referred to as "petroil".
Primary drive Description of the drive from the crankshaft to the clutch. Usually by gear or chain.
PS Pfedestärke - a German interpretation of BHP.
PSI Pounds-force per square inch. Imperial measurement of tyre pressure and cylinder pressure measurement.
PTFE Polytetrafluroethylene. A low friction substance.

Pulse secondary air injection system A process of promoting the burning of excess fuel present in the exhaust gases by routing fresh air into the exhaust ports.

Q

Quartz halogen bulb Tungsten filament surrounded by a halogen gas. Typically used for the headlight **(see illustration)**.

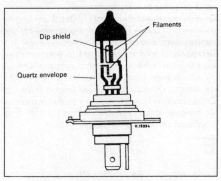

Quartz halogen headlight bulb construction

R

Rack-and-pinion A pinion gear on the end of a shaft that mates with a rack (think of a geared wheel opened up and laid flat). Sometimes used in clutch operating systems.
Radial play Up and down movement about a shaft.
Radial ply tyres Tyre plies run across the tyre (from bead to bead) and around the circumference of the tyre. Less resistant to tread distortion than other tyre types.
Radiator A liquid-to-air heat transfer device designed to reduce the temperature of the coolant in a liquid cooled engine.
Rake A feature of steering geometry - the angle of the steering head in relation to the vertical **(see illustration)**.

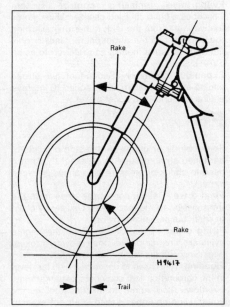

Steering geometry

Rebore Providing a new working surface to the cylinder bore by boring out the old surface. Necessitates the use of oversize piston and rings.

Rebound damping A means of controlling the oscillation of a suspension unit spring after it has been compressed. Resists the spring's natural tendency to bounce back after being compressed.

Rectifier Device for converting the ac output of an alternator into dc for battery charging.

Reed valve An induction system commonly used on two-stroke engines.

Regulator Device for maintaining the charging voltage from the generator or alternator within a specified range.

Relay A electrical device used to switch heavy current on and off by using a low current auxiliary circuit.

Resistance Measured in ohms. An electrical component's ability to pass electrical current.

RON (Research Octane Number) A measure of a fuel's resistance to knock.

rpm revolutions per minute.

Runout The amount of wobble (in-and-out movement) of a wheel or shaft as it's rotated. The amount a shaft rotates 'out-of-true'. The out-of-round condition of a rotating part.

S

SAE (Society of Automotive Engineers) A standard for the viscosity of a fluid.

Sealant A liquid or paste used to prevent leakage at a joint. Sometimes used in conjunction with a gasket.

Service limit Term for the point where a component is no longer useable and must be renewed.

Shaft drive A method of transmitting drive from the transmission to the rear wheel.

Shell bearings Plain bearings consisting of two shell halves. Most often used as big-end and main bearings in a four-stroke engine. Often called bearing inserts.

Shim Thin spacer, commonly used to adjust the clearance or relative positions between two parts. For example, shims inserted into or under tappets or followers to control valve clearances. Clearance is adjusted by changing the thickness of the shim.

Short-circuit An electrical condition where current shorts to earth (ground) bypassing the circuit components.

Skimming Process to correct warpage or repair a damaged surface, eg on brake discs or drums.

Slide-hammer A special puller that screws into or hooks onto a component such as a shaft or bearing; a heavy sliding handle on the shaft bottoms against the end of the shaft to knock the component free.

Small-end bearing The bearing in the upper end of the connecting rod at its joint with the gudgeon pin.

Spalling Damage to camshaft lobes or bearing journals shown as pitting of the working surface.

Specific gravity (SG) The state of charge of the electrolyte in a lead-acid battery. A measure of the electrolyte's density compared with water.

Straight-cut gears Common type gear used on gearbox shafts and for oil pump and water pump drives.

Stanchion The inner sliding part of the front forks, held by the yokes. Often called a fork tube.

Stoichiometric ratio The optimum chemical air/fuel ratio for a petrol engine, said to be 14.7 parts of air to 1 part of fuel.

Sulphuric acid The liquid (electrolyte) used in a lead-acid battery. Poisonous and extremely corrosive.

Surface grinding (lapping) Process to correct a warped gasket face, commonly used on cylinder heads.

T

Tapered-roller bearing Tapered inner race of caged needle rollers and separate tapered outer race. Examples of taper roller bearings can be found on steering heads.

Tappet A cylindrical component which transmits motion from the cam to the valve stem, either directly or via a pushrod and rocker arm. Also called a cam follower.

TCS Traction Control System. An electronically-controlled system which senses wheel spin and reduces engine speed accordingly.

TDC Top Dead Centre denotes that the piston is at its highest point in the cylinder.

Thread-locking compound Solution applied to fastener threads to prevent slackening. Select type to suit application.

Thrust washer A washer positioned between two moving components on a shaft. For example, between gear pinions on gearshaft.

Timing chain See **Cam Chain.**

Timing light Stroboscopic lamp for carrying out ignition timing checks with the engine running.

Top-end A description of an engine's cylinder block, head and valve gear components.

Torque Turning or twisting force about a shaft.

Torque setting A prescribed tightness specified by the motorcycle manufacturer to ensure that the bolt or nut is secured correctly. Undertightening can result in the bolt or nut coming loose or a surface not being sealed. Overtightening can result in stripped threads, distortion or damage to the component being retained.

Torx key A six-point wrench.

Tracer A stripe of a second colour applied to a wire insulator to distinguish that wire from another one with the same colour insulator. For example, Br/W is often used to denote a brown insulator with a white tracer.

Trail A feature of steering geometry. Distance from the steering head axis to the tyre's central contact point.

Triple clamps The cast components which extend from the steering head and support the fork stanchions or tubes. Often called fork yokes.

Turbocharger A centrifugal device, driven by exhaust gases, that pressurises the intake air. Normally used to increase the power output from a given engine displacement.

TWI Abbreviation for Tyre Wear Indicator. Indicates the location of the tread depth indicator bars on tyres.

U

Universal joint or U-joint (UJ) A double-pivoted connection for transmitting power from a driving to a driven shaft through an angle. Typically found in shaft drive assemblies.

Unsprung weight Anything not supported by the bike's suspension (ie the wheel, tyres, brakes, final drive and bottom (moving) part of the suspension).

V

Vacuum gauges Clock-type gauges for measuring intake tract vacuum. Used for carburettor synchronisation on multi-cylinder engines.

Valve A device through which the flow of liquid, gas or vacuum may be stopped, started or regulated by a moveable part that opens, shuts or partially obstructs one or more ports or passageways. The intake and exhaust valves in the cylinder head are of the poppet type.

Valve clearance The clearance between the valve tip (the end of the valve stem) and the rocker arm or tappet/follower. The valve clearance is measured when the valve is closed. The correct clearance is important - if too small the valve won't close fully and will burn out, whereas if too large noisy operation will result.

Valve lift The amount a valve is lifted off its seat by the camshaft lobe.

Valve timing The exact setting for the opening and closing of the valves in relation to piston position.

Vernier caliper A precision measuring instrument that measures inside and outside dimensions. Not quite as accurate as a micrometer, but more convenient.

VIN Vehicle Identification Number. Term for the bike's engine and frame numbers.

Viscosity The thickness of a liquid or its resistance to flow.

Volt A unit for expressing electrical "pressure" in a circuit. Volts = current x ohms.

W

Water pump A mechanically-driven device for moving coolant around the engine.

Watt A unit for expressing electrical power. Watts = volts x current.

Wear limit see **Service limit**

Wet liner A liquid-cooled engine design where the pistons run in liners which are directly surrounded by coolant **(see illustration)**.

Wet liner arrangement

Wheelbase Distance from the centre of the front wheel to the centre of the rear wheel.

Wiring harness or loom Describes the electrical wires running the length of the motorcycle and enclosed in tape or plastic sheathing. Wiring coming off the main harness is usually referred to as a sub harness.

Woodruff key A key of semi-circular or square section used to locate a gear to a shaft. Often used to locate the alternator rotor on the crankshaft.

Wrist pin Another name for gudgeon or piston pin.

Note: *References throughout this index are in the form - "Chapter number" • "page number"*

Preserving Our Motoring Heritage

< The Model J Duesenberg Derham Tourster. Only eight of these magnificent cars were ever built – this is the only example to be found outside the United States of America

Almost every car you've ever loved, loathed or desired is gathered under one roof at the Haynes Motor Museum. Over 300 immaculately presented cars and motorbikes represent every aspect of our motoring heritage, from elegant reminders of bygone days, such as the superb Model J Duesenberg to curiosities like the bug-eyed BMW Isetta. There are also many old friends and flames. Perhaps you remember the 1959 Ford Popular that you did your courting in? The magnificent 'Red Collection' is a spectacle of classic sports cars including AC, Alfa Romeo, Austin Healey, Ferrari, Lamborghini, Maserati, MG, Riley, Porsche and Triumph.

A Perfect Day Out

Each and every vehicle at the Haynes Motor Museum has played its part in the history and culture of Motoring. Today, they make a wonderful spectacle and a great day out for all the family. Bring the kids, bring Mum and Dad, but above all bring your camera to capture those golden memories for ever. You will also find an impressive array of motoring memorabilia, a comfortable 70 seat video cinema and one of the most extensive transport book shops in Britain. The Pit Stop Cafe serves everything from a cup of tea to wholesome, home-made meals or, if you prefer, you can enjoy the large picnic area nestled in the beautiful rural surroundings of Somerset.

> John Haynes O.B.E., Founder and Chairman of the museum at the wheel of a Haynes Light 12.

< The 1936 490cc sohc-engined International Norton – well known for its racing success

The Museum is situated on the A359 Yeovil to Frome road at Sparkford, just off the A303 in Somerset. It is about 40 miles south of Bristol, and 25 minutes drive from the M5 intersection at Taunton.

Open 9.30am - 5.30pm (10.00am - 4.00pm Winter) 7 days a week, *except Christmas Day, Boxing Day and New Years Day*

Special rates available for schools, coach parties and outings Charitable Trust No. 292048